# WRITINGS OF THE YOUNG MARX
## ON PHILOSOPHY AND SOCIETY

LOYD D. EASTON is currently Professor of Philosophy and Department Chairman at Ohio Wesleyan University. He received his B.A. from DePauw University, his M.A. and Ph.D. from Boston University. He has studied at Harvard and Glasgow universities and has been Visiting Professor of Philosophy at Ohio State University and Methodist Theological School in Ohio. He is the immediate past President of the Ohio Philosophical Association.

KURT H. GUDDAT was born in Berlin, Germany. He immigrated to the United States in 1951 and received his B.A. from Eastern New Mexico University, his M.A. and Ph.D. from Ohio State University. He is currently Professor of German and Department Chairman at Ohio Wesleyan University and has previously taught at Ohio State University, Montana State University, and Southern Illinois University.

# Writings of the Young Marx on Philosophy and Society

TRANSLATED AND EDITED BY
LOYD D. EASTON AND KURT H. GUDDAT

Anchor Books
Doubleday & Company, Inc.
Garden City, New York

*Writings of the Young Marx on Philosophy and Society* was published simultaneously in a hardcover edition by Doubleday & Company, Inc.

Anchor Books edition: 1967

# PREFACE

The past decade brought a spate of books, essays, and commentaries on Marx's early thought, here and abroad, with startlingly diverse claims about its relation to Hegel, Christianity, existentialism, humanism, democracy, and his and Engels' mature views. We concluded that a comprehensive collection of Marx's early writings in translation was needed to make available in English what Marx actually said in the dozen years prior to the *Communist Manifesto*. In making our selection from some 2200 pages of *Marx-Engels Historisch-Kritische Gesamtausgabe* (1927–32), the fullest but not complete publication of Marx's early writings, we aimed at major writings—"major" not only as most often cited or quoted but as revealing characteristic positions and turning points in Marx's thought. A number of essays and chapters which we excluded are described or quoted in the Introduction and headnotes.

Where we had doubts about the accuracy of the texts, we consulted the original manuscripts and first editions at the International Institute of Social History in Amsterdam, as well as editions of Marx's early writings published by Cotta and by Kröner in Stuttgart and by Dietz in Berlin. With *The German Ideology*, however, our translation generally follows the reading of the original manuscript supplied by Professors H.-J. Lieber and P. Furth, editors of the *Karl-Marx-Ausgabe* (Stuttgart: Cotta-Verlag, 1962–   ). We also consulted existing translations.

Editorial additions are indicated by the customary square brackets, but we omitted these from several titles which we supplied or amplified. Other editorial marks are explained in footnotes. Except for "Defense of the Moselle

Correspondent," all articles and all chapters or sections of book-length writings are translated in their entirety, without internal abridgment.

The pages to follow are fully our joint product, though initiative for the writing often reflected our respective special interests, philosophy and German literature. We acknowledge with gratitude a grant from Ohio Wesleyan University which facilitated research and consultations in Europe. Our thanks also go to Dr. Marvin Farber, editor, for permission to use portions of "Alienation and History in the Early Marx" (*Philosophy and Phenomenological Research*, December 1961) in the Introduction, and to Drs. Hans-Joachim Lieber and Peter Furth of the Free University in Berlin for permitting us to use their reading of "Die deutsche Ideologie." For encouragement and counsel we thank Dr. Maximilien Rubel who has long stressed the need for a complete and exact edition of Marx's writings. For facilitating our research we convey our gratitude to the staffs of the Beeghly Library at Ohio Wesleyan University and the International Institute of Social History in Amsterdam. Not least, our thanks go to Mrs. Douglas Mullins for special efforts, cheerfully given, in typing the manuscript, and to Mrs. Robert Muladore for secretarial help.

*Delaware, Ohio*    L. D. E.
*November 1966*    K. H. G.

# CONTENTS

# WRITINGS OF THE YOUNG MARX
## ON PHILOSOPHY AND SOCIETY

# INTRODUCTION

Karl Marx's writings prior to *The Communist Manifesto*, published most completely in the *Marx-Engels Gesamtausgabe* from 1927 to 1932, reveal his philosophical premises in Hegel and Feuerbach and the genesis of his epoch-making historical materialism. They deal at length with the nature of religion, freedom of the press, the relation of the state to democracy, the "alienation" of man, humanism in opposition to philosophical idealism, the overcoming of alienation through communism, and the relation of communism to historical *Praxis*.

With such themes Marx's early writings have appealed to a variety of interests and have had a variety of uses. Philosophers have reinterpreted Marx's thought to find him essentially an idealist—even a metaphysical egoist—in his view of history, a pragmatist in his recurrence to practical activity, or an existentialist in his account of man as a suffering subject reacting against an alien system of ideas and institutions. Social scientists have been attracted to Marx's views on democracy in relation to a centralized state and to his ideas on "alienated labor" in relation to the problem of a humane organization of work. In Western Europe Marx's early thought has been used to reformulate the relation between democracy and socialism, and in Communist countries it has been employed to defend workers' self-government and individual freedom against Stalinist bureaucracy. The variety of appeal and uses of Marx's early thought has resulted in a veritable literary industry on the subject and suggests that acquaintance with his early writings is at least a prerequisite to grasping the compass of his thought as well as the background of the *Manifesto*,

*Critique of Political Economy, Capital,* and other mature publications.

Some interpreters have dismissed Marx's early writings as "mere preliminaries" or "juvenilia," citing Engels' "embarrassed" remark made in the 1890s that they were as unimportant as Marx's youthful poetry and unreadable in their semi-Hegelian language. But Marx himself regarded them as important in their own right and the basis of his mature thought. In the classical statement of his "leading thread," the preface to the *Critique of Political Economy* of 1859, Marx noted that his first effort to resolve his doubts about the relation of socialism to economics was a critical revision of Hegel's philosophy of law, the "Critique of Hegel's Philosophy of the State," written in the summer of 1843, and the "Introduction to the Critique of Hegel's Philosophy of Law," published in 1844. With these writings he came to the conclusion "that neither legal relations nor forms of the state could be understood by themselves or explained from the so-called general evolution of the human mind, but that they are rooted in the material conditions of life whose totality Hegel, following the English and French of the eighteenth century, summed up under the term 'civil society,' and the anatomy of civil society is to be sought in political economy."

In 1851 Marx edited the first part of a two-volume collection of his works beginning with his first published essay, his "Comments on the Latest Prussian Censorship Instruction" of 1842. The collection was to include essays from the *Rheinische Zeitung,* the "Introduction to the Critique of Hegel's Philosophy of Law" and essay "On the Jewish Question" from the *Deutsch-Französische Jahrbücher,* and inaccessible writings from other journals up to 1848.[1] Only the first part of the first volume was ever published, but Marx's plans indicate the importance he placed on his early writings.

---

[1] Cf. D. Rjazanov and V. Adoratskij (eds.), *Marx-Engels Gesamtausgabe* [hereafter MEGA], (Berlin, 1927–   ), Abt. I, Bd. 1¹, pp. xi–xii; Engels on Marx's early writings, *Reminiscences of Marx and Engels* (Moscow, n.d.), pp. 330–31; and Marx and Engels, *Letters to Americans* (New York, 1953), p. 151.

### *Humanitarianism and Liberalism of a Young Hegelian*

From his final term at the Trier *Gymnasium* in 1835 to his resignation as editor of the *Rheinische Zeitung* in 1843, Marx's writings widely expressed a strong, humanitarian social concern. At first that concern was grounded in Christianity. Later it was based on the philosophy of Hegel. With his university studies in philosophy and first publications on social issues, he became increasingly hostile to Christianity and turned his liberal interpretation of Hegel toward democracy.

In "Reflections of a Youth on Choosing an Occupation," an examination essay at the *Gymnasium,* Marx takes "the welfare of humanity" as his main principle. "Man's nature," he declares, "makes it possible for him to reach his fulfillment only by working for the perfection and welfare of his society." Such a criterion is not only confirmed by history and experience, but "religion itself teaches us that the ideal for which we are all striving sacrificed itself for humanity." Thus Marx put Christianity at the center of his humanitarianism. Though his parents had descended from a long line of rabbis, Marx had been baptized into the Evangelical Church of Prussia at the age of six, his father having become a Christian eight years before. His elementary school and the *Gymnasium* had required the study of Christianity. In another examination essay (MEGA, I, 1², 171–74), Marx referred to the brotherhood of man as being rooted in the union of the faithful with Christ. Developing the parable of the vine and the branches, he concluded that through love of Christ "we turn our hearts at the same time to our brothers, whom He has bound more closely with us, for whom He also sacrificed himself." Even at this time, however, Marx's humanitarian aspiration was tempered by a sense of social limitation. He anticipated his mature thought in saying that "we cannot always choose the vocation to which we believe we are called. Our social relations, to some extent, have already begun to form before we are in a position to determine them."

After two years of university life at Bonn and Berlin, Marx reports a basic shift in his thinking in the 1837 "Letter to His Father." He has turned away from romantic poetry toward philosophy, and in philosophy has gone from Kant and Fichte "into the clutches" of Hegel. Disturbed by the conflict between what is and what ought to be, he has decided to seek "the Idea in the real itself." He studies Hegel from end to end, discusses Hegel's philosophy in the Berlin Doctors' Club, and writes a dialogue on "the godhead manifested as a concept per se, as religion, as nature, and as history." The conclusion of the dialogue is the premise of Hegel's system. Thus Marx became a Hegelian. He saw the actual world as the embodiment of reason, the manifestation of an all-embracing Idea as its developing wholeness.

During the next two to three years Marx became increasingly critical of Christianity. This attitude seems to have stemmed more from his humanitarian sympathies and aspirations than from philosophical considerations. Marx was aware that Strauss and Bauer had come to regard the miracles of the New Testament as messianic myths. But this could readily be absorbed in Hegel's philosophy; the basic themes of Christianity could be seen as the Idea manifest in historically developed forms of "imaginative presentation." Marx seems to have been particularly offended by the callousness to human welfare he saw in orthodox, supernaturalistic Christianity functioning as a branch of the Prussian monarchy. In the following decade he bitterly assailed the King of Prussia's "Christian statecraft" toward pauperism and a weavers' revolt, the mores of Christianity and Judaism in the degrading effects of money and trade, and the "social principles of Christianity" of the *Rheinische Beobachter*—principles which sneakily preach sin and self-contempt to justify slavery and oppression while "the proletariat, not wanting to be treated as canaille, needs its courage, confidence, pride, and independence more than its daily bread." But even at the end of his university studies, according to one report, he viewed "the Christian religion as one of the most immoral" of all religions. His humanitarian sympathies had already been directed to "the most numerous and poorest class" by the doctrines of Saint-Simon to which he had been exposed in Trier through his father and in Berlin through the lectures of Eduard Gans. Saint-Simon, moreover, had specifically criticized existing Christianity for its failure to ameliorate the condition of the poorest class.[2]

Marx's criticism of religion and Christianity in particular became more explicit with his doctoral dissertation on "The Difference Between the Democritean and Epicurean Philosophy of Nature." In the Foreword to the dissertation[3] Marx noted his adherence to Hegel, who had correctly defined the general features of the philosophies of Democritus and Epicurus. He also indicated his adherence to a radical interpretation of Hegel like that of Bruno Bauer for whom the Idea was a function of human self-consciousness, not a transcendent or supernatural entity. On this basis Marx followed Epicurus in regarding the crowd's opinions of the gods as impious and linked philosophy with Prometheus' hatred of all the gods who gave ill for good. Prometheus, said Marx, is "the noblest of saints and martyrs in the calendar of philosophy." This judgment implicitly expressed Marx's ethical commitment and humanitarianism, which he had earlier based on Christianity. Prometheus was the god who brought fire to earth and aided man in defiance of Zeus. Instead of Christ, who had become mythical in the thought of Strauss and Bauer, Marx directed himself to Prometheus to express his commitment to human welfare.

Marx's Notes to the Doctoral Dissertation further express his criticism of Christianity. The second of these Notes takes issue with D. F. C. Baur's book on *The Christian Element of Platonism* and insists that there is a marked difference between philosophy personified in Socrates and religion personified in Christ. The "exaltation" in philoso-

[2] Cf. T. B. Bottomore and M. Rubel (eds.), *Karl Marx, Selected Writings in Sociology and Social Philosophy* (London, 1956), p. 9; Claude Henri Saint-Simon, "The New Christianity," in *Socialist Thought*, eds. A. Fried and R. Saunders (New York, 1964), pp. 82–97.

[3] MEGA, I, 1¹, 9–10, translated in Marx and Engels, *On Religion* (Moscow, 1957; New York, 1964), pp. 13–16.

phy transmits the flame of knowledge and nurtures a universal perspective on nature and history while religious exaltation is only a "hot-water bottle for some individual souls." Plato's myths reveal his common ground with historic Christianity which is "the completed philosophy of transcendence," severing the Absolute from its immersion in the actual world. In these matters, Marx indicates in the last of his Notes, the "ontological argument" can be of little help. Hegel's inversion of this argument at best disproves God's transcendence. The ontological argument is actually a tautology which only says that what I conceive as actual for me is an actual conception which "really matters," but this is incompatible with any divine transcendence.

In these criticisms of religion Marx was using an interpretation of Hegel similar to that which Bruno Bauer had used against Hegel's own support of Christianity as the fullest manifestation of the Absolute Idea. Marx was entirely in agreement with—and probably helped to write—Bauer's anonymous pamphlet, *The Trumpet of the Last Judgment over Hegel the Atheist and Antichrist*, published in November 1841. This pamphlet depicted Hegel as identifying God with universal spirit in self-consciousness, as favoring philosophy independent of theology, as admiring the pantheism of Spinoza, and as being a revolutionary whose view of reason in history condemned existing institutions as passing failures. In this spirit Marx's "Nodal Points in the Development of Philosophy" sees philosophy after Hegel as having reached a turning point to become practical, primarily ethical, so it "turns against the apparent world." This practical work, Marx explains in "Philosophy after Its Completion," is essentially criticism "which measures individual existence against essence, particular actuality against the Idea." Adhering to the Idea, the liberal party in criticism seeks out "the deficiency of the world to be made philosophical" and thus transcends philosophy itself. "Criticism" in this sense became a main strand in Marx's writings to 1843 and remained in his views as the "rational kernel" he always retained from Hegel, the dialectical pattern of history. In opposition to transcendental Christianity, the Idea as the development of human self-consciousness and reason in actuality became the foundation of Marx's humanitarian aspirations.

In his first published essay of social criticism, "Comments on the Latest Prussian Censorship Instruction," Marx goes into detail on the inconsistencies of a new directive to relax prevailing regulations. Marx finds that restriction on expressions of political tendency assumes the government alone to possess reason and stifles reason in its more universal form, the community as a whole. Further, censorship is incompatible with the very essence of law, publicity and universality. Law pertains only to deeds and acts, not thoughts and motives included in "the sacredness and inviolability of subjective conviction." Defects of the press should be left to the cure that freedom brings and not to the cuts of the censor. Thus Marx turned the Idea as a truly ethical state against the existing actuality of censorship, toward liberal democracy.

"Luther as Arbiter Between Strauss and Feuerbach" signalizes the beginning of Marx's attachment to Ludwig Feuerbach whose *Essence of Christianity* he had studied on leaving the university. Marx appeals to Luther to decide between Feuerbach and Strauss on miracles. Feuerbach comes out the victor because Luther takes religion to be "immediate truth" or "Nature," that is, "confident trust" and "hearts that are intrepid and unafraid," and this immediate truth of human feeling rather than mediating speculation as in Strauss is the substance of Feuerbach's definitions of "providence," "miracle," and "faith." With this position Marx not only expressed distrust of Hegelian speculative idealism but endorsed a naturalistic view of religion affiliated with an emerging existentialism, an insistence on the primacy of immediate experience over concepts for getting at things "as they are." "There is no other road to *truth* and *freedom*," Marx concludes, "except that leading *through* the stream of fire [the *Feuer-bach*]." Later, especially from 1843 to 1845, Marx followed that road closely as he used Feuerbach's view of "alienation" to criticize abstract speculation in Hegel and put Hegel's dialectical method on a new foundation.

In spite of his distrust of Hegelianism in religion, Marx

continued to follow Hegel's social thought at a number of points in his contributions to the *Rheinische Zeitung* even as he departed from Hegel in the direction of liberal democracy. "The Philosophical Manifesto of the Historical School of Law" shows the consequences of taking mere existence, past or present, as the norm for laws of property and marriage. Such a position leads to a relativism which justifies slavery, animalism, and arbitrary power because it sceptically rejects the norm of rationality in legal institutions. Here Marx was closely following Hegel whose *Philosophy of Law* (§ 3) had criticized a leader of the Historical School for not indicating whether Roman slavery met the "demands of reason" and for confusing historical development with development from the concept. Marx's criticism was based on "the structures of human rationality."

In writing on "The Centralization Question," Marx indicates that a "philosophical answer" cannot be an imagined ideal or verbal solution. "Philosophy must seriously protest when it is confused with imagination." True criticism, rather, must analyze the question itself in terms of the actualities of history. Though Marx did not refer to Hegel, he was closely following his thought. Hegel had prominently condemned utopian solutions and abstract ideals as substitutes for reason in history.

In "The Leading Article in No. 179 of the *Kölnische Zeitung*," Marx answers criticisms of his view on freedom of the press, particularly freedom to discuss religion. This gives him another opportunity to insist on the superiority of philosophy to religion. Athens and Rome, Marx argues, reached their heights only when philosophy had displaced religion. He challenges the notion that even fetishism has an elevating quality. It is "the *religion of sensuous appetites*" in which the worshiper projects his wishes into a thing. Criticizing a wood-theft law a few months later, Marx noted how forest owners made a fetish of wood. He returned to this theme from time to time to expose self-deceptions about the state and commodities. Now he suggests that fetishism involves a mistaken devaluation of man's consciousness and reason, a criticism implied in Hegel's idealism. Marx particularly follows Hegel in viewing education as the transformation of individual impulse into universal aims, in describing philosophy as "the living soul of a culture," and in arguing for the separation of church and state. Substantially agreeing with Hegel, he derives the state from "reason in society," not reason in the individual, and describes it as "the great organism in which legal, ethical, and political freedom has to be actualized and the individual citizen simply obeys the laws of his own reason, human reason, in the laws of the state."

"Communism and the Augsburg 'Allgemeine Zeitung,'" Marx's first article as editor in chief, answers charges that the *Rheinische Zeitung* had been "flirting with communism." He sides with liberalism, noting that he can hardly endorse "socialist-communist" ideas on labor and division of land when they are being spread by reactionaries. Communism does involve issues of European significance and deserves serious study because ideas won by intelligence and forged in conscience are chains to which we must submit. From this position Marx threw himself into the study of socialism about which, he later admitted, he knew almost nothing.

Marx's comments "On a Proposed Divorce Law" go into detail on the confusions of existing regulations and reflect the influence of Hegel as they stress the "ethical substance" of marriage in opposition to the individual caprice or private pleasure of easy divorce. Marx allows that when a marriage does not correspond to its concept, it may be recognized by the state as dead. In holding that law as recognition of this ethical death must be "the conscious expression of the will of the people" involving "reverence for man," Marx departed from Hegel in the direction of democracy. This direction was apparent in a short series of articles, written at the same time about standing committees in the Prussian assembly (MEGA, I, 1¹, 321–35). From Hegel's view of the state as a spiritual organism substantiating freedom, Marx argued that such committees should not represent special class interests or minorities but all the people. "Representation," Marx held, "is not to be representation of some substance which is not the people but must be viewed only as *self-representation,* as the state's action, which is distinct from general manifestations of political life only through the universality of its content." In a true state, Marx concluded, there is no landed property, industry, or "matter" which might bargain with the state. Only as such elements are politically transformed can they become "spiritual forces" deserving a voice in the state. "The state permeates the whole with spiritual nerves, and it must be everywhere apparent that not matter but form, not nature without the state but the nature of the state, not the *unfree thing* but the *free man* dominates."

"Defense of the Moselle Correspondent" deals more directly with "material interests" in relation to the state as it analyzes the economic distress of the vintagers in the Moselle valley. Like his earlier essay on a wood-theft law, this one reveals Marx's humanitarian concern as he speaks for "the impoverished, the socially and politically deprived masses." Alleviation of the distress of the vintagers, Marx argues, requires action from the state but also a universal "participation in the interests of the fatherland" that can transcend bureaucracy, truly represent the citizen, and manifest itself in a free press. In substance, Marx was saying, it requires liberal democracy. Later he referred to his "Defense of the Moselle Correspondent" and earlier essay on a wood-theft law as his first "embarrassed" efforts to deal with "material interests." They became the impetus to his subsequent study of economics much as "Communism and the Augsburg 'Allgemeine Zeitung'" impelled him to study socialism. Some results of these studies became apparent in his next writings.

## Feuerbachian Criticism of Hegel

The second phase of Marx's early writings—the summer of 1843 to the end of 1844—coincided mainly with his exile in Paris where he began his influential collaboration with Engels, intensively studied classical economics, and frequently met with socialist thinkers and workers. In this period the dominant influence on Marx's thought was that of Ludwig Feuerbach, who provided a view of "alienation" and its correlative "humanism" to be used against

Hegel's idealism, against identification of every event and object with the development of a transcendent Absolute Idea. Through criticism of Hegel and on the basis of Feuerbach's humanism Marx espoused democracy and its fulfillment in socialism. This fulfillment, however, was premised on the historical and dialectical movement of the working class, the proletariat. In this respect Marx retained the view of "reason in society" he had acquired from Hegel.

Early in his "Critique of Hegel's Philosophy of the State," Marx introduces the idea of "alienation" that had been developed by Feuerbach through internal criticism of Hegel's dialectic. By "alienation" Marx meant, in general terms, that the projections of human experience in thought or social institutions are misleadingly separated from man in abstract speculation and acquire a harmful power over him in his social life, dividing him from himself and his fellow men so that he is never truly whole and never truly "at home." Marx specifically charges that the "dependence" of family and civil society on the state in Hegel's *Philosophy of Law* (§ 262) is a relationship not in experienced actuality but only in something external and alien. "Actuality," Marx says, "is not experienced as it is itself but as another actuality. Common experience is not subject to the law of its own spirit but to an alien spirit." Hegel's mistake is a result of reversing subject and predicate in respect to the Idea and its content, while "development takes place on the side of the predicate," which is the real content of the Idea. Thus Hegel's method is "mystification," the alienation of abstract concepts from the concrete connections of experience.

Here Marx was following Feuerbach's attack on speculation which had appeared in *The Essence of Christianity* and subsequently in the *Anekdota* along with his own first essay on censorship. The speculative philosopher, Feuerbach charged, sees nature, religion, and philosophy itself as mere predicates of the Idea, but "we need only to convert the predicate into the subject to get at the pure, undisguised truth." Feuerbach saw Hegel's idealism as the apotheosis of abstraction that "alienates man from himself" because it inverts the real relation of thought to its object.[4] Following Feuerbach against Hegel, Marx looks to "empirical actuality" and "common experience" for the content of the Idea. He becomes an empiricist to avoid Hegel's mystification which connects things "in the abstract sphere of logic." In parts of the "Critique" omitted from the translation to follow, however, Marx firmly adhered to the liberal "party of the Idea." He accused Hegel of uncritically accepting the status quo as the truth of the Idea, as being a genuine state. This was internal criticism of Hegel from Hegelian premises.

Further, Marx uses the idea of alienation to criticize Hegel's dismissal of sovereignty of the people. Hegel had repeatedly insisted that the idea of the state requires unity of form and content, universality and particularity. These conditions, Marx argues, are met only in democracy, which is "the true unity of the general and the particular." Without democracy the "far removed existence of the political state" only affirms the alienation of property, family, and civil society. Marx sees this alienation as essentially religious. In *The Essence of Christianity* Feuerbach had interpreted religion as involving man's projection of his deepest satisfactions and values into an ideal, heavenly realm whose substance must be returned to man. Now Marx sees in the "state as such" an instance of this projection and alienation. The state is "the religious sphere," "the heaven of universality," in contrast to the people's actual, mundane life. But democracy, Marx argues, can resolve this alienation of political life through self-government. In democracy there is "self-determination of the people," and the constitution is "man's and the people's *own* work." In democracy "man does not exist for the law, but the law exists for man." With the achievement of democracy in this sense, the political state as such disappears because the alienation of ordinary life from a "heavenly universality" is overcome.

On this basis Marx condemns Hegel's treatment of the civil service as "bureaucracy," a theological "illusion of

[4] Cf. Ludwig Feuerbach, *Kleine philosophische Schriften* (Leipzig, 1950), pp. 56, 59, 144, 149; *The Essence of Christianity*, trans. G. Eliot [M. Evans], (New York, 1957), ch. I, § 2.

the state," "something apart from and alien to the nature of civil society." The resolution of this alienation is simply the further application of democracy involving "the capacity of the universal class to be actually universal, that is, to be the class of every citizen." For the implementation of democracy Marx insists on "unlimited voting" to overcome the alienation between the "heavenly universality" of the state on the one hand and life in civil society on the other. "The reform of voting," Marx concludes, "is the *dissolution* of the state, but likewise the *dissolution of civil society*." It is the dissolution of civil society, because civil society—the realm of economic interests, labor, private property, and class distinctions, which Hegel characterized after Hobbes as "the war of all against all"—is authentically universalized. It is transcended in democracy, in "socialized man as a particular constitution." Here was Marx's first conception of socialism in outline. It included the dissolution of civil society—the dissolution of the existing organization of labor and industry—with the achievement of democracy as self-government through unrestricted voting.

In addition to the influence of Feuerbach, this position reflected Marx's study of Spinoza's argument for democracy in the *Tractatus Theologico-Politicus* and Thomas Hamilton's suggestion that democracy, as shown by developments in the United States, would lead the working class to overcome the power and concentrated wealth of the capitalists.[5] Marx reaffirmed this view of democracy two years later in "Points on the Modern State and Civil Society," translated below from his Notebooks containing the well-known "Theses on Feuerbach." After linking the French Revolution with the "presumption of the political sphere," after distinguishing between centralized "state administration and local government," Marx concludes his "Points" with the statement: "*Suffrage*, the struggle to *overcome* the state and civil society."

In his essay "On the Jewish Question," Marx further de-

[5] Cf. M. Rubel, "Notes on Marx's Conception of Democracy," *New Politics*, 1 (Winter 1962), 80–85; "Le Concept de démocratie chez Marx," *Contrat social*, 6 (1962), 2–8.

velops the theme of political alienation. Substituting Feuerbach's idea of man's "species-life" for Hegel's concept of "universality," he describes the split between man's "heavenly" political life and his actual, earthly life in civil society. In the former, man "regards himself as a *communal being;* but in *civil society,* he is active as a *private individual,* treats other men as means, reduces himself to a means, and becomes the plaything of alien powers." Thus Marx was becoming as much concerned about alienation within civil society as alienation in relation to the state. He finds alienation especially apparent in money which, like all religious objects, becomes a fetish with an independent power that diminishes man and detracts from his personal worth. Judaism and Christianity in practice are vivid expressions of this alienation. Hence, full human emancipation, a full resolution of this alienation, cannot come with bills of rights making religion merely a private affair. Such rights do not go beyond "the egoistic man, the man withdrawn into himself, his private interest and his private choice, and separated from the community as a member of civil society," as shown in America. Political emancipation through bills of human rights, Marx allows, is a great step forward. But it fails to answer man's social nature and fails to make his species-life real. Full emancipation requires democracy where the sovereignty of man has become "a tangible reality, a secular maxim." With Christianity as a religion, that sovereignty remains a "chimera, dream, and postulate." The basis of democracy is thus "not Christianity but the *human ground* of Christianity"—a statement revealing the positive content of Marx's criticism of religion. At this point Marx was as little or as much a Christian as Feuerbach for whom the "true atheist" was not the man who denies God but the one for whom the predicates attributed to God are nothing. For Marx the preciousness, brotherhood, and unity of man in his species-life were everything. He was committed to central values of Christianity as human and natural values. On this basis he describes "full human emancipation" in the following terms:

Only when the actual, individual man has taken back into himself the abstract citizen and in his everyday life, his individual work, and his individual relations has become a *species-being,* only when he has recognized and organized his own powers as *social* powers so that social force is no longer separated from him as *political* power, only then is human emancipation complete.

This conclusion has been identified as the point at which Marx became a socialist, but its substance had already been achieved earlier in his view of democracy whereby civil society is transformed into "socialized man" through unrestricted voting.

In the "Introduction to the Critique of Hegel's Philosophy of Law," Marx further applies Feuerbach's view of alienation and finds in the proletariat the lever for the full human emancipation he earlier identified as democracy. With Feuerbach, Marx sees man as the basis of religion, but man must be understood concretely and socially as *"the world of men,* the state, society." Marx had already complained that Feuerbach was "too much concerned with nature and too little with politics." Hence, "the immediate *task of philosophy* which is in the service of history," Marx insists, "is to unmask human self-alienation in its *unholy forms* now that it has been unmasked in its *holy form.*" This requires criticism of law and politics and transcendence of philosophy by putting it into practice with "the *categorical imperative to overthrow all conditions* in which man is a degraded, enslaved, neglected, contemptible being." But the actualization of philosophy in practice requires action against the German status quo by a sphere of civil society having a universal character, a universal human title, "that cannot emancipate itself without emancipating itself from all other spheres of society, thereby emancipating them"—namely, the proletariat.

Marx's selection of the proletariat as the key to full human emancipation was undoubtedly influenced by many factors—his reading on the proletariat in Lorenz Stein and Flora Tristan, his discussions with socialists in Paris, his own financial distress in exile, and his close contact with

French workers, among whom, said Marx, "the brother-hood of man is no phrase but a truth." Marx's preoccupa-tion with Hegel was also a factor. He had read in Hegel's *Philosophy of Law* (§ 244) that with development of in-dustry "a great mass of people sinks below a certain necessary level of subsistence and thereby loses the sense of justice, integrity, and the honor to exist by one's own activity and labor. This produces the proletariat [*Pöbel*] which in turn facilitates the concentration of excessive wealth in a few hands." Further, Marx's discussion of the proletariat followed Hegel's dialectic—namely, a class in chains is to destroy all chains, a particular class is to end classes, the complete loss of humanity is to redeem hu-manity.

Thus Marx was beginning to supplement Feuerbach by using Hegel's dialectic of reason to formulate and resolve alienation. This is apparent in "An Exchange of Letters," which launched the *Deutsch-Französische Jahrbücher*. Crit-icizing the socialism of Weitling, Proudhon, and others as one-sided "abstractions" from "the reality of true human nature," Marx calls for criticism of existing political de-velopments:

> Reason has always existed, but not always in rational form. The critic, therefore, can start with any form of theoretical and practical consciousness and develop the true actuality out of the forms *inherent* in existing actuality as its ought-to-be and goal. As far as actual life is concerned, the *political state* especially contains in all its *modern* forms the demands of reason, even where the political state is not yet conscious of socialis-tic demands. . . . We develop new principles for the world out of the principles of the world.

Thus Marx viewed socialism not as a dogmatic anticipa-tion of the future but as the fulfillment of historical reason which criticism, the measurement of actuality against the Idea, was to bring to light. This fulfillment requires an awakening of the feeling of human dignity. "Only this feel-ing," writes Marx, "which disappeared from the world with the Greeks and with Christianity vanished into the blue mist of heaven, can again transform society into a community of men to achieve their highest purpose, a democratic state." Thus Marx firmly linked the achievement of socialism with the achievement of democracy.

In the "Excerpt-Notes of 1844" and "Economic and Philosophic Manuscripts," Marx prominently uses the idea of "alienation" to analyze labor and the economic relationships of existing society and to refine his conception of socialism. The "Manuscripts" specifically criticize Hegel's speculative method in the "critical theology" of Strauss and Bauer for being a clear case of the "alienation of man's nature." In this respect Marx follows Feuerbach, "the true conqueror of the old philosophy." He adopts Feuerbach's "positive humanistic and naturalistic criticism" to deal with speculative alienation.

With Feuerbach, Marx holds that genuine thought as opposed to abstract speculation is rooted in sense perception, the object, nature involving the relation of man to man. On this basis he seems to be calling for a thoroughly empirical, scientific sociology and predicts that natural science and the science of man will become "one science." He refers to this position as "naturalism or humanism." It is to be distinguished from both idealism and materialism but unites the truth of each. Its provision for the element of subjectivity, for "the immediate" in sense perception and feeling, along with its warning that "society" must not be established as an abstraction over and against the individual, has particularly appealed to contemporary existentialists. But without special note of the fact, Marx goes beyond Feuerbach to identify this humanism with the history of industry and society. He insists that man's senses and varied needs are themselves the products of history. For socialist man, Marx holds, "world history is only the creation of man through human labor and the development of nature for man." This practical and sensuous relation to nature disposes of the need for a transcendent creator. "Atheism" implies the affirmation of man.

In more detail than the "Excerpt-Notes of 1844," the "Manuscripts" analyze the characteristic sphere of civil society related to man's economic life, labor, and its relationship to commodities. Marx finds man alienated from himself both in the process of labor and in its product which belongs to "other men." In this respect he particularly leans on Hegel's *Phenomenology of Spirit* (ch. VI, B, i) where wealth and state power are viewed as alienations overcome in the movement of experience toward absolute knowledge. Marx warmly endorses Hegel's great insight that man is the historical product of his own work in a process of alienation and its resolution. Hegel's mistake was to treat that process speculatively, as a development of knowledge, a dialectical movement of abstract concepts, rather than as a dialectical development in actual, perceptible, historical practice.

With the "Manuscripts" Marx further develops his view of socialism in relation to man's alienation in labor and private property. He opposes the "crude" communism of Proudhon and Fourier which seeks to universalize private property (even of women), abstract from talent, negate man's personality, and force the situation of the laborer on all men because it fails to see the basis of property in man's alienation. In Marx's view, man's alienation can be overcome only through "a complete and conscious restoration of man to himself within the total wealth of previous development" to achieve "the *rich,* deep, and *entirely sensitive* man as its enduring actuality." Such a "whole man" lives not through the favor of another but through his own social action in a "real community" where the five senses and the "spiritual or moral senses (will, love, etc.)" are objectively unfolded to confirm and realize his individuality. The earlier "Excerpt-Notes" held that such a realization of individuality is possible only if production does not presuppose possession and profit. Then, said Marx in terms of Feuerbach's humanistic Christianity, production would provide that mutuality in which I would be "affirmed in your thought as well as your love." Though Marx did not relate this achievement to democracy, the relation is implicit in his reference to the "whole man" as realizing "generic life" and as being self-directed in the overcoming of his alienation in the state. The achievement of such a "real community," however, is not simply a matter of personal will and action. It is no "abstraction from the objective world" but rather "the actual emergence, the actual future realization for man of his nature and his nature as actual." Thus Marx was moving beyond Feuerbach's ethical humanism to put his ultimate reliance on the movement of history manifesting the dialectic of labor and industry.

Marx wrote his "Critical Notes on 'The King of Prussia and Social Reform'" for the Paris *Vorwärts* while he was at work on the "Manuscripts" in order to refute Ruge's view, occasioned by a Silesian weavers' revolt, concerning the relation between social reform and political action. Though Marx probably exaggerated the significance of the revolt, his "Critical Notes" importantly amplified his view of socialism.

Using the view of the state he developed earlier, Marx insists that political administration cannot fundamentally remedy social evils because the state is based on the contradiction between general interests and the unsocial nature of civil life manifest in private property, industry, and the mutual plundering of different civil groups. Against "this debasement, this *slavery of civil society*," the modern state is impotent, and rival political parties always blame social misery only on their opponents or "defects of administration." What is needed is not so much political revolt with "irrational and useless uprisings suppressed in blood" as social revolution expressing the "protest of man against dehumanized life," against separation from the "*real community* of man" rather than from the abstract political state. Socialism does require political action against the existing ruling power and existing social conditions. "But where its *organizing activity* begins, where its *own aim* and *spirit* emerge, there socialism throws the *political* hull away." Here Marx was crystallizing his conclusion that socialism involves a truly universal human community reflected in labor and industry rather than a deceptively universal state presupposing the "slavery of civil society." He was insisting on a democracy that would include but go beyond politics and the state.

*Criticism and Appropriation of Hegel and Feuerbach*

In the third phase of Marx's early development—from the end of 1844 to the completion of *The Poverty of Philosophy* shortly before *The Communist Manifesto*—there emerged a distinct combination of ideas from Feuerbach and Hegel, which became the core of Marx's mature thought and the "leading thread," as he called it, of all his subsequent writings. In these years Marx adopted, in part, Feuerbach's humanism and his appeal to sense perception, and used these positions against Hegel. At the same time he retained Hegel's view of "reason in society," the dialectic of history, but saw this as inherent in man's sensuous activity, his labor and social practice, not in the Idea. Further, he saw this dialectical movement as entailing the achievement of socialism. This combination, however, had been foreshadowed in the "Introduction to the Critique of Hegel's Philosophy of Law" and the "Manuscripts" of 1844.

*The Holy Family* was the first product of Marx's collaboration with Engels after their long, enthusiastic meeting in Paris, though most of its chapters were written by Marx. In its underlying perspective it essentially agreed with the "Manuscripts" of 1844 and might well be put at the end of the previous phase of Marx's writings. Its Foreword identified the authors' position as "real humanism," that is, the philosophy of Feuerbach, which pits "real individual man" against "Spirit" or "Self-consciousness" as involved in the speculative idealism, the "disguised theology," of Bruno Bauer, Edgar Bauer, and their followers.[6] But *The Holy Family* is more explicit than previous writings as to how Marx was still a Hegelian in his social dialectic and how he came to call his view "materialism." Though its polemics involve much hairsplitting and verbal byplay on views which were expiring or unimportant even in 1845, it also contains some of Marx's most vivid writing.

The early part of *The Holy Family* defends Proudhon, with whom Marx often discussed Hegel's dialectic, against

---

[6] Cf. MEGA, I, 3, 179, or Marx and Engels, *The Holy Family*, trans. R. Dixon (Moscow, 1956), pp. 15–16.

the "critical criticism" of Edgar Bauer. Marx finds a "great scientific advance" in Proudhon's view that "political economy moves in a continuous contradiction to its basic premise, private property, a contradiction analogous to that of a theologian who constantly gives a human interpretation to religious ideas and thereby contradicts his fundamental assumption, the superhuman character of religion." Proudhon particularly reveals the contradiction between the humane appearance of economic conditions and their inhumane reality.

Extending Proudhon's insight, Marx finds a dialectical connection between property and poverty by virtue of their actual internal movement. Proletariat and wealth are antitheses, the poles of a dialectic. Both manifest private property and depend on one another. They represent the same human self-alienation, but the propertied class is comfortable in this alienation while the proletariat, in Hegel's words, is abased and indignant at its inhuman existence. It is driven to destroy the antithesis. Marx sees this dialectical movement not as a speculative relationship but as an economic process in which "private property is driven towards its own dissolution but only through a development which does not depend on it, of which it is unconscious, which takes place against its will, and which is brought about by the very nature of things." The action of the proletariat in this process "is prescribed, irrevocably and obviously, in its own situation in life as well as in the entire organization of contemporary civil society."

For such a view of the movement of history and civil society, Marx was obviously indebted to Hegel. His conception of the class struggle, the resolution of man's self-alienation, and the pattern of necessity in historical action were simply applications of Hegel's dialectic. In this respect Marx was more Hegelian than Bauer. But for Marx the dialectic was not a speculative movement of thought and ideas; rather it was a movement of actual, perceptible events and relationships. In this respect he adhered to Feuerbach.

In writing on "The Mystery of Speculative Construction," Marx insists that to think of "Fruit" as true "Substance," "*self-activity* of the absolute Subject," or "*inner Process*" is to elaborate a devious conceptual invention which simply renames the ordinary, experienced properties and relations of ordinary apples, pears, and strawberries. Marx allows, however, that Hegel himself "very often gives an *actual* presentation, a presentation of the *matter* itself, within his *speculative* presentation." Further, abstract speculation leads Bauer and his cohorts to treat history as "a person apart, a metaphysical subject of which human individuals are merely bearers." Contrasting "Spirit" to "Mass" they ignore the effective role of interests in history and resolve the "*practical* self-alienations of the mass" by a movement of ideas, as Hegel did in his *Phenomenology*. Bruno Bauer at least correctly sees, as Hegel did not, that the Absolute Spirit makes history "only in consciousness, in the opinion and conception of the philosopher, only in speculative imagination." But Ludwig Feuerbach, notes Engels in his contribution to *The Holy Family*, not only destroyed the speculative approach to history in the old "dialectic of concepts," but made clear that

> *History* does *nothing*, it "possesses *no* colossal riches," it "fights *no* battles"! Rather it is *man*, actual and living man who does all this, who possesses and fights; "history" does not use man as a means for *its* purposes as though it were a person apart; it is *nothing* but the activity of man pursuing his ends.

In the section of *The Holy Family* on the "Critical Battle Against French Materialism," Marx further indicates his reliance on Feuerbach's empiricism which rooted thought in sense experience as opposed to abstract speculation. Like Pierre Bayle, Feuerbach saw in speculative metaphysics the last prop of traditional theology. In Marx's view materialism, the radical enemy of theology and metaphysics, is at bottom the view that "our knowledge and ideas originate from the world of the senses" as Bacon, Hobbes, and Locke had insisted. With the French followers of Locke, materialism flowed directly into socialism and communism. If man forms all his knowledge from the world of sense, it follows, says Marx, that the empirical world must be so arranged that man experiences what is truly human in it. "If man is formed by circumstances, then his circumstances must be made human." In this way, Marx claims, Fourier, Babeuf, and Owen "developed the doctrine of *materialism* as a doctrine of *real humanism*, the *logical* basis of *communism*."

At several points in this treatment of materialism Marx's transitions are questionable. The rootage of knowledge in sense experience did not imply for Locke or Berkeley that everything is matter. Nor did it for Marx a year earlier. Like Feuerbach before him, Marx misleadingly applied to a theory of knowledge a label better reserved for a theory of the substance or stuff of things. Further, the rootage of knowledge in sense perception does not logically imply that the perceptible world ought to be changed and made more humane. What "is" as sensuous fact does not imply what "ought to be." Marx's use of "materialism" as a synonym for "real humanism," however, does reveal that behind his socialism was a moral commitment to the dignity and preciousness of every man.

In his well-known and much-analyzed "Theses on Feuerbach," which Engels called "the brilliant germ of a new world view," Marx criticizes Feuerbach and moves toward a unique combination of Feuerbach and Hegel. He refers to Feuerbach's philosophy as "materialism" and finds it lacking the active element, the element of practical activity, he had earlier found in Hegel. But Marx also rejects Hegelian "activity" as abstract, detached from sensuous objects and events. "Practical activity," then, becomes his central idea. It must change man's circumstances if man is to be changed. It must resolve the self-alienation of the secular world in civil society to achieve "socialized humanity." Feuerbach provides no guidance in these directions because, Marx indicates, he sees man only as "species" and not as an "ensemble of social relations" within the "historical process." Thus practical activity in history, historical practice, becomes the fulcrum of Marx's thought.

Several of Marx's main themes up to this point—alienation, the state, labor, and history—are more extensively and concretely developed in *The German Ideology* which Marx and Engels wrote together in 1845–46, though Engels later noted that Marx had already arrived at the main features of his view in the spring of 1845 so the theory "rightly bears his name." In the first section of *The German Ideology* to follow, Marx observes that man's own activity in government, wealth, and culture becomes to him an alien power, standing over against him instead of being ruled by him. The remedy is communism, a "real community" in which the contradiction between the separate individual or family and the interest of all has been overcome by healing the cleavage between production and consumption, between intellectual and manual labor, arising from division of labor in modern industry. This requires the abolition of the state, social classes, and all existing forms of association that express man's self-alienation. The alien and seemingly independent powers that fetter men—the state, class, industry, religion—are to be brought under their control so there is nothing independent of self-active, associated individuals.

This remedy for alienation rounds out Marx's earlier view of democracy and full human emancipation. But it is not, we are now warned, a speculative conclusion. Its foundation is rather "real individuals, their actions, and their material conditions of life," and such premises can be verified "in a purely empirical way." This empiricism from Feuerbach, however, does not save him from criticism. Marx accuses him of having an "abstract" view of human nature, of seeing man's nature as something fixed and isolated. Earlier Marx had praised and adopted Feuerbach's view of man as a "species-being." He had agreed with Feuerbach that "the essence of man exists only in community, in the unity of man with man." What then was Feuerbach's deficiency? Specifically, he lacked a historical view of man and particularly a dialectical view of man's development in relation to industry and labor. Hence his remedy for man's alienation could only be an ideal to be contemplated, an ideal "ought" as suggested in the preface to *The Essence of Christianity*. For Marx the overcoming of man's alienation in communism was something different. It was "the *real* movement which abolishes the present state of affairs." In short, it was the dialectic of reason in history manifest in the movement of labor, industry, and the social classes within civil society. Thus Feuerbach's deficiency was corrected by the "rational kernel" from Hegel to which Marx later referred in his preface to *Capital*.

Engels emphasized this debt to Hegel in a review of the *Critique of Political Economy,* first published in America by August Willich in the *Cincinnati Republikaner, Organ der Arbeiter* (September 15, 1859). Hegel's dialectic, Engels insisted, was scarcely less important in Marx's position than the economic basis of society. Willich, in turn, saw Marx's use of Hegel's dialectic as its proof and as evidence that Hegel was "the greatest philosopher of the nineteenth century." With all his criticism of Hegel, then, Marx retained an essential aspect of his thought—the dialectic of reason in history—and grafted it onto the empiricism he took from Feuerbach in criticism of speculative "mystification."

This appropriation of Hegel is apparent in *The Poverty of Philosophy* in which Marx "answered" Proudhon's *Philosophy of Poverty* and gave what he called the first "scientific" presentation of his theory for a final settlement with German philosophy.

Marx finds all the illusions and confusions of "speculative philosophy" in Proudhon's method, his adaptation of Hegel's dialectic. Proudhon transforms historic relations of production into a dialectic of abstract categories and pre-existing eternal ideas. He does not see that the same men who change their social relations as they change their mode of production also produce ideas and categories that are historical products, no more eternal than the relations they express. Failing to grasp the real basis of ideas and categories, Proudhon finds their medium to be "general reason" or "social genius" whose "providential purpose" is to affirm the good side of economic contradictions, particularly Proudhon's own ideal of equality, and eliminate the bad. Thus in the manner of a speculative philosopher Proudhon reifies ideas and categories and their dialectical movement as well.

In making these criticisms of Proudhon, Marx proceeded from the objections to speculative philosophy he had adopted from Feuerbach. At the same time, however, he adhered to the core of Hegel's thought, the dialectic. In subsequent letters of 1865 and 1868 Marx criticized Proudhon for not having grasped "the secret of scientific dialectic" and called Hegel's dialectic "the basic form of all dialectic." "Feuerbach," wrote Marx, "has much to answer for" in the disrepute of Hegel's dialectic, in its being treated as a "dead horse." The section of *The Poverty of Philosophy* to follow favorably compares Hegel's dialectic with Proudhon's and widely uses it to formulate "the real movement of things" in history. Marx sees feudal production as based on a contradiction expressed in class antagonisms moving toward the resolution of the contradiction. Again, he finds in bourgeois relationships of production a double, antagonistic character producing both wealth and poverty, release and repression, an increasingly wealthy class and an ever growing proletariat. But the dialectic here is not a relationship of ideas and categories; it is the pattern of the historical development of relationships of production. Hence, the socialism foreshadowed in this development is not a "utopian" system of ideas designed to help the oppressed classes but rather a product of an observable "historical movement." The extensive and fundamental use of dialectic in *The Poverty of Philosophy* substantially supports Franz Mehring's conclusion that Marx "went beyond Feuerbach by going back to Hegel."

## Humanism versus Dialectic in History

Marx's combination of ideas from both Feuerbach and Hegel gave his thought an impressive force and scope. It also created internal tensions that come to the surface in disturbing ambiguities and ambivalences of principle. One such ambiguity revolves around the status of the individual person—the "principle of subjectivity," to use Hegel's phrase—in Marx's view of socialism and history.

In adhering to Feuerbach's "real humanism," Marx

committed himself to empiricism and existentialism. With Feuerbach he held that genuine thought must be rooted in "sensuous consciousness," "sensibility," or "nature" which has a social dimension in the relation of "man to man." Thus he gave priority to direct experience, to "immediacy," over against derivative general ideas and abstractions. His existentialism appears in his emphasis on man and man's action as having an inescapably "subjective" dimension, as distinctly differing from a thing, object, or logical category. The "Manuscripts" of 1844 see man as a sensuous, limited, and suffering being as well as a being "for itself," a species-being. Marx particularly warns against establishing "society" as an abstraction over against the individual. The individual is a social being as the subjective, experienced existence of society. This aspect of Marx's thought, it has been noted, is distinctively "existentialist" because it preserves "subjectivity" in necessary correlation with "objectivity."[7]

Under the impact of Feuerbach, Marx's thought had a distinctive moral bent, a source of its great appeal. Since the basis of religion, government, and the whole structure of civilization is man and man's action, not the Absolute Idea, it followed that man's alienation is not a problem to be solved by speculative thought which, like the Owl of Minerva, takes flight only after dusk has fallen. Nor is it to be left to the processes of history. Defending Feuerbach against Hegelians who would "transform man himself into a category," Marx saw history as man's action and labor. It does not, in Engels' words, "use man as a means for *its* purposes as though it were a person apart; it is *nothing* but the activity of man pursuing his ends." From this point of view Marx could insist, in Kantian terms, that man's alienation is essentially a question of "the *categorical imperative to overthrow all conditions* in which man is a degraded, enslaved, neglected, contemptible being." Such a "categorical imperative" appears in the context of Marx's criticism of religion and reveals the un-

---

[7] Cf. J.-P. Sartre, *Literary and Philosophical Essays*, trans. A. Michelson (New York, 1962), pp. 219 n, 245–50; P. Tillich, "Man in a Technical Society," *Perspectives* (Summer 1962), 118.

derlying point of that criticism. With Feuerbach, Marx saw religion as an inverted, compensatory expression of human values. It is "the heart of a heartless world . . . the spirit of spiritless conditions." But the natural and social values for which religion invertedly stands—a world with heart and conditions congenial to spirit—are not denied. They are unmistakably affirmed as values to be actualized. Marx's criticism of religion particularly reveals his moral dedication to the wholeness of man and the dignity he may achieve as the alien powers of state, industry, and class are brought under his associated control.

Echoes of this moral humanism in Marx's later writings are his well-known charges that capitalism degrades human beings, turns men into commodities, and transforms human relations into a cash nexus. His discussion of the "fetishism of commodities" in *Capital* reinstates alienation in economic terminology. A commodity is mysterious because "a definite social relation between men" has assumed "the fantastic form of a relation between things." The humanistic theme animates Marx's vision of socialism as "an association," not a special political power or state, "in which the free development of each is the condition of the free development of all" and "the development of human power is its own end." Marx's early writings repeatedly refer to the organized state and bureaucracy as a reflection of man's alienation to be overcome in communism where there is nothing but self-active, associated individuals. This is the background of his "anarchistic" anticipation of the "withering away" of the state and the basis of his belief in 1871 that a truly socialist society was manifest in the "self-government of producers" of the Paris Commune, an extension of the co-operative principle advocated by Proudhon.[8] This "fuller democracy" involving worker control of industry was the mature Marx's answer—or better, one of his answers—to the problem of alienated labor.

These echoes of Marx's humanism indicate the prominence in his thought of the "principle of subjectivity," as Hegel called it. He was asserting that man is an end in

[8] Cf. Marx, *The Civil War in France* (New York, 1940), pp. 18–22, 56–62.

himself, an end restricting the use of all means and thus setting limits to the action of state, class, political party, or any other social institution. In this respect one might well agree with the frequent assertion that Marx was a "child of the Enlightenment," a proponent of the "principles of 1789" who sought to substantiate that emphasis on the individual person and his self-direction which characterizes liberal democracy.

This side of Marx's thought has appeared at a number of points in the democratic Socialist movement—for example, in Bernstein's "revisionism" which attacked Marx's reliance on Hegel and viewed socialism as extending the moral aims of liberal democracy, in the "back to Kant" movement of continental socialists, and in the views of W. E. Walling who, in the heyday of American socialism around 1910, opposed "society as God" and based his opposition to "absolutism" on John Dewey's deference to "the concrete thing as experienced." Today an increasing number of socialists believe that preoccupation with consumption and income distribution neglects society's most important product—the kind of men it produces. Accordingly, they revive Marx's preoccupation with "alienated labor" and concentrate on transformation of work.

But as Marx corrected Feuerbach by "going back" to Hegel's dialectic of history, he adopted positions which undercut the humanistic side of his thought and his adherence to the "principle of subjectivity." He made man's alienation simply a present fact and his reconciliation a future fact. To set his own view apart from "utopianism," he dismissed "alienation" in *The Communist Manifesto* as a "philosophical phantasy" and increasingly insisted that socialists "preach no morals" and "have no ideals to realize." To correct Feuerbach, for whom "the Idea" had only moral significance and facts were properly distinguished from commitments, Marx identified what "ought to be" with the dialectical movement of history. With this identification he not only deprived himself of the moral leverage for criticizing history which was implicit in his humanism, but also provided a justification for anything and everything that happens, no matter how cruel or inhuman. When the "collective activity of men" and the "results of history" become the final arbiter of all human action, there is no ground for setting limits to the action of the state or any other social institution through the principle that man is an end in himself, restricting the use of all means. Such a principle, Marx frequently agreed with Hegel, is "abstract" and "impotent." By comparison, the "results of history" are concrete and potent, but if they are the only mark of what "ought to be," then anything and everything that happens is morally justified.

As Marx identified socialism with the "real movement" of history, he increasingly viewed history as something independent of men's actions, likened its laws to those of nature which work with "iron necessity towards inevitable results," and viewed it as a dialectical relation of classes and entities such as "proletariat," "civil society," and "bourgeoisie." Within this perspective, especially in terms of achieving class power, even "the State" as such becomes important. As Marx was finishing the first volume of *Capital*, he still thought of socialism as he had in the *Manifesto* and Communist League Circular of 1850, as "decisive centralization of power in the hands of the State," lamenting to Engels that Proudhon's followers wanted to make a company of communes "but not a State." This direction in Marx's thought gave first place precisely to those features of Hegel's system which, under Feuerbach's influence, he had condemned as "abstractions" and forms of alienation. While the movement of "civil society"—the social relations involved in the production and exchange of commodities—had displaced the movement of the Absolute Idea, man was nonetheless a subcategory of the dialectic of history. This aspect of Marx's thought is especially apparent in the Bolshevik cult of history—in Lenin's appeals, despite his voluntarism, to "the reign of law" in "world history," in Trotsky's deference to the "indeferable demands of history" in "the will of events," and in Khrushchev's references to "the historical course of development" as proving the superiority of Soviet Communism and justifying intervention in Hungary.

This side of Marx's thought is incompatible with the

existentialism of his early views because it eliminates the element of subjectivity or "immediacy" in man's action and absorbs him in an objective order of happenings. Marx's early empiricism is equally undercut by the "rational kernel" of dialectic he appropriated from Hegel. When Joseph Dietzgen, whom Marx introduced to the International Workingmen's Association as "our philosopher," developed from Feuerbach a view of knowledge that strikingly anticipated Ernst Mach and contemporary "logical empiricism," Marx specifically criticized it for not having absorbed Hegel.[9] The distance of Marx's mature thought from empiricism is strikingly revealed in Marcuse's *Reason and Revolution,* where the socialist "realm of freedom" is seen as negating the "necessity" on which historical materialism is based to become manifest as "reason determining itself." Here socialism indeed becomes "a chapter in logic" such as Marx had dismissed in 1843.

Some final qualifications are needed on Marx's relation to Hegel in regard to the "principle of subjectivity" and the status of the individual. In his essay "On the Jewish Question," Marx saw the "inalienable rights of man" as forms of alienation, as satisfactions of the "egoistic man, of man separated from other men and the community." One might argue that their substance will be preserved as they are *aufgehoben,* transcended, in the true community where social force is no longer separated from man as political power. But Marx increasingly identified these rights with capitalism as ideological reflections of capitalists' class interest, and the capitalist class, of course, was to disappear under communism. Sometimes he condoned the phraseology of "inalienable rights" but only as a tactical concession since the working class "has no ideals to realize."[10] Hegel, too, thought that these rights would have to be

---

[9] Cf. Marx and Engels, *Selected Correspondence,* trans. D. Torr (New York, 1942), p. 253; L. D. Easton, "Empiricism and Ethics in Dietzgen," *Journal of the History of Ideas,* 19 (1958), 77–83; H. A. Marcuse, *Reason and Revolution* (New York, 1954), pp. 271, 315–30, *et passim.*

[10] Marx, *Critique of the Gotha Program* (New York, 1938), pp. 10, 18–21. Cf. *Capital* (Chicago, 1906), Vol. I, p. 195, on capitalism as "a very Eden of the innate rights of man."

transcended, but he gave attention to the preservation of their substance in his views on freedom of inquiry, rights of Quakers, choice in employment, and separation of church and state.[11] Marx came to neglect "the principle of subjectivity" because, in going back to Hegel to get beyond Feuerbach, he went back to only part of Hegel. The "rational kernel" he picked up from Hegel was only a kernel. For Hegel the dialectic of history was subordinate to the development of the Idea in art, religion, and philosophy. This enabled him to insist repeatedly that individuality, the element of subjectivity, is inherently eternal and divine as an intrinsic part of the Absolute Idea.[12] For Marx, however, the dialectic of history had no such superstructure and hence no systematic support for the principle of subjectivity. In this respect he was less of a "child of the Enlightenment," less a proponent of the "principles of 1789" than Hegel, and the implications of his thought are more congenial to totalitarianism than to the emphasis on the individual person and his self-direction which characterizes liberal democracy.

[11] Cf. Hegel, *Philosophy of Right*, § 270, 124, 66.
[12] Cf. Hegel, *The Philosophy of History*, trans. J. Sibree (New York, 1956), pp. 33, 37, 39, 250–52; *Philosophy of Right*, § 270.

# HUMANITARIANISM AND LIBERALISM
## OF A YOUNG HEGELIAN

# REFLECTIONS OF A YOUTH ON CHOOSING AN OCCUPATION (1835)

[The following examination essay is one of two in German which Marx wrote shortly before his graduation from the Trier *Gymnasium* on September 24, 1835. In tone it is suffused by a spirit of dedication to the perfection and welfare of all humanity. It reveals a special respect for the life devoted to ideas and a hint of Marx's characteristic mature view that our social relations have begun to form before we can determine them. Marx's second examination essay on "The Union of the Faithful with Christ" also reflected a lofty humanitarian idealism as Marx found the ground of that union in human aspiration and its effects in a genuine love of men "beautifully shaping and elevating life." The examiner found "Reflections of a Youth" marred by unusual expressions, but the state examining committee certified Marx as ready to enter the university on the basis of general good conduct, good or superior performance in German and classical languages, competence in Christian doctrine, a good knowledge of mathematics, and a passing knowledge of physics. At the *Gymnasium* Marx had been exposed to high standards and a liberal atmosphere. A number of his teachers were in disfavor with the secret police. The headmaster and Marx's father were members of a liberal literary society. Marx's father had left Judaism for Christianity in 1816 and was attached to the Enlightenment spirit of Frederick the Great.]

Nature has assigned to the animal the sphere of its activity, and the animal acts calmly within it, not striving beyond, not even surmising that there is another. To man, too, the Deity gave a general goal, to improve mankind and himself, but left it up to him to seek the means by which he can attain this goal, left it up to him to choose the position in society which is most appropriate and from which he can best elevate both himself and society.

This choice is a great privilege over other creatures

but at the same time an act which can destroy man's entire life, defeat all his plans, and make him unhappy. Hence, a youth who is beginning a career and who does not wish to leave his most important concerns to chance certainly sees his foremost duty in considering this choice seriously.

Everyone has a goal which appears to be great, at least to himself, and is great when deepest conviction, the innermost voice of the heart, pronounces it great; for the Deity never leaves man entirely without a guide; the Deity speaks softly, but with certainty.

This voice, however, is easily drowned out, and what we thought to be inspiration may have been created by the fleeting moment and again perhaps destroyed by it. Perhaps our fantasy is inflamed, our emotions excited; phantoms move before our eyes, and eagerly we rush to the goal, believing that the Deity pointed it out to us. But what we ardently pressed to our breast soon repels us, and we see our whole existence destroyed.

We must seriously ask ourselves, therefore, whether we are really inspired about a vocation, whether an inner voice approves of it, or whether the inspiration was a deception, whether that which we took as the Deity's calling to us was self-deceit. But how else could we recognize this except by searching for the source of our inspiration?

Everything great glitters, glitter begets ambition, and ambition can easily have caused the inspiration or what we thought to be inspiration. But reason can no longer restrain one who is lured by the fury of ambition. He tumbles where his vehement drive calls him; no longer does he choose his position, but rather chance and luster determine it.

Then we are not called to the position where we can most shine. It is not the one which in the long succession of years during which we may hold it will never make us weary, subdue our zeal, or dampen our inspiration. Soon we shall see our wishes unfulfilled and our ideas unsatisfied. We shall have a grievance against the Deity and curse humanity.

But not only ambition can cause a sudden inspiration

about a position; we may have embellished it with our fantasies, embellished it to the highest point that life can offer. We have not analyzed it, not considered the entire burden and great responsibility to be placed upon us. We have regarded it only from a distance, and distance deceives.

In this matter our own reason cannot be the counselor. Neither experience nor profound observation supports our reason, which is deceived by emotion and blinded by fantasy. But where shall we look for support when our reason leaves us in the lurch?

Our heart calls upon our parents who have walked the path of life, have experienced fate's severity.

And if our inspiration still endures, if we still love that position and believe we are called to it after we have tested it objectively, perceived its burden, and become acquainted with its encumbrances—then we may strive for it, then inspiration does not deceive us, nor does overeagerness rush us.

But we cannot always choose the vocation to which we believe we are called. Our social relations, to some extent, have already begun to form before we are in a position to determine them.

Even our physical nature often threateningly opposes us, and no one dare mock its rights!

To be sure, we can lift ourselves above it, but then we fall all the faster. We then venture to construct a building on rotten foundations, and our entire life is an unfortunate struggle between the intellectual and the physical principle. When one cannot calm the elements fighting in himself, how can he stand up against life's tempestuous urge, how is he to act calmly? Out of calmness alone can great and beautiful deeds emerge. Calmness is the only soil on which ripe fruits thrive.

Although we cannot work for long, and seldom joyfully, with a physical nature inappropriate to our position, the thought of sacrificing our welfare to duty, of acting with weakness, yet with strength, always arises. However, if we have chosen a position for which we do not possess the talents, we shall never be able to fill it properly, we shall soon recognize with shame our own incapability and say to ourselves that we are a useless creature, a member of society who cannot fill his post. The most natural result, then, is self-contempt, and what feeling is more painful, what can less be displaced by anything the external world offers? Self-contempt is a serpent which eternally gnaws in one's breast, sucks out the heart's lifeblood, and mixes it with the poison of misanthropy and despair.

A deception about our aptitude for a position we have examined closely is a misdeed which revengefully falls back on ourselves, and even though it may not be censured by the external world, provokes in our breast a pain more terrible than the external world can cause.

When we have weighed everything, and when our relations in life permit us to choose any given position, we may take that one which guarantees us the greatest dignity, which is based on ideas of whose truth we are completely convinced, which offers the largest field to work for mankind and approach the universal goal for which every position is only a means: perfection.

Dignity elevates man most, bestows a high nobleness to all his acts, all his endeavors, and permits him to stand irreproachable, admired by the crowd and above it.

Only that position can impart dignity in which we do not appear as servile tools but rather create independently within our circle. Only that position can impart dignity which requires no reproachable acts, reproachable not even in appearance—a position which the best person can undertake with noble pride. The position which guarantees this the most is not always the highest, but it is always the best.

Just as a position without dignity lowers us, we certainly succumb to the burden of one based on ideas we later recognize as false.

Then we see no aid except in self-deception, and what a desperate rescue is the one that guarantees self-betrayal!

The vocations which do not take hold of life but deal, rather, with abstract truths are the most dangerous for the youth whose principles are not yet crystallized, whose conviction is not yet firm and unshakable, though at the same time they seem to be the most lofty ones when they have taken root deep in the breast and when we can sacrifice life and all striving for the ideas which hold sway in them.

They can make him happy who is called to them; but they destroy him who takes them overhurriedly, without reflection, obeying the moment.

But the high opinion we have of the ideas on which our vocation is based bestows on us a higher standpoint in society, enlarges our own dignity, makes our actions unwavering.

Whoever chooses a vocation which he esteems highly will carefully avoid making himself unworthy of it; therefore, he will act nobly because his position in society is noble.

The main principle, however, which must guide us in the selection of a vocation is the welfare of humanity, our own perfection. One should not think that these two interests combat each other, that the one must destroy the other. Rather, man's nature makes it possible for him to reach his fulfillment only by working for the perfection and welfare of his society.

If a person works only for himself he can perhaps be a famous scholar, a great wise man, a distinguished poet, but never a complete, genuinely great man.

History calls those the greatest men who ennobled themselves by working for the universal. Experience praises as the most happy the one who made the most people happy. Religion itself teaches us that the ideal for which we are all striving sacrificed itself for humanity, and who would dare to destroy such a statement?

When we have chosen the vocation in which we can contribute most to humanity, burdens cannot bend us because they are only sacrifices for all. Then we experience no meager, limited, egotistic joy, but our happiness belongs to millions, our deeds live on quietly but eternally effective, and glowing tears of noble men will fall on our ashes.

*Marx.*

# LETTER TO HIS FATHER: ON A
# TURNING-POINT IN LIFE (1837)

[After two years of university life—a desultory year at Bonn with too much wine and a duel and then a year at "the work-house," the University of Berlin—Marx reviewed the course of his interests. In the following candid letter to his father he reveals his deepest feelings about his family and Jenny von West-phalen, to whom he had become secretly engaged in the summer of 1836, much to his father's pleasure. He also records major shifts in his thinking. He has turned his back on romantic poetry with its intensity of feeling, flashing phrases, and forlorn maidens for the sake of more restrained reflection. That reflection leads him away from the idealism of Fichte and Kant to Hegel's view that the actual social world already manifests reason, an all-embracing Idea, as its developing wholeness. Marx becomes an active, vocal member of the Doctors' Club at the University of Berlin, a group of "Young Hegelians" concerned with showing, after Strauss, that the true basis of Christianity is to be found in historical experience and ultimately in man's social needs.]

Berlin, November 10

Dear Father,

There are moments in life which mark the close of a period like boundary posts and at the same time definitely point in a new direction.

At such a point of transition, we feel compelled to contemplate the past and the present with the eagle eye of thought to become aware of our actual position. Indeed, world history itself loves such a retrospect, and reflects upon itself, often producing the semblance of a retrogression or standstill, while in reality it has merely eased itself back in an armchair to comprehend itself and penetrate intellectually its own act, the act of the mind.

In such moments, however, the individual becomes lyri-

cal, for every transformation is to some extent a swan song,
to some extent the overture to a great new poem, which
strives to gain shape in tints still blurred but brilliant. Yet,
we should like to erect a memorial to what already has
been experienced so it may regain in sentiment the place
which it lost in the world of action; and where could we
find a holier site than in the heart of our parents, the most
clement judge, the most ardent participator, the sun of
love, whose fire warms the innermost center of our endeavors! How could much that is objectionable and
blameworthy better find compensation and pardon than by
becoming manifestation of an essentially necessary condition? How, at any rate, could the often hostile turn of
chance and aberration of the spirit escape the reproach of
being due to a twisted heart?

When, therefore, at the close of a year here, I now
glance back upon what has happened and in this way, dear
Father, answer your very affectionate letter from Ems, allow me to contemplate my circumstances, how I regard
life in general as the expression of reflection taking shape
in all directions—in science, art, private matters.

When I left you, a new world had just opened for me,
the world of love, at first a love that was frenzied with
yearning and void of hope. Even the journey to Berlin,
which otherwise would have extremely delighted me,
would have incited me to contemplate nature, would have
inflamed me with the joy of living, left me cold. It even
depressed me profoundly, for the rocks I saw were no
rougher, no harsher, than the feelings of my soul; the big
cities were not more lively than my blood; the tables in
the inns were not more overladen, the food not more indigestible than were the contents of my imagination; and,
to conclude, art was not so beautiful as Jenny.

Having arrived in Berlin, I broke all existing ties, re-
luctantly made very few visits, and sought to immerse myself in science and art.

In my state of mind at that time, lyrical poetry inevitably
had to be my first concern, at any rate the most agreeable
and most obvious; but, in accord with my position and
whole previous development, it was purely idealistic. A re-

mote beyond, such as my love, became my heaven, my art. Everything real grew vague, and all that is vague lacks boundaries. Onslaughts against the present, broad and shapeless expressions of unnatural feeling, constructed purely out of the blue, the complete opposition of what is and what ought to be, rhetorical reflections instead of poetic thoughts but perhaps also a certain warmth of sentiment and a struggle for movement characterize all the poems in the first three volumes I sent to Jenny. The whole horizon of a longing which sees no frontiers assumed many forms and frustrated my effort to write with poetic conciseness.

But poetry could only be, should only be, a companion. I had to study jurisprudence, and above all I felt an urge to wrestle with philosophy. The two were so closely connected that I read Heineccius, Thibaut, and the sources in schoolboy fashion, quite uncritically. I translated, for instance, the first two books of the Pandects into German, but I also tried, in studying law, to work out a philosophy of law. I prefixed, as introduction, some metaphysical propositions and developed this ill-starred opus as far as the topic of public law—a work of nearly three hundred pages.

Particularly here I was greatly disturbed by the conflict between what is and what ought to be, a conflict peculiar to idealism, and this gave rise to the following hopelessly inaccurate classification. First of all, what I gratuitously christened "metaphysics of law"—that is, principles, reflections, determinative concepts—was severed from all actual law and from any actual form of law as in the writings of Fichte, only in my case in a more modern and less substantial fashion. Furthermore, the unscientific form of mathematical dogmatism—where the subject wanders about the topic, argues hither and thither, while the topic itself is never formulated as something rich in content, something alive—was from the first a hindrance to the comprehension of the truth.

The nature of the triangle induces the mathematician to construct it, demonstrate its properties, but it remains a mere idea in space and undergoes no further development. We must put the triangle beside another form. Then it assumes different positions, and the other form with its various relative positions endows the triangle with different relations and truths. On the other hand, in the concrete expression of the living world of thought—as in law, the state, nature, philosophy as a whole—the object itself must be studied in its development; there must be no arbitrary classifications; the rationale of the thing itself must be disclosed in all its contradictoriness and find its unity in itself.

As a second part there followed the philosophy of law, that is, as I then saw the matter, the study of development of ideas in positive Roman law, as if positive law in the development of its ideas (I do not mean in its purely finite determinations) could be anything different from the formulation of the concept of law which the first part was to include.

On top of this I had divided this part into a formal and a material doctrine of law. The former was to describe the pure form of the system in its succession and interaction, the classification and the scope; the latter, on the other hand, the content, the condensation of the form in its content. This was an error which I share with Herr von Savigny, as I was to find out later when reading his scholarly work on possession, but with the difference that he speaks of formal determinate concepts as "finding the place which this or that doctrine occupies in the suppositional Roman system" and of material determinate concepts as "the doctrine of positivity which the Romans ascribe to a concept established this way," whereas I understood by form the necessary architectonic of the formulations of the concept and by matter the necessary quality of these formulations. My mistake was that I believed one could and must develop the one apart from the other, with the result that I achieved no genuine form but a desk with a number of drawers I subsequently littered with sand.

The concept is, after all, the intermediary between form and content. In a philosophical disquisition on law, therefore, the one must arise out of the other because form can only be the continuation of content. Thus I finally did arrive at a classification, though the subject lends itself at most to superficial and shallow classification, but the spirit of law and truth had perished. All law was subdivided into covenanted and uncovenanted. I take the liberty of writing down the schema, with the exception of the *ius publicum* which is also dealt with in the formal part, to acquaint you with it better.

I
*Ius privatum*

II
*Ius publicum*

### I  *Ius privatum*

A.  About conditional covenanted private law
B.  About conditional uncovenanted law

A. *About conditional covenanted private law: a)* Personal law; *b)* Property law; *c)* Personal property law.

#### a) Personal law

I. On the basis of encumbered contract; II. on the basis of secured contract; III. on the basis of open contract.

##### I. *On the basis of encumbered contract.*

2. Contract of agreement (societas); 3. *Contract of service* (locatio conductio)

##### 3. Locatio conductio

1. As referring to operae
   *a)* Actual locatio conductio (I mean neither the Roman renting nor leasing);
   *b) mandatum*
2. As referring to usus rei
   *a)* As to land: *usus fructus* (again not in the merely Roman meaning);
   *b)* As to buildings: *habitatio*

##### II. *On the basis of secured contract.*

1. Arbitration or mediation contract. 2. Securance contract.

##### III. *On the basis of open contract.*

##### 2. *Contract by consent*

1. fide iussio; 2. negotiorum gestio

3. Deed

1. donatio; 2. gratiae promissum

b) Property law

I. *On the basis of encumbered contract.*

2. permutatio stricte sic dicta.

1. Actual permutatio; 2. mutuum (usurae); 3. *emptio, venditio*

II. *On the basis of secured contract.*

pignus.

III. *On the basis of open contract.*

2. commodatum; 3. depositum.

But why should I continue filling pages with things I have discarded? The whole is permeated with trichotomous classifications, penned with wearisome prolixity. I misused the Roman notions most barbarously in order to force them into my system. Still, to some extent at least, I gained a conspectus of my topic and an affection for it.

At the close of the discussion of material private law, I saw the fallaciousness of the whole, which in its fundamental schema borders on the Kantian, though differing wholly from Kant in matters of detail. Once more I realized that I could not make my way without philosophy. Hence, I was again able, with good conscience, to throw myself into the arms of philosophy, and I wrote a new basic metaphysical system. Upon its completion I was again constrained to recognize its futility and that of all my previous endeavors.

Meanwhile I had acquired the habit of making excerpts from all the books I was reading, from Lessing's *Laocoön*, Solger's *Erwin*, Winckelmann's *History of Art*, Luden's *German History*. While doing this, I scribbled down some reflections. At the same time I translated Tacitus' *Germania*, Ovid's *Tristium libri*. With the aid of grammar books I began the private study of English and Italian, but as yet have not achieved anything. I read Klein's book on criminal law and his *Annals,* and a lot of the most recent literature, though the latter only incidentally.

At the end of the semester, I once more sought the dance of the muses and the music of satyrs. Already in the last pages I sent you, idealism plays its part in the form of forced humor (Skorpion and Felix) and in an unsuccessful dramatic fantasy (Oulanem), until at length it takes an entirely different direction and changes into pure formal art, for the most part without any stimulating objects and without any lively movement of ideas.

Nevertheless, these last poems are the only ones in which suddenly, as if by the wave of a magician's wand—it was shattering at the beginning—the realm of true poetry flashed open before me like a distant faery palace, and all my creations collapsed into nothing.

During the first semester I was awake many a night, engaged in these multifarious occupations. I went through many struggles and experienced much stimulation from within and without. Yet, in the end, I found that my mind had not been greatly enriched while I had neglected nature, art, and the world, and had alienated my friends. My body apparently reacted. A physician advised a stay in the country, and so for the first time I traversed the whole spread-out town and went through the gate to Stralow. I did not anticipate that I, an anemic weakling, should there ripen into a man with a robust and solid frame.

A curtain had fallen, my holy of holies had been shattered, and new gods had to be found.

Setting out from idealism—which, let me say in passing, I had compared to and nourished with that of Kant and Fichte—I hit upon seeking the Idea in the real itself. If formerly the gods had dwelt above the world, they had now become its center.

I had read fragments of Hegel's philosophy and had found its grotesque craggy melody unpleasing. I wished to dive into the ocean once again but with the definite intention of discovering our mental nature to be just as determined, concrete, and firmly established as our physical

—no longer to practice the art of fencing but to bring pure pearls into the sunlight.

I wrote a dialogue of about twenty-four pages, entitled "Cleanthes, or the Starting Point and the Necessary Progress of Philosophy." Here, in a way, art and science, which had been severed, were reunited. And now, an energetic wanderer, I set out for the main task, a philosophic-dialectical discussion of the godhead manifested as a concept per se, as religion, as nature, and as history. My last sentence was the beginning of the Hegelian system, and this task—for which I had acquainted myself to some extent with natural science, Schelling, and history, and which (since it was to be a new logic) is written in such a [ . . . ?] fashion that even I myself now can scarcely make head or tail of it—this darling child of mine, nurtured in moonlight, bears me like a false-hearted siren into the clutches of the enemy.

Because of my vexation, I was for several days quite unable to think. Like a lunatic I ran around in the garden beside the Spree's dirty water "which washes the soul and dilutes tea." I even went out hunting with my host and then returned hotfoot to Berlin, wishing to embrace every loafer at the street corners.

Thereafter I carried on positive studies only: Savigny's study on ownership, [Anselm] Feuerbach's and Grolmann's works on criminal law, Cramer's *De verborum significatione,* Wenning-Ingenheim's pandect system and Mühlenbruch's *Doctrina Pandectarum* (which I am still reading), and finally some of Lauterbach's works, books on civil law and especially on ecclesiastical law. As regards this last, I have read through and made extracts from almost all the first part of Gratian, *Concordia discordantium canonum,* as well as its appendix, and Lancelotti's *Institutiones.* Then I translated part of Aristotle's *Rhetoric,* read *De dignitate et augmentis scientiarum* of the famous Bacon of Verulam, occupied myself intensively with Reimarus whose work on the mechanical instincts of animals I followed through with delight. Next I came to German law, but mainly concerned myself with the capitularies of the Franconian kings and the letters of the popes to them.

From grief over Jenny's illness and because of the futility of my lost labors, from consuming vexation at having to make an idol of a view I detest, I fell sick, as, my dear Father, I have previously related. Having recovered, I burned all my poems, my sketches for novellas, etc., under the illusion that I could refrain from anything of the kind —and there is as yet no evidence to the contrary.

While out of sorts, I had got to know Hegel from beginning to end, and most of his disciples as well. Through several meetings with friends in Stralow I became a member of a Doctors' Club to which some instructors and my most intimate friend in Berlin, Dr. [Adolf] Rutenberg, belong. In discussions many a conflicting opinion was voiced, and I was more and more chained to the current world philosophy from which I had thought to escape. But all tones were muted and a fit of irony possessed me as was natural after so many negations. Jenny's silence added to this, and I could not rest until I had become up-to-date and acquired the current scientific view by some poor productions such as *The Visit*.

If I have perhaps failed to explain this last semester clearly to you as a whole and in all its details, if I left its shadings hazy, you will forgive me, dear Father, on account of my eagerness to speak of the present.

Herr [Adalbert] von Chamisso has sent me a piddling note in which he informs me of his "regret that his Almanac can make no use of my contributions, having long since gone to press." I swallowed his note in anger. Wigand, the bookseller, has forwarded my plan to Dr. Schmidt, manager of Wunder's Warehouse of Good Cheese and Bad Literature. I am enclosing Wigand's letter; Schmidt has not answered yet. Meanwhile I have by no means abandoned the plan, all the more since all the aesthetic notables of the Hegelian school have promised to co-operate, induced by Instructor [Bruno] Bauer who is important among them and by my coadjutor Dr. Rutenberg.

As to the question of a career as an official, dear Father, I have recently made the acquaintance of an assistant judge, Schmidthänner by name, who advises me to enter upon this after passing the third of my law examinations.

The plan appeals to me, since I really prefer jurisprudence to any study of administration. This gentleman told me that from the Münster provincial court of appeal he and many others had in three years attained the position of assistant judge, which, he says, is not difficult—provided, of course, that one works hard—since in that part of the world the stages are not as they are in Berlin and elsewhere strictly marked out. If, as assistant judge, one obtains the doctorate, there are excellent chances of speedy appointment as professor extraordinary. This is what happened to Herr Gärtner in Bonn after he had written a mediocre book on provincial law-codes, his only other title to fame being that he proclaims himself a member of the Hegelian school of jurists. But, dear Father, best of fathers, can't we talk all this over face to face? Eduard's condition, dear Mother's trouble, your own indisposition—I hope it is nothing serious—all combine to make me want to hurry home without delay. It is virtually imperative that I should. Indeed, I should already be with you, were I not in doubt as to your approval.

Believe me, my dear Father, this is not a selfish wish (though I should be so happy to see Jenny again). I am driven rather by a thought I cannot put into words. Actually in some respects it would be difficult for me to come; but such considerations, as my darling Jenny writes, all give way to the fulfillment of sacred duties.

I beg you, dear Father, whatever you may decide, not to show this letter—or at any rate this page of it—to Mother. My unexpected arrival may perhaps cheer the great, magnificent woman.

My letter to her was written long before Jenny's dear letter arrived, so I may unwittingly have written too much about unsuitable matters.

In the hope that the clouds which hang over our family will gradually disperse; that I shall be permitted to share your sufferings and mingle my tears with yours, and perhaps in your presence show the deep affection, the immeasurable love, which I often have not been able to express as I should like; in the hope that you too, dear and eternally beloved Father, mindful of my storm-tossed feelings, will forgive me when my heart must often have seemed to have gone astray as the burdens of my spirit stifled it; in the hope that you will soon be fully restored to health and I shall be able to clasp you in my arms to tell you all I feel,

I remain always your loving son,

*Karl.*

Forgive the illegible handwriting and defective style, dear Father. It is nearly four o'clock, the candle has burned out, and my eyes are clouded. Restlessness has overwhelmed me. I shall not be able to lay the specters haunting me until I am in your dear presence.

Please give my best love to my sweet Jenny. I have already read her letter a dozen times, finding new charms in it each time. In every respect, style included, it is the most beautiful letter I can imagine a woman writing.

# NOTES TO THE
# DOCTORAL DISSERTATION (1839–41)

[Preparing for an academic career which never materialized, Marx began work late in 1839 on his dissertation, "The Difference Between the Democritean and Epicurean Philosophy of Nature," and was awarded the doctorate by the University of Jena on April 15, 1841. The dissertation compared two representatives of the Greek "philosophy of self-consciousness" about whom Hegel was correct in outline though lacking in details. Marx found Epicurus' concept of the atom superior to Democritus' more empirical view because it implied independence, freedom, and an "energizing principle" for experience.

The first and second of the following notes are preparatory studies for the dissertation and a larger work, never finished, on "the Epicurean, Stoic, and Sceptical philosophies in relation to the whole of Greek speculation." Marx sees philosophy after Hegel as being like that after Aristotle—practical-minded, turning against the apparent world. Distrusting religion as Epicurus had, Marx commends philosophical over religious "exaltation" and relates Plato's myths to Christianity through "transcendence" in both. The third note belongs to the dissertation and the fourth to its appendix. Marx holds that philosophy in practice is "criticism" as measuring actuality against the Idea. Adhering to the Idea, the liberal party in criticism seeks out "the deficiency of the world to be made philosophical" and thus transcends philosophy itself. In the last note Marx rejects transcendent divinity as he criticizes the "ontological argument" in relation to historic religions and social beliefs but carelessly in relation to Kant.]

## Nodal Points in the Development of Philosophy

Just as the νοῦς of Anaxagoras acquires movement with the Sophists (where the νοῦς in reality becomes the non-being of the world) and this immediate *daemonic movement* as such is manifested in Socrates' daimonion, the practical action of Socrates in turn becomes general and ideal in Plato, and the νοῦς extends itself to a realm of ideas. With Aristotle this process is again confined to a particularity which, however, has now become the actual, conceptual particularity.

Just as there are nodal points in philosophy that in themselves rise to concretion, form abstract principles into a totality, and thus interrupt a straight-line continuation, so there are also moments when philosophy turns its eyes to the external world. No longer reflectively but like a practical person, it spins intrigues with the world, emerges from Amenthes' transparent realm, and throws itself on the bosom of the mundane siren. That is the Shrovetide of philosophy, whether it be clothed in the dog's garb of the Cynic, the vestment of the Alexandrine, or the gauzy spring tunic of the Epicurean. Putting on character masks is then essential for philosophy. As we have been told that Deukalion at the creation of man cast stones over his shoulder, philosophy casts back its eyes (its mother's bones being shiny eyes) when its heart has been strengthened to create a world. Just as Prometheus, having stolen fire from heaven, begins to build houses and settle on the earth, so philosophy, having extended itself to the world, turns against the apparent world. So now with the Hegelian philosophy.

As philosophy has closed itself into a complete, total world—the outline of this totality is in general conditioned by its development, the basis of the form which reverses itself in a practical relationship to actuality—the totality of the world is implicitly split, and this split is driven to extremes because spiritual existence has become free, enriched to universality. The heartbeat has implicitly become in a concrete way the characteristic of the whole organism. The diremption of the world is not causal while its sides are totalities. Hence, the world is self-divided as opposed to a total philosophy, one in itself. The manifestation of the activity of this philosophy is thereby also split and contradictory; its objective universality reverts to subjective forms of individual consciousness in which it lives. Common harps will sound under any hand; aeolian harps, only when the storm strikes them. But one must not let himself be misled by the storm that follows a great world-philosophy.

He who does not comprehend this historical necessity must consequently deny that man can still live after a total philosophy, or he must take the dialectic of measure as such for the highest category of self-knowing Spirit and maintain with some of our mistaken Hegelians that *mediocrity* is the normal manifestation of the absolute Spirit. But a mediocrity which pretends to be a regular manifestation of the Absolute has itself fallen into a lack of measure, namely, a measureless pretension. Without this necessity it is incomprehensible how after Aristotle a Zeno, an Epicurus, even a Sextus Empiricus could come forth, or after Hegel the fundamentally groundless and paltry efforts of more recent philosophers.

In such times, fearful souls take the reverse point of view of valiant commanders. They believe they are able to repair the damage by decreasing forces, by dispersal, by a peace treaty with real needs, while Themistocles, when Athens was threatened with devastation, persuaded the Athenians to leave it for good and found a new Athens on the sea, on another element.

Furthermore, we must not forget that the time following such catastrophes is an iron one, happy if the battles of titans mark them, lamentable if the time is like the lamely limping centuries of great epochs of art, busied with casting in wax, plaster, and copper that which once leapt from the Carraran marble as did Pallas Athena from Zeus's head. Titanlike, however, are the times that follow an implicitly total philosophy and its subjective forms of development, for the diremption—its unity—is tremendous. Thus, Rome came after the Stoic, Sceptic, and Epicurean philosophies. They are unhappy and iron, for their gods are dead, and the new goddess still has immediately the dark form of Fate, of pure Light or pure Darkness. She still lacks the day's colors. The kernel of this unhappiness is that the soul of the time, the spiritual Monas, in itself satiated and ideally formed in all aspects, can recognize no actuality which has already developed without it. The happy element in such unhappiness, then, is the subjective form, the modality in which philosophy as subjective consciousness relates itself to actuality.

Thus, for example, the Epicurean, Stoic philosophy was the happy fortune of its time. Similarly the hawk moth seeks the lamp light of privacy when the sun has set.

The other aspect, more important for the historian of philosophy, is the fact that this reversal of the philosophers, their transubstantiation in flesh and blood, is distinguished by the characteristic which an implicitly total and concrete philosophy bears like a birthmark. It is at once a retaliation for those who in their abstract one-sidedness believe that, for example, Hegel's philosophy passed judgment on itself because Hegel approved the sentencing of Socrates as necessary, because Giordano Bruno had to atone for the fire of his spirit on the smoky fire of the pyre. But it is important, philosophically speaking, to stress this aspect since from the specific form of this reversal deductions can be made as to the immanent determination and world-historical character of the course of philosophy. What formerly appeared as growth is now determinateness; implicitly existing negativity has become negation. Here we observe, as it were, the curriculum vitae of a philosophy focused to the subjective point, just as one can conclude a hero's life story from the way he died. Since I hold the Epicurean philosophy as such a form of Greek philosophy, this might here at the same time justify my procedure. Instead of beginning with elements taken from preceding Greek philosophies as conditions in the life of the Epicurean philosophy, I shall make deductions from the latter to the former and thus allow Epicurean philosophy itself to express its own position.

## Platonism and Christianity

To extract more fully the subjective form of Platonic philosophy I shall examine closely some of Professor Baur's views in his work, *The Christian Element of Platonism.* Thus we can arrive at some conclusions while bringing to light some opposing views at the same time.

*The Christian Element of Platonism or Socrates and Christ*, by D. F. C. Baur. Tübingen, 1837.

Baur says on page 24:

"Viewed in respect to their starting point, Socratic philosophy is related to Christianity as self-knowledge is related to knowledge of sin."

It seems to us that this comparison between Socrates and Christ proves the opposite of what should be proved, the opposite of a similarity between Socrates and Christ. To be sure, self-knowledge and knowledge of sin are related to each other as general and particular, specifically as philosophy and religion. This is the position of every philosopher, whether of antiquity or the modern period. It would be more a matter of the eternal division of the two areas than their unity, thus indicating, to be sure, a relationship because every division is a division of unity. That would only be saying that the philosopher Socrates is related to Christ as a philosopher is related to a teacher of religion. If only a similarity or analogy is presented between grace and the Socratic midwifery, the Socratic irony, this only means that the contradiction, not the analogy, is pushed to extremes. The Socratic irony as Baur and Hegel conceive it, the dialectical trap whereby common sense is lured from its motley ossification not into what is comfortable and better known but into the truth immanent within it—this irony is nothing but the form of philosophy subjectively related to ordinary awareness. The fact that in Socrates it has the form of an ironical and wise man is a result of the fundamental character of Greek philosophy and its relation to actuality; for us, the irony in Friedrich von Schlegel has been taught as an immanent, universal formula, a philosophy as it were. But for the objective content, Heraclitus, who not only despised but even hated common sense, also Thales, who taught that everything is water—while every Greek knew that he could not live by water alone—and similarly Fichte with his world-creating Ego—though even Nicolai saw that he could not create a world—in short, every philosopher who defends immanence against the empirical person is an ironist as well.

In grace, on the other hand, in the recognition of sinfulness, not only the subject who has been brought to this recognition with grace is an empirical person, but also the one granting it and the one rising from the recognition of sinfulness are empirical persons.

If there is an analogy here between Socrates and Christ it would be that Socrates is philosophy personified and Christ is religion personified. Merely a general relationship between philosophy and religion is not involved here, but rather the question is how philosophy incarnate is related to religion incarnate. That they are related to one another is a very vague truth or rather the general condition of the question, not the particular ground of the answer. In this attempt to establish a Christian element in Socrates, the relationship of the eminent personalities, Christ and Socrates, is no more specific than the relationship of a philosopher to a religious teacher in general. There is the same emptiness when the universal ethical structure of the Socratic Idea, the Platonic state, is connected with the universal structure of the Idea and when Christ as a historic individuality is pre-eminently brought into connection with the church.

(The important consideration is missed that Plato's Republic is something produced by Plato while the church is something totally distinct from Christ.)

If the Hegelian thesis accepted by Baur is correct that Plato maintained Greek substantiality in his Republic against the encroaching principle of subjectivity, then Plato is diametrically opposed to Christ who maintained this subjectivity against the existing state, which he characterized as purely secular and thus unholy. The real distinction between the Platonic Republic and the Christian Church is not that the former remained an ideal while the latter achieved reality, but rather the reverse in that the Platonic Idea followed as reality while the Christian Idea preceded reality.

In general it would be more correct to say that Platonic elements are found in Christianity rather than Christian elements in Plato, particularly since historically the earliest church fathers—for example, Origen, Herennios—proceeded in part from the Platonic philosophy. In respect to philosophy it is noteworthy that the first class in Plato's Republic is that of learned men or philosophers. In the Republic the Platonic Ideas are similar to the Christian Logos (p. 38), Plato's doctrine of recollection is similar to the Christian regeneration of man in his original image (p. 40), the Platonic downfall of the soul is similar to the Christian lapse into sin (p. 43), and there is the myth of the soul's pre-existence.

That myth is concerned with the conscience in Plato, Plato's transmigration of the soul, and the relation to the stars.

Baur says on page 83:

"There is no other philosophy in antiquity which has the character of a religion so much as Platonism has."

This would follow from Plato's definition of the "task of philosophy" (p. 86) as a λύσις, ἀπαλλαγή, χωρισμός [delivery or separation] of the soul from the body, as a form of dying and μελετᾶν ἀποθνῄσκειν [getting used to death].

"Indeed, the one-sidedness of Platonism lies in that redemptive power which is again and again, in the final analysis, attributed to philosophy" (p. 89).

One might accept Baur's view that no philosophy in antiquity has more the character of a religion than Platonism. But this would only mean that no other philosopher taught philosophy with more religious exaltation and that for no other philosopher did philosophy more have the character and form of a religious cult. For more intensive philosophers like Aristotle, Spinoza, and Hegel, philosophy had a more universal form, less absorbed in empirical emotion. But nevertheless Aristotle's exaltation as he praises θεωρία [contemplation] as the highest, τὸ ἥδιστον καὶ ἄριστον [the most satisfying and best], or admires the rationality of nature in the treatise περὶ τῆς φύσεως ζωϊκῆς [concerning nature as animate] [Arist. De partibus animalium, Bek. 645a], and particularly Spinoza's exaltation as he speaks of viewing things sub specie aeternitatis, of the love of God or the liberty of the human spirit, or even Hegel's exaltation in developing the eternal realization of the Idea, the immense organism of universal spirit—this exaltation is more intense, more ardent, and more beneficial for the mind formed in universality. While religious exaltation is consumed at its highest point in ecstasy, philosophical exaltation is transmitted as the pure, ideal flame of science. Hence the former has been only the hot-water bottle for some individual souls while the latter has been the animating spirit of world-historical developments.

One can thus concede that in Christianity as the apex of religious development there is more agreement with the subjective form of Platonism than with the other ancient philosophies. Conversely and on the same ground one must also conclude that in no philosophy can the antithesis between what is religious and philosophical be expressed more clearly, because in what is religious, philosophy appears in the mode of religion and in what is philosophical, religion appears in the mode of philosophy.

Further, Plato's views on the salvation of the soul prove nothing, since every philosopher seeks to release the soul from its empirical limitation; the analogy with religion would then be only a deficiency in philosophy, to be considered as the task of philosophy while it is only the condition of a solution, only the beginning of the beginning.

Finally, there is no deficiency or one-sidedness in Plato when he ultimately attributes this redemptive power to philosophy, rather this is the one-sidedness that makes him a philosopher and not a theologian. There is no one-sidedness of Platonic philosophy except that by which it is uniquely and specifically philosophy, and thus he again transcends the formula we rejected of a task for philosophy which would not be its own.

"In the tendency to give philosophical truth an [objective] foundation independent of the subjectivity of the individual, lies the reason why Plato, as he develops truths of highest ethico-religious interest, also presents them in mythical form" (p. 94).

Is anything clarified this way? Doesn't this include in essence the question of the reason for this reason? It is being asked, in effect, why Plato feels the need to give philosophical truth a positive and at first mythical basis. Such an attempt is the most astonishing thing that can be said of a philosopher when he does not find the objective force in his system itself, in the eternal power of the Idea. Hence Aristotle called mythology a gnomology.

Externally, the answer here can be found in the subjective or dialogic form of the Platonic system and in irony. The utterance of the individual which is valid as such in opposition to opinions or individuals needs a purchase whereby subjective uncertainty becomes objective truth.

But it can further be asked why this mythologizing is found in dialogues pre-eminently developing ethico-religious truths while the purely metaphysical Parmenides is free of it. It can be asked why the positive basis is mythical and depends on myths.

And here we come to the solution. In developing definite ethical and religious questions, or even questions of natural philosophy as in the *Timaeus,* Plato is not satisfied with his negative interpretation of the Absolute. It is not enough to plunge everything into the depths of a night where, as Hegel says, all cows are black. Here Plato avails himself of a positive interpretation of the Absolute. And its essential, self-grounded form is myth and allegory. Where the Absolute stands on one side and limited positive actuality on the other, and the positive is still to be maintained, it becomes the medium of absolute light which bursts into a fabulous display of color. The finite and positive signifies something other than itself. It has a soul in itself for which this transformation is miraculous. The entire world has become a world of myths. Every form is an enigma. And this has reappeared even in our time by virtue of a similar law.

This positive representation of the Absolute with its mythico-allegorical garb is the fountainhead and heartbeat of the philosophy of transcendence, a transcendence that is as essentially related to immanence as it is distinct from it. Here indeed is the affinity of Platonism with every positive religion, particularly with Christianity, which is the completed philosophy of transcendence. Here also is one of the respects in which a deeper connection can be made between historic Christianity and the history of ancient philosophy. With this positive interpretation of the Absolute it would follow that for Plato an individual as such, Socrates, was the mirror and the myth of Wisdom. Plato calls him the philosopher of Death and Love. This is not to say that Plato superseded the historical Socrates. The positive interpretation of the Absolute goes with the subjective character of Greek philosophy, with the concept of the wise man.

Death and Love are myths of the negative dialectic because the dialectic is the simple inner light, the penetrating eye of Love, the inner soul which is not crushed through the material dissolution of life. It is the inner place of the spirit. Thus Love is the myth of the dialectic. But the dialectic is also the torrent which shatters multiplicity and its limits, which overthrows autonomous forms to plunge everything into the one sea of eternity. Hence the myth of the dialectic is Death.

The dialectic is thus Death but at the same time the vehicle of what is living, the flowering in the garden of spirit. It is the effervescing in the bubbling tumbler of innumerable suns from which the flower of a spiritual fire blooms. Hence Plotinus calls it the means to the ἅπλωσις [opening] of the soul and immediate union with God, an expression in which the θεωρία [contemplation] of Aristotle is united with the dialectic of Plato. But as these concepts in Plato and Aristotle are virtually predetermined and not developed from immanent necessity, their immersion in empirical, individual consciousness appears with Plato as a state of *ecstasy*.

## Philosophy after Its Completion

In regard to Hegel, too, it is out of mere ignorance that his disciples explain this or that determination of his system by accommodation and the like or, in a word, *morally*. They forget that a very short time ago they enthusiastically adhered to all aspects of his one-sidedness; clear evidence of this fact is found in their own writings.

If they really were so much affected by the completed scientific knowledge they received that they submitted to it with naïve, uncritical trust, how unconscionable it is to reproach the master with having a hidden motive behind his insight—the master for whom scientific knowledge was not something received but something evolving as his own intellectual life's blood pulsed to its outmost periphery. Doing this, they throw suspicion on themselves, as though formerly they were not serious, and they combat their own former position in the form of ascribing it to Hegel. They forget, however, that he stood in direct, substantial relationship to his system, and they in a reflected relationship.

It is conceivable that a philosopher commits this or that apparent non sequitur out of this or that accommodation. He himself may be conscious of it. But he is not conscious that the possibility of this apparent accommodation is rooted in the inadequacy of his principle or in its inadequate formulation. Hence, if a philosopher has accommodated himself, his disciples have to explain *from his inner essential consciousness* what for him had *the form of an exoteric consciousness*. In this way what appears as progress of consciousness is progress of knowledge as well. It is not that the particular consciousness of the philosopher is suspect; rather, his essential form of consciousness is constructed, raised to a particular form and meaning, and at the same time superseded.

Incidentally, I regard this unphilosophical turn made by a large segment of the Hegelian school as a phenomenon that will always accompany the transition from discipline to freedom.

It is a psychological law that the theoretical mind, having become free in itself, turns into practical energy. Emerging as *will* from Amenthes' shadow-world, it turns against worldly actuality which exists outside it. (It is important, however, from the philosophical point of view, to specify these aspects more clearly, because deductions about a philosophy's immanent determination and world-historical character can be made from the particular manner of this turn. Here we see, as it were, its curriculum vitae narrowed down, brought to the subjective point.) The *practice* [*Praxis*] of philosophy, however, is itself *theoretical*. It is *criticism* which measures individual existence against essence, particular actuality against the Idea. But this *direct realization* of philosophy is burdened with contradictions in its innermost essence, and this essence manifests itself in appearance and puts its stamp thereon.

While philosophy, as will, turns toward the apparent world, the system is reduced to an abstract totality, that is, it becomes one side of the world facing another. Its relation to the world is reflexive relation. Enthusiastic in its drive to realize itself, it enters into tension with everything else. The inner self-contentedness and roundedness is broken down. The former inner light becomes a consuming flame turning outward. The consequence, hence, is that the world's becoming philosophical is at the same time philosophy's becoming worldly, that its realization is at the same time its loss, that what it combats outside is its own inner defect, that just in this combat philosophy itself falls into the faults which it combats in its opponent, and that it transcends these faults only by falling victim to them. Whatever opposes it and what philosophy combats is always the very same thing as philosophy, only with reversed factors.

This is the one side, when we look at the matter *purely objectively,* as immediate realization of philosophy. But there is also a *subjective* side—actually only a different form of the other side. This is *the relation of the philosophical system* which is actualized to its intellectual supporters and to the individual self-consciousnesses in which its progress becomes manifest. From the relationship that lies in the realization of philosophy in opposition to the world it is apparent that these individual self-consciousnesses always have *a double-edged demand,* of which one edge turns against the world, the other against philosophy itself. For what appears objectively as a relationship reversed in itself, appears to them as a double, self-contradictory demand and action. Their liberation of the world from nonphilosophy is at the same time their own liberation from the philosophy which fettered it as a definite system. Being themselves involved in action and the immediate energy of development, and hence, as far as theory is concerned, not yet beyond that system, they sense only the contradiction with the plastic self-identity of the system and are unaware that by turning against it, they merely actualize its particular moments.

Finally, this duality of philosophical self-consciousness manifests itself in double directions which are diametrically opposed. The one, which we may generally call the *liberal* party, adheres to the Concept and the principle of philosophy as its main determination; the other to its *Non-concept*, the element of reality. This second direction is *positive philosophy*. The act of the former is criticism; hence, precisely the turning outward of philosophy. The act of the latter is the attempt to philosophize, thus the turning inward of philosophy. It grasps the deficiency as immanent to philosophy, while the former conceives it as a deficiency of the world to be made philosophical. Each of these parties does exactly what the other wants to do, and what each one itself does not want to do. But the former, with its inner contradiction, is conscious in general of principle and aim. In the second appears perversity, so to speak, insanity as such. In content only the liberal party makes real progress, because it is the party of the Concept while positive philosophy is capable of achieving merely demands and tendencies whose form contradicts its meaning.

What seems to be, first of all, philosophy's wrong relation to and diremption with the world, turns secondly into a diremption of the individual philosophical self-consciousness in itself and finally appears as philosophy's external separation and duality, as two opposed philosophical directions.

It is understood that in addition a lot of subordinate, trifling, unoriginal forms appear, which perhaps hide behind a philosophical giant of the past—but one soon notices the donkey under the lion's skin; the whiny voice of a perennial puppet cries in comic contrast to the mighty voice that fills centuries, say Aristotle's, having made itself his unwelcome mouthpiece; it is, as if a mute person wanted to acquire a voice with the aid of an enormous megaphone —or, armed with double spectacles, some Lilliputian stands on the extremity of the giant's posterior, announces amazedly to the world what an astoundingly new view is offered from his point of vantage and ridiculously endeavors to demonstrate that the Archimedean point, the ποῦ στῶ on which the world hinges, can be found not in the pulsating heart but in the firm and solid area on which he stands. Thus originate hair-, toe-, excrement-philosophers, and others who represent an even worse position in Swedenborg's mystical world-man. According to their nature, however, all these clams fall into the two directions stated, these being their element. In regard to these directions, I shall elsewhere explain completely their relationship to each other and to Hegel's philosophy, as well as the particular historical moments in which this development is manifest.

## Reason and the Proof of God

"*Weak* reason, however, is not reason which knows no objective God, but *wants* to recognize one" (Schelling, "Philosophical Letters on Dogmatism and Criticism" in *Philosophical Writings*, Vol. I, Landshut, 1809, p. 127, Letter II). In general, Herr Schelling would be well advised to recall his first writings. For instance, he says in the piece on the Self as the principle of philosophy: "If we assume, for example, that insofar as *God* defined as object is the *real basis* of our nature, then God *himself* enters *the sphere of our knowledge* as object and hence cannot be the ultimate point for us on which this entire sphere depends" (*loc. cit.*, p. 5). And we remind Herr Schelling of the concluding sentence of his letter mentioned above: "**It is time** to acquaint the *new* humanity with **freedom of mind** and **no longer tolerate its crying about its lost restrictions**" [*] (*loc. cit.*, p. 129). If it was already time in A.D. 1795, how about the year 1841?

This may be the place to recall a topic that has become almost notorious, *the proofs for the existence of God. Hegel* completely inverted these theological proofs, that is to say, he refuted them in order to substantiate them. What kind of clients have to be killed by their own attorney so that

[* Boldface type identifies Marx's emphasis in the quotation.]

he can spare them from sentence? Hegel interprets, for example, the inference from the world to God in the form: "Since contingency does *not* exist, God or the Absolute does." But the theological proof reverses this: "Since contingency truly exists, God exists." God is the guarantee for the contingent world. In this, it is obvious, the converse is also being asserted.

The proofs for the existence of God are nothing but *empty tautologies.* For example, the ontological proof merely asserts: "What I conceive for myself as actual (realiter), is an actual conception for me," really matters to me. In this sense *any God,* heathen as well as Christian, has had real existence. Did not old Moloch rule? Was not the Delphic Apollo an actual force in Greek life? Here even Kant's critique means nothing. If someone conceives that he has a hundred dollars, if this conception is not merely incidental and subjective for him, if he believes in it, then the hundred conceived dollars have the same value for him as a hundred real ones. He will contract debts on the basis of his imagination, which will really *matter, just as all of humanity has incurred debts on the basis of its gods.* On the contrary, Kant's example could have strengthened the ontological argument. Real dollars have the same existence imagined gods have. Has a real dollar any mode of existence other than in conception, though in man's general or rather communal conception? Take paper money into a country where this use of paper is not known, and everyone will laugh at your subjective concept. Come with your gods into a country where other gods prevail, and people will prove to you that you are a victim of fictions and abstractions. Quite right. If someone had taken a Wendish god to the ancient Greeks, he would have found proof for the non-existence of this god, because this god did not exist for the Greeks. *What a certain country is for foreign gods, the country of reason is for God altogether— namely, a place where God no longer exists.*

On the other hand, the proofs for the existence of God are nothing but *proofs for the existence of the essentially human self-consciousness and logical explications of it.*

Take the ontological argument. What existence is immediate in being thought? Self-consciousness.

In this sense all proofs for the existence of God are proofs for his *non-existence;* they are *refutations* of all conceptions of a god. Valid proofs would have to state, on the contrary: "Since nature is imperfect, God exists." "Since a non-rational world exists, God exists." "Since there is no rationale in things, God exists." What else does this mean except that *God exists for the man to whom the world is non-rational and who is therefore non-rational himself? In other words, non-rationality is God's existence.*

"When you presuppose the **idea** of an **objective god,** how can you speak of *laws* which **reason** produces *from itself,* since **autonomy** can be attributed only to an *absolutely* **free being?**" (Schelling, *loc. cit.,* p. 198.)

"It is a crime against humanity, to conceal principles which are generally communicable." (*Ibid.,* p. 199.)

# COMMENTS ON THE LATEST
# PRUSSIAN CENSORSHIP INSTRUCTION

[Having received his doctorate, Marx hoped to get a teaching post at Bonn University with his friend Bruno Bauer, but as the campaign of the Prussian government to dismiss Bauer accelerated, Marx gave up the idea of teaching and turned to writing, specifically to writing on a sensitive political issue. The result was the following article, Marx's first, completed in February 1842 for the *Deutsche Jahrbücher* edited by Arnold Ruge. When censorship killed the *Jahrbücher*, Ruge published Marx's article—along with pieces by Bauer, Feuerbach, and Köppen—in Switzerland in the *Anekdota* of February 1843, the first and only issue.

With a wide-ranging verbal facility Marx slashes at the inconsistencies and confusions of a new instruction to censors, which was supposed to relax prevailing regulations. He argues that the new instruction necessarily threatens the integrity of the writer and all inquiry. It suppresses criticism of religion and converts morality into police-regulated manners, the opposite of morality for Kant, Fichte, and Spinoza. Restriction on the "tendency" of political writing is particularly dangerous. It goes beyond the proper sphere of law—acts and only acts—to undermine "the sacredness and inviolability of subjective conviction." Its basis is the "haughty conceit of a police state concerning its officials," an "unethical and materialistic view of the state," which denigrates the people and views one organ of society as the sole locus of reason. But in a truly ethical state "the view of the state is subordinated to its members, even if they oppose an organ of the state or the government." Thus Marx was beginning to turn Hegel's premise about the state as the ethical embodiment of reason in the direction of liberal democracy, against some of Hegel's conclusions and the existing Prussian monarchy.]

We are not among those malcontents who even before the enactment of the new Prussian censorship edict exclaim: *Timeo Danaos et dona ferentes* [I fear Greeks bearing gifts (Virgil)]. Since criticism of a law already passed is permitted in the new Instruction even if the criticism is directed against the government, we will begin with such criticism and deal with the Instruction itself. *Censorship is official criticism;* its norms are critical norms and must therefore not be withheld from criticism, the very field they belong to.

Everybody will certainly be able to approve of the *general tendency* expressed at the beginning of the Instruction:

"In order to free the press, **even at this early time,**[*] from undue limitations not intended by the Highest Authority, His Majesty the King, in an Order addressed to the Royal State Ministry and dated the 10th of this month, deigned to disapprove of any improper censorship in the field of journalism, and with regard to the value of and need for frank and loyal publicity empowered us again to remind the censors that they should pay proper attention to Article II of the Censorship Edict of October 18, 1819."

Certainly! Once censorship is a necessity, frank and liberal censorship is even more so.

What must bother us to some extent right away is the *date* of the law referred to. It is dated October 18, 1819. How come? Is it perhaps a law that circumstances had to minimize? This does not seem to be the case. For the censors are *"again"* reminded to pay attention to it. Until 1842, therefore, the law existed but it was not observed; for in order to free the press *"even at this early time"* from undue limitations not intended by the Crown the law is resurrected.

The press—this is a direct implication of the introductory sentence—was until now subject to undue limitations *despite the law*.

Now, does this speak *against the law* or *against the censors?*

We are hardly *permitted* to claim that it speaks against the latter. For twenty-two years illegal actions have been committed by an office which controls what is of highest

[* Boldface type identifies Marx's emphasis in the quotation.]

concern to the citizens, *their minds,* an office regulating not only the behavior of individual citizens but even the behavior of the public mind. That is more than the Roman censors did! Should such disloyalty and such unscrupulous conduct of the highest civil servants be possible in the Prussian state, which is so well-administered and so proud of its administration? Or has the state, in perpetual delusion, appointed the most unfit persons to the most difficult positions? Or is it perhaps that the subjects of the Prussian state have no recourse in protesting against illegal measures? Are all Prussian journalists so uneducated and stupid that they are not familiar with laws that concern their livelihood, or are they too cowardly to demand that the laws be observed?

If we blame the *censors,* we compromise not only their honor but also the honor of the Prussian state and of Prussian writers.

Because of the lawless behavior of the censors for twenty years despite the statutes, the argumentum ad hominem is offered that the press needs other guarantees for such irresponsible individuals besides those general regulations. It has been proved convincingly that there is a basic fault in censorship, a fault no law can remedy.

But if the censors were capable and *if the law was no good,* why resurrect it again to do away with the very evil it has caused?

Or is it perhaps that the *objective mistakes* of an institution are to be blamed on *individuals* so that the semblance of improvement is achieved without a real improvement? It is this kind of *pseudo-liberalism* that is apt to make concessions under pressure and that sacrifices persons to maintain the institution, the tools, the object. The attention of a superficial public is thus diverted.

External exasperation is turned into exasperation against persons. With a change of personnel one claims to have a change in substance. Our attention is focused on individual censors, away from censorship as such, and those little journalists in the service of progress-by-order hurl as petty epithets against those who have been disfavored as they give great compliments to the government.

We encounter an additional difficulty.

Some newspaper correspondents consider the Censorship Instruction to be a new censorship edict. They are mistaken, but their error is forgivable. The Censorship Edict of October 18, 1819, was to be in force until 1824 only. To this day it would have remained a provisional law, except that we now learn from the Instruction that it was never observed.

The Edict of 1819 was an *interim* measure, the difference being that the definite time of five years was expected while in the new Instruction no time limitation is indicated. Furthermore, *laws on the freedom of the press* were expected *then* while *now laws of censorship* are expected.

Other correspondents regard the Censorship Instruction as a brushing up of the old Censorship Edict. Their error will be evident in the examination of the Instruction itself.

We regard the Censorship Instruction as the *anticipated spirit* of a probable censorship law. We find this exactly in the spirit of the Censorship Edict of 1819 in which *state laws* and *regulations* are of equal importance for the press (see the Edict, Article XVI, No. 2).

But let us return to the Instruction.

"According to this law," that is, Article II, "censorship shall not impede any serious and restrained pursuit of truth. It shall not put undue compulsion on writers and shall not hinder the unrestricted sale of books."

The pursuit of truth not to be impeded is qualified as being *serious* and *restrained*. Both modifications point to something outside the content of the pursuit rather than to the matter to be investigated. They detract from the pursuit of truth and bring into play an unknown third factor. If an investigation must constantly attend to this third factor, an irritation supported by law, will such pursuit not lose sight of the truth? Isn't it the first duty of the person in search of truth that he proceed to it directly without glancing left or right? Don't I forget the substance if I must never forget to state it in a prescribed form?

Truth can be as little restrained as light, and in relation to what should it be restrained? In relation to itself? *Verum index sui et falsi* [Truth, the test of itself and of falsehood (Spinoza)]. Hence, *in relation to falsehood?*

If restraint shapes the character of inquiry it is a criterion for shying away from truth rather than from falsity. It is a drag on every step I take. *With inquiry, restraint is the prescribed fear of finding the result,* a means of keeping one from the truth.

Furthermore, truth is universal. It does not belong to me, it belongs to all; it possesses me, I do not possess it. A *style* is my property, my spiritual individuality. *Le style, c'est l'homme.* Indeed! The law permits me to write, only I am supposed to write in a style different from *my own.* I may show the profile of my mind, but first I must show the *prescribed mien.* What man of honor will not blush at this effrontery and rather hide his head under his toga. At least it is conceivable that under the toga there is the head of a Jupiter. The prescribed mien is nothing but *bonne mine à mauvais jeu.*

You admire the charming variety, the inexhaustible wealth of nature. You do not demand that the rose smell like the violet. But the richest of all, the mind, is to exist only in *one* way? I may be humorous, but the law orders that I write seriously. I may be forward, but the law orders that my style be restrained. *Grey on grey* is to be the only permissible color of freedom. Every dewdrop in the sun glitters in an infinite play of colors, but the light of the mind is to produce only one, only the *official color,* no matter in how many individuals and in which objects it may be refracted. The essential form of mind is *brightness* and *light,* and you want to make *shadow* its only appropriate manifestation. It is to be dressed only in black, and yet there are no black flowers. The essence of mind is *always truth itself,* and what do you make its essence? *Restraint.* Only a good-for-nothing holds back, says Goethe, and you want to make the mind a good-for-nothing? Or do you mean the restraint of genius of which Schiller speaks? Then you will first have to transform all citizens and chiefly all censors into geniuses. But the restraint of genius does not lie in the language of culture permitting no accent and no dialect. Rather it speaks the accent of the substance of things and the dialect of their nature. It is a matter of forgetting restraint and unrestraint, and of crystallizing things. The general restraint of the mind is reason, that universal liberality which is related to *every nature* according to *its essential character*.

Furthermore, if *seriousness* is not to fit into the definition of Tristram Shandy where it is deceitful behavior of the body to cover up the deficiencies of the soul, and if seriousness should mean *substantial* earnestness, then the entire regulation cancels itself. For I treat the ridiculous seriously when I treat it as ridiculous, and the most serious lack of intellectual restraint is to be restrained about a lack of restraint.

Serious and restrained! What wavering and relative concepts! Where does seriousness end, and where does levity begin? Where does restraint leave off, and where does lack of restraint start? We are dependent upon the *temperament* of the censor. Prescribing a temperament for the censor would be just as wrong as prescribing a style for the writer. If you wish to be logical in your aesthetic criticism, prohibit the pursuit of truth in a *too serious* and *too restrained* manner, for the greatest seriousness is the most ridiculous thing, and the greatest restraint is the bitterest irony.

Finally, all this proceeds from a completely wrong and abstract view of *truth*. All purposes of journalistic activity are subsumed under the one general concept of "*truth*." Even if we disregard the *subjective* side, namely that one and the same object appears differently in different individuals and expresses its various aspects in as many various intellects, shouldn't *the character of the object* have some influence, even the slightest, on the inquiry? Not only the result but also the route belongs to truth. The pursuit of truth must itself be true; the true inquiry is the developed truth whose scattered parts are assembled in the result. And the nature of inquiry is not to change according to the object? When the object is humorous, inquiry is supposed to appear serious. When the object is touchy, inquiry is to be restrained. Thus you injure the rights of the object

HUMANITARIANISM AND LIBERALISM

as you injure the rights of the subject. You grasp truth abstractly and make the mind an *inquisitor* who dryly *records the proceedings.*

Or is this metaphysical torment unnecessary? Is *truth* to be understood in such a way that it is constituted by *governmental order,* and is *inquiry* a superfluous and obnoxious third element which cannot be entirely rejected *for reasons of etiquette?* It almost appears that way. For inquiry is understood a priori as being *opposed* to truth and appears therefore with the suspicious official patina of seriousness and restraint a layman is supposed to display before a priest. Administrative reasoning is the only rationality in politics. Under certain circumstances concessions are to be made to other reasoning and idle talk, but at the same time this reasoning ought to be conscious of the concession and of its real groundlessness: restrained and subservient, serious and boring. When Voltaire says, "Tous les genres sont bons, excepté le genre ennuyeux," the boring type becomes the only type as we can easily observe in the "Proceedings of the Rhenish States." Why not rather the good old German legal style? You are to write freely, but every word is to be a curtsy before liberal censorship, which lets your serious and restrained words pass. By no means should you lose a consciousness of humility!

The *legal emphasis* is not placed on truth, but on restraint and seriousness. Hence, everything causes concern, seriousness, restraint, and above all a kind of truth under whose vague scope a very definite, very doubtful truth appears to be hidden.

"Censorship," the order continues, "is by no means to be carried out with a narrow-mindedness that would go beyond this law."

By *this law* is meant first of all Article II of the Edict of 1819, but later the Instruction refers to the *"spirit"* of the Censorship Edict in general. Both regulations can be easily combined. Article II is the *concentrated spirit* of the Censorship Edict whose structure and specifications are found in the other Articles. We believe that we can best characterize the spirit through *its following manifestation:*

Article VII. "The freedom from censorship granted SO FAR to the Academy of Sciences and to the universities is herewith suspended for five years."

§ 10. "The present temporary regulation is to be effective for five years, starting today. Before the expiration date Parliament is to investigate thoroughly how the regulations on freedom of the press, as stated in Article 18 of the Act, might be uniformly applied. A definite law on the legal limits of freedom of the press in Germany is to follow soon."

A law which suspends *freedom of the press* where it still exists and precludes it through *censorship* in areas where it was to be achieved cannot exactly be called a law favorable to the press. Section 10 confesses that a temporary *censorship law* is to be enacted, instead of the promise of *freedom of the press* to be achieved at some time, as mentioned in Article 18 of the Act. This quid pro quo at least reveals that the character of the time prescribed limitations on the press and that the Edict owes its origin to distrust of the press. The quid pro quo is even excused: it is termed temporary in that it is valid for only five years. Unfortunately it lasted twenty-two.

The next line of the Instruction contains the contradiction that on the one hand censorship is not to be applied so as to exceed the Edict, while on the other hand the procedure is described as follows: "The censor may permit a frank discussion of domestic matters."

The censor *may;* he does not have to; it is not a necessity. But this careful liberalism transgresses not only the spirit but also definite specifications of the Censorship Edict, and in a very definite way. Article II of the old Censorship Edict, after all, does not permit a *frank discussion* of anything, not of Prussian nor even of *Chinese* matters.

The commentary on the security of the Prussian state and the federated German states says, "This concerns all attempts to present those parties in a favorable light which work toward an overthrow of the constitution in any given country."

Does this permit a *frank* discussion of Chinese or Turkish public affairs? If such remote references might endanger the volatile security of the German federation, how much more so might a disapproving word about *domestic* matters?

If the Instruction thus departs from the spirit of Article II of the Censorship Edict on the liberal side, it equally departs *from the Edict on the illiberal side* and adds *new restrictions of the press* to the old ones. The liberal *departure,* by the way, whose *substance* will become evident later, is already suspect in *form* as the consequence of Article II, cleverly cited only in its *first half* while the censor is referred to the *Article itself.*

Article II of the Edict reads: "The purpose" (of censorship) "is to control whatever opposes the **fundamental principles** of religion **WITHOUT REGARD** to the opinions and doctrines of **particular** religious groups and sects permitted in the state."

Rationalism still prevailed in 1819 and generally viewed religion as religion according to reason. This *rationalistic viewpoint* is also the viewpoint of the Censorship Edict which, however, is so illogical as to take an irreligious point of view while it aims to protect religion. It is contradictory to the fundamental principles of religion to separate those principles from its positive content and specific quality, for every religion believes it is different from other *illusory* religions by virtue of its *particular nature,* and is the *true religion* by virtue of its *specific quality.* In quoting Article II the new Censorship Instruction omits the *limiting clause* regulating particular religious groups and sects. But it does not stop here and offers the following addition: "Nothing will be tolerated which opposes **Christian** religion in general or a **particular doctrine** in a **frivolous** and **hostile** manner."

The old Censorship Edict does not mention *Christian* religion at all. On the contrary, it distinguishes religion from *any* religious group or sect. The new Censorship Instruction not only changes religion to *Christian* religion, but even *adds particular doctrine.* What a monster from our new Christian scientific attitude! Who can deny that it has forged new chains for the press? Religion is to be attacked *neither in general nor in particular*. Or do you believe that the words "frivolous" and "hostile" make these chains into a chain of roses? How cleverly put: *frivolous, hostile*. The adjective "frivolous" appeals to the citizen's sense of propriety and is the exoteric term in the public view; but the adjective "hostile" is whispered into the censor's ear and becomes the legal interpretation of frivolity. We will find more examples of this finesse in the Instruction: a subjective word which makes the public blush, and an objective word for the censor which makes the writer pale. In this way one can set lettres de cachet to music.

And in what strange contradictions the Censorship Instruction gets entangled! Only that part of an attack is frivolous which involves particular surface aspects without being profound and serious enough to get to the substance. The very move against any *particular thing* is frivolous. As an attack on Christian religion in its fundamentals is forbidden, only a frivolous attack is possible. In reverse, the attack on the fundamental principles of religion, on its substance and upon particulars *insofar as they are manifestations* of that substance is a hostile attack. Religion can be attacked only in *a hostile or frivolous* way; there is no third way. This illogicality in which the Instruction is entangled, however, is only something *apparent* because it is based on the deceptive notion that an attack *of any kind* on religion is permitted. Only one objective look is needed to recognize this deception. Religion is not to be attacked *at all*, neither in a hostile nor frivolous manner, not in general or in particular.

Since the Instruction in open contradiction to the Censorship Edict of 1819 newly enchains the *philosophical press*, it should at least be so logical as to free the *religious press* from the old chains put on by that rationalistic Edict. The additional purpose of censorship is "to oppose the fanatical injection of religious convictions into politics and the ensuing intellectual confusion."

To be sure, the new Instruction cleverly fails to mention this provision in the *commentary*, but it does include it in the *quotation of Article II*. What does fanatical injection of religious convictions into politics mean? It means that specific religious convictions can determine the state and that the *particular nature of religion* can become *the norm of the state*. The old Censorship Edict could rightly oppose this confusion, for it left the particular religion and its specific content to criticism. The old Edict was based on the shallow and superficial *rationalism* you despise. In basing the state on *faith* and *Christianity* and wanting a *Christian state,* how can you expect censorship to prevent this intellectual confusion?

The confusion of political and Christian-religious principles has indeed become an *official denomination.* Let us briefly clarify this confusion. As Christianity is the only recognized religion, your state contains Catholics and Protestants. Both make the same demands on the state and have the same duties to it. They disregard their religious differences and agree in demanding that the state be the actualization of political and legal rationality. However, you want a *Christian state.* If your state is only *Protestant,* it becomes for the *Catholic* a church to which he does not belong, which he must reject as heretical, and whose essence he finds obnoxious. The reverse would be true if the state were Catholic. And if you make the *general spirit of Christianity* the *particular* spirit of the state, you would decide on the basis of your Protestant background *what* the universal spirit of Christianity might be. You want to determine *what the Christian state* is to be, although recent events teach you that some government officials cannot draw the line between religion and secularity, between state and church. Not the *censors* but the *diplomats* had to *negotiate* about this *confusion;* they did not have to *make decisions* about it. Finally, you are in a *heretical* position when you reject particular dogma as unessential. When you call your state *universally Christian,* you are confessing with a diplomatic twist that it is *un-Christian.* You should forbid that religion be drawn into politics—but you do not want to do that because you wish to base the state on faith rather than on free reason, with religion constituting for you the *general sanction of the positive.*

Or you should permit the *fanatical* injection of religion into politics. Religion might be politically active in its *own way,* but you do not want that either. For religion is to support secular matters without the latter's being subject to religion. Once religion is drawn into politics, it becomes an insufferable, indeed an *irreligious* presumption to want to determine *on secular grounds how* religion has to operate within politics. If one allies himself with religion from religiosity, one must give religion the decisive voice in all matters. Or do you perhaps understand by religion the *cult of your own sovereignty and governmental wisdom?*

The *orthodoxy* of the new Censorship Instruction comes into conflict with the *rationalism* of the old Censorship Edict in an additional way. The Edict also includes within the purpose of censorship the suppression of "whatever offends **morality** and good conduct." The Instruction *quotes* this from Article II. But although the *commentary* makes additions in regard to religion, it contains omissions in regard to morality. To offend *morality* and *good conduct* is now to injure "discipline, morals, and outward loyalty." One observes that *morality as morality,* as the *principle of a world* with its own laws, has *disappeared;* external manifestations such as *police-regulated honorability* and *conventional good manners* have taken its place. Credit where credit is due: this shows real consistency. The specifically Christian legislator *cannot recognize morality* as an independent sphere sanctified in itself, for he derives the inner universal essence of morality from religion. Independent morality offends the basic principles of religion, and particular concepts of religion are opposed to morality. Morality recognizes only its own universal and rational religion, and religion only its own particular and positive morality. Following the Instruction, censorship will have to repudiate such intellectual heroes of morality as Kant, Fichte, Spinoza for being irreligious and threatening discipline, morals, and outward loyalty. All of these moralists proceed from a principled opposition between morality and religion, because *morality,* they claim, is based on the *autonomy,* and *religion* on the *heteronomy* of the human spirit. From these undesirable new aspects of censorship—

on the one hand the relaxation of the moral conscience and on the other hand the tightening of the religious conscience—we now turn to something more pleasant, to the *concessions*.

> "Writings which evaluate the entire political administration or its individual branches, evaluate laws already passed or yet to be passed, reveal mistakes and errors, indicate or propose improvements are not to be censored because they conflict with the viewpoint of the government so long as their form is decent and their **tendency** is **well-intentioned**."

Restraint and seriousness of the investigation—both the Censorship Edict and the new Instruction contain this requirement. But the latter is not satisfied with the *decent* form and the truth of the contents. The *TENDENCY* has become the main criterion, the pervading thought, while the Edict does not contain *the word* tendency at all. The Instruction does not say what tendency amounts to, but how significant this tendency is can be seen from the following excerpt:

> "It is an **absolute** requirement that the *tendency* of the criticism of governmental measures be well-intentioned and not spiteful or malevolent. The censors must have good will and the insight enabling them to distinguish one from the other. They have to pay special attention to the form and tone of the language used and must not permit publication of writings if **their tendency** is harmful because of passion, violence, and presumptiousness."

According to this statement the writer is subject to the *most horrible terrorism*, to *jurisdiction based on suspicion*. *Tendentious* laws, laws without objective norms, are laws of terrorism, such as those created by Robespierre because of emergencies in the state and by Roman emperors because of the rottenness of the state. Laws that make the *sentiment* of the acting person the main criterion, and not the *act as such*, are nothing but *positive sanctions* of *lawlessness*. It would be better to act like the czar of Russia who had everybody's beard shaved off by Cossacks rather than like the person who makes the idea of wearing a beard the criterion for shaving it off.

Only by *expressing* myself and by entering the sphere of actuality do I enter the legislator's sphere. As far as the law is concerned I do not exist and am not subject to law except in *my* acts. They alone concern the law; only because of them do I demand the right to exist, a *right of actuality* that makes me subject to *actual law*. But a tendentious law does not punish me for my acts, but for my *motive*. It is an insult to the honor of the citizen, a mockery directed against my existence.

I may turn and twist myself as much as possible—the evidence is not important. My existence is suspect; my innermost being, my individuality, is considered to be *evil*, and I am *punished* for that. The law does not penalize me for wrongs I commit but rather for wrongs I do not commit. In fact, I am punished because my actions are *not illegal*, for in this way alone a mild and well-meaning judge is compelled to consider my *evil sentiment*, which I am clever enough not to bring out into the open.

A law like that is *not a law of the state* for the *citizenry*, but a *law of a party against another party*. The tendentious law cancels the equality of the citizens before the law. It divides rather than unites; and all dividing laws are reactionary. It is not a law; it is a *privilege*. One person may do what another person may not do, and not because the latter lacks the objective capability for the action, say like a child who cannot draw up contracts, but rather because his intentions are suspect. In an *ethical state the view of the state* is subordinated to its members, even if they *oppose an organ of the state* or the *government*. But a society in which *one* organ thinks of itself as the only, exclusive possessor of reason and morality on the state level, a government that in principle opposes the people and assumes that *their subversive attitude* is universal and normal, the evil conscience of a faction—such a government invents tendentious laws, *laws of revenge*, against an attitude existing only in the members of the government themselves. Such laws are based on a lack of character and on an unethical and materialistic view of the state. They are indiscreet outcries of bad conscience. And how can a law of this sort be enforced? Through means more outrageous than the law itself: through *spies* or through a priori decisions saying that entire literary movements must be considered suspect, in which case one must find out to which movement an individual belongs. In a tendentious law the *legal form contradicts* the *content;* the *government* issuing it passionately denounces the very thing it represents itself, a subversive attitude. Similarly such a government constitutes, so to speak, an institution *opposed* to its own laws, using two yardsticks. Lawfulness on the one side is unlawfulness on the other. *Such laws are the opposite of what they proclaim to be law.*

The *new Censorship Instruction* is entangled in this dialectic. It is contradictory to force the censors to do the very thing that is condemned as subversive when it takes place in the press.

The Instruction, for example, forbids writers to suspect the sentiment of individuals or entire classes, and in the same breath it orders the censors to group all citizens as to whether they are suspect or unsuspect, malevolent or well-meaning. The criticism forbidden for the press becomes the day-to-day duty of the governmental critic. But that is not all. So far as the content is concerned the subversive element in the press formerly appeared as something particular and yet universal, that is, handed over to universal judgment, so far as the form is concerned.

But now the matter is reversed. Now the particular is justified *in regard to its content;* what is subversive appears as the view and law of the state, as particular in regard to its form, inaccessible to the light of day, banned from the open public, and concealed in the bureau of a governmental critic. The Instruction, for example, aims to protect religion, but it violates the most universal of all religions: the sacredness and inviolability of subjective conviction. It replaces God as the judge of the heart with the censor. It prohibits offensive utterances and defamatory judgments on individuals, but every day it exposes you to the defamatory and offensive judgment of the censor. The Instruction aims to suppress the gossip of malevolent or poorly informed individuals; yet it forces the censor to rely on such gossip and spying by poorly informed and malevolent individuals. It resorts to such means as degrading a judgment in the realm of objective content into one of subjective opinion and arbitrariness. The intention of the state is not to be suspected, but the Instruction proceeds from the public's suspicion against the state. A critical attitude is not to be hidden, so it appears, but the Instruction itself is based on false pretense. Patriotism is to be promoted, but on the basis of a philosophy debasing nationality. We are to act within the legal boundaries of and with respect for the law, but at the same time we are to obey institutions that make us lawless and replace law with arbitrariness. We are to acknowledge the principle of personality to such an extent that we trust the censor despite deficient censorship, and you violate the principle of personality to such an extent that you ask for judgments not based on acts but only on opinions about the meaning of such acts. You demand restraint, and you proceed from the enormous unrestraint of making the civil servant a spy of the heart, an omniscient person, philosopher, theologian, the Delphic Apollo. On the one hand, you force us to acknowledge unrestraint, on the other, you forbid us unrestraint. The real unrestraint consists of assigning the perfection of a group to special individuals. The censor is a special individual; the press, though, constitutes the group. You order us to have trust, and you bestow legal powers on distrust. You place so much confidence in your political institutions that you think they will turn a weak mortal, the civil servant, into a saint who can do the impossible. But you distrust your political organism to such a degree that you fear the isolated opinion of a private person; after all, you are treating the press as a private person. You demand of the officials that they act impersonally, without anger, passion, narrow-mindedness, and human frailty. But you suspect that impersonal *ideas* are full of personal intrigues and subjective baseness. The Instruction demands unlimited confidence in officialdom, but it proceeds from unlimited distrust toward private persons. Why shouldn't we return the same coin?

Why shouldn't we suspect officialdom? It is the same in regard to character. An unprejudiced person will have more respect for the character of a public critic than for that of a secret critic.

Whatever is thoroughly evil will remain so, no matter which individual represents the evil, a private critic or one employed by the government. The only difference is that in the latter case evil is authorized and regarded as a necessity on a higher level, which brings about goodness on a lower.

The *censorship of tendentiousness* and the *tendentiousness of censorship* constitute the *gift of the new liberal Instruction*. Nobody will blame us when we now turn with some distrust to further regulations stated in the Instruction.

"Offensive utterances and defamatory judgments on individuals are not suitable for print." Not suitable for print! Instead of this gentle phrasing we should have liked to receive objective definitions for what is considered offensive and defamatory.

"The same applies to casting suspicion on attitudes of individuals or" (a weighty "or"!) "entire classes, and to the use of the names of political parties and persons." This means also that the grouping by categories, the attack on entire classes, the use of names of political parties—and man, like Adam, must give everything a name so that it exists for him—are necessary categories for the political press,

> "Because every disease, as Dr. Sassafras says,
> Must first be identified by name,
> Before it can be handled with success."

All this refers to *personalities*. How are we to do it? We must not attack an individual person, a class, a general group, a moral person. The state rightfully does not want to suffer injuries and be involved in personalities. But by that easy "or" the universal is also grouped with persons. By that "or" the universal is placed in the center, and by way of an insignificant "and" we finally learn that only persons were meant. It is easy to arrive at the conclusion: the press is not permitted to keep a check on officials and institutions as a group.

> "If censorship is exercised in the spirit of the Censorship Edict of October 18, 1819, and in accordance with these further instructions, loyal and frank publicity will have sufficient elbowroom, and it is to be expected that a more active participation in the interests of the fatherland will be achieved and that patriotism will grow."

We will admit that in accordance with these instructions more than sufficient elbowroom is provided for loyal publicity—"*loyal*" by censorship definition of course. The word "elbowroom," too, is well chosen, because that room is granted a press satisfied with playful shadow-boxing. Whether this applies to *frank* publicity and where the *frankness* is to come from we shall leave to the reader's acumen. As to the *expectations* expressed in the Instruction, *patriotism* may very well be promoted, just as the sending of a cord heightens the Turkish nationalistic sentiment. But whether the press, as restrained as it is serious, will awaken some participation in the interests of the fatherland, we shall leave to the press itself; a lean press cannot be fattened with China. But it is possible that we take the passage too seriously. Perhaps we will understand the whole matter better when we regard the sentence as the clasp in the chain of roses. It is possible that this liberal clasp bears a pearl of very doubtful value. Let's pursue this. Everything depends on the context. Promoting patriotism and awakening participation in the interests of the fatherland, both being *expectations* in the passage of the Instruction quoted above, can be easily changed into *orders* involving a *new compulsion* for our poor consumptive *daily papers*.

> "It is to be hoped in this way that political literature and the daily press will recognize their tasks more clearly than before, acquire more material as well as gain a more dignified tone, and abstain in the future from playing on the curiosity of their readers by printing gossip, insinuations, and meaningless reports taken from foreign newspapers and written by malevolent and poorly informed correspondents. —Censorship must combat this tendency."

It is to be *hoped* in the way indicated that political literature and the daily press will recognize their tasks more clearly than before, etc. However, *better recognition* cannot be ordered. It is a fruit still awaited, and hope remains just hope. But the Instruction is much too practical to be satisfied with pious hopes and vain wishes. While the press gains the hope of improving itself by *this new support* of the benevolent Instruction, it also loses what it still possesses while hoping for the improvement. The press fares like poor Sancho Panza from whom the court physician withheld all food so that an upset stomach would not make him incapable of performing the duties demanded by the Duke.

We cannot let the opportunity pass without challenging the Prussian writers to emulate this kind of loyal style. The introductory clause reads, "It is to be hoped in this way *that* . . ." The "that" governs a long series of regulations, viz., that political literature and the daily press recognize their tasks more clearly than before, that they gain a more dignified tone, etc., etc., that they abstain from printing meaningless reports taken from foreign newspapers, etc. All these regulations are expressed as hopes. But the conclusion, connected by a *dash*, "censorship must combat this tendency" saves the censor the boring job of waiting for the desired improvement of the daily press and empowers him to strike out anything disagreeable without much ado. This is an *amputation* rather than a *cure*.

> "To achieve this goal it is necessary that great caution be employed in the licensing of new papers and new editors so that the daily press is in the hands of men who are completely irreproachable and whose scientific qualifications, reputation, and character vouch for the seriousness of their endeavor and for their loyalty."

Before discussing this paragraph in detail we should like to make a general observation. The licensing of new editors, which means the licensing of all future editors, is entirely left to the *"great caution"* exercised by *state offices* and censorship, while the old Censorship Edict, though with some restrictions, left the choice of the editor *up to the publisher:*

"Article IX. The Superior Censorship Office is empowered to inform the publisher of a newspaper that the editor in question is not as trustworthy as required, in which case the publisher must employ another editor **or,** if he **wishes to keep** him, must set up **bond** for him, the amount **to be determined** upon recommendation of said Superior Censorship Office by one of Our state ministries mentioned above."

An entirely different depth, a *romanticism* of the spirit, as it were, is expressed in the new Censorship Instruction. While the old Censorship Edict prescribes external and prosaic bonds which can be set legally and by which even an ill-favored editor can be licensed, the Instruction deprives the publisher of a newspaper of *any personal preference* and refers to the preventive prudence of the government, the great caution and the intellectual profundity of the office, and internal and subjective criteria that cannot be defined externally. But since such *romantic* indefiniteness, sensitive inwardness, and subjective exuberance often suddenly shift into the realm of the *purely external* —in the sense that the external contingency appears bathed in wonderful glory and in illusory depth and splendor and no longer with prosaic definiteness and delineation—the Instruction too will hardly escape this *romantic fate.*

The editors of the daily press—all journalism falls into this category—are to be men who are completely irreproachable. The first criterion for the complete irreproachability is *"scientific qualification."* Not the slightest doubt, however, exists as to the censor's scientific qualification to pass judgment on scientific qualifications of any sort. If it is true that Prussia has such a tremendous number of universal geniuses who are well known to the government— every city has at least one censor—why don't these encyclopedic minds come out as writers? If these officials, overwhelming in number and so powerful by knowledge and genius, would rise all of a sudden and by sheer weight crush those wretched writers who are active in one genre of writing only, and even there without officially tested qualifications, the confusion in the press could be terminated better than can be done by censorship. Why are these skilled men so silent when they could act like the Roman geese saving the Capitol by their cackle? They must be men of great reserve. The scientific public does not know them, but the government does.

And even if they are men such as no state could ever find—for no state has entire classes of universal geniuses and polyhistorians—how much more gifted must be those selecting them! They must have some secret information enabling them to testify to the universally scientific qualifications of officials otherwise unknown in the republic of science! The higher we climb in this *bureaucracy of intelligence,* the more remarkable are the minds we meet. Is it worth the trouble and is it practical for a state having such potential pillars of a perfect press to appoint these men *guardians* of a deficient press, to debase what is perfect to a means for controlling what is not perfect?

The more censors you employ, the more chances of improvement you take away from the press. You remove healthy people from your army in order to make them doctors for the sick.

Stamp the ground as Pompey did, and an armored Pallas Athena will emerge from every government building. The shallow daily press will collapse entirely before the *official press.* The existence of light suffices to refute darkness. Let your light shine and don't put it under a bushel. Instead of the deficient censorship, which is problematic to you too, give us a perfect press willing to obey your orders; the *Chinese* state has been serving as a model for centuries.

However, isn't it a sound intellectual criterion to make *scientific qualifications* the only requirement for writers of the daily press, instead of conventional privilege and favoritism? Isn't that an objective rather than subjective criterion?

Unfortunately the Censorship Instruction interrupts our panegyric. In addition to the requirement of scientific qualifications we have that of *rank and character*. Rank and character!

Character, mentioned immediately after rank, almost seems to be a by-product of rank. Let us keep *social standing* in mind, above all! It is boxed in between scientific qualification and character so that one is almost tempted to doubt its right to exist by itself.

The *general* requirement of scientific qualification: how *liberal!* The *specific* requirement of rank: how *illiberal!* Scientific qualification combined with rank: how *pseudo-liberal!* Since scientific qualification and character are quite indefinite and rank is very definite, why shouldn't we conclude that logically and necessarily the indefinite will lean on the definite and find support there? Would it be a great mistake of the censor to interpret the Instruction as saying that the *external form* of scientific qualification and public character constitute *rank,* especially since the censor's own rank makes his view the official one? Without this interpretation one could not understand why scientific qualification and character are not sufficient and why rank is a necessary third requirement. Since one and the same person will rarely—or never—have all three qualifications, the censor finds himself in a dilemma. Somebody, after all, has to edit newspapers and periodicals. Scientific qualification and character, in absence of rank, can be a problem for the censor; they are indefinite. He must be amazed, understandably, that such qualities can exist apart from rank. On the other hand, may the censor have doubts as to character and scientific knowledge despite established reputation? In this case he would place more confidence in his own judgment than in that of the state, while in the other case he would favor the writer over the state. Should a censor be so tactless and malevolent? We don't think so, and it certainly is not expected of him. Since in *case of doubt rank* is the decisive criterion, it is altogether the *absolute* criterion.

We have seen that the Instruction conflicts with the *Edict* because of its *orthodoxy;* a similar conflict arises from the Instruction's *romanticism* and *tendentious* poesy. The *bond in money,* a prosaic and real guarantee, becomes a bond in thought, but in terms of the very *real* and *individual* rank which acquires a magic fictitious significance. The meaning of the guarantee changes altogether. No longer does the publisher *select* the editor for whom *he* vouches; now the bureau selects the editor, vouching for him itself. The old Edict sees the editor's work safeguarded by the bond put up by the publisher. The Instruction, however, does not concern itself with the editor's *work* but with his *person*. It requires a certain personality which the *publisher's money* is to provide. The new Instruction is just as vague as the Edict. The only difference is found in the fact that the Edict expresses and delineates what is prosaically definite, while the Instruction lends an imaginary spirit to what is externally most contingent and expresses what is merely individual with the pathos of universality.

But although this romantic Instruction, in regard to the editor, gives the tone of the most spirited indefiniteness to what is most externally definite, in regard to the censor it gives the tone of legal definiteness to what is most vaguely indefinite.

"Equal caution must be applied in appointing the censors so that only men of tested loyalty and **ability** are chosen who completely deserve the honorable confidence required. They must be loyal and intelligent at the same time, men who know how to separate the form from the substance of the matter and who can overlook with self-confidence and **tact** minor objections which are not justified in view of the **purport** and direction of the entire article."

What rank and character is for the writer, is for the censor tested loyalty, since rank is present to begin with. More important, though, is the fact that *scientific capability* is required of the writer, while only *ability* without further modification is required of the censor. Apart from politics the old Edict is rationalistic and in Article III requires *"scientifically educated"* and even *"enlightened"* censors. Both modifications are omitted in the Instruction. And while the *capability* of the writer is understood to be a definite, developed, and realized capability, the censor needs only a *predisposition for capability*, ability in general. This means that a *predisposition for capability* is to *control real capability*, although logically the reverse should be true. Finally, let us note in passing that the censor's ability is not defined in detail as to *subject-matter*, thus becoming quite *ambiguous*.

Furthermore, the task of censorship is to be given to men "who completely deserve the honorable confidence required." No further discussion is needed for this pleonastic pseudo-directive which says that only trustworthy men should be appointed, that they will *completely deserve* the honorable confidence, the trust placed in them, a very complete trust, to be sure, etc.

Finally, the censors are to be men "loyal and intelligent at the same time, men who know how to separate the form from the substance of the matter and who can overlook with self-confidence and tact minor objections which are not justified in view of the purport and tendency of the entire article."

Farther above, on the other hand, the Instruction states:

"In regard to this" (i.e. the investigation of the tendency) "the censors have to pay special attention to the form and tone of the language used and must not permit publication of writings if their tendency is harmful because of passion, violence, and presumptuousness."

On the one hand, then, the censor is to judge the *tendency from the form*, on the other, the *form from the tendency*. The *content* as a criterion for censorship already disappeared, as we have observed; now the *form* disappears too. As long as the tendency is good, *faults in form* are to be overlooked. Even if the article is not written very seriously and restrainedly, even if it appears to be violent, passionate, presumptuous, who would take offense at the *rough form?* One must know how to separate the *form* from the *substance*. Any semblance of definiteness had to disappear; the Instruction had to end with a *complete contradiction*. Anything revealing the tendency must first be qualified by and recognized from the tendency. The violence of the patriot is sacred zeal, his passion is the irritability of a lover, his presumptuousness is devoted participation, too boundless to be moderate.

*All objective norms* have been abandoned; the *personal* relationship is left; and the censor's *tact may* be called a guarantee. What can the censor violate, then? Tact. But tactlessness is no crime. What is threatened for the writer? His existence. What state ever made the existence of an entire profession dependent upon the tact of individual officials?

Let us say it again: *all objective norms have been abandoned*. The tendency constitutes the content for the writer, demanded and prescribed; a formless opinion is the object. The tendency as the subject, as an opinion of an opinion, is tact, the only directive for the censor.

Although the censor's arbitrariness is concealed behind pseudo-factual directives (the right to act on the basis of mere opinion, after all, is the right to be arbitrary), the Instruction clearly states that the *Superior Censorship Office* may act arbitrarily. *This confidence placed in the Director* is the ultimate *guarantee for the press*. The essence of censorship is thus based on the haughty conceit of a police state concerning its officials. The public is not given credit for having a sound mind and a good will to do the most simple thing. But even the impossible is to be possible for the officials.

This fundamental fault permeates all our institutions. In criminal proceedings, for example, judge, prosecutor, and defense lawyer are *one person*. This contradicts all findings of psychology. But the official is above psychological laws; the public, though, is subject to them. A deficient principle in the state may be excused; but a dishonestly inconsequential principle is inexcusable. The difference between the *responsibility* of officials and that of the public should correspond to the difference between officials and public. It is exactly here that the principle is abandoned, although it could be put into practice. The opposite is done.

The censor, too, is prosecutor, lawyer, and judge in one person. The censor is entrusted with the *administration of the mind*. He is *not held responsible*.

Censorship could acquire some *provisional* legal aspects

if it were subject to our *regular courts*. That is not possible because we have no objective censorship laws. The worst is that censorship is again censored, as for example by a director or by a commission.

Everything said about the relationship between the press and censorship applies also to the relationship between ordinary censorship and censorship by higher authority and to the relationship between the writer and the superior censor, even though an *intermediary* exists. It is the same relationship on a higher level, the strange error of abandoning subject-matter and replacing it with persons. If this sort of *dictatorship* were loyal it would dissolve itself. Everything would be based on the same compulsion and the same reaction. Censorship by high authority would have to be censored in turn. To escape this vicious circle one decides to be disloyal, and unlawfulness begins on the third or ninety-ninth level. Because officialdom is hazily conscious of this fact, it attempts to place unlawfulness at such a high level that it is no longer visible, thinking that it disappears.

The real *cure* would be the *abolition of censorship*. It is a bad institution, but institutions are more powerful than men. It makes no difference whether we are right or wrong, for the Prussian writers will *gain* something *from the new Instruction:* either in *real freedom* or in *ideal freedom,* in awareness.

*Rara temporum felicitas, ubi quae vilis sentire et quae sentias dicere licet.*

[How rare the fortunate times in which you can think what you wish and say what you think. (Tacitus)]

# LUTHER AS ARBITER
# BETWEEN STRAUSS AND FEUERBACH

[Marx wrote the following brief essay in late January 1842 to answer articles in the *Deutsche Jahrbücher für Wissenschaft und Kunst* which questioned Feuerbach's advance over D. F. Strauss in theology. Marx may have intended his essay as a substitute for longer ones promised to the *Anekdota* but never finished. The articles in the *Deutsche Jahrbücher,* presumably written by Max Stirner, were signed "A Berliner" and "Also a Berliner," so Marx signalized his position by "No Berliner." Here, for the first time, Marx explicitly indicates his attachment to Ludwig Feuerbach and appeals to Luther to decide between Strauss and Feuerbach on miracles. Feuerbach, who referred to himself as Luther II, comes out the winner because for Luther religion was "confident trust," "hearts that are intrepid and unafraid," and hence an "immediate truth" of human feeling rather than mediating philosophical speculation as in Strauss. Thus Marx not only expressed a distrust of Hegelian speculation, even in its left-wing form, but endorsed a naturalistic view of religion affiliated with a nascent existentialism, with an insistence on the priority of immediate experience over any scheme of concepts for getting at things "as they are."]

Strauss and Feuerbach! Which one of the two is right in regard to the recently mentioned question of the concept of miracle? Strauss who still views the matter as a theologian and therefore with prepossession, or Feuerbach who views it as a non-theologian and therefore without prepossession? Strauss who looks at the matter as it *appears* through the eyes of speculative theology, or Feuerbach who looks at it as it *is?*

Is it Strauss, who does not arrive at a final judgment about miracle yet assumes a special power of the Spirit through miracle, distinct from wish—as if wish were not this power of the Spirit assumed by him or the power of man; as if, for example, the wish to be free were not the *first* act of liberty? Or is it Feuerbach, who makes short shrift of the matter and says that miracle is the realization of a natural or human wish in a supranaturalistic way? Which one of the two is right? Let us ask Luther to make the decision, a very good authority, an authority greater, infinitely, than all Protestant dogmas altogether, because with Luther religion was *immediate truth,* was *Nature,* so to speak.

Luther says, *for example*—and innumerable similar quotations could be cited from him—concerning the resurrection of the dead in Luke 7:

> "We ought to regard the work of our Lord Jesus Christ in a different way and as something *higher* than the work of man, for His works are described for us so that we may recognize by them what kind of Lord He is, namely *a Lord and God who can help where nobody else is able to help,* where no man is so exalted, no man fallen so deep, that the Lord could not help him, no matter what the need be." "And what is *impossible for our Lord and God* that we could not with confidence trust in Him to do it? After all He *created* heaven and earth and *everything out of nothing.* Every year he fills the trees with cherries, plums, apples, and pears, and *needs nothing for doing so.* For anyone of us it would be impossible, when there is snow in the winter, to produce a single little cherry out of the snow. But God is the person who *can accomplish everything,* who can *bestow life on what is dead,* and who can *command to exist what does not exist.* In summary, no matter how deep anything may have fallen, it has not fallen so deep that our Lord and God could not lift it and set it up. It is necessary that we recognize such works done by God and know that *nothing* is impossible for him, so *that, when matters go badly, we learn to rely without fear upon His omnipotence.* May the Turks come or another *misfortune,* let us remember that there is a Helper and Savior with a hand that *is almighty and can help.* That is the *right, true faith."* "*Boldly trust in God* and *do not despair.* For what I and other people cannot do, He can do. *If I and other people can no longer help, He*

*can help me and even save me from death,* as the 68th Psalm says, *We have a God who helps* and the *Lord who saves us from death.* Let our hearts, therefore, always be boldly confident in God and keep to Him. The hearts that serve God rightly and love Him are hearts that are intrepid and unafraid." "We shall trust in *God* and His *Son Jesus Christ.* For *what we cannot do, He can do. What we do not have, He does have. When we cannot help ourselves, He can help and will do so gladly and willingly,* as can be seen here." (Luther's [*Sämtliche Schriften und*] *Werke,* Leipzig, 1732 [Part XVI], pp. 442–45.)

In these few words you have an *apology* for Feuerbach's whole book [*The Essence of Christianity*]—an apology for the definitions of *Providence, Omnipotence, Creation, Miracle,* and *Faith* as given in that book. Shame on you, you Christians, noble and common, educated and uneducated Christians, *shame* on you, that an *antichrist* had to show you the essence of Christianity in its true, unveiled form! And I advise you, speculative theologians and philosophers: free yourselves from the concepts and prepossessions of existing speculative philosophy if you want to get at things differently, as they are, that is to say, if you want to arrive at the *truth.* And there is no other road for you to *truth* and *freedom* except that leading *through* the stream of fire [the *Feuer-bach*]. Feuerbach is the *purgatory* of the present times.

*No Berliner.*

# THE PHILOSOPHICAL MANIFESTO OF THE HISTORICAL SCHOOL OF LAW

[In late April 1842, Marx became a contributor to the *Rheinische Zeitung*, a paper established by well-to-do businessmen to compete with the pro-Catholic *Kölnische Zeitung*. There were several Hegelians from Berlin on the editorial board of the *Rheinische Zeitung*, including Adolf Rutenberg whom Marx had known well in the Doctors' Club. In his first contribution Marx discussed the debates in the Rhenish Diet on freedom of the press. A writer's work, Marx insisted, is an end in itself, not a means, and "the first freedom of the press must be its emancipation from commerce." Further, a free press is required for progress in changing public law to meet social needs. As Marx was writing on the Diet, perhaps some weeks earlier, he finished the following article from which the section on marriage was deleted by the censor. In criticizing Hugo, the "source" of the Historical School, Marx was also criticizing Savigny who had recently been appointed Legislative Minister of Prussia. Extensively quoting from Hugo, Marx draws the consequences of taking bare existence, past or present, as the norm for law in property, the state, and marriage. Such a position sceptically rejects the norm of rationality in legal institutions and leads to a relativism that justifies slavery, animalism, sexual promiscuity, and "the law of arbitrary power." This criticism of the Historical School was similar to Hegel's as presented by Eduard Gans, the professor who had most impressed Marx in Berlin. Hegel criticized Hugo for not telling whether Roman slavery satisfied the "demands of reason" and for confusing historical development with development from the concept. In his dissertation Marx had espoused criticism as the measurement of actuality against the Idea. Now he appeals to "the structures of human rationality."]

The *historical school* is ordinarily viewed as a *reaction* against the *frivolous spirit* of the *eighteenth* century. The spread of this view is inversely related to its truth. The eighteenth century, rather, brought forth only *one* product whose *essential character* is frivolity, and this *single frivolous* product is the *historical school*.

The historical school has made a shibboleth of the study of sources. Its fondness for sources has become so extreme that it advises the ship's captain not to sail in the mainstream but rather on its source. So it will be appropriate for us to trace the historical school to *its sources*, to [Gustav] *Hugo's natural law*. The school's *philosophy* presupposes its development, so we can hardly find philosophy in the development as such.

A common fiction of the eighteenth century viewed the state of nature as the true condition of human nature. People wanted to see ideas of Man with their own eyes and created *Natural Men, Papagenos,* whose innocence even included their feathered skins. In the last decades of the eighteenth century, people sought primitive wisdom among *natives,* and everywhere birdcatchers imitated the songs of the Iroquois and other Indians, hoping to snare the birds themselves with these tricks. The true basis of all these eccentricities was the fact that *crude* conditions are naïve Flemish paintings of *actual* conditions.

The *natural man of the historical school,* still unaffected by any romantic culture, is *Hugo*. His textbook on *natural law* is the *Old Testament* of the historical school. *Herder's* view that natural men are *poets* and the *sacred* books of natives are *poetic* makes no difference, although Hugo uses the most trivial and sober prose. For as every century has its peculiar nature, it also produces its peculiar natural men. If Hugo does not *write poetry*, he still creates *fiction*, and *fiction* is the *poetry of prose* corresponding to the prosaic nature of the eighteenth century.

In designating Herr Hugo as the ancestor and creator of the historical school we act in the *very spirit* of the school as proved by the most famous historical jurist's *program* for Hugo's doctoral anniversary [Friedrich Karl von Savigny's *The Tenth of May, 1788: A Contribution to the History of Jurisprudence,* Berlin, 1838]. In calling Herr Hugo a child of the eighteenth century, we are even proceeding in Herr Hugo's *spirit,* as he himself testifies: he identifies himself as a *disciple* of Kant and calls his natural law an offshoot of *Kantian philosophy*. At this point we take up his *Manifesto*.

Hugo *misinterprets* the master *Kant* in saying that since we cannot know what is *true*, we consequently let pass as *entirely valid* what is *untrue* if it merely *exists*. Hugo is a *sceptic* concerning the *necessary essence* of things so that he can be another [E. T. A.] *Hoffmann* concerning their *contingent appearance*. In no way does he seek to prove that what is *positive* is *rational;* he does seek to prove that what is *positive* is *not rational*. With self-satisfied industry he pulls together evidence from all corners of the world to prove that positive institutions such as property, the state, marriage, etc., are not informed by any rational necessity, that they even *contradict* reason, and that at best one can *bicker* about them pro and con. This *method* can in no way be ascribed to an accident of Hugo's personality. It is rather the *method of his principle*, the *frank, naïve, direct* method of the historical school. If what is *positive* is to be *valid because* it is *positive,* then I must *prove* that what is *positive* is *not* valid *since* it is *rational*. And how could I prove this better than by showing that the non-rational is positive and the positive is non-rational, by showing that what is positive does not exist *through* reason but *in spite of* it? If *reason* were the *norm of what is positive*, then *what is positive* would not be the *norm of reason*. "Though this be madness, yet there is method in 't." Hugo *desecrates* everything that is sacred to lawful, moral, political man. He smashes what is sacred so that he can revere it as a *historical relic;* he violates it before the *eyes of reason* so that he can later honor it before the *eyes of history;* at the same time he also wants to honor *historical eyes*.

Just as Hugo's *principle* is *positive,* that is, *uncritical,* so is his *argumentation*. He recognizes *no distinctions. Everything that exists* is an *authority* for him; every authority is a *reason* for him. In one paragraph he quotes *Moses* and *Voltaire, Richardson* and *Homer, Montaigne* and *Amnon, Rousseau's* "Contrat social" and *Augustine's* "De civitate Dei." *Nations* are likewise equated with one another. The *Siamese* who regards it an eternal law of nature that his king should have a gossip's mouth sewn up and have a clumsy orator's mouth cut open to his ears is, according to Hugo, as *positive* as the *Englishman*, who considers it one of the paradoxes of politics that his king, on his own, would levy a tax of one penny. The shameless *Conci* who runs around naked or at most covered with mud is as positive as the *Frenchman* who not only clothes himself but clothes himself elegantly. The *German* who raises his daughter as the jewel of the family is not more positive than the *Rajput* who kills her so that he won't have to feed her. In brief: *the pimple is as positive as the skin*.

Something is positive in this place, something else is positive in another; one thing is as non-rational as another; just accept what is positive in your framework.

*Hugo*, therefore, is a *perfect sceptic*. The *scepticism* of the *eighteenth century* concerning *the rationality of existing conditions* with him becomes *scepticism* concerning the *existence of reason*. He accepts the *Enlightenment; in what is positive he no longer sees anything rational, but only so that he won't have to see in what is rational anything positive*. He believes that the appearance of reason is extinguished in the positive, so the positive can be recognized *without* the appearance of reason. He believes that *imitation flowers* have been plucked from the necklace so that the *real necklace* can be worn without flowers.

*Hugo* is related to *other men of the Enlightenment* of the eighteenth century just as the *dissolution of the French state* in the lewd *court of the Regent* [Philippe II] is related to the dissolution of the French state in the *National Assembly*. Dissolution on both sides! At the Court, dissolution appears as *lewd frivolity* which includes and mocks the hollow mindlessness of existing conditions. This frivolity, dispensing with all rational and ethical bonds, carries on *its game* with the rotten debris, only to be driven and dissolved by this very game. It is the *rotting of the world at that time, a world enjoying itself*. In the *National Assembly*, on the other hand, the *dissolution* appears as the *separation of the new spirit* from *old forms* no longer *worthy* and *capable* of holding that spirit. It is the *self-confidence of new life* which *shatters what is shattered* and *discards what is discarded.* If *Kant's philosophy* is rightly to be regarded as the *German theory* of the French Revolution, *Hugo's natural law* is the *German theory* of the French Ancien Régime. In Hugo we encounter again all the *frivolity* of those *roués,* the *nasty scepticism* which is insolent toward ideas and most humble toward palpabilities. It senses its cleverness only when it has killed the *spirit* of what is positive. It then possesses the purely positive as residue and feels comfortable in these *animalistic* conditions. Assessing the weight of the evidence, Hugo will find, with his infallibly sure instinct, that everything rational and ethical in institutions is *doubtful* for reason. To *his reason* only *what is animalistic* appears *indubitable.* But let us listen to our man of the Enlightenment with the standpoint of the Ancien Régime. We must learn Hugo's views from Hugo himself. To all his thought belongs an αὐτὸς ἔφα [he said it himself].

## Introduction

"*Juristically,* the *only distinguishing feature* of *man* is his *animal* nature."

## The Chapter on Freedom

"The fact that *a rational being cannot voluntarily cease being a rational being,* i.e. a being which can and ought to act rationally—even this is a *limitation of freedom.*"

"*Absence of freedom* changes *nothing* in the animal and rational nature of the *unfree* and *other men. All* the *duties of conscience* remain. *Slavery* is possible not only *physically* but also *rationally.* Any inquiry teaching us the opposite must involve some misunderstanding. To be sure, slavery is not *peremptorily legal,* i.e., it is not based on animal, rational, or civic nature. Slavery, however, can be *provisional law* just as *anything* added by the adversaries can be provisional law. This is shown by a comparison of that law with *private law* and *public law.*" The proof: "In regard to his *animal* nature a man *owned* by a wealthy person aware of his needs and of losing something with him is obviously more secure against deprivation than the poor man used by his fellow citizens as long as he can be used, etc." "The right to *mistreat* and *mutilate* serfs is not essential, and *even though such acts do occur,* they are *not much worse* than those suffered by the poor. And as far as the *body* is concerned they are not so bad as *war* from which serfs as such must always be exempt. One finds *beauty* more in a *Circassian slave girl* than in a *beggar's girl.*" (Listen to the old fellow!)

"For man's *rational* nature, serfdom is better than poverty in that a serf-holder will undertake the education of a capable serf out of a *well-calculated economy* before he will concern himself with a beggar's child. Especially with a *constitution* a serf is spared numerous kinds of oppression. Is the slave less fortunate than the prisoner of war whose guard is unconcerned except to be responsible for him for a while, or less fortunate than the forced laborer over whom the governing régime has placed an overseer?"

"It is still a matter of controversy whether slavery in itself promotes or hinders *propagation.*"

## The Chapter on Marriage

"In a *philosophical* treatment of positive law, *marriage* has commonly been regarded as *more essential* and *rational* than it would appear in *an unsystematic approach.*" To be sure, *sexual satisfaction* in marriage is proper for Herr Hugo. He even deduces a *salutary moral* from this: "As from innumerable other relationships, one *should have observed* also from marriage that it is not always *unethical to treat the human body as a means to an end.* Some people, and probably even *Kant himself,* misunderstood this expression."

But the sanctification of the sex drive through *exclusiveness,* the restraint of the drive through law, the *ethical beauty* which turns nature's command into an ideal moment of spiritual union—the *spiritual essence* of marriage—

this is what is *suspect* in marriage for Herr Hugo. But before we follow further his *frivolous shamelessness,* let's for a moment hear a French *philosopher* as opposed to a *historical* German:

> "In renouncing for one man that mysterious reserve whose divine law she carries in her heart, she gives herself to that man. In momentary abandon she suspends for his sake that modesty which never leaves her. For him alone she discards the veils which elsewhere are her sanctuary and her finery. From this stems the intimate trust in her husband, the result of an exclusive relationship which can exist only between her and him without her feeling dishonored. From this stems the husband's appreciation of a sacrifice and that mixture of desire and deference for one who only seems to submit to him, even in sharing his pleasures. From this stems everything moral in our social order."

Thus the liberal *French* philosopher, *Benjamin Constant!* And now let us hear the servile historical German:

> "Much *more suspect* is another reference to the effect that *outside of marriage* the *satisfaction of the sex drive* is *not* permissible. Our *animal nature is opposed to this limitation.* Our *rational* nature is even more so because," . . . guess what! . . . "because a person would have to be *virtually omniscient* to foresee the consequence of committing himself to satisfy one of the most powerful drives with only one particular person: that would mean *challenging God."* "The *sense of beauty, free* by its very nature, should be restrained, and what depends on it should be completely separated from it."

You can see *what* school our *Young Germans* [free-thinking writers influenced by Heinrich Heine and Ludwig Börne] have attended.

> "This arrangement clashes with our *civic* nature in that . . . finally the *police* undertake an *almost insurmountable task."* What a clumsy philosophy, not to pay equal attention to the *policemen* themselves!

> "Everything stated in the detailed provisions of the marriage law shows that marriage remains a *very*

*imperfect institution,* regardless of the principles applied."

"The limitation of the sex drive to marriage, *on the other hand,* has *also* the *important* advantage that *infectious diseases* are usually avoided. *Marriage* spares the government a lot of *trouble.* Finally there is the *important consideration* that what is a *matter of private law* is *already what is uniquely common.*" "*Fichte* says: The unmarried person is only *half* a person." "I am very sorry," says Hugo, "to have to insist that such a beautiful dictum—putting even me above Christ, Fénelon, Kant, and Hume—is a *gross exaggeration.*"

"As far as monogamy and polygamy are concerned, it *obviously* depends on the *animal* nature of man"!!

## The Chapter on Education

We learn right away "that the art of educating is not less opposed to education in the family in its juristic relationships than the *art of loving* is opposed to *marriage.*"

"The confinement of education to such a relationship is by far not so questionable as is the confinement in the satisfaction of the sex drive. This is so because education may be transferred by contract to a third person. Thus, whoever might feel a great drive [to educate] could easily satisfy it, although not with the *certain* desired *person.* But it is already contrary to reason that a person to whom one would never entrust a child could educate the child and exclude others on the strength of *such a relationship.*" "Finally, the element of *compulsion* is present here, too, because the one doing the educating is not permitted by positive law *to relinquish this relationship,* and partly because the one being educated is forced to have himself educated by the one responsible for the education." "The actuality of this relationship rests mainly on the *mere accident* of birth which must be related to the *father* through *marriage.* This *mode of origin* is patently not very rational, since it usually entails a *partiality* which stands in the way of a good education. That this mode of origin is not at all necessary is apparent from the fact that orphans too are educated."

## The Chapter on Private Law

In § 107 we are told that the *"necessity of private law is something presumed."*

## The Chapter on Public Law

"It is a *sacred duty of conscience to obey* the *authority in power."* "So far as the *division of governmental power* is concerned, *no* single constitution is peremptorily *legal;* but *every* constitution is *provisionally legal, no matter how the governmental power is distributed."* Hasn't Hugo proved that man can even throw off the *last fetter of freedom,* the fetter of being a *rational* being?

These few excerpts from the *philosophical manifesto of the historical school* will suffice, we believe, to render a historical judgment on this school instead of unhistorical fancies, vague emotional dreams, and deliberate fictions. These excerpts will suffice for deciding whether *Hugo's followers* are *called upon* to be the *legislators of our time* [as suggested in Savigny's title, *On the Call of Our Time for Legislation and Jurisprudence,* Heidelberg, 1814]. With time and culture, the *rough family tree* of the historical school was befogged by the *incense of mysticism,* fantastically carved up by *romanticism,* and engrafted with *speculation.* Much *scholarly* fruit was shaken down from the tree, dried, and ostentatiously stored away in the vast warehouse of German erudition. But only very little *criticism* is needed to recognize sordid old ideas behind all the fragrant modern phrases of our enlightener from the Ancien Régime and to recognize his slovenly triviality behind all the excessive unction.

While Hugo states that *"juristically, the distinguishing feature of man* is his *animal* nature" and hence law is *animalistic* law, educated *modern* writers substitute *"organic"* for the crude and frank *"animalistic,"* for who would immediately think of *animal organism?* While Hugo says that there is *no rationality* in *marriage* and other *ethico-legal* institutions, the *modern* gentlemen say that these institutions are *projections* of a higher *"positive"* rationality, *not structures of human rationality*. And so it is with everything else. With equal crudity they *all* enunciate *one* result: *The law of arbitrary power*.

The juristic and historical theories of *Haller, Stahl, Leo* and like-minded writers are to be regarded only as *codices rescripti* of *Hugonian natural law* which, as we plan to show on some other occasion, again reveal the old *original text* after some *critical analysis*. Every *trick of embellishment* is all the more vain as we still possess the *old Manifesto* which is surely *quite intelligible* even if it is not *intelligent*.

# THE CENTRALIZATION QUESTION

[Having condemned the Historical School for justifying every institution on the ground of its mere existence through custom and tradition, Marx rejects the opposite approach in the following unfinished and unpublished reply to Moses Hess who had succeeded Rutenberg as editor of the *Rheinische Zeitung*. Hess had maintained that in a nation of just men the central power of the state would live in its members and disappear as such. Marx rejects this substitution of an imagined ideal for a philosophical answer to the question. He was aware that Hegel had prominently condemned utopian solutions and abstract ideals as substitutes for reason in history. "True theory," Marx wrote to a sponsor of the *Rheinische Zeitung,* "must be developed and clarified in concrete circumstances and existing conditions."]

*The centralization question in itself and in relation to the supplement to No. 137 of the* Rheinische Zeitung, *Tuesday, May 17, 1842.*

"Germany and France in regard to the centralization question" with the signature ÷ ÷. "Whether the **power of the state** is to **emanate** from one point or whether every province, every community, is to administer itself, and the central government is to govern the individual parts of the state as the power of the whole only when the state is to be represented externally—on this question opinions are still widely divided."

As with every question justified by its content and hence rational, it is the fate of a question of the day that the *question*, not the *answer*, constitutes the main difficulty. True criticism, therefore, does not analyze the answers but the questions. Just as the solution of an algebraic equation is found the moment the problem is put in its purest and sharpest form, any question is answered the moment it has become an *actual* question. World history itself has only one method: to answer and settle old questions through new ones. The verbal puzzles of any given period, therefore, are easily found. They are the questions of the day, and if the intention and the insight of each individual play an important role in the answers, if a sharp view is necessary to separate what belongs to the individual and what to the period, the *questions*, on the other hand, are the open, ruthless voices of a period, transcending all individualities. They are its mottoes, the *supremely practical* proclamations of its psychic state. Hence, in any period, reactionaries are good barometers for its intellectual condition, just as dogs are good for scenting something out. The public believes that the reactionaries *make up* the questions. Hence it believes that the question does not *exist* if this or that obscurantist does not oppose a modern trend or put something in question. The public itself, therefore, considers the reactionaries the true men of progress.

"Whether the power of the state is to emanate from one point," that is, whether *one point* is to govern, or whether every province, etc., is to govern itself, and the central government as the power of the whole "externally" is to appear only externally—the centralization question cannot possibly be grasped in this way. The author assures us that "regarded from a higher point of view, this question collapses as being empty"; for "if man actually is what according to his nature he should be, individual freedom is in no way different from universal freedom." "Hence, if we presuppose a nation of the just, the question under discussion cannot be raised at all," "the central power would live in all its members, etc., etc." "Just as any external law, any positive institution, etc., would in general be superfluous, so would any central power of the state, etc. Such a society would not be a state, but the ideal of humanity." "Viewing our social life from a high philosophical standpoint can make the solution of the most difficult problems of the state amazingly easy. Theoretically, such a solution of the problems is quite correct; indeed, it is the only correct one. But we are not concerned here with the theoretical answer to the centralization question, but with a practical answer, indeed only an empirical and relative answer, etc."

The author of the article begins with a *self-criticism* of his question. Considered from a higher standpoint it does not exist, but at the same time we learn that from this high standpoint all laws, positive institutions, the central power of the state, and finally the state itself disappear. The author rightly praises the "amazing ease" with which this point of view can be oriented, but it is wrong to call such a solution "theoretically quite correct, indeed the only correct one." He wrongly calls this standpoint "philosophical." Philosophy must seriously protest when it is confused with imagination. The fiction of a nation "of the just" is as alien to philosophy as the fiction of "praying hyenas" is alien to nature. The author substitutes "his abstractions" for philosophy. [Here the manuscript breaks off.]

# THE LEADING ARTICLE IN NO. 179
## OF THE *KÖLNISCHE ZEITUNG:*
### RELIGION, FREE PRESS, AND PHILOSOPHY

[In Marx's first contribution to the *Rheinische Zeitung* he had criticized debates in the Rhenish Diet on freedom of the press. His views on censorship evoked a reply from the *Kölnische Zeitung* which he answered in early July 1842 with the following article expressing his views on religion, freedom of the press, the nature of philosophy, and the relation of church to state. The editor of the *Kölnische Zeitung* had claimed that the height of a nation's life coincides with the vitality of religion. Marx insists that Athens and Rome reached their heights when philosophy displaced religion. Marx challenges the notion that even fetishism has an elevating quality. It is "the religion of sensuous appetites," a devaluation of man's consciousness and reason, in which the worshiper projects his wishes into a thing. Criticizing a wood-theft law four months later, Marx noted how forest owners had made a fetish of wood. He returned to this theme in subsequent writings to expose man's alienation and self-deception in relation to the state and commodities. In what follows Marx particularly agrees with Hegel in viewing education as transformation of individual impulse into universal aims, in regarding philosophy as "the living soul of a culture," and in arguing for separation of church and state. In substantial agreement with Hegel, Marx derives the state from "reason in society," not reason in the individual. Hence, the state is to be viewed as a "great organism" in which reason—"human reason"—is actualized as law and freedom.]

On a previous occasion we complimented the *Kölnische Zeitung* as being, if not the "paper of Rhineland intelligence" [*Blatt der rheinischen Intelligenz*], at least the Rhineland "Advertiser" [*Intelligenzblatt*]. Above all we saw in its "leading political article" a means, as wise as it was select, of disgusting the reader with politics so that he would all the more eagerly turn to the vigorous, industriously pulsating and often belletristically piquant domain of advertising, so that here too the motto would be *per aspera ad astra,* through politics to oysters [*Austern*]. But the beautiful balance between politics and advertising, which the *Kölnische Zeitung* has thus far known how to maintain, has lately been upset by what could be called "advertisements of the political industry." In the initial uncertainty as to where this new species should be inserted, it happened that an advertisement was transformed into a leading article and the leading article into an advertisement of the kind called a "denunciation" but which, if paid for, is merely an "advertisement."

In the north it is customary to treat guests to exquisite liqueurs before lean meals. We are all the more willing to follow this custom with our northern guest and give him spirits before the meal since in the meal itself, in the "ailing" [*leidenden*] article in No. 179 of the *Kölnische Zeitung,* we find no spirits whatsoever. So we first serve up a scene from Lucian's *Conversations of the Gods* in a "popular" translation since there will be at least *one* among our readers who is no Hellene.

## Lucian's *Conversations of the Gods*

### XXIV. Hermes' Complaints

#### Hermes, Maia

*Hermes.* Is there, dear Mother, in the entire heaven a god more troubled than I am?

*Maia.* Speak not so, my son!

*Hermes.* Why should I not? I, who have a multitude of affairs to attend to, must always work alone and submit to so many servile duties? I must rise in the earliest hours of the morning and clean out the dining hall, arrange the cushions in the council room, and when everything is in order wait on Jupiter and spend the whole day running errands as his messenger. Immediately on my return, covered with dust, I must serve the ambrosia. And what is most annoying is that I am the only one who is given no peace even at night, for then I must escort the souls of the dead to Pluto and serve as attendant at their judgment. It is not enough for me to work during the day when I attend the *gymnastics,* serve as *herald* at the assemblies of the people, and help popular orators learn their speeches. No, I who am distracted by so many matters must also take care of the *entire business of the dead*.

Since his expulsion from Olympus, Hermes has been going on with his "servile duties" and the whole business of the dead by force of habit.

Whether it was Hermes himself or his son, the goat-god Pan, who wrote the ailing article in No. 179, we shall leave the reader to decide, reminding himself that the Greek Hermes was the god of eloquence and logic.

"To disseminate philosophical and religious views by means of newspapers or to combat them in newspapers appears to us equally inadmissible."

As the old fellow thus chattered on, it was easy for me to note that he [Karl Heinrich Hermes, editor of the *Kölnische Zeitung*] was bent on a tiresome litany of oracles, but I calmed my impatience, for why should I not believe that perceptive man who is so unconstrained as to speak out his opinion quite candidly in his own house, and I read on. And lo and behold, this article, which cannot be reproached with a single philosophical view, certainly has the tendency to combat philosophical views and disseminate religious ones.

Of what use is an article which challenges its own right to exist and introduces itself with a declaration of its incompetence? The verbose author will answer us. He explains how his bombastic articles are to be read. He limits himself to giving fragments whose "concatenation and interconnection" he leaves to "the penetration of the reader" —the most appropriate method for the kind of advertising with which he occupies himself. So we shall "concatenate and interconnect," and it is not our fault if the rosary does not become a string of pearls.

The author clarifies himself:

"A party which makes use of these means" (spreading and combating philosophical and religious views in newspapers) "thereby shows, in *our* opinion, that its intentions *are not honorable* and that it is less interested in teaching and enlightening the people than in attaining some *other ulterior purposes.*"

This being *his* opinion, his article can have nothing else in view than the achievement of ulterior purposes. These "ulterior purposes" will not remain hidden.

The state, says the author, has not only the right but also the duty "to silence *non-professional* babblers." He is talking about the *opponents* of his views, for he has long argued with himself that he is a *professional* babbler.

It is, therefore, a question of a further sharpening of censorship in religious affairs, a new police measure against the press which has scarcely begun to breathe freely.

"In our view the state can be reproached with undue forbearance rather than undue strictness."

But the author of the leading article remembers that it is dangerous to reproach the state. Hence he addresses himself to the authorities, and his accusation against freedom of the press becomes an accusation against the censors for applying "too little censorship."

"So far a blameworthy forbearance has been shown —*not, to be sure, by the state* but by '*particular authorities*'—in allowing the newer philosophical school to make the most unseemly attacks upon Christianity in public papers and other printed writings not intended exclusively for scientific circles."

Again the author pauses and remembers that scarcely a week ago he found too little freedom of the press in the freedom of censorship. Now with compulsion of censors he finds too little censorship compulsion.

This must again be set aright.

"As long as censorship exists it has the strictest duty to excise such repulsive spoutings of youthful presumption as have recently and repeatedly offended our eyes."

Such weak eyes! Such weak eyes! And the "weakest eye will be offended by an expression which can only be intended for the comprehension of the broad masses."

If lightened censorship allows repulsive spoutings to appear, what then can be expected from freedom of the press? If our eyes are too weak to bear the "presumption" [*Übermut*] of the censored press, how could they be strong enough to bear the "audacity" [*Mut*] of the free press?

"As long as censorship exists it has the strictest duty to . . ." And once it no longer exists? The statement must be interpreted: It is the strictest duty of the censorship to exist as long as possible.

And again the author reminds himself:

> "It is not our function to act as *public* prosecutor and therefore we refrain from any closer specification."

What a heavenly kindness the man has! He refrains from closer "specification," but only by very close and distinct indications could he establish and show what *his* view wants; he lets drop only vague, half-whispered words of suspicion; it is not his function to act as *public* prosecutor, it is his function to be a *hidden accuser*.

For the last time the unfortunate man reminds himself that his function is to write liberal leading articles, that he should portray a "loyal friend of freedom of the press." He therefore jockeys himself into his last position:

> "We could not refrain from protesting against a procedure which, if it is not a result of casual negligence, can have no other purpose than to compromise in the public eye a freer activity of the press and give the game to its opponents who are afraid of losing by playing strictly fair."

This champion of freedom of the press, as bold as he is penetrating, says that censorship, if it is not the English leopard with the inscription "I sleep, wake me not," has undertaken this "godless" procedure to compromise a freer activity of the press in the public eye.

Is there any further need to compromise an activity of

the press that makes the censorship take notice of *"casual negligencies"* and expects to get good repute in the public eye from the *"censor's penknife"*?

This activity can be called "free" only to the extent that the license of shamelessness is sometimes called "free," and is it not the shamelessness of folly and hypocrisy to try to pass as a champion of a freer press and at the same time teach that the press will slip into the gutter the moment two policemen stop holding its arms?

And what do we need censorship for, what do we need this leading article for, if the philosophical press discredits itself in the public eye? Of course the author does not want to restrict *"the freedom of scientific inquiry"* in any way.

> "In our day *scientific inquiry* is rightly allowed the widest and most unlimited scope."

But the following pronouncement will show what notion our man has of scientific inquiry:

> "There must be a sharp distinction between what is required by the freedom of scientific inquiry that can only benefit Christianity itself and what is outside the limits of scientific inquiry."

Who should decide the limits of scientific inquiry if not scientific inquiry itself! According to the leading article limits should be prescribed for scientific knowledge. Thus the leading article knows an *"official reason"* that does not learn from scientific inquiry but teaches scientific inquiry and that, like an educated providence, gives the length every hair can have to transform a scientific beard into one of world significance. The Leading Article believes in the scientific inspiration of censorship.

Before we further pursue these "foolish" explanations of the leading article on "scientific inquiry," let us regale ourselves for a moment with Herr H[ermes'] *"philosophy of religion,"* his "own science"!

> "Religion is the foundation of the state as well as the most indispensable condition of every social organization not directed merely at achieving some ulterior purpose."

*Proof:* "In its crudest form as *childish fetishism* it elevates man in some degree above sensuous appetites which, if he lets himself be entirely dominated by them, *debase him to an animal* and make him incapable of achieving any higher purpose."

The leading article calls fetishism the *"crudest* form" of religion. It thus holds what is established by all men of "scientific research" even without its assent, that *"animal worship"* is a *higher* religious form than fetishism. But doesn't animal worship degrade man below the animal and make the animal man's god?

And this matter of "fetishism"! Genuine penny magazine learning! Fetishism is so far from raising man *above* the appetites that it is on the contrary "the *religion of sensuous appetites."* The fantasy of the appetites deceives the fetish worshiper into believing that a "lifeless object" will give up its natural character to gratify his desires. The crude appetite of the fetish worshiper therefore *smashes* the fetish which ceases to be its most devoted servant.

"In those nations which have achieved a higher historical importance, the prime of their national life coincides with the highest development of their religious temper and the decline of their greatness and power with the decline of their religious culture."

By exactly reversing the author's assertion, we get the truth. He has turned history upside down. Greece and Rome are certainly countries of the highest "historical culture" in the ancient world. Greece's highest internal development came at the time of Pericles, its highest external peak, with Alexander. In Pericles' time the sophists and Socrates, who may be called philosophy incarnate, had supplanted religion with art and rhetoric. Alexander's time was the time of Aristotle who rejected the eternity of the "individual" spirit and the God of positive religions. And then Rome! Read Cicero! Epicurean, stoic, or sceptical philosophy was the religion of cultured Romans when Rome reached the zenith of its history. If with the decline of ancient states their religions disappear, this needs no further explanation because the "true religion" of the ancients was the cult of "their nationality," of their "state." It was not the decline of the ancient religions that brought the downfall of the ancient states but the decline of the ancient states that brought the downfall of the old religions. And such ignorance as that of the leading article proclaims itself the "legislator of scientific inquiry" and writes "decrees" for philosophy.

> "The entire ancient world was bound to collapse because the progress of its peoples in scientific development necessarily entailed the discovery of the errors on which their religious views rested."

Thus according to the leading article the whole ancient world perished because scientific inquiry revealed the errors of the old religions. Would the ancient world not have declined if inquiry had ignored the errors of the old religions, if the author of the leading article had recommended the elimination of Lucretius' and Lucian's writings to the Roman authorities?

For the rest we take the liberty of adding to Herr H[ermes'] learning by means of a note.

As the downfall of the ancient world was approaching, there was established the *School of Alexandria* which sought to prove by force "the eternal truth" of Greek mythology and its complete agreement "with the results of scientific inquiry." Emperor Julian also belonged to that trend which thought it could make the newly appearing temper disappear if it kept its eyes closed. But let us keep only to Herr H[ermes'] results! In the religions of antiquity "the faint notions of the divine were veiled in the darkest night of error" and therefore could not resist scientific inquiry. With Christianity the situation is reversed, as any thinking machine will maintain. To be sure, H[ermes] says:

> "The best results of scientific inquiry have thus far served only to confirm the truths of the Christian religion."

Apart from the fact that every philosophy of the past without exception was accused of apostasy by the theologians—even that of the devout Malebranche and the inspired Jakob Böhme; apart from the fact that Leibniz was accused by the Brunswick peasants as being a *"Löwenix"* (*non-believer*) and by the Englishman Clarke and Newton's other followers as being an atheist; apart from the fact that Christianity, as the most competent and consistent of the Protestant theologians maintain, cannot be consonant with reason because "secular" and "spiritual" reason contradict each other, a point which Tertullian classically expressed in saying, *Verum est, quia absurdum est* [It is true because it is absurd]; apart from all this how can one prove the agreement of scientific inquiry with religion except by forcing scientific inquiry to resolve itself into religion, so that it follows its own course? Another force is no proof anyway.

If, of course, you acknowledge beforehand as scientific inquiry only what agrees with your own view, it is easy for you to prophesy; but then what advantage does your assertion have over that of the Indian Brahmin who proves the holiness of the Vedas by reserving for himself alone the right to read them!

Yes, says H[ermes], "scientific inquiry." But any inquiry that contradicts Christianity "stops halfway" or "takes a wrong turn." Can anyone argue more conveniently?

Once scientific inquiry "has *'made clear'* to itself the content of its findings, it will never clash with the truths of Christianity," but at the same time the state must ensure that this *"making clear"* is impossible, since inquiry must never appeal to the powers of comprehension of the masses, that is, must never become popular and clear *to itself*. Even if it is attacked by unscientific investigations in all the papers of the monarchy it must be discreet and quiet.

Christianity precludes the possibility of "any new decline," but the police must keep watch that philosophizing newspaper writers do not bring on a decline; it must keep a very strict watch. In contest with truth, error will of itself be recognized as such without needing suppression by an external power; but the state must make this contest easier for truth by depriving the champions of "error" not indeed of internal freedom, which it cannot take away from them, but the possibility of this freedom, the possibility of its existence.

Christianity is certain of its victory, but according to Herr H[ermes] it is not so certain that it can disdain the help of the police.

If from the outset everything which contradicts your faith is error and must be treated as such, what is there to distinguish your claims from those of the Mohammedans, from the claims of any other religion? Must philosophy adopt different principles for every country in accordance with the saying "different countries, different customs" so as not to contradict the ground truths of dogma? Must it believe that in one country $3 \times 1 = 1$, in another that women have no souls, in a third that beer is drunk in heaven? Is there no *universal human* nature just as there is a universal nature of plants and heavenly bodies? Philosophy asks what is true not what is accepted as such, what is true for all men not what is true for individuals: its metaphysical truths do not recognize the boundaries of political geography; its political truths know too well where the "boundaries" begin, to confuse the illusory horizon of particular world and natural outlooks with the true horizon of the human mind. H[ermes] is the weakest of all the defenders of Christianity.

His only proof in support of Christianity is Christianity's *long existence*. Has not philosophy also existed from Thales to the present, and has it not now, according to H[ermes] himself, greater claims and a greater opinion of its own importance than ever?

How, in the end, does H[ermes] prove that the state is a "Christian" state, that instead of being a free association of moral human beings it is an association of believers, and that instead of aiming at the actualization of freedom it aims at the actualization of dogma? "Our European states all have Christianity as their foundation."

The *French* state too? The *Constitution*, Article 3, does not say that "all Christians" or "only Christians" but *"tous les Français* are equally eligible for civil and military positions."

The Prussian *Civil Code* also says, Part II, Section XIII:

> "The *primary* duty of the supreme state authority is to maintain both external and internal peace and security and to safeguard each and every one in what is his from force and interference."

According to Paragraph 1, however, the supreme state authority unites in himself all "duties and rights of the state." It does not say that the primary duty of the state is the suppression of heretical error for salvation in another world.

But if some European states are actually founded upon Christianity, do those states conform to their concept, is the "pure existence" of a condition already the rightness of that condition?

In the view of our H[ermes] it is, for he reminds the supporters of Young Hegelianism "that according to the laws predominantly in force in the state a marriage *without the church's consecration* is regarded as *concubinage* and punished as such by *police* courts."

So if "marriage without the church's consecration" is regarded on the Rhine according to the Napoleonic Code as "marriage" and on the Spree according to the Prussian Civil Code as "concubinage," the "police court" punishment must argue for the "philosophers" that what is right in one place is wrong in another, that not the Napoleonic Code but the Prussian Civil Code has the scientific and ethical, the rational concept of marriage. This "philosophy of police court punishment" may be convincing in other places. It is not convincing in *Prussia*. For the rest, how little the Prussian Civil Code is inclined to "holy" matrimony is shown by Paragraph 12, Part II, Section 1.

> "Nevertheless, a marriage which is allowed by laws of the region loses none of its *civil* validity by the fact that the dispensation of the spiritual authorities has not been requested or has been denied."

Here [in Prussia], too, marriage is partly emancipated from the "spiritual authorities" and its "civil" validity is distinct from its "ecclesiastical."

It is obvious that our great Christian philosopher of the state has no very "high" view of the state.

"Since our states are not merely *legal associations* but at the time true *educational institutions* extending their care to a *wider* field than institutions devoted to the education of youth," etc., "all public education," Hermes says, "rests on the foundation of Christianity."

The education of our schoolchildren is based just as much on the ancient classics and science in general as on the catechism.

According to H[ermes] the state is distinguished from a children's home not by content but by size—it extends its "care" more widely.

But the true "public" education of the state is rather the rational and public actuality of the state. Even the state educates its members by making them part of the state, by transforming the aims of the individual into universal aims, by transforming raw impulse into ethical inclination, by transforming natural independence into spiritual freedom, and by the individual finding his satisfaction in the life of the whole and the whole in the attitude of the individual.

The leading article, in contrast, makes the state not an association of free men mutually educating one another but a crowd of grown-ups destined to be educated from above and to pass from the "narrow" schoolroom to the "broader" one.

This theory of education and tutelage is here presented by a friend of freedom of the press who in his love for *la belle* freedom notes the "negligences of the censorship," who knows how to depict the "capability of comprehension of the masses" in the appropriate place (perhaps the comprehension of the masses has *lately* seemed so precarious to the *Kölnische Zeitung* because they have forgotten how to comprehend the advantages of the "unphilosophical newspaper"?) and who advises the educated to have one view on stage and another off!

As the leading article shows us its *"short"* view of the state, it will now document for us its *low view "of Christianity."*

> "All the newspaper articles in the world will never convince a population which on the whole feels well and happy that it is in a miserable condition."

Indeed! The *material* feeling of well-being and happiness is more proof against newspaper articles than the saving, all-conquering certainty of faith! H[ermes] does not sing "A mighty fortress is our God." The truly believing heart of the "great masses" is probably more exposed to the corrosion of doubt than the refined wordly culture of the "few."

H[ermes] fears "even incitement to insurrection in a *well-ordered* state" less than in a "well-ordered church" though the latter may be led by the "spirit of God" to all truth. A fine believer, and what grounds he has! Political articles, he says, are within the comprehension of the masses, and philosophical articles are beyond it!

If we finally compare the leading article's hint—"the *half-*measures recently applied against Young Hegelianism have had the results half-measures usually have"—with the *ingenuous* wish that the most recent doings of the Hegelians might pass by "without *too unfavorable* results" for them, we can understand Cornwall's words in *King Lear:*

> He cannot flatter, he—
> An honest mind and plain,—he must speak truth!
> An' they will take it, so; if not, he's plain.
> These kind of knaves I know, which in this plainness
> Harbour more craft and more corrupter ends,
> Than twenty silly ducking óbservants,
> That stretch their duties nicely.

We would think we were insulting the readers of the *Rheinische Zeitung* if we supposed they would be satisfied with the more comical rather than serious show of a one-time liberal, "a young man of days gone by," being sent back to where he belongs. We want to say a few words on *"the matter itself."* As long as we were engaged in a polemic against the ailing article, it would not have been right to interrupt its process of self-annihilation.

Next the question is raised: "Should philosophy discuss religious matters even in newspaper articles?"

We can answer this question only by criticizing it.

Philosophy, above all German philosophy, has a tendency toward solitude, toward systematic seclusion, toward dispassionate self-examination which from the outset puts it in opposition to and estranges it from the ready-tongued, alive-to-events newspapers whose only satisfaction is information. In its systematic development philosophy is unpopular, and to the untutored eye its secret weaving within itself seems to be an occupation as overstrained as it is impractical. It is taken to be a professor of magic whose incantations sound pompous because they are incomprehensible.

In accordance with its character philosophy has never taken the first step toward replacing its ascetic priestly vestments by the light conventional garb of the newspapers. But philosophers do not grow out of the earth like mushrooms; they are the fruit of their time, of their people whose most subtle, precious and invisible sap circulates in philosophical ideas. The same spirit that builds philosophical systems in the brain of the philosophers builds railroads by the hands of the workers. Philosophy does not stand outside the world any more than man's brain is outside him because it is not in his stomach; but philosophy, to be sure, is in the world with its brain before it stands on the earth with its feet, while many other human spheres have long been rooted in the earth and pluck the fruits of the world long before they realize that the "head" also belongs to this world or that this world is the world of the head.

Since every genuine philosophy is the spiritual quintessence of its time, the time must come when philosophy comes into contact and mutual reaction with the actual world not only internally by its content but also externally through its appearance. Then philosophy ceases to be a specific system compared with other specific systems, it becomes philosophy in general compared with the world, it becomes the philosophy of the present world. The formalities which attest that philosophy has achieved this importance, that it is the living soul of a culture, that philosophy is becoming worldly and the world philosophical, have been the same in all times: we may open any history book and will find with stereotyped fidelity the simplest rituals again and again unmistakably marking the introduction of philosophy into drawing rooms and priests' studies, into the editorial offices of newspapers and the antechambers of courts, into the hatred and love of the people of the time. Philosophy is introduced into the world by the yelling of its enemies who betray their internal infection by their noisy call for help against the blaze of ideas. This yelling of its enemies has the same meaning for philosophy as the first cry of a child for the anxious ear of its mother. It is the cry of life of ideas which have burst open the orderly, hieroglyphic husk of the system to become citizens of the world. The Corybantes and Cabiri, who announce to the world with the roll of drums the birth of baby Zeus, first turn against the religious party of philosophers, partly because their inquisitorial instinct can secure a firmer hold on this sentimental side of the public and partly because the public, to which the opponents of philosophy also belong, can touch the ideal sphere of philosophy only with its ideal feelers—and the field of religious ideas is the only one in whose value the public believes almost as much as it believes in the system of material wants—and finally because religion carries on a polemic not against a specific system of philosophy but against philosophy of the specific systems in general.

The genuine philosophy of the present does not differ in respect to this fate from the genuine philosophies of the past. This fate is rather a proof which history owed to the truth of philosophy.

And for six years German papers have been drumming against the religious party [D. F. Strauss and followers] in philosophy, calumniating, distorting, and bowdlerizing it. The *Allgemeine Augsburger* sang bravuras; almost every overture played the theme that philosophy was not worth being discussed by the sage lady, that it was the idle boasting of youth, a fad for blasé coteries. But in spite of all that it could not be gotten rid of and there was still more drumming, for in her anti-philosophical caterwauling the *Augsburger* plays only *one* instrument, the monotonous kettledrum. All German papers, from the *Berliner politisches Wochenblatt* and *Hamburger Correspondent* to the obscure locals and the *Kölnische Zeitung* sounded off on Hegel and Schelling, Feuerbach and Bauer, *Deutsche Jahrbücher,* etc. Finally the public became curious to see the Leviathan with its own eyes, all the more as semi-official articles threatened philosophy that it would have a legal syllabus officially prescribed for it. And that was the moment philosophy appeared in the papers. It had long kept silent in face of the self-satisfied superficiality that boasted in a few stale journalistic phrases that it could blow away like soap bubbles years of study of genius, the hard-won fruits of self-sacrificing solitude, and the results of that invisible but slowly expanding effort of contemplation. Philosophy had even *protested against the newspapers* as being an unsuitable terrain, but finally had to break its silence. It became a newspaper correspondent and—an unprecedented diversion!—suddenly the garrulous purveyors of newspapers became aware that philosophy is no food for the newspaper public. Hence they could not refrain from drawing the attention of governments to the unfairness of bringing philosophical and religious issues into the sphere of newspapers, not to enlighten the public but to attain ulterior ends.

What could philosophy say so bad about religion or about itself that your newspaper clamor had not long ago imputed to it in worse and more frivolous terms? It needs only to repeat what you unphilosophical Capuchins have preached about it in thousand upon thousands of polemics and it has said the worst.

But philosophy speaks differently about religious and philosophical subjects than you have. You speak without having studied them, it speaks after study. You appeal to passion, it appeals to reason. You curse, it teaches. You promise heaven and earth, it promises nothing but truth. You demand faith in your faith, it demands not faith in its results but the test of doubt. You alarm, it calms. And truly, philosophy is worldly-wise enough to know that its results flatter the desire for pleasure and egoism of neither the heavenly nor earthly world. The public, however, which loves truth and knowledge for its own sake will be able to measure itself in judgment and morality against ignorant, servile, inconsistent, and paid scribblers.

To be sure somebody or other may misinterpret philosophy as a result of his wretched intellect or views, but do not you Protestants believe that Catholics misinterpret Christianity, do you not reproach the Christian religion for the shameful times of the eighth and ninth centuries, the eve of St. Bartholomew or the Inquisition? There are clear proofs that the hatred of Protestant theology for philosophers arises largely out of philosophy's tolerance toward the particular confession as such. Feuerbach and Strauss were reproached more for holding that Catholic dogmas were Christian than that the dogmas of Christianity were not dogmas of reason.

But if particular individuals cannot digest modern philosophy and perish from philosophical indigestion, nothing more is proved against philosophy than what the occasional blowing up of a few passengers by a steam boiler proves against laws of mechanics.

The question of whether philosophical and religious matters are to be discussed in newspapers resolves itself in its own emptiness.

If such questions already interest the public as *news*, they have become *questions of the day*. Then the point is not whether they should be discussed but where and how—whether within the family circle and the hotels, within the schools and churches but not by the press, whether by opponents of philosophy but not by philosophers, whether in the clouded language of private opinion but not in the clarifying words of public rationality. Then the point is whether what lives in actuality belongs in the realm of the press, and it is no longer a question of the particular content of the press but the general question of whether the press should really be the press, that is, a free press.

From the first question we entirely separate the second: "Should the newspapers deal with politics philosophically in a so-called Christian state?"

If religion has a political quality and becomes an object of politics, there seems to be hardly any need to mention that the newspapers not only may, but must, discuss political affairs. It seems from the outset that the wisdom of the world, philosophy, has more right to concern itself with the order of the world, with the state, than the wisdom of the other world, religion. The issue here is not whether there should be philosophizing about the state but whether that philosophizing should be done well or badly, philosophically or unphilosophically, with prejudice or without, consciously or unconsciously, consistently or inconsistently, in a fully rational or half rational way. If you make religion into a theory of state law, you make religion itself a kind of philosophy.

Did not Christianity above all separate church and state? Read St. Augustine's *De civitate Dei,* study the church fathers and the spirit of Christianity, and then tell us whether the church or the state is the "Christian State"! Does not every moment of your practical life give the lie to your theory? Do you consider it wrong to go to court if you are cheated? But the apostle writes that that is wrong. Do you offer your right cheek if you are struck on the left, or do you not bring legal action for assault? Yet the Gospel forbids that. Do you not claim your reasonable right in this world, do you not complain at the smallest increase in taxes, are you not beside yourself at the slightest infringement of your personal liberty? But you have been told that present suffering is nothing compared with future glory, that suffering in patience and bliss in hope are the cardinal virtues.

Are not most of your legal proceedings and the majority of civil laws concerned with property? But you have been told that your treasures are not of this world. Or if you refer to giving Caesar the things that are Caesar's and God the things that are God's, do not treat Mammon alone as the Caesar of this world but concede at least as much to free reason, and the "activity of free reason" is called philosophizing.

When a quasi-religious alliance of states was first formed in the Holy Alliance and religion was to be the motto of Europe, *the Pope* showed deep sense and complete consistency in refusing to join it, for in his view the universal Christian link among nations should be the Church and not diplomacy, not a worldly alliance of states.

The genuinely religious state is the theocratic state. The prince of such states must be either the God of religion, Jehovah himself as in the Jewish state, the representative of God, the Dalai Lama as in Tibet, or finally, as Görres rightly demands of Christian states in his most recent work, they must completely submit to a church which is "infallible." For if there is no supreme head of the church as in Protestantism, the domination of religion is nothing but the religion of domination, the cult of the government's will.

Once a state includes a number of confessions with equal rights, it cannot be a religious state without violating particular confessions; it cannot be a church which condemns members of another confession as heretics, makes every piece of bread depend on faith, and makes dogma the link between particular individuals and civil life in the state. Ask the Catholic inhabitants of "poor green Erin," ask the Huguenots before the French Revolution. They did not appeal to religion, for their religion was not the state religion. They appealed to the "Rights of Humanity," and philosophy interprets the Rights of Humanity. Philosophy demands that the state be the state of human nature.

But the half and narrow rationalism which is as unbelieving as it is theological says that the universal Christian spirit must be the spirit of the state regardless of confessional differences! It is the greatest irreligion and the presumption of secular reasoning to separate the general spirit of religion from positive religion. This separation of religion from its dogmas and institutions is the same as asserting that the universal spirit of law must prevail in the state without regard to definite laws and positive institutions of law.

If you presume to stand so far above religion as to have the right to separate the general spirit of religion from its positive *embodiments,* what reproach have you for the philosophers if they want to make this separation complete and not halfway, if they call the human rather than Christian spirit the universal spirit of religion?

Christians live in states with differing constitutions, some in a republic, others in an absolute monarchy, and still others in a constitutional monarchy. Christianity does not decide on the *quality* of constitutions since it knows no distinction among them. It teaches as religion must: Submit to authority, for *every authority* is ordained by God. The justice of state constitutions is therefore to be decided not on the basis of Christianity, not on the basis of the state's own nature and essence, not from the nature of Christian society but from the nature of human society.

The Byzantine was the properly religious state, for dogmas were there matters of state. But the Byzantine state was the worst of states. The states of the Ancien Régime were the most Christian states, but they were nevertheless states of the "royal will."

There is a dilemma which "sound" common sense cannot withstand.

Either the Christian state corresponds to the concept of the state as the actualization of rational freedom, and then nothing else can be demanded for it to be Christian than that it be rational; then it suffices to develop the state from reason in human relations, a task philosophy accomplishes. Or, the state of rational freedom cannot be developed out of Christianity; then you will yourselves concede that this development does not lie in the tendency of Christianity, since Christianity does not want a bad state and any state is a bad state which is not the actualization of rational freedom.

Answer the dilemma as you will, you must admit that the state is not to be derived from religion but from the rationale of freedom. Only the crassest ignorance can maintain that the theory which makes the state-concept independent is a passing fancy of modern philosophers.

Philosophy has done nothing in politics that physics,

mathematics, medicine, every science has not done in its own sphere. Bacon of Verulam declared theological physics to be a virgin consecrated to God and barren; he emancipated physics from theology and she became fertile. You have no more to ask the politician than the doctor whether he has faith. Immediately before and after the great discovery of the true solar system by Copernicus, the law of gravitation of the state was discovered. The center of gravity of the state was found in the state itself. The various European governments sought to apply this result, at first with superficiality of practice, to the balance of power among states. Similarly Machiavelli and Campanella earlier, and Hobbes, Spinoza, and Hugo Grotius later, down to Rousseau, Fichte, and Hegel began considering the state from the human viewpoint and developed its natural laws from reason and experience. They did not proceed from theology any more than Copernicus let himself be influenced by Joshua's command that the sun stand still over Gideon and the moon over the valley of Ajalon. Modern philosophy has only continued the work begun by Heraclitus and Aristotle. Thus it is not reason in modern philosophy you are attacking but the ever modern philosophy of reason. To be sure, the ignorance that discovered age-old ideas about the state in the *Rheinische* or *Königsberger Zeitung* yesterday, or perhaps the day before, considers the ideas of history as fancies which occurred overnight to certain individuals since they are new to it and came to it overnight. Such ignorance forgets that it has assumed the old role of the doctor of the Sorbonne who considered it his duty to accuse Montesquieu publicly because Montesquieu was so frivolous as to maintain that political quality rather than the excellence of the church was the highest quality in the state. Such ignorance forgets that it has assumed the role of Joachim Lange who denounced Wolff because his doctrine of predestination would lead to desertion among soldiers and thus to a relaxation of military discipline and finally to the dissolution of the state. Finally, this ignorance forgets that the Prussian *Civil Code* came precisely from the philosophical school of "that wolf" and the Napoleonic Code came not from the Old Testament but from the ideas of Voltaire, Rousseau, Condorcet, Mirabeau, Montesquieu, and the French Revolution. Ignorance is a demon and we fear that it will yet produce more than one tragedy. In the frightening dramas of the royal houses of Mycenae and Thebes the greatest Greek poets rightly represented ignorance as tragic fate.

While the earlier philosophers of state law derived the state from drives of ambition and gregariousness, or from reason—though not reason in society but rather in the individual—the more ideal and profound view of modern philosophy derives it from the idea of the whole. It considers the state as the great organism in which legal, ethical, and political freedom has to be actualized and in which the individual citizen simply obeys the natural laws of his own reason, human reason, in the laws of the state. *Sapienti sat* [Sufficient for the wise].

In conclusion we extend a further philosophical word of farewell to the *Kölnische Zeitung*. It was reasonable of it to take to itself a "former" liberal. One can be both liberal and reactionary at the same time in the most comfortable way, if one only is skillful enough to address the liberals of the recent past who know no other dilemma than that of Vidocq—"prisoner or jailer." It was still more reasonable that the liberal of the recent past should combat the liberals of the present. Without parties there is no development, without division, no progress. We hope that with the leading article in No. 179 a new era has begun for the *Kölnische Zeitung,* the era of character.

# COMMUNISM AND THE AUGSBURG "ALLGEMEINE ZEITUNG"

[On the day Marx was appointed editor in chief he wrote the following reply to charges that the *Rheinische Zeitung* had been "flirting with communism" in reprinting an article from Wilhelm Weitling's magazine on housing and reporting speeches in Strasbourg that reflected the "socialist-communist ideas" of Charles Fourier. In Marx's judgment communism involves issues of European significance, which cannot be dealt with in a simple phrase. But when existing communist principles on land and labor are being spread by reactionaries rather than liberals, he can hardly grant their theoretical validity and even less want their practical realization. What is needed is criticism, serious study, of the writings of Leroux, Considérant, and particularly Proudhon because ideas are harsh masters of men. From this position, Marx turned to the study of French socialism about which, he said later, he did not know enough "to hazard an independent judgment."]

*Cologne,* October 15. Issue 284 of the Augsburg paper makes the faux pas of finding the *Rheinische Zeitung* to be a Prussian *communist,* to be sure not a real communist but someone who fancifully coquets and platonically flirts with communism.

The reader may decide whether this ill-mannered fancy of the Augsburger is fair or whether this idle illusion of an excited imagination is connected with speculations and diplomatic affairs—after we have presented the alleged corpus delicti.

The *Rheinische Zeitung* is said to have printed a communistic essay on Berlin family dwellings, accompanied by the following remark: This report *"might not be without interest for the history of this important current issue."* According to the Augsburger's logic the *Rheinische Zei-*

*tung "presented such dirty linen with approval."* If I say then, for example: "The following report in *Mefistofeles* on the household affairs of the Augsburg paper might not be *without interest* for this pretentious paper's history," am I recommending *dirty "clothes"* for a colorful wardrobe? Or should we maintain that communism is not an important current issue, because it is not a matter for the attention of the Crown, because communism wears dirty linen and does not smell of rose water.

But the Augsburg paper has good reason to be irritated at our misunderstanding. The significance of communism does not lie in its being a current issue of highest moment for France and England. Communism has *European significance*, as indicated recently by the Augsburg paper. One of its Paris correspondents, a convert who treats history as a baker treats botany, has the notion that monarchy in its fashion must seek to appropriate socialist-communist ideas. Now you understand the irritation of the Augsburger who will never forgive us for revealing communism to the public in its *unwashed* nakedness. Now you understand the dogged *irony* with which we are told that we *recommend* communism, which had the happy elegance of being discussed in the Augsburg paper.

The second accusation against the *Rheinische Zeitung* deals with the end of a report on the communistic speeches given at the congress in Strasbourg, because the sister-papers of Cologne and Augsburg had shared the booty, the *former* talking about the *proceedings* of the congress and the *latter* about the scholars' *meals*. The exact wording of the passage in question reads:

> The middle class of today is in the same position as the nobility was in 1789. At that time the middle class claimed the privileges belonging to the nobility, and got them. *Today the class which possesses nothing demands to share in the wealth of the middle class presently in control.* The middle class, however, is better prepared against an assault than the nobility of '89, and it is to be expected that the problem will be solved peacefully.

Bülow-Cummerow, the former *Berliner politisches Wochenblatt,* Dr. Kosegarten, and all the feudalistic writers confess with saddest indignation that Sieyès' prophecy has come true and that the third estate has become everything and wants to be everything. It is a fact that the class possessing nothing today *demands* to share in the wealth of the middle class—a fact clearly evident in the streets of Manchester, Paris, and Lyons, without the talk in Strasbourg and the silence in Augsburg. Does the Augsburger really believe that indignation and silence refute the facts of the time? The Augsburger *persists in fleeing.* The Augsburger escapes from sticky issues and hopes that the dust left behind and invectives muttered in flight will confuse the uncomfortable issue as well as the comfortable reader.

Or is the Augsburger angry at our correspondent's expectation that the indefeasible conflict will be solved *"peacefully"?* Does the Augsburger reproach us for not having immediately given the correct prescription and not having put into the surprised reader's pocket a clear-cut report on the difficult solution for the problem? We don't know how to solve with *one* phrase problems on which *two* nations are at work.

My dear Augsburger! With reference to communism you give us to understand that Germany now has very few independent people, that nine tenths of the better educated youths beg the state for their future bread, that our rivers are neglected, that shipping has declined, that our once burgeoning centers of trade are no longer prosperous, that Prussia makes very slow progress toward free institutions, that the surplus of our population helplessly wanders away and ceases to be German among foreigners—and for all these problems there is not a single prescription, no attempt to become *"clearer about the means to achieve"* the great act which is to redeem us from all these sins! Or don't you expect a peaceful solution? It almost appears that another article from Karlsruhe, in the same issue, points in that direction when you pose for Prussia the sticky question of the Customs Union: *"Does anyone believe that such a crisis would pass like a squabble over smoking in the Tiergarten?"* The reason you offer for your disbelief is *communistic*. *"Let a crisis arise in industry; let millions in capital be lost; let thousands of workers go hungry."* How inopportune came our *"peaceful expectation,"* after you had decided *to have* a bloody crisis *arise*. Probably for this reason your article on Great Britain, by your own logic, points *with approval* to the demagogic physician, Dr. M'Douall, who emigrated to America because *"nothing can be done about that dynasty after all."*

Before leaving we would like to call your attention in passing to your own wisdom. With your method of phrasing things you can hardly avoid not *having* an idea now and then, but just for that reason you *speak up*. You find that the polemic by M. Hennequin of Paris [a Fourierist] against the division of land puts him in surprising harmony with the still autonomous nobility. Wonder, says Aristotle [*Met.* 982b], is the beginning of philosophizing. You ended at the beginning. Otherwise would the surprising fact have escaped you that in Germany communistic principles are spread not by the liberals but rather by your *reactionary* friends?

Who talks about *labor corporations?* The reactionaries. The laboring class is to form a state within the state. Do you find it striking that such ideas, brought up to date, go as follows: "The state is to be transformed into the laboring class"? If the laborer's class is to be the state for him, but if the modern laborer, like any modern man, understands and can understand the state only as a sphere shared by all his fellow citizens—how can you synthesize both ideas in any other way except in a *labor state?*

Who attacks the *division of land?* The reactionaries. In a recently published feudalistic writing on division of land Kosegarten goes so far as to call *private property* a *privilege*. That is *Fourier's* principle. Once there is agreement on principles, can't there be controversy on implications and applications?

The *Rheinische Zeitung,* which cannot even concede *theoretical reality* to communistic ideas in their present form, and can even less wish or consider possible their *practical realization,* will submit these ideas to thorough criticism. If the Augsburger wanted and could achieve more than slick phrases, the Augsburger would see that writings such as those by Leroux, Considérant, and above all Proudhon's penetrating work can be criticized only after long and deep study, not through superficial and passing notions. We do not agree with the Augsburger who finds the *"reality"* of communistic *ideas* not in *Plato* but in an *obscure acquaintance* who, with some merit in scientific research, gave up the entire fortune at his disposal at the time and washed his confederates' dishes and polished their boots, fulfilling the will of father Enfantin [utopian socialist and follower of Saint-Simon]. Because of this disagreement we have to take such *theoretical* works all the more seriously. We are firmly convinced that it is not the *practical effort* but rather the *theoretical explication* of communistic ideas which is the real *danger.* Dangerous practical *attempts,* even *those on a large scale,* can be answered with *cannon,* but *ideas* won by our intelligence, embodied in our outlook, and forged in our conscience are chains from which we cannot tear ourselves away without breaking our hearts; they are demons we can overcome only by submitting to them. But the Augsburg paper knows nothing of the *troubled conscience* evoked by a rebellion of man's subjective wishes against his objective *understanding, because it possesses neither* understanding *nor conscience.*

# ON A PROPOSED DIVORCE LAW

[The following discussion of proposed changes in the divorce law appeared in the *Rheinische Zeitung* on December 19, 1842, a few weeks after Marx's first meeting with Engels and his break with the Berlin "Young Hegelians." Marx's reception of Engels was cool, probably because he identified Engels with the "Free Ones" of Berlin whose public buffooneries had become notorious. In response to requests from Berlin for space in the *Rheinische Zeitung* Marx demanded less vagueness and opposed smuggling "socialist and communist dogmas—a new outlook on the world—into casual columns of dramatic criticism." The following discussion criticizes existing divorce laws for being a patchwork of expedients as well as an inconsistent combination of religious and civil conceptions of marriage. In opposition to those who view marriage as a matter of individual pleasure or caprice, Marx follows Hegel in stressing the "ethical substance" of marriage in the family and children. He objects to easy divorce but allows that when a marriage does not correspond to its concept it may properly be recognized by the state as being dead. In holding that law as recognition of this ethical death must be "the conscious expression of the will of the people" involving "reverence for man," Marx departs from Hegel and reveals his early commitment to democracy.]

## *Criticism of a Criticism: Editorial Footnote to an Article*

The preceding criticism of the draft of a divorce law is written from the viewpoint of *Rhenish* jurisprudence, while the earlier criticism (see the supplement to No. 310 of the *Rheinische Zeitung*) was based on the standpoint of Old Prussian jurisprudence and its practice. There remains a third kind of criticism: criticism from a standpoint that is deliberately universal, the standpoint of *philosophy of law*.

It will no longer suffice to examine separate grounds for divorce pro and con. It will be necessary to develop the concept of marriage and its implications.

Both articles presented thus far equally repudiate the mixing of religion with law. They do not explain, however, the extent to which the essence of marriage is or is not intrinsically religious. They cannot explain how the consistent legislator must necessarily act, guided by the essential nature of things, not stopping with the empty abstraction of a definition of that nature. If a legislator considers spiritual sacredness and not human ethics as the essence of marriage, if he replaces self-determination by determination from above, inner natural dedication by a supernatural sanction, and loyal submission to the nature of the relationship by passive obedience to commandments —commandments transcending the nature of that relationship—can he be blamed for subjugating marriage to the church which is entitled to realize the demands and claims of a religion? Can he be blamed when he puts secular marriage under the supervision of spiritual authority? Isn't that a simple and necessary consequence? We are deceiving ourselves when we believe we can refute the religious legislator by demonstrating the contradiction between this or that regulation and the secular nature of marriage. The religious legislator does not argue against the abolition of secular marriage. Rather, he argues against the secular nature of marriage and attempts to cleanse it of this secularity or, if this is not possible, to make this secularity ever aware of its limitations, point out that it is merely tolerated, and break the sinful strength of its results.

The standpoint of *Rhenish* jurisprudence sharply brought out in the criticism mentioned earlier, however, is entirely insufficient. It will not do to divide marriage into two kinds, spiritual and secular, so that one is assigned only to the church and the conscience of particular individuals while the other is assigned to the state and the legal consciousness of its citizens. In finding two different spheres, one does not transcend the contradiction. Rather, one creates a contradiction and an unresolved collision between these spheres themselves. Can one restrict the legislator to a dualism, to a dualistic world-view? Isn't the conscientious, religious legislator compelled to elevate to the only power in the actual world and in secular forms that which he knows as the only truth and that which he worships as the only power in the spiritual world and religious forms? If in this respect the basic deficiency of Rhenish jurisprudence is apparent—namely, that its dualistic world-view does not even superficially prevent the most severe collisions by separating conscience from the consciousness of law, but rather acts as a splitting force, separating the legal world from the world of spirit, law from spirit and jurisprudence from philosophy—the great instability of Prussian jurisprudence is even further and most unambiguously manifest in its opposition to the proposed law.

If it is true that no legislature can decree what is ethical, it is even truer that no legislature can recognize it as legal. Statute law is based on an intellectual abstraction intrinsically lacking content, an abstraction which absorbs the natural, legal, and ethical content as external matter, as matter intrinsically lawless, and then attempts to shape, modify, and arrange this spiritless and lawless matter for an external purpose. Statute law does not treat the objective world according to its innate principles but according to capricious, subjective whims and intentions that have nothing to do with the matter itself. The Prussian jurists showed precious little insight into the nature of statute law. They criticized particular manifestations of its existence but not its essential nature. They were hostile to its reforming tendency but not to the form and method of the new proposed divorce law. They believed they might find proof of bad laws in bad ethics. Above all else we demand that the criticism be critical of itself and not overlook the difficulty of its subject.

## The Proposed Divorce Law

In regard to the *proposed divorce law* the *Rheinische Zeitung* has taken a *completely isolated* position. So far no one has demonstrated that it is untenable. The *Rheinische*

*Zeitung* agrees with the bill in considering the present Prussian marriage law unethical, the numerous and frivolous reasons for divorce inappropriate, and the procedure used so far not commensurate with the dignity of the matter—criticisms that could also be leveled against all Prussian legal proceedings. On the other hand, the *Rheinische Zeitung* raises the following main objections against the new bill: (1) Instead of a *reform* a mere *revision* has taken place, since the Prussian statute law has been retained as fundamental and thereby considerable indecision and insecurity have arisen; (2) Marriage is treated by the legislature not as an *ethical* but as a *religious* and *ecclesiastical* institution, and thus the *secular* nature of marriage has not been recognized; (3) The legal procedure is seriously deficient and made up of an external composition of contradictory elements; (4) On the one hand, there is police severity contradicting the concept of marriage, but on the other hand, there is too much indulgence toward so-called reasons of equity; (5) The entire bill leaves much to be desired in logic, precision, clarity, and thoroughness.

When the opponents of the bill point to one of these deficiencies, we agree with them but can in no way approve their unconditional apology for the old system. Let us again reiterate the statement made earlier: "If the legislature cannot decree what is ethical, it can even less recognize what is unethical as legal." When we ask about the basis of the argument of *these* opponents (not the opponents of the ecclesiastical view and critics of the other deficiencies noted), they always talk of the misery of spouses bound to each other against their will. They take an eudaemonistic view. They think only of two individuals and forget the *family*. They forget that nearly every dissolution of a marriage is the dissolution of a family and that the children and what belongs to them should not be dependent on arbitrary whims, even from a purely legal point of view. If marriage were not the basis of the family, it would not be subject to legislation, just as friendship is not. Those opponents, therefore, take into account *only* individual will, or rather the *caprice* of the spouses; they do not consider the *will of marriage*, the ethical substance of this relationship. The legislator, however, must consider himself a naturalist. He does not *make* laws; he does not invent them; he only formulates them. He expresses the inner principles of spiritual relationships in conscious, positive laws. The legislator would have to be accused of gross arbitrariness if he permitted his whims to replace the nature of things. But it is his right to regard it as gross arbitrariness if private persons want their whims to prevail against the nature of things. Nobody is forced to enter into a marriage, but everybody must be forced to make up his mind that he will obey the laws of marriage when he enters into it. A person entering into marriage does not *make* or *invent* it just as a swimmer does not invent nature and the laws of water and gravity. Marriage, therefore, cannot yield to his arbitrariness; rather, his arbitrariness must yield to marriage. Anyone who arbitrarily breaks a marriage maintains that arbitrariness, *lawlessness, constitutes the law of marriage,* for no reasonable person would be so presumptuous as to consider his acts privileged acts, acts appropriate for *him alone.* Instead, he will pass them off as legal acts *appropriate for all.* What do you oppose then? Legislation by arbitrariness. But you certainly won't want to turn arbitrariness into law at the very moment you accuse the legislator of arbitrariness.

Hegel says: *Implicitly* and in accordance with its concept, marriage should be indissoluble, but *only* implicitly, that is, only in accordance with its concept. This says nothing which is *peculiar* to marriage. All ethical relationships are by *their very concept* indissoluble, as one can easily find by assuming their *truth.* A *true* state, a *true* marriage, a *true* friendship is indissoluble; but there is no state, no marriage, no friendship that completely corresponds to its concept. Actual friendship even within the family is *dissoluble;* the actual state in world history is dissoluble; and so is actual marriage in the state. No ethical *existence* corresponds to its *essence,* or at least does not *have to* correspond to it. In nature itself there is dissolution and death when a particular existent no longer fully corresponds to its essential determination. World history decides whether a state is so much at odds with the idea of the state that it no longer deserves to continue. Similarly the state decides under which conditions an *existing* marriage has ceased to be a marriage. Divorce is nothing but the declaration that a marriage is *dead* and that its existence is only pretense and deception. It is obvious that neither the arbitrariness of the legislator nor that of private persons can decide whether or not a marriage is dead. Only the *nature of things* can do that, for a *death certificate,* as is well known, depends on factual evidence and not on the *wishes* of the interested parties. Now, as precise unmistakable proof is required for *physical* death, the legislator can declare an *ethical* death only in the presence of the most indubitable symptoms, since to conserve the life of ethical relationships is not only his right but also his *duty,* the duty of his self-preservation.

The *guarantee,* however, that the *conditions* will be fairly substantiated under which the *existence* of an ethical relationship no longer corresponds to its *essence* and is no longer commensurate with reliable knowledge and universal insight—this guarantee will be present only when law is the conscious expression of the will of the people, created with and through it. Let us add a word about making divorce easier or more difficult: Do you consider a natural body healthy, sound, and truly organized if any external shock, any injury, would destroy it? Wouldn't you feel offended if it were an established axiom that your friendship could not withstand the smallest accidents and *would have to* dissolve on account of any crotchet? In regard to marriage, however, the legislator can only determine when it *may* be dissolved, though essentially it already is *dissolved.* The judicial dissolution can be only the recording of the inner dissolution. The viewpoint of the legislator is the viewpoint of necessity. Believing marriage to be strong enough to withstand many collisions without harm, the legislator shows *reverence* for marriage and recognizes its deeply ethical nature. Compliance with the wishes of individuals would become harshness against their essential nature, against their ethical rationality which is embodied in ethical relationships.

Finally, we can call it only rashness when states with

*strict divorce laws* are accused of *hypocrisy;* the Rhineland is *proud* to be included among them. Only a person
with a horizon below the ethical decay around him can
venture such accusations. Here in the Rhineland we find
them ridiculous and at best consider them as proof that
even the *concept* of ethical relationships can be lost and
any ethical fact can be taken as a *fairy tale* and lie. This
is precisely the immediate consequence of laws which have
been decreed without reverence for man—a mistake one
cannot overcome by passing from material disdain to ideal
disdain and by demanding unconscious obedience to a
supra-ethical and supernatural authority instead of conscious subordination to ethico-natural forces.

# From DEFENSE OF THE MOSELLE
CORRESPONDENT: ECONOMIC DISTRESS
AND FREEDOM OF THE PRESS

[The following paragraphs present the leading ideas and principles of Marx's articles, written in the first weeks of 1843, on the economic distress of the Moselle vintagers. Censorship prevented completion of the articles, and the Prussian government suspended the *Rheinische Zeitung* as of April 1. Later Marx referred to this writing and an earlier essay on a wood-theft law as his first "embarrassed" effort to deal with "material interests," the impetus to his study of economics. In both he spoke for "the impoverished, the socially and politically deprived masses." The essay on the wood-theft law emphasized its harshness and injustice to the poor to protect the interests of a class, the forest owners, rather than the interest of all. In writing about the Moselle vintagers Marx gave many pages of factual details, omitted below, to verify conditions of economic distress. These conditions, he argues in the translation to follow, are not so much the result of personal action as of objectively determined relationships. Their alleviation requires, in addition to action from the state, a universal "participation in the interests of the fatherland" transcending bureaucracy, representing the citizen, and coming to life in a free press. Thus Marx was beginning to see the economic dimension of social problems as related to political change in the direction of liberal democracy.]

With reference to my article in No. 346 of the *Rheinische Zeitung,* dated "Bernkastel, December 10"—in which I claimed that the people on the Moselle enthusiastically hailed the greater freedom of the press effected by the Royal Cabinet Order of December 24, 1841, because of their especially oppressed situation—the president of the Rhine Province says the following:

> "If that article is to make sense, the Moselle people must have been forbidden to discuss freely and publicly their emergency, the causes of it as well as the

remedies. I doubt that this is the case. For nothing can have been more desirable for the authorities in their efforts to remedy the acknowledged emergency of the vintagers than a discussion of the conditions there, as open and free as possible." "I would be obliged to the writer of that article, if he would kindly state the instances where even before the enactment of the Highest Cabinet Order of December 24 of last year a free and open discussion of the emergency of the inhabitants along the Moselle was prevented by the authorities."

Farther down he notes: "The assertion made in the article quoted that the vintagers' cries for help have for some time been considered by the authorities as *insolent screams* is untruthful, to begin with."

My response will proceed as follows: I will try to prove

(1) that a free press is a *necessity* because of the particular nature of the emergency on the Moselle, the rights of the press as stated in the Royal Cabinet Order of December 24, 1841, being completely *irrelevant;*

(2) that my assertion would be absolutely correct, even if *no special* obstruction to "free and public discussion" took place before the enactment of the Cabinet Order, and that the great interest of the inhabitants of the Moselle valley in the Royal Cabinet Order and in the freer development of the press effected by the Order is understandable;

(3) *that very special* circumstances did prevent a "free and public discussion."

The entire context will show, then, whether I told the truth or a lie when I claimed that "For a long time the authorities had doubts about the vintagers' *desolate* situation, and they considered their cries for help as insolent screams."

ad (1) In the investigation of *political* conditions one is too easily tempted to overlook *the objective nature of the relationships* and to explain everything from the *will* of the persons acting. There are *relationships,* however, which determine the actions of private persons as well as those of individual authorities, and which are as independent as are the movements in breathing. Taking this objective standpoint from the outset, one will not presuppose an exclusively good or bad will on either side. Rather, one will observe relationships in which only persons appear to act at first. As soon as it is demonstrated that something was *necessitated* by conditions, it will not be difficult to figure out under which *external* circumstances this thing *actually* had to come into being, and under which other circumstances it could not have come about although a need for it was present. One can determine this with almost the same certainty as a chemist determines under which *external* circumstances some substances will form a compound. We stated that "a free press is a *necessity* because of the *particularity* of the emergency on the Moselle"; we submit that our presentation is far from being personal.

The *emergency* in the Moselle area cannot be regarded as *simple*. There will always be at least *two* sides that we must keep in mind: the private person and the state. The Moselle area is not located outside the state; it follows that its emergency is not outside the realm of the state administration. It is the *relationship* on both sides that forms the *actual* condition of the Moselle area.

[Marx here presents in detail, through two subsequent issues of the *Rheinische Zeitung,* the report of Tax Inspector von Zuccalmaglio on Moselle conditions and the sharp reply to that report from the Vintagers' Association. Marx concludes that "an administration exists for the country, not the country for an administration," and then demands that "the state provide the atmosphere in which the Moselle vintager can live and thrive." Hence, the emergency on the Moselle is at the same time an emergency in administration.]

To resolve the difficulty the administration and the administered both need a *third* element, which is *political* without being official and bureaucratic, an element which at the same time represents the citizen without being directly involved in private interests. This resolving element composed of a *political mind* and a *civic heart* is a *free press*.

ad (2) [ . . . ] The following sentences in the Censorship Edict [of 1819] inform us most clearly about the content and character of *political literature* and the *daily press:*

> "It is to be *hoped* in this way that *political literature* and the *daily press* will recognize their tasks *more clearly* than before, acquire a more *dignified* tone, and abstain *in the future* from playing upon the *curiosity* of their readers by printing meaningless reports taken from foreign newspapers, etc., etc. . . . . It is to be expected that a *more active* participation in the interests *of the fatherland will be achieved* and that *patriotism* will grow."[*]

The gist of this seems to be the following: Even though no *specific* measures prevented a free and open discussion, the *general condition* of the Prussian press itself was an insurmountable obstacle. When we summarize the excerpts, the censorship instruction says: censorship was much concerned and constituted an *external* barrier to a free press; with this went an *internal* limitation, for the press had given up its courage and any attempt to rise above the reporting of the news. Finally, people did not sufficiently *participate in the interests of the fatherland* and had lost their *patriotism*, the creative force for a free and open press, as well as the condition of popular acceptance of a free and open press, the atmosphere without which the press is hopelessly sick.

If measures taken by the authorities can create an *unfree* press, it is on the other hand *beyond the power of the authorities* to secure a free and open discussion of special problems, *because* of the general lack of freedom of the press; for even frank comments on some matters, filling the columns of newspapers, could not produce *universal* participation and could not achieve true publicity. [ . . . ]

When a segment of the population, especially the majority, encounters a striking and terrifying misfortune, and nobody discusses and treats it as a phenomenon *worthy of consideration*, the people affected must conclude that others are not *permitted* to speak out, or do not *wish* to

[* Marx here abridges and provides emphasis for two previous quotations from the Censorship Edict of 1819.]

speak out because the matter seems unimportant to them. But even the most uneducated vintager feels a need for cognizance of his misfortune and the sharing of it in spirit, hoping that with all people thinking and many speaking about his misfortune, some will take action. If the conditions on the Moselle could have been discussed freely and openly, this discussion would not have *taken place* anyway. People believe only in what exists in *actuality,* in a free press that actually exists, not in a free press that might exist. *Before* the enactment of the Royal Cabinet Order, the people on the Moselle had been aware of their distress, had heard doubts about their need, and had known nothing like a free and open press. *After* the enactment of the Cabinet Order, they saw such a press take shape out of nowhere. Their conclusion that the Royal Cabinet Order was the *only* cause for this development of the press seems to have been a very popular conclusion. At least they welcomed it because it met their *real* needs. Even when we disregard the aspect of popularity, a critical examination will yield the same result. The introductory words of the Censorship Order of December 24, 1841, read: *"His Majesty the King* deigns to *disapprove explicitly* of any improper coercion in journalism, and *with the recognition of the value of and the need* for free and decent publications, etc. . . ."* These introductory words bestow upon the press special *royal* recognition and thus *political significance.* The fact that *one* royal statement can be so effective that it was hailed by the people on the Moselle as a statement of magic power and as a panacea for all ailments seems to attest to the genuinely royalistic sentiment of the people there and to their unbridled and overflowing gratefulness.

ad (3) Here, too, we must first of all emphasize the guiding viewpoint in our presentation and recognize the power of the general *relationships* in the *will* of the acting persons. In the *special* circumstances which prevented a free and open discussion of the conditions on the Moselle, we must see the *factual embodiment* and *evident manifestation* of the *general* relationships as already shown above, that is, the *particular* attitude of the administration to the Moselle area; the general condition of the daily press and of public opinion; and finally the prevailing political spirit and its system. If these conditions, as it appears, were the *general, invisible,* and *compelling* forces of the time, we hardly need to point out that they had to act as *such,* had to become actual facts, and be *expressed* as individual acts that were only *apparently* arbitrary. [ . . . ]

It is not our aim to give a complete rundown of all *special circumstances,* for this would mean to write the history of the Moselle area since 1830. We believe that it is sufficient to demonstrate that the free and open word came into conflict with *special* obstacles, and *in all its forms:* in the form of *speech,* in the form of *writing,* in the form of *print,* print *not yet censored* as well as print already *censored.* [ . . . ]

We are justified in calling the vintagers' *"cries for help"* just that, not only in the *figurative* but also in the *literal* sense. A *government report* and *criminal proceedings* have shown that these cries had been called unreasonable. The description of the emergency had been regarded as a gross exaggeration based on egoistic and evil motives, and the complaint had been interpreted as an *"insolent,* disrespectful criticism of the law." Loud *cries,* which disregard the facts, stem from evil motives, and involve *insolent* criticism of the law, can certainly be called "screams," and "insolent screams." This is not such a farfetched or even *untruthful* assertion. It is only a logical conclusion.

# FEUERBACHIAN CRITICISM OF HEGEL

# CRITIQUE OF HEGEL'S PHILOSOPHY OF THE STATE (1843)

[With the prospects of an editor's salary from the *Deutsch-Französische Jahrbücher* to be published in Paris, Marx married Jenny von Westphalen and moved into the house of his mother-in-law in Kreuznach. There he finished the following critique of Hegel's philosophy of law which had engaged his attention for over a year. Marx's analysis of Hegel's sections 257 to 260 is missing in the manuscript. In his previous writings on the state Marx had followed Hegel at a number of points. Now he subjects Hegel's view to a detailed criticism. Part of the time Marx's criticism is internal, showing how Hegel's constitutional monarchy does not agree with his premise that the state is the unity of the universal and the particular, form and content. Marx also shows how Hegel's conclusions involve a speculative reversal of subject and predicate resulting in "mystification." In this, Marx follows Feuerbach's critique of speculation, most fully developed in his "Preliminary Theses Toward Reform of Philosophy" which had appeared in the *Anekdota* along with Marx's first essay on censorship. The speculative philosopher, Feuerbach charged, sees nature, religion, and philosophy itself as mere predicates of the abstract Idea, but "we need only to convert the predicate into the subject to get at the pure, undisguised truth." With this perspective and sharp internal criticism Marx challenges Hegel's view of the state in relation to civil society, his view of democracy, and his treatment of bureaucracy and voting. Marx emphasizes the cleavage between civil society as the battlefield of individual interests on the one hand and the state—apart from democracy —as an ideal and alien universality on the other. In other sections omitted from the translation below, Marx described labor as "the basis on which the spheres of civil society rest and move" and criticized Hegel's view of property as an "illusion of family life" that converts owners into "property of property."]

### Root Errors of Political Speculation: On Hegel's § 261–69

§ 261. "In contrast with the family and civil society, the spheres of private rights and private welfare, the state is **from one point of view**[*] an *external* necessity and their higher authority; its nature is such that their laws and interests are subordinate to it and dependent on it. **On the other hand,** however, the state is their *immanent* aim; its strength lies in the unity of its universal end and aim with the particular interest of individuals, in the fact that individuals have *duties* to the state in proportion as they have rights (§155)."

The paragraph above informs us that *concrete freedom* consists in the identity (to be achieved, on both sides) of the system of particular interests (of family and civil society) with the system of general interests (of the state). The relationship of these spheres will now be determined more closely.

On the one hand, the state is an *"external* necessity" in contrast to the sphere of family and civil society, an authority to which "laws" and "interests" are "subordinate" and upon which they depend. The fact that the state, in contrast to family and civil society, is an *"external* necessity" is inherent partly in the category of "transition" and partly in their *conscious relationship* to the state. The "subordination" to the state still completely corresponds to this relationship of *"external* necessity." But what Hegel understands by "dependence" is indicated in the sentence found in the Remark on this paragraph:

"It was Montesquieu above all who kept in view the thought of **dependence** of laws, in particular laws concerning the rights of persons, on the specific character of the state and the philosophical perspective of treating the part only in its relation to the whole."

[* Boldface type indicates underlining by Marx alone in Hegel's paragraphs.]

Hegel thus speaks here of the *inner* dependence or essential determination of private right, etc., upon the state. At the same time, however, he subsumes this dependence under the relationship of *"external* necessity" and juxtaposes it to the other relationship in which family and civil society are related to the state as their *"immanent* aim."

By "external necessity" we must understand that "laws" and "interests" of family and society must give way in the event of collision to the "laws" and "interests" of the state, that they are subordinate to the state, that their existence is dependent upon the state's existence, or that even the will and laws of the state appear to the "will" and "laws" of the family and civil society as a necessity!

Hegel, however, does not speak here of perceptible collisions. He speaks of the relationship of *"spheres* of private right and welfare of family and civil society" to the state. He is concerned with the *essential relationship* of these spheres themselves. Not only their "interests" but also their "laws" and their "essential determinations" are "dependent" upon the state, "subordinate" to it. The state is related to their "laws and interests" as a "higher *authority."* Their "interest" and "law" are the state's "subordinates." They live in "dependence" on it. Just because "subordination" and "dependence" are *external* relationships limiting and hindering independence, the relationship of "family" and of "civil society" to the state is one of *"external* necessity," a necessity which moves against the inner nature of the matter. The fact itself that "the laws concerning the rights of persons" depend "on the specific character of the state" and are modified by it, is thus subsumed under the relationship of *"external necessity,"* especially because "civil society and family" in their true or independent and complete development are presupposed, as particular "spheres," for the state. *"Subordination"* and *"dependence"* serve as expressions for an "external," *forced,* apparent identity. As a logical expression for this identity Hegel correctly employs the phrase *"external necessity."* With "subordination" and "dependence" Hegel has further developed one side of the divided identity, namely, the aspect of alienation within unity. "On the other hand, however, the state is their *immanent* aim; its strength lies in the unity of its *universal end and aim* with the *particular interest* of individuals, in the fact that individuals have *duties* to the state in proportion as they have rights."

Here Hegel poses an unresolved *antinomy. On the one side,* external necessity; *on the other side,* immanent aim. The unity of the state's *universal end and aim* with the *particular interest of individuals* is to mean that *their duties* and their *rights* in regard to the state are identical (thus, for example, the duty to respect property coincides with the right to have property). This identity is explained in the Remark [on § 261] as follows:

> "*Duty* is primarily a relation *to* something which for me is *substantive,* absolutely universal. A right, on the other hand, is simply the *embodiment* of this substance and thus is the *particular aspect* of it, my *particular* freedom. Hence, at abstract levels, right and duty appear to be parceled out on different sides or in different persons. In the state as something ethical, as the interpenetration of the substantive and the particular, my obligation to what is substantive is at the same time the embodiment of my particular freedom. This means that in the state, duty and right are *united in one and the same relation.*"

§ 262. "The actual Idea, Spirit, divides itself in its finitude into two ideal spheres of its notion, family and civil society, in order to leave behind its ideality and to become **explicitly infinite** actual Spirit. It lends to these spheres the material of its finite actuality—i.e. individuals as a *mass*—in such a way that this lending appears *mediated* in the individual by circumstances, caprice, and his personal choice of his station in life."

Translating this into prose, we arrive at the following: The ways in which the state is mediated with family and civil society are "circumstances, caprice, and the individual's own choice of his station in life." The state's rationality thus has nothing to do with the distribution of its content as family and civil society. The state emerges from them in an unconscious and arbitrary way. Family and civil society appear as nature's dark ground, from which the state's light is kindled. By the term "content of the state" is understood the *functions* of the state, insofar as family and civil society as parts of the state participate in it.

This development is remarkable in two ways.

1. Family and civil society are grasped as *conceptual spheres* of the state, and thus as spheres of its *finitude,* as its *finitude.* It is the state which *divides* itself into them and *presupposes* them, and *does* this "in order to leave behind its ideality and to become *explicitly infinite* actual Spirit." "It divides itself in order to. . . ." It *"thus lends* to these spheres the material of its actuality, *in such a way that* this lending, etc., *appears* mediated." The so-called "actual Idea" (Spirit as infinite, actual Spirit) is represented as if it acted by a specific principle and with specific intent. It divides itself into finite spheres. It does this "in order to return into itself, to exist for itself," in such a way that it directly is as it is in actuality.

Here, the logical, pantheistic mysticism is strikingly apparent.

The *actual* relationship is: "that the lending of the content of the state is mediated in the individual by circumstances, caprice, and personal choice of his station in life." This fact, this *actual relationship,* is expressed in speculation as *appearance* or *phenomenon.* These circumstances, this caprice, this choice of position in life, this *actual mediation* are merely the *appearance* of *mediation,* which the actual Idea undergoes and which takes place behind the curtain. Actuality is not expressed as it is itself but as another actuality. Common experience is not subject to the law of its own spirit but to an alien spirit, whereas the actual Idea is based not on an actuality developed from itself but rather on common experience.

The Idea is thoroughly subjectivized. The *actual* relationship of family and civil society to the state is grasped as their *inner imaginary* activity. Family and civil society are the presuppositions of the state; they are really the active forms. But in speculation this is reversed. As the Idea is subjectivized, the actual subjects—civil society, family, "circumstances, caprice, etc."—become *unactual,* objective moments of the Idea, meaning something else.

[2. ?] The lending of the content of the state "to the individual through circumstances, caprice, and his own choice of his relation in life"—these are expressed not as what is genuine, necessary, and generally justified in and for itself. They are not *as such* presented as rational. But they become rational again only in that they are presented as an *apparent* mediation, in that they are left just as they are, but at the same time acquire the meaning of a determination of the Idea, a result, a product of the Idea. The distinction lies not in the content, but in the method or in the *manner of speaking*. There is a double history, an esoteric and an exoteric. The content lies in the exoteric part. The interest of the esoteric part is to rediscover in the state the history of the logical Concept. Actual development, however, proceeds in the exoteric side.

*Rationally,* Hegel's assertions simply mean:

Family and civil society are parts of the state. The content of the state is distributed to them through "circumstances, caprice, and one's own choice of his station in life." Citizens of the state are members of families and members of civil society.

"The actual Idea, Spirit, *divides itself* in *its finitude* into two ideal spheres of its Concept, family and civil society" —hence, the division of the state into family and civil society is *ideal,* that is, necessary, belonging to the essence of the state. Family and civil society are actual parts of the state, actual spiritual manifestations of will. They are the state's particular modes of existence. Family and civil society themselves *comprise* the state. They are its dynamism. According to Hegel, on the other hand, they are *produced* by the actual Idea. It is not their own life that binds them into the state; rather, it is the life of the Idea that has discerned them from itself; and thus they are the finitude of the Idea; they owe their particular existence to a spirit different from their own; they are determinations made by a third party, not self-determinations; consequently they are thus determined as "finitude," as the very *finitude* of the "actual Idea." The purpose of their particular existence is not particular existence itself, but the Idea separates from itself these presuppositions "in order to leave behind its ideality and to become explicitly infinite actual Spirit," that is, there can be no political state without the natural basis of the family and the created basis of civil society; they are a conditio sine qua non for the state. But the conditioning factor is presented as the conditioned, the determining is presented as the determined, and the producing is presented as the product of its product. The actual Idea is debased only in the "finitude" of family and civil society so that it may enjoy and manifest its infinitude by transcending them. The actual Idea "*thus* lends to these spheres" (in order to achieve its purpose) "the material of this its finite actuality" (of this? of which? these spheres are already its "finite actuality," its "material"), "individuals as a mass" ("the individuals, the mass" here are the content of the state; "the state consists of them"; this very existence of the state is expressed here as an act of the Idea, as a "distribution" made by the Idea with its own content; the fact is that the state emerges from the mass existing as members of families and civil society, while speculation sees this fact as act of Idea, not as the Idea of the mass, but as act of a subjective Idea different from the fact itself) "in such a way that this lending to the individual" (formerly only the lending of the individual to the spheres of family and civil society was mentioned) "appears mediated by circumstances, caprice, etc." Empirical actuality is thus understood as it is. It is also pronounced rational, but it is not rational through its own rationality but rather because the empirical fact in its empirical existence has another meaning than its own. The initial fact is not taken as such but rather as a mystical result.

Actual existence becomes the phenomenon, but the Idea has no other content but this phenomenon. Further, the Idea has no other purpose but the logical one: "to become explicitly infinite actual Spirit." The entire mystery of Hegel's philosophy of law and of his philosophy in general is laid out in this paragraph.

§ 263. "In these spheres in which the elements of Spirit, individuality and particularity, have their **immediate** and **reflected** reality, Spirit is present as their

objective universality **illuminating them** as the power
of reason in the region of necessity [§ 184], i.e. as
the *institutions* considered above."

§ 264. "Individuals *en masse* contain in themselves
spiritual natures and thus two aspects: at one extreme,
*related individuality* as knowing and willing, and at
the other extreme, *universality* as knowing and willing
what is substantial. Hence, they attain their right in
both these aspects only insofar as they are actualized
both as private and substantial persons. In those
spheres [of family and civil society] individuals acquire
their right in the first of these two aspects directly.
In the other aspect they find their essential self-
consciousness in social institutions, the *universal* implicit in their particular interests, and in the corporation they give their interests a pursuit and activity
directed to a universal end."

§ 265. "These institutions make up the *constitution*,
i.e. developed and actualized rationality *in terms of
particularity*. They are, therefore, the firm foundation
of the state as well as of individuals' trust in and senti-
ments toward the state. They are the main pillars of
public freedom, because in them particular freedom
is realized and rational, and therefore the union of
freedom and necessity is *implicitly* in them."

§ 266. "*But* Spirit is objective and actual to itself
not merely as this" (which?) "necessity . . . but as
the *ideality* and core of this necessity. Hence this substantial universality is its *own* object and purpose, and
that necessity therefore is in the same measure its own
object and purpose in the *form* of freedom."

The transition from family and civil society to political
state is such that the Spirit of those spheres, which is *implicitly* the Spirit of the state, relates itself as such to itself
and is *actual* to itself as their core. The transition, therefore, is not derived from the *particular* nature of the family, etc., and the particular nature of the state, but from the
*general* relationship of *necessity* and *freedom*. This is the
very same transition which is accomplished from the sphere
of essence into the sphere of Concept in [Hegel's] Logic.

The same transition is made in [Hegel's] Philosophy of Nature from the inorganic into life. The same categories always provide the soul of either one of these spheres. It only depends on finding for the particular concrete definitions the corresponding abstract ones.

§ 267. "The *necessity* in ideality is the inner self-*development* of the Idea. As *subjective* substantiality, it is **political** *sentiment*. In distinction from this, as *objective* substantiality, it is the *organism* of the state, the specifically *political* state and *its constitution*."

The *subject* here is "the necessity in ideality," the "Idea in itself." The *predicate* is *political sentiment* and the *political constitution*. In plain language: *Political sentiment* is the subjective *substance* of the state, the *political constitution* is the *objective*. The logical development from family and civil society to state is thus *appearance* only, for it does not proceed in the same way as family sentiment, civic sentiment, the family institution, and social institutions as such are related to and linked with political sentiment and political constitution.

There is no transition at all in Spirit's existing "not only as this necessity and as a *realm of appearance*" but rather being actual as "ideality," explicitly as the soul of this realm and having particular existence, because the soul of the family exists explicitly as love, etc. Pure ideality of an actual sphere, however, could exist only as *systematic knowledge*.

It is important that Hegel always converts the Idea into the subject and the particular actual subject, such as "political sentiment," into the predicate. But the development always takes place on the side of the predicate.

Section 268 contains a fine exposition on political *sentiment, patriotism,* which has nothing in common with its logical development, except that Hegel defines this sentiment *"only"* as "a product of the institutions existing within the *state,* because rationality is *actually* present in them." Conversely these institutions are just as much an *objectification* of political sentiment. Cf. the Remark [by Hegel] on this paragraph.

§ 269. "This sentiment gets its specifically determined *content* from the various aspects of the state as **organism.** This *organism* is the development of the Idea into its distinctions and their objective actuality. **Hence** these different aspects are the *various powers* and the functions and spheres of these powers. Thereby the **universal** continually *engenders* itself—*necessarily* so because they are determined by the *nature of the concept*—and *maintains* itself because the universal is the presupposition of its own production. This organism is the *political constitution.*"

The political constitution is the organism of the state, or: the organism of the state is the political constitution. The fact that the various aspects of an organism are necessarily connected as the result of the nature of the organism—that is a mere tautology. And if the political constitution is defined as an organism, the fact that the various aspects of the constitution and the various powers are organically determined and rationally related to one another—that is also a tautology. It is a great step forward to view the political state as an organism, to view the diversity of powers no longer as an [in]organic but as a living and rational distinction. But how does Hegel present this discovery?

1. "This *organism* is the development of the Idea into its distinctions and their objective actuality." He does not say: This organism of the state is its development into distinctions and their objective actuality. The real point is: The development of the state or of the political constitution into distinctions and their actuality is an *organic* development. The *actual distinctions* or the *various aspects of the political* constitution are the premise, the subject. The predicate is their determination as *organic*. Instead, Hegel makes the Idea the subject and takes the distinctions and their actuality as its development, its product. But conversely, the Idea must be developed out of the actual distinctions. What is here organic is just the *idea of the distinctions,* its ideal determination.

[2. ?] The *Idea,* however, is spoken of as a subject, developing itself to *its* distinctions. In addition to the reversal of subject and predicate, it appears that here some other idea is discussed as the organism. Hegel proceeds from the abstract Idea whose development in the state is the *political constitution*. He does not concern himself with the political idea but with the abstract Idea in its political element. By saying, "This organism (namely, of the state, political constitution) is the development of the Idea into its distinctions, etc.," we know nothing at all yet of the *specific idea* of the political constitution. With equal truth we can make the same statement about an *animal* organism as about a *political* organism. What is the *distinction* between these two? Nothing follows from such a general definition. A definition that does not give differentia specifica is *no* definition. The main thing is to rediscover "the Idea" itself, the "logical Idea" in each element, whether it be the idea of the state or of nature. The actual subjects, such as the "political constitution" here, become mere *names,* so that we have only the semblance of actual cognition. They are and remain unconceptual definitions because they are not conceived according to their specific essence.

"*Hence* these different aspects are the *various powers* and the functions and sphere of these powers." The adverb "*hence*" gives the appearance of a conclusion, a derivation and development. But we must ask, "How come 'hence'?" The fact "that the various aspects of the state as organism" are "the various powers" and "the functions and sphere of these powers" is an empirical fact; the fact that they are parts of an "organism" is a philosophical "predicate."

We note here a stylistic peculiarity of Hegel which frequently recurs and is a result of his mysticism. The entire paragraph reads:

| | |
|---|---|
| "This sentiment gets its specifically determined content from the **various aspects** of the state as **organism. This** *organism* is the development of the Idea into its distinctions and their objective actuality. **Hence these different aspects** are the *various powers* and the | (1) "This sentiment gets its specifically determined content *from the various aspects* of the state as organism." "These different aspects are . . . the *various powers* and the functions and spheres of these powers." |

functions and spheres of these powers. Thereby the universal continually *engenders* itself—*necessarily* so because they are determined by the *nature of the Concept*—and *maintains* itself because the universal is the presupposition of its own production. This organism is the *political constitution*."

(2) "This sentiment gets its specifically determined content from the various aspects of the state as *organism*. *This organism* is the development of the Idea into its distinctions and their objective actuality ... Thereby the universal continually *engenders* itself—*necessarily* so because they are determined by the *nature of the Concept*—and *maintains* itself because the universal is the presupposition of its own production. —*This organism* is the *political constitution*."

We see that Hegel links the broader definitions with two subjects—to the "various aspects of the organism" and to the "organism." In the third sentence the "various aspects" are defined as the "various powers." The inserted word *"hence"* gives the appearance that these "various powers" are derived from the second assertion about the organism as the development of the Idea.

Hegel then continues discussing the "various powers." The statement that the universal continually "engenders" and thus maintains itself is nothing new, because it is already implied in the definition of the universal as "aspects of the organism," as "organic" aspects. Rather, this definition of the "various powers" is nothing but a different way of saying that the organism is "the development of the Idea into its distinctions, etc."

To say that this organism is "the development of the Idea into its distinctions and their objective actuality" is the same as saying that it is the development into distinctions so that "the universal" (the universal here is the same as the Idea) "continually maintains itself, *engenders* itself —*necessarily* so because they are determined by the *nature of the Concept*—and *maintains* itself because the universal is the presupposition of its own production." The latter is just a closer explication of "the development of the Idea into its distinctions." With this, Hegel still has not gone one step beyond the general concept of "Idea" and at most of "organism" in general (for only this particular idea is the point in question). Can Hegel validly conclude that "this organism is the political constitution"? Why not conclude: "This organism is the solar system"? After all, he later defines "the various aspects of the state" as the "various powers." The assertion that "the various aspects of the state are the various powers" is an empirical truth and cannot be presented as a philosophical discovery; in no way does it result from a previous development. By defining the organism as the "development of *the* Idea," by speaking of the distinctions of *the* Idea, and then by inserting the concretum of "various *powers*," Hegel manages to make it appear that a *determinate* content has been developed. He simply cannot attach the phrase *"this* organism" to the assertion that "this sentiment gets its specifically determined content from the various aspects *of the state as organism,"* but only the phrase *"the* organism is the development of the Idea, etc." What he says is true of any organism, and there is no predicate making the subject *"this"* relevant. The final result he is seeking is the definition of the *organism* as the *political constitution.* He establishes no link *by which one* could get *from the general idea of organism to the determinate idea of the state organism or the political constitution,* and there will never be such a link. At the beginning he speaks of "the various aspects of the state organism" which he later specifies as "the various powers." Thus he merely says: *"The various powers of the state organism,"* or *"the state organism of the various powers"* is—the *"political constitution"* of the *state.* He does not make the link to *"political* constitution" from "organism," "the Idea," its "distinctions," etc., but from the presupposed concept: "various powers," *"state* organism."

Actually, Hegel has only resolved the "political constitution" into the general abstract idea of "organism," but in his opinion—and only apparently so—has he developed the specific from the "general Idea." He converted the subject of the Idea into a product, a predicate. He does not develop his thinking from the object, but he develops the object by a sort of thinking that he manages, and manages in the abstract sphere of logic. It is not a matter of developing the determinate idea of political constitution, but rather of connecting political constitution with the abstract Idea, establishing its place as part of (the Idea's) life history—an obvious mystification.

Another determination is that the "various powers are determined by the *nature of the concept*"; that therefore the universal engenders them *"necessarily."* The various powers are thus not determined through their "own nature," but through something foreign to them. Furthermore, the *necessity* is not derived from their own essence and still less established critically. Their fate is predestined through the "nature of the concept" sealed in the sacred files of the Santa Casa [the Inquisitorial prison] (of logic). The soul of objects, here that of the state, exists and is predestined prior to the body which actually exists only in appearance. The "concept" is the son in the "Idea," the father of God, the driving force, the determining and differentiating principle. "Idea" and "concept" are here autonomous abstractions.

### Sovereignty and Democracy: On Hegel's § 279

§ 279. "Sovereignty, at first simply the *universal* thought of this ideality [of the state's sovereignty in relation to all particular authorities within it] *exists* only as *subjectivity* certain of itself and as abstract and hence ungrounded *self-determination* of the will,

(1) "Sovereignty, at first simply the universal thought of this ideality [of the state's sovereignty in relation to all particular authorities within it] *exists* only as *subjectivity* certain of itself [ . . . ]. Genuine subjectivity exists only as a *subject, personality*

containing the ultimate basis of decision. This is the individual aspect of the state as such whereby the state is *one*. But genuine subjectivity exists only as a *subject*, personality only as a *person*, and in the constitution which has matured into genuine rationality each of the three moments of the concept has its *explicitly actual*, separate form. Hence, this absolutely distinct moment of the whole is not individuality in general, but one individual, the *monarch*."

only as a person. In the constitution which has matured into genuine rationality each of the three moments of the concept has [ . . . ] explicitly actual, separate form."

(2) Sovereignty "exists only [ . . . ] as abstract and hence ungrounded *self-determination* of the will, containing the ultimate basis of decision. This is the individual aspect of the state as such, whereby the state is *one* [ . . . ] (and in the constitution that has matured into genuine rationality each of the three moments of the concept has its *explicitly actual*, separate form). Hence, this absolutely distinct moment of the whole is not individuality in general, but one individual, the *monarch*."

The first statement means only that the universal thought of this ideality whose sorry existence we have already noted would have to be the self-conscious effect of subjects and as such exist for and in them.

If Hegel had proceeded from actual subjects as the bases of the state he would not need to let the state be subjectivized in a mysterious way. "But genuine subjectivity," says Hegel, "exists only as a *subject*, personality only as a *person*." This too is a mystification. Subjectivity is a determination of the subject, personality a determination of the person. Instead of grasping them as predicates of their subjects, Hegel makes the predicates self-sufficient and in a mystical way has them later transformed into their subjects.

The existence of the predicates is the subject: thus the subject is the existence of subjectivity, etc. Hegel makes the predicates, the objects, self-sufficient, but separated from their actual self-sufficiency, from their subject. Later the actual subject then appears as a result, while one should proceed from the actual subject and pay attention to its objectivization. Hence the mystical substance turns into the actual subject and the real subject appears as something else, as a moment of mystical substance. Just because Hegel proceeds from predicates of universal determination instead of the real Ens (ὑποκείμενον, subject) and because a vehicle for these determinations must exist, the mystical idea becomes this vehicle. This is the dualism: Hegel considers the universal not as the actual essence of what is the actual-finite, that is, what is existing and determinate, and he considers the actual Ens not as the *genuine subject* of the infinite.

Here Hegel first considers sovereignty, the essence of the state, as something self-sufficient and objectifies it. Then, of course, he must make this object into the subject. But this subject then appears as the self-embodiment of sovereignty, while the sovereignty is nothing but the objectified spirit of the state as subject.

Setting aside this basic defect of development, let us consider the first sentence of the paragraph. As it stands, it means nothing but the following: sovereignty, the idealism of the state as person and as "subject" obviously exists in the form of many persons and many subjects, because no single person exhausts the sphere of personality and no single subject exhausts the sphere of subjectivity. What kind of idealism of the state would exist as the communal soul of the state as *one* person, *one* subject, instead of being the actual self-consciousness of the citizens? Hegel does not develop anything further from this proposition. But let us now consider the second statement included in the first sentence. Hegel wants to present the monarch as the actual "God-man," as the *actual embodiment* of the Idea.

"Sovereignty . . . *exists* only . . . as abstract and hence ungrounded *self-determination* of the will, containing the ultimate basis of decision. This is the *individual aspect* of the state as such, where the state is *one* . . . In the constitution which has matured into genuine rationality each of the three moments of the concept has its *explicitly actual*, separate form. *Hence* this absolutely distinct moment of the whole is not individuality in general, but one individual, the *monarch*."

We have already called attention to this sentence. The moment of resolving—of arbitrary decision, arbitrary because it is definite—is the *monarchial power of the will* in general. The idea of *monarchial power*, as Hegel develops it, is nothing but the *idea* of what is *arbitrary*, of the *decision* of the will.

Taking sovereignty as the idealism of the state, as the actual determination of the parts through the idea of the whole, Hegel then makes sovereignty the "*abstract* and hence *ungrounded* self-determination of the will, containing the ultimate basis of decision. This is the *individual aspect* of the state as such." Formerly he spoke of subjectivity, now he speaks of individuality. The sovereign state must be *one, one individual* possessing individuality. The state is *one* "not only" in this individuality; individuality is only the *natural* moment of its unity, the state's *natural determination*. "*Hence* this absolutely distinct moment is not individuality in general, but one individual, the *monarch*." How come? Because "each of the three moments of the concept has its *explicitly actual*, separate form." A moment of the concept is "singleness." However, this is still not *one individual*. And in what kind of constitution would universality, particularity, and singleness have "its *explicitly actual*, separate form"? Since we are dealing with the state, with society, and not generally with an abstraction, we may even adopt Hegel's classification. What would follow? The citizen determining the universal is legislator; deciding what is single, *actually* exercising his will, he is monarch. What is this to mean: *The individuality of the state's will* is "one *individual*," a particular individual distinct from all others? *Universality* too, the legislature, has "explicitly actual, separate form." Couldn't we conclude that "these particular individuals are the legislature"?

*The common man:*

2. The monarch possesses sovereign power, sovereignty.

3. Sovereignty does what it wants to do.

*Hegel:*

2. The *sovereignty* of the state is *the* monarch.

3. Sovereignty is "the abstract and hence ungrounded *self-determination* of the will, containing the ultimate basis of decision."

Hegel converts every attribute of the constitutional monarch in present-day Europe into absolute self-determinations of the *will*. He does not say: the monarch's will is the ultimate decision; but he says: the will's ultimate decision is—the monarch. The first assertion is empirical. The second twists empirical fact into a metaphysical axiom.

Hegel mixes the two subjects, sovereignty "as subjectivity certain of itself" *and* sovereignty "as the *ungrounded* self-determination of the will, as the individual will," in order to develop the "Idea" as *"one* individual."

Of course, self-certain subjectivity must *actually* exercise its will, exercise it also as unity, as individual. But who has ever doubted that the state acts through individuals? If Hegel had wanted to develop the idea that the state must have *one* individual as the representative of its individual unity, he did not propose the *monarch* for this purpose. As the *positive* result of the examination of this paragraph we can only say:

In the state the *monarch* is the moment of *individual will,* of ungrounded self-determination, of arbitrariness.

Hegel's Remark on this paragraph is so noteworthy that we must look at it more closely.

"The immanent development of a science, the *derivation of its entire content* from the simple *concept* . . . is peculiar in that one and the same concept, will in this instance, being abstract at the beginning because it is the beginning, preserves itself while consolidating its determinations, likewise merely through itself, thus achieving a concrete content. Hence it is the basic moment of personality, at first abstract in immediate rights, which has progressed through its various forms of subjectivity, and here, in absolute rights, in the state as complete, concrete objectivity of will, is the *personality of the state* and its *certainty of itself*. This transcends all particular elements in the self per se, cuts short the weighing of the possible pros and cons, *terminates* these particular elements through the statement, 'I will,' and begins all action and actuality."

First of all, it is not "peculiar to science," that the fundamental concept of anything always reappears.

Further, no *progress* has taken place. *Abstract personality* was the subject of abstract rights. It has not changed. As *abstract personality* it is still the *personality of the state*. Hegel should not have been surprised that an *actual person* —and persons constitute the state—reappears everywhere as its essence. He should have been surprised about the contrary, even more so about the fact that a person as a person of the state reappears in the same thin abstraction as does a person of private rights.

Hegel here defines the monarch as "the personality of the state and its certainty of itself." The monarch is "personified sovereignty," "sovereignty become human," the consciousness of the state incarnate, whereby all other persons are excluded from this sovereignty, from such personality, and from the consciousness of the state. At the same time, though, Hegel is unable to give this personified sovereignty any other content than "I will," the moment of arbitrariness in willing. "Reason of state" and "consciousness of the state" is a "single" empirical person excluding all others, but this personified reason has no content except the abstraction, "I will." *L'Etat, c'est moi.*

"But personality, subjectivity in general, **furthermore**, as infinitely self-relating, only has *truth*—its most immediate truth as a person, as a subject existing for itself—and what exists for itself is likewise just *a unit*."

Since personality and subjectivity are only predicates of a person and a subject, they, of course, exist only as person and subject; and a person is a *unit*. But, as Hegel should have continued, the *unit* has truth only as *many units*. The predicate, the essence, never exhausts the ranges of its existence in *one unit* but rather *in many units*.

Instead, Hegel concludes:

"The personality of the state is actual only as a *person,* the *monarch.*"

So, because subjectivity exists only as subject, and subject only as unit, the personality of the state is actual only as one person. A fine conclusion! Hegel could just as well conclude: because a single individual is a unit, the human species is only a single individual.

> "Personality expresses the concept as such; at the same time, the person contains the concept's actuality; and only with this determination is the concept *idea,* truth."

*Personality,* however, is only an abstraction without the person, but the person is only the *actual idea* of personality in its particular species-existence, *as persons.*

> "A so-called *moral* person, a society, community, or family, however inherently concrete it may be, has personality only as a moment abstractly within and has not therein achieved the truth of its existence. The state, though, is precisely the totality in which the moments of the concept achieve actuality according to their particular truth."

There is a lot of confusion in this sentence. Hegel considers a *moral* person, society, etc., abstract, the very species-formations, in which the *actual person* particularly manifests its actual content, objectifies himself, and abandons the abstraction of "person as such." Instead of recognizing this *actualization* of the person as the most concrete thing possible, Hegel favors the state: "the moment of the concept," "singleness," achieves a mystical "particular existence." In Hegel what is rational is not found in the reason of the actual person becoming actual but rather in the moments of an abstract concept becoming actual.

> "The concept of the monarch is therefore the most difficult of all for raisonnement, i.e. for the reflective method employed by Understanding, because raisonnement is stuck in isolated categories and hence knows only particular reasons, finite points of view, and *deductive* argumentation. Thus it presents the dignity of

the monarch as something *deduced* not only in form but also in substance. But the concept of the monarch is not something deduced but rather *absolutely self-originating*. Most relevant to this point" (obviously!) "is the idea of regarding the monarch's right as based on the authority of God, for the authority of God contains the unconditional character of the monarch's right."

To some degree any necessary particular existence is "absolutely self-originating"; the monarch's lice as well as the monarch himself. With this Hegel says nothing special about the monarch. But if Hegel means that something should hold for the monarch which is specifically different from all other objects of scientific knowledge of philosophy and law, this is plain foolishness and correct only insofar as the *"one* person-idea" is something to be deduced from imagination and not from Understanding.

"We may speak of *sovereignty of the people* in the sense that a people after all is independent *in relation to others* and constitutes a state of its own," etc.

This is a triviality. If the monarch is the "actual sovereignty of the state," "the monarch" would have to be considered an "independent state" also in relation to others, even without the people. Should he be sovereign, however, he represents the unity of the people, and he is then only a representative, a symbol of the sovereignty of the people. The sovereignty of the people does not exist through him, but he exists through it.

"We can also speak of *internal sovereignty* residing in people, providing we are only speaking of the *whole,* just as we have shown above (§ 277, 278) that sovereignty belongs to the *state.*"

As if the people did not constitute the actual state! The state is an abstraction. Only the people is a concrete fact. And it is peculiar that Hegel attributes a living quality such as sovereignty to a concrete fact only with stipulations and reservations, although he attributes it to an abstraction without any stipulations.

"But the sovereignty of the people, as in *antithesis to the sovereignty existing in the monarch*—that is the usual sense of sovereignty of the people, as it has become known in modern times. In this antithesis the sovereignty of the people is one of confused notions which are rooted in the *wild* idea of the *people*."

The "confused notions" and the *"wild* idea" are here only Hegel's. To be sure, if sovereignty *exists* in the monarch, it is foolishness to speak of an antithetical sovereignty in the people, for the concept of sovereignty implies that sovereignty can have no double or conflicting existence. But:

1. The question is: Isn't sovereignty as absorbed in the monarch an illusion? Sovereignty of the monarch or of the people, that is the question.

2. We can speak also of a sovereignty of the people *in antithesis to sovereignty existing in the monarch*. But then we do not deal with *one and the same sovereignty* manifesting itself in two aspects, but we are dealing with two *completely opposed concepts of sovereignty*, of which one is such that it can exist in a *monarch*, and the other is such that it can exist only in a *people*. We may ask likewise: Is God the sovereign or is man? One of these alternatives is an untruth, even if it is an existing untruth.

"*Without* its monarch and **thereby** the necessary and immediate *organization* of the whole, the people is a formless mass and no longer a state. It no longer has *any* of the determinations which are present only in an *organized* whole—sovereignty, government, courts, magistrates, classes, and so on. Since such moments bearing on an organization and on the political life appear in a people, the people ceases to be this indeterminate abstraction which by way of a merely popular notion is called the people."

This whole thing is a tautology. When a people has a monarch and a necessary and immediate organization with him, that is, when the people is organized as a monarchy, it certainly is a formless mass when taken out of this organization, and a merely popular notion.

"If by popular sovereignty is meant a *republic* and even more specifically a democracy . . . we can no longer speak of such a notion in the face of the developed idea [of the state]."

This is correct, of course, as long as one has only "such a notion" and no "developed idea" of democracy.

Democracy is the truth of monarchy; monarchy is not the truth of democracy. Monarchy is necessarily democracy as an inconsequence and excrescence, the monarchial aspect is not an inconsequence of democracy. Democracy can, monarchy cannot, be conceived in its own terms. In democracy none of the aspects acquires any other meaning than the appropriate one. Each is actually only an aspect of the whole demos. But in monarchy a part determines the character of the whole. The entire constitution must conform to a fixed point. Democracy is the generic constitution. But monarchy is a modification and indeed a bad one. Democracy is content and form. Monarchy *might* be only form, but it falsifies the content.

In monarchy, the whole, the people, is subsumed under one of its particular modes of existence, under political constitution. In democracy the *constitution itself* appears only as *one* determination, and indeed the self-determination of the people. In monarchy we have the people of the constitution; in democracy the constitution of the people. Democracy is the solution of the *problem* of all constitutions. In democracy the constitution is always based on its actual foundation, on *actual man* and the *actual people,* not only *implicitly* and in its essence, but in its *existence* and actuality. Here the constitution is man's and the people's *own* work. The constitution appears as what it is: the free product of man. One could say that in some respect this is true also of constitutional monarchy, but the specific difference in democracy is that here the *constitution* is only *one* particular moment of the people and that the *political constitution* in itself does not form the state.

Hegel proceeds from the state and makes man into the state subjectivized. Democracy proceeds from man and makes the state into man objectivized. Just as religion does not create man, but man creates religion, so the constitution does not create the people, but the people create the constitution. In some respects democracy is related to all other forms of state, as Christianity is related to all other religions. Christianity is religion κατ' ἐξοχήν, the *essence of religion*, deified man as a *particular* religion. Similarly democracy is the *essence of every* constitution, socialized man as a *particular* constitution. Democracy is related to other constitutions as a species is related to its modifications. Only, in democracy the species itself is existent as a *particular* modification distinct from existences that do not correspond to their essence. Democracy is the Old Testament of all other forms of state. Man does not exist for the law, but the law exists for man. In democracy there is *particular human existence*, while in other forms of state man is the *particular juridical existence*. This is the basic uniqueness of democracy.

All other *state formations* are a certain, definite, *particular form of state*. In democracy the *formal* principle is at the same time the *material* principle. Only democracy, therefore, is the true unity of the general and the particular. In monarchy, for example, and in a republic as only a particular form of state, political man has his particular existence alongside unpolitical man, private man. Property, contract, marriage, civil society here appear as *particular* modes of existence alongside the *political* state (Hegel develops this quite correctly for these *abstract* forms of state, only he *believes* that he develops the idea of the state). They appear as the *content* related to the *political state* as the *organizing form*, actually only as determining, limiting understanding, contentless in itself, at one time affirmative, at another time negative. In democracy the political state, as it stands beside this content and is distinguished from it, is itself only a *particular* content as a people's particular *form of existence*. In monarchy, for example, this particularity, the political constitution, means the *universal* dominating and determining everything particular. In democracy the state as particular is *only* particular, as universal as the actual universal, that is, it is nothing determinate in contrast to any other content. Recently the French have conceived of this in such a way that the *political state disappears* in true democracy. This is correct insofar as the political state as such, as constitution, no longer applies to the whole.

In any other state than democracy the *state*, the *law*, the *constitution* is the dominant factor even without actually dominating, that is, without materially penetrating the content of other non-political spheres. In democracy the constitution, the law, the state itself insofar as it is politically constituted, is only a self-determination of the people and a particular content of the people.

It is quite obvious then that all forms of the state have democracy *for* their truth and hence are untrue if they are not democracy.

In the ancient states the political state formed the state's content by the exclusion of the other spheres. The modern state is an accommodation between the political and the unpolitical state.

In democracy the *abstract* state has ceased being the dominating factor. The struggle between monarchy and republic is itself still a struggle inside the abstract state. The *political* republic is democracy inside the abstract form of state. Democracy's abstract form of state is, hence, the republic. Here, however, it ceases to be the *merely political* constitution.

Property, etc., in short, the entire content of law and state is the same in North America and in Prussia, with few modifications. In North America the *republic* is thus a mere *form* of the state as monarchy is here. The content of the state remains outside these constitutions. Hegel is right, therefore, when he says: the political state is the constitution, that is, the material state is not political. There is only an external identity here; a mutual determination takes place. Of the various phases in a people's life the most difficult was the formation of the political state, the constitution. It emerged as universal reason in contrast to other spheres, and as the aspect most removed from these spheres. The historical problem then was their revindication, but the particular spheres are not aware that their private nature coincides with the distant nature of the constitution or political state, and the far removed existence of the political state is nothing but the affirmation of their own alienation. Up to now the *political constitution* has been the *religious sphere*, the *religion* of the people's life, the heaven of their universality in contrast to the particular *mundane existence* of their actuality. The political sphere was the state's only sphere within the state in which both content and form were a generic content and the genuine universal, but in such a way that its content became formal and particular because these spheres stood in contrast to each other. *Political life* in the modern sense of the word is the *scholasticism* of a people's life. *Monarchy* is the completed expression of this alienation. The *republic* is the negation of alienation within alienation. It is obvious that a political constitution as such is formed only where the private spheres have achieved independent existence. Where trade and property are unfree and still not independent, the political constitution also is unfree and still not independent. The Middle Ages were the *democracy of unfreedom.*

The abstraction of the *state as such* belongs only to modern times because the abstraction of private life belongs only to these times. The abstraction of the *political state* is a modern product.

In the Middle Ages there was the serf, the fief, the guild, the scholastic corporation, etc., that is to say, in the Middle Ages property, trade, society, man was *political.* The material content of the state was set by its form. Each private sphere had a political character or was one political sphere, and politics was characteristic of the private spheres. In the Middle Ages the political constitution was the constitution of private property but only because the constitution of private property was political. In the Middle Ages the life of the people and the life of the state were identical. Man was the actual principle of the state, but it was man as *unfree.* Thus it was the *democracy of unfreedom,* perfected alienation. The abstract, reflected antithesis belongs only to the modern world. The Middle Ages is *actual* dualism; the modern period is *abstract* dualism.

"At the previously mentioned stage with the division of constitutions into democracy, aristocracy, and monarchy—at the view of a **substantial unity** still **remaining in itself and still not having arrived at its infinite differentiation and deepening within itself**—the moment of the *final self-determining decision of the will* does not emerge explicitly into its *own actuality* as an *immanent* organic moment of the state."

Initially in monarchy, democracy, and aristocracy there is as yet no political constitution in contrast to the actual, material state or to the other content of the people's life. The political state does not appear as yet as the *form* of the material state. Either the res publica is the actual private life and the actual content of the citizens, as was the case in Greece where the political state as such was the only true content of their life and will and a private man was a slave; or the political state is nothing but the private arbitrariness of a particular individual, as was the case in Asiatic despotism, where the political state, like the material one, was a slave. The difference between the modern state and those states with a substantial unity of state and people does not exist in the fact that the various aspects of the constitution achieved *particular* actuality, as Hegel has it, but rather that the constitution itself has achieved *particular* actuality alongside actual popular life and that the political state has become the *constitution* of the rest of the state.

### Civil Society and Bureaucracy: On Hegel's § 287–97

§ 287. "We distinguish between the monarch's **decision** and its **execution** and **application,** or in general the continuance and maintenance of past decisions, existing laws, regulations, institutions for common purposes, and the like. The *governing power* implicitly embraces this task of *subsuming* [the particular under the universal] and this power includes also the powers of *the judiciary and the police*. The latter powers have a more immediate bearing on the particulars of civil society and manifest the universal interest in these aims."

The customary explanation of the governing power. The only *unique* thing in Hegel is that he *co-ordinates governing power*, police power, and *judicial power*, while others treat administrative and judicial powers as antitheses.

§ 288. "The common *particular* interests fall within civil society and lie outside the state proper as completely existent universal (§ 256). Their administration is in the hands of municipal, commercial, and professional corporations (§ 251) and their officials, directors, managers, and the like. On the one hand, the corporations deal with *private property* and matters of *interest* to these *particular* areas, and in this respect their authority depends upon the confidence of their equals and commonalties. On the other hand, the corporations must be subordinate to the higher interests of the state. For the filling of the offices, therefore, there will generally be a combination of popular election by those interested, with appointment and confirmation by a higher authority."

A simple description of the empirical condition in several countries.

§ 289. "The *maintenance* of the *state's universal interest* and of *legality* in these particular rights and the re-establishment of these rights on the basis of this interest and legality require the service of deputies of the governing power: namely, the executive *civil servants* and the higher advisory officials organized in committees which converge at the top level and have contact with the monarch."

Hegel has not *developed* the governing power. But even if he had, he did not prove that the governing power is more than *a function* and a *determination* of the citizen. He has only deduced it as a *particular separate* power by considering the "particular interests of civil society" as such, "lying outside the completely existent and universal interest of the state."

"Just as civil society is the battleground of the individual interests of each against all, so here takes place the conflict of private interest with the particular matters of common concern and the conflict of both of these together against the higher perspective and organization of the state. The corporation spirit, engendered when particular spheres gain their title to rights, is at the same time converted into the spirit of the state, since it finds in the state the means for maintaining its particular ends. This is the **secret** of the citizens' patriotism in the respect that they know the state as their substance, *because* the state maintains their particular spheres of interest together with the title, authority, and welfare of these spheres. Since the *rooting* of the *particular in the universal* is *immediately* contained in the corporation spirit, that spirit is the depth and the strength which the state possesses in *sentiment*."

This is noteworthy

1. because of the definition of civil society as bellum omnium contra omnes;

2. because *private egoism* is revealed as the *"secret of the citizens' patriotism"* and as the "depth and strength of the state in sentiment";

3. because the "citizen," the man of particular interests in contrast to the universal, the member of civil society, is considered to be a "fixed individual," while the state in "fixed individuals" stands opposed to the "citizens."

Hegel should have defined "civil society" as well as "family"—hence also the subsequent "political qualities" —as determinations of any given political individual. But it is not the same individual which develops a new determination of his social essence. It is the will's essence which is supposed to develop its determinations from itself. Distinct, separate, and empirical political existences are taken to be immediate incarnations of one of these determinations.

Hegel makes the universal as such autonomous, immediately puts it on the same basis as empirical existence, and uncritically takes limited existences for the expression of the Idea.

Hegel contradicts himself here only insofar as he does not consider "man in family" to be as much a fixed faction and as much excluded from other qualities as the citizen.

§ 290. "There is also a *division of labor* in **governmental affairs** [ . . . ]. The organization of officials, therefore, has the formal, but difficult task of arranging matters in such a way that from below, where civil life is *concrete*, it should be governed in a concrete way and that this activity is divided into *abstract* branches. These are dealt with by special officials in distinct departments whose operations at the lower level converge again in concrete supervision as they do in the supreme governing power."

The *Addition* to this paragraph is to be considered below.

§ 291. "The nature of governmental affairs is *objective* and already explicitly fixed by their substance (§ 287), to be carried out and actualized by *individuals*. Between governmental affairs and individuals there is no immediate **natural** link. Hence individuals are not predetermined by native endowment and birth to hold office. The objective fact in their appointment to office is the recognition and proof of ability—a proof guaranteeing that the state is satisfied, and a proof which at the same time is the only condition that any citizen has the **chance** of becoming part of the universal class of civil servants."

§ 292. "Since the objective criteria are not based on genius (as in art, for example), there is by necessity an indefinite *plurality* of candidates among whom the preference for a particular individual is not determinable with absolute precision. This subjective aspect of selecting and appointing the individual to an office and empowering him to transact public business, this uniting of individual and office both always fortuitous in relation to each other, belongs to the crown as the deciding and sovereign power in the state."

§ 293. "The particular affairs of state which the **crown** entrusts to officials, constitute a part of the *objective* aspect of the sovereignty residing in the monarch. The specific *differentiation* among the officials is also determined by the subject matter. While the activity of the officials is a fulfillment of their duty, their office is also a right exempt from contingency."

The only noteworthy item here is the *"objective* aspect of the sovereignty *residing* in the monarch."

§ 294. "When the individual is appointed to an official position by a sovereign act (§ 292), his tenure is conditional on the fulfillment of his duties, the essential part of his office. *As the result* of this essential part he finds the livelihood, the assured satisfaction of his particular interests (§ 264), and the release of external circumstances and official activity from other subjective dependency and influence."

"The service of the state," Hegel says in his Remark, "requires [ . . . ] the renunciation of selfish and capricious satisfaction of subjective purposes. By this very renunciation there is created the right to find satisfaction in dutiful achievement, and only in that. So far as public business is concerned, here lies the link between universal and particular interests, constituting the concept of the state and its inner stability (§ 260)." "The assured satisfaction of particular needs removes the external pressure which may induce a man to seek ways and means of satisfying his needs at the expense of official activity and duty. Those who are entrusted with the affairs of state find in its universal power the protection against another subjective matter, against the private passions of the governed whose private interests, etc., are injured as the universal interest prevails against them."

§ 295. "The security of the state and its subjects against the misuse of power by authorities and officials lies immediately in their hierarchy and accountability, but also in the rights of societies and corporations. Thereby the injection of subjective caprice into the power given to the official is implicitly checked, and the control from above which does not extend to the conduct of individuals is supplemented from below."

§ 296. "Direct *ethical* and *intellectual* education— in balance with the mechanical activity of acquiring the so-called sciences of matters connected with administration, with the requisite service training in the actual work, etc.—in part makes impartiality, uprightness, and politeness *customary* in civil servants. The *size* of the state is another main factor because it weakens the weight of family ties and other private bonds and diminishes and dampens revenge, hatred, and other passions. In the occupation with the large interests present in the large state these subjective interests disappear by themselves and the habit is created of thinking in terms of general interests, points of view, and activities."

§ 297. "The members of the government and the civil servants constitute the main part of the *middle class* where is found the educated intelligence and the consciousness of right in the mass of a people. The **institutions of sovereignty** from above and the **rights of corporations** from below prevent the middle class from assuming the isolated position of an aristocracy and using its education and skills as means for arbitrariness and tyranny."

"*Addition*. Political consciousness and superior education are prominent in the middle class to which civil servants belong. This class, therefore, is the main pillar of the state as to honesty and intelligence." "Developing this middle class is a prime concern of the state. But it can happen only in an organization like the one described here: by giving authority to particular, relatively independent spheres and by creating a **corps of officials** whose arbitrariness is checked by the authorized spheres. Action in terms of universal right and the habit of such action is the result of the antithesis created by these spheres, independent by themselves."

What Hegel says about the "governing power" does not deserve the name of a philosophical development. Most of the paragraphs could be taken verbatim from the Prussian Civil Code. Yet the actual administration is the most difficult point of the development.

Since Hegel already vindicated "police" and "judicial" power for the sphere of *civil society,* the *governing power* is nothing but that administration which he develops as *bureaucracy*.

The *"self-administration"* of civil society in *"corporations"* presupposes bureaucracy. Hegel's only additional requirement is that the choice of administrators, superiors, etc., be *mixed*, with the initiative coming from the citizens and the confirmation from the particular governing power (Hegel's *"higher* confirmation").

Above the sphere serving the "maintenance of the state's universal interest and of legality" are to be *"deputies* of the governing power," the "executive civil servants," and the "officials organized in committees," all converging in the "monarch."

In "governmental affairs" a "division of labor" takes place. The individuals must prove their ability in governmental matters, by passing examinations. The choice of *particular* individuals for political office is the prerogative of the crown. The allocation of these matters is "determined by the subject matter." Holding office is the duty and the life vocation of civil servants. Therefore, the state must *pay* them *salaries*. The guaranty against the malfeasance of the bureaucracy is partly its hierarchy and accountability, partly the authorization given to communities, corporations. Bureaucracy's humaneness partly depends on "direct ethical and intellectual education," partly on the "size of the state." The officials constitute the "main part of the middle class." Both the "institutions of sovereignty from above" and "the rights of corporations from below" are a safeguard against "aristocracy and tyranny." The "middle class" is the class of "education." That is all. Hegel gives us an empirical description of bureaucracy, partly as it actually is, partly as bureaucracy thinks of itself. And that is the end of the difficult chapter on "governing power."

Hegel proceeds from the *separation* of the "state" and "civil" society, from "particular interests" and the "completely existent universal." And bureaucracy is indeed based on *this separation*. Hegel proceeds from the premise of "corporations." And bureaucracy indeed presupposes *corporations* or at least the "corporation spirit." Hegel develops no *content* for bureaucracy, only some general definitions of its *"formal"* organization. And indeed bureaucracy is only the "formalism" of a content lying outside.

The *corporations* are the materialism of bureaucracy, and bureaucracy is the *spiritualism* of the corporations. The corporation is the bureaucracy of civil society; bureaucracy is the corporation of the state. In actuality, therefore, bureaucracy as the "civil society of the state" stands opposed to the "state of civil society," the corporations. When "bureaucracy" is a new principle, when the universal interest of the state starts to become something "apart" by itself and thereby an "actual" interest, bureaucracy conflicts with the corporations just as any consequence conflicts with the existence of its presuppositions. But as soon as actual political life emerges and civil society frees itself from the corporations by its own rational impulse, bureaucracy tries to restore them. For as soon as the "state of civil society" falls, the "civil society of the state" also falls. The spiritualism disappears with the materialism opposed to it. The consequence struggles for the existence of its presuppositions, as soon as a new principle struggles not against the *existence* but against the *principle* of this existence. The same spirit that creates the corporation in society, creates bureaucracy in the state. The spirit of bureaucracy is attacked along with the spirit of the corporation. If bureaucracy earlier attacked the existence of corporations to make room for its own existence, it now attempts to sustain forcefully the existence of the corporations so as to preserve the corporation spirit, which is its own spirit.

"Bureaucracy" is the *"state formalism"* of civil society. It is the "state's consciousness," the "state's will," the "state's power," as *a corporation,* hence a *particular, closed* society in the state. (The "universal interest" can maintain itself as a "particular" in relation to particulars only so long as the particular can maintain itself as a "universal" in relation to universals. Bureaucracy, therefore, must protect the *imaginary* universality of the particular interest, namely the corporation spirit, so as to protect the *imaginary* particularness of the universal interest, namely its own spirit. The state must be a corporation as long as the corporation wants to be a state.) Bureaucracy, however, wants the corporation as an *imaginary* power. To be sure, the individual corporation also wishes to maintain its *particular* interest against bureaucracy, but it *wants* bureaucracy against other corporations, against other particular interests. Bureaucracy as the *completed corporation,* therefore, is victorious over the *corporation* as uncompleted bureaucracy. Bureaucracy denigrates the corporation as mere appearance, or rather wants to denigrate it, but it wants this appearance to exist and believe in its own existence. The corporation is the attempt of civil society to become the state; but bureaucracy is the state which in actuality has become civil society.

The "state formalism" of bureaucracy is the "state as formalism," and Hegel has described it as such formalism. Since this "state formalism" constitutes itself as an actual power and becomes its own *material* content, it is obvious that "bureaucracy" is a web of *practical* illusions or the "illusion of the state." The spirit of bureaucracy is thoroughly Jesuitical and theological. The bureaucrats are the state's Jesuits and theologians. Bureaucracy is the priest's republic.

Since bureaucracy is the "state as formalism" in its *essence,* it is also the state as formalism in its *purpose.* For bureaucracy the actual purpose of the state therefore appears as a purpose *against* the state. The spirit of bureaucracy is the "formal state spirit." Bureaucracy makes the "formal state spirit" or the *actual* spiritlessness the categorical imperative. Bureaucracy considers itself the ultimate finite purpose of the state. Since bureaucracy converts its "formal" purposes into its contents, it everywhere comes in conflict with "real" purposes. It is, therefore, compelled to pass off what is formal for the content and the content for what is formal. The purposes of the state are changed into purposes of bureaus and vice versa. Bureaucracy is a circle no one can leave. Its hierarchy is a *hierarchy of information.* The top entrusts the lower circles with an insight into details, while the lower circles entrust the top with an insight into what is universal, and thus they mutually deceive each other.

Bureaucracy is the imaginary state beside the real state, the spiritualism of the state. Hence everything has a double meaning, a real and a bureaucratic meaning, just as knowledge and also the will are something double, real, and bureaucratic. What is real is dealt with in its bureaucratic nature, in its otherworldly spiritual essence. Bureaucracy possesses the state's essence, the spiritual essence of society, as its *private property*. The universal spirit of bureaucracy is the *secret*, the mystery sustained within bureaucracy itself by hierarchy and maintained on the outside as a closed corporation. The open spirit and sentiment of patriotism, hence, appear to bureaucracy as a *betrayal* of this mystery. So *authority* is the principle of its knowledge, and the deification of authority is its *sentiment*. But within bureaucracy *spiritualism* becomes a *crass materialism*, the materialism of passive obedience, of faith in authority, of the *mechanism* of fixedly formal activity, fixed principles, views, and traditions. For the individual bureaucrat the state's purpose becomes his private purpose of *hunting for higher positions* and *making a career* for himself. In one respect he views actual life as something *material*, for *the spirit of this life has its separate existence* in bureaucracy. Bureaucracy, therefore, must aim to make life as material as possible. In another respect, life insofar as it becomes the object of bureaucratic treatment is material for him, for his spirit is not his own, his purpose lies outside, his particular existence is the existence of the bureau. The state then only exists in various fixed bureau-spirits whose connection is subordination and passive obedience. *Actual* knowledge seems lacking in content, just as actual life seems dead, since this imaginary knowledge and this imaginary life pass for real. So the bureaucrat must treat the actual state Jesuitically, no matter whether this Jesuitism is conscious or unconscious. It is necessary, though, that the Jesuitism, aware of its antithetical position, then achieves self-consciousness and becomes intentional.

While the bureaucracy is in one sense this crass materialism, its crass spiritualism is shown in its trying *to do every-*

*thing,* that is, in its making *will* the causa prima, because it is merely *active* particular existence, derives its content externally, and thus can demonstrate its existence only through forming and limiting this content. For the bureaucrat the world is a mere object of his concern.

If Hegel calls the governing power the *objective* side of sovereignty residing in the monarch, this is correct in the same sense as the Catholic church was the *real particular existence* of the Holy Trinity's sovereignty, content, and spirit. In bureaucracy the identity of the state's interest and particular private purpose is established in such a way that the *state's interest* becomes a *particular* private purpose opposed to other private purposes.

The transcendence of bureaucracy can mean only that the universal interest becomes the particular interest *in actuality* and not, as with Hegel, merely in thought and *abstraction.* This is possible only when the *particular* interest becomes *universal.* Hegel proceeds from an unreal antithesis and hence develops it only to an imaginary identity really antithetical to itself. Such an identity is the bureaucracy.

Now let us pursue his development in detail.

The only philosophical definition Hegel presents concerning the *governing power* is that of *"subsumption"* of the individual and the particular under the universal, etc.

Hegel is satisfied with that. On one side: the category of the "subsumption" of the particular, etc. This category must be actualized. Then he takes any of the empirical existences of the Prussian or modern state (as it is in toto), which among other things also actualizes this category, although its specific nature is not expressed in this way. Applied mathematics is also subsumption, etc. Hegel does not ask whether this is the rational and adequate mode of subsumption. He sticks only to *one* category and is content to discover a corresponding existence for it. Hegel gives *his logic a political body;* he does not give the *logic of the body politic* (§ 287).

Concerning the relationship of corporations and communities to the government, we learn first that their *administration* (the designation of the magistracy) requires "generally a combination of popular election by those interested, with appointment and *confirmation by a higher authority*." The *combined selection* of community and corporation officials would thus be the *first relationship* between civil society and the state or governing power, its *first identity* (§ 288). According to Hegel himself, this identity is very superficial, a mixtum compositum, a "*combination*." As superficial as this identity is, the antithesis is as sharp. "Since these matters" (i.e. of the corporation, the community, etc.) "on the one hand are *private property* and matters of *interest* to these *particular* areas, and in this respect their authority depends upon the confidence of their equals and commonalties; since on the other hand the corporations must be subordinate to the *higher interests of the state,*" there results the so-called "*combined selection.*"

The administration thus has the antithesis: *Private property and the interest of particular areas as opposed to the higher interest of the state: antithesis between private property and state.*

We need not mention that the resolution of this antithesis in the *combined selection* is a mere *accommodation,* a treaty, a *confession* of the unresolved dualism, itself a *dualism* or "*combination.*" The *particular* interests of the corporation and communities have a dualism within *their own areas* which also shapes the character of their *administration.*

"But the antithesis becomes obvious in the relationship of these *common particular* interests," etc., which "lie outside the *state* as completely existent universal" to this "*state as completely existent universal.*" Further, it is obvious again within this area.

"The maintenance of the state's universal interest and of legality in these particular rights and the re-establishment of these rights on the basis of this interest and legality requires the *service* of *deputies* of the *governing power:* namely, the *executive civil servants* and the higher advisory officials organized in *committees* which converge at the top level and have contact with the monarch" (§ 289).

Incidentally we call attention to the establishment of governmental *committees,* which are not known in France, for example. *"Insofar"* as Hegel mentions these officials as *"advisory," "insofar"* is it indeed obvious that they are "organized in committees."

Hegel has the "state proper," the "governing power," move into the "service" of the "state's universal interest and of legality, etc." within civil society through "deputies." According to him these "governing deputies" are particularly the "executive civil servants," the *true "representation of the state"* not "of," but "against civil society." Thus the antithesis of state and society is fixed. The state does not reside in but outside civil society. The state makes contact with civil society only through its *"deputies,"* to whom *"service of the state"* is entrusted within this area. The antithesis is not transcended through these "deputies," but becomes a "legal" and "fixed" antithesis. With the deputies against civil society the "state" amounts to something apart from and alien to the *nature* of civil society. "Police," "courts," and "administration" are not deputies of civil society itself, which maintains its *own* universal interest in them and through them, but they are deputies of the state to safeguard the state against civil society. Hegel further makes this *antithesis* explicit in the frank Remark [on § 289] considered earlier.

"The nature of governmental affairs is *objective* and already explicitly fixed [ . . . ]" (§ 291).

Does Hegel conclude that for this very reason they do not require a "hierarchy of information" and that they can be completely carried out by "civil society itself"? On the contrary.

He makes the profound comment that they are to be carried out by "individuals" and that between "governmental affairs and these individuals there is no immediate *natural* link." This alludes to princely power which is nothing but the *"natural power of arbitrariness"* and thus can be *"born."* The "princely power" is nothing but the representative of the aspect of nature in will, of the "dominance of *physical nature in the state."*

The "executive civil servants" differ essentially from the "prince" through acquiring their office.

"The objective factor in their appointment to office" (i.e. in state employment) "is the recognition" (subjective arbitrariness lacks this aspect) "and proof of ability—a proof guaranteeing that the state is satisfied, and a proof which at the same time is the only condition that *any citizen* has the *chance* of becoming part of the *universal* class of civil servants." This *chance* of any citizen to become a civil servant is thus the second affirmative relationship between civil society and the state, the *second identity*. It is very superficial and dualistic. Any Catholic has the chance to become a priest (i.e. to divorce himself from the laity as well as the world). Is priesthood, therefore, as a power separate and beyond, any less opposed to the Catholics? The fact that anyone has the chance to acquire the right to *another* sphere merely proves that *his own* sphere has not actualized this right.

What counts in the genuine state is not the chance of any citizen to devote himself to the universal class as something special, but the capacity of the universal class to be actually universal, that is, to be the class of every citizen. But Hegel proceeds from the premise of a pseudo-universal, an illusory-universal class, from the premise of universality as a particular class.

The identity Hegel has set up between civil society and the state is the identity of *two hostile armies*, where any soldier has the "chance" to join the "enemy" through "desertion." Thus does Hegel correctly describe the existing empirical situation.

## Representation and Voting:
### On Hegel's § 308

§ 308. "The other part of the estates [in contrast to the agricultural class] is the *mobile* side of *civil society*. This element can come forth only through *deputies*, externally because of the number of its members, but essentially because of the nature of its character and occupation. Since these deputies are deputies of civil society, it follows that their appointment is made by civil society *as such*—civil society not dispersed into atomic units and not only gathered momentarily and impermanently for a single and temporary act, but rather organized into associations, communities, and corporations. These groups, already constituted for other purposes, in this way acquire a connection with politics. The existence of the estates and their assembly has a constitutional guarantee of its own in the fact that they are **entitled** to send deputies at the summons of the crown, while the agricultural class is entitled to appear in person" (§ 307).

Here we find a *new* distinction within civil society and its estates: a *mobile* part and an *immobile* part (landed property). This distinction has also been presented as *space* and *time,* conservative and progressive, etc. [in Hegel's previous paragraphs]. Incidentally, through groups like the corporations Hegel makes the *mobile* part of society into a *stable* part.

The second distinction consists in the fact that the first part of the *estates* as developed above, the *landlords* as such, are legislators; that the legislative power is an attribute of their empirical personal existence; that they act in their *own* capacity and not as *deputies.* In the second part of the estates, however, *election* and *selection of deputies* take place.

Hegel states two reasons why this *mobile* part of civil society can enter the political state and legislative power only through *deputies.* Hegel himself calls the *great number* of this part, the first reason, *external* and relieves us of any need for a reply.

But the *essential* reason, so he claims, is the "nature of its character and occupation." "Political activity and occupation" is something alien to "the nature of its character and occupation."

Hegel plays again his old song about these estates as *"deputies* of civil society." Their appointment, according to Hegel, must be made by civil society *as such.* Rather, civil society must do this for what it is *not,* because it is *unpolitical* and here would perform a *political* act as something *essential to it* and proceeding from itself. With this, civil society is "dispersed into atomic units" and "only gathered momentarily and impermanently for a single and temporary act." First of all, its *political* act is *single and temporary* and can appear that way in its being carried out. It is an act of political society which produces a *hub-bub*. It is an *ecstasy* of political society and must *appear* as such. Secondly, Hegel was not bothered by the fact—he even construed it as necessary—that civil society, only as a *second society deputized by it, materially* separates itself from its civil actuality and makes itself what it is *not*. How can he dispose of this *formally*?

Hegel says that society's associations, etc., which are already constituted for other purposes, acquire a "connection *with politics*" through the fact that society is ordered into corporations, etc. But either they acquire a significance which is *not* their significance, or their connection as such *is* political and does not *"acquire"* the political coloration, as developed above. Rather, "politics" acquires its connection in this way. By designating only this part of the estates as that of the "deputy," he has unwittingly stated the nature of the two Chambers (and at a point where they do have the relationship he indicated). The Chamber of Deputies and the Chamber of Peers (or whatever they may be called) are here not separate instances of one principle but belong to *two* essentially *separate principles* and social orders. The Chamber of Deputies is here the *political constitution* of civil society in the modern sense; the Chamber of Peers, in the sense pertaining to *estates*. In terms of estates and *politics* the Chamber of Peers and the Chamber of Deputies represent civil society in opposition. The one is the *existing* principle of civil society, pertaining to estates; the other is the actualization of the *abstract political* existence of civil society. Hence, it is obvious that the latter cannot come *into being* again as representation of *estates*, corporations, etc., for it simply does not represent the existence of civil society pertaining to estates but rather the existence pertaining to politics. Furthermore, it is obvious that only the part of civil society pertaining to estates, "landed property as sovereign," hereditary nobility, is seated in the former Chamber, for this part is not *one* estate among other estates. Rather, the estate principle of civil society as actually social, hence political, principle exists *merely* in that part which is *the* estate. Civil society then represents its medieval existence in the chamber *of the estates,* its *political* (modern) existence in the Chamber of Deputies. The only progress beyond the Middle Ages consists in the fact that the *politics pertaining to estates* has been downgraded into a separate political existence alongside the politics *of citizenship.* The *empirical* political existence which Hegel has in mind (*England*) has a meaning quite different from the one he imputes to it.

The French Constitution is a step forward here too. To be sure, it has reduced the Chamber of Peers to a mere formality. But this Chamber, *within the principle* of constitutional monarchy, as Hegel has pretended to develop it, can only be a *formality* by its very nature, a *fiction* of harmony between prince and civil society, between *legislative power* or *political state with itself,* as a particular and thus again *contrasting* existence.

The French left the *life tenure* of the peers intact in order to express their independence equally from government and the people. But they abolished the *medieval* expression—*hereditariness.* Their step forward consists of the fact that they no longer have the *Chamber of Peers* emerge from *actual civil* society, but have created it in *abstraction* from civil society. They have the selection of peers proceed from the *existing* political state, from the *prince,* without binding him to any other civil quality. The honor of being a *peer* in this *constitution* is really a political *estate in civil society,* created from the standpoint of the *political state* as abstraction. But it appears more as *political decoration* than an actual *estate* with particular rights. The Chamber of Peers during the Restoration was a reminiscence. The Chamber of Peers during the July Revolution is an *actual* creature of constitutional monarchy.

Since in modern times the idea of the state could appear in no other way but in the *abstraction* of the *"merely* political state" or of the *abstraction of civil society from itself,* from its actual condition, it is to the merit of the French that they have marked and produced this *abstract actuality* and thus the *political* principle itself. The abstraction for which they are blamed is a genuine consequence and the product of a *patriotism rediscovered* in an opposition, to be sure, but in necessary opposition. Thus the merit of the French here is that they have established the Chamber of Peers as a *unique* product of the political state and have in general made the political principle in its *uniqueness* the determining and effective element.

Hegel also says that in the selection of deputies, as he construes it, in "entitling corporations, etc., to send deputies . . . the *existence* of the estates and their assembly has a constitutional guarantee of its own." The *guarantee of the existence* of the estates' assembly, their truly *original* existence, thus becomes the *privilege* of the corporations, etc. Saying this, Hegel completely reverts to the medieval point of view and has entirely abandoned his abstraction of the political state as the sphere of the state as such, the "completely existent universal."

In the modern sense, the *existence* of the *estates' assembly* is the *political existence* of civil society, the *guarantee* of its political presence. The doubting of its existence is thus *doubt about the presence of the state.* With Hegel, "patriotism"—the essence of legislative power—is guaranteed by "independent private property"; similarly the *existence* of civil society is guaranteed by the "privileges of corporations."

But the one element pertaining to the estates is rather the *political privilege* of civil society, or civil society's *privilege* to be *political.* This element thus can never be the privilege of a particular mode of civil society and still less find its guarantee in that mode, because it *should* be, rather, the universal guarantee.

In this way Hegel reverts to the point where he ascribes to the "political state" a precarious actuality contingent in *relation to something else* instead of describing it as the highest, completely existent actuality of social existence. He does not describe "political state" as the true existence of the other sphere, but rather permits it to find *its true ex-*

*istence* in the other sphere. Everywhere the political state needs the guarantee of outside spheres. It is not actualized power. It is a *supported* impotence. It is not the power over these supports, but the power of support. The support is the element of power.

What sort of existence would need a guarantee outside of itself? And at the same time be the *universal* guarantee, its actual guarantee? In the development of the legislative power Hegel everywhere retreats from the philosophical standpoint to the other standpoint which fails to investigate the matter *in its own terms*.

If the existence of the estates needs a guarantee, then they constitute *no actual*, but only a *fictitious political existence*. In constitutional states, *law* guarantees the existence of the estates. This existence is *legal* existence as the actuality of *association in the state*, dependent on the nature of the state as universal, and not on the power or powerlessness of various corporations and associations. (Only here should the corporations, etc., particular areas of civil society, come into existence. Again Hegel *anticipates* this universal existence as privilege, as the presence of these particular areas.)

Political law as the law of corporations, etc., completely contradicts political law as *political*, as the law of the state and citizenship. After all, political law should not be the law of this existence as particular; it should not be the law as this particular existence.

Before we discuss the category of *election* as the political act by which civil society decides upon its political representation, let us look at some additional definitions taken from the Remark on this paragraph.

"The idea that all as individuals should participate in deliberating and deciding on political matters of general concern because everyone is a member of the state, because the state's concerns are the concern of *all*, and because they have a *right* to participate with their knowledge and will—this idea resulted in the intention to put the *democratic* element *without any rational form* into the organism of the state which would need such a form to be an organism. This idea

occurs so readily because it stops at the *abstract* definition of being a member of the state; and superficial
thinking clings to abstractions."

First of all, Hegel calls "being a member of the state
an *abstract* definition," although it is the highest and *most
concrete* social definition of the legal person, of the member of the state—and this even in accordance with the *Idea,*
the *meaning* of his own development. To stop at the "definition of being a member of the state" and to conceive of
the individual in terms of this definition does not after all
seem to be the "superficial thinking that clings to abstraction." However, it is not the fault of this thinking that the
"definition of being a member of the state" is *"abstract";*
it is the fault of Hegel's train of thought and of actual
modern conditions which presuppose the separation of actual life from political life and turn the quality of the state
into an "abstract definition" of actual political participation.

The immediate participation of *all* in deliberating and
deciding on political matters of general concern according
to Hegel incorporates "the *democratic* element *without
any rational form* into the organism of the state which
would *need* such a form to be an organism." In other
words, only a state organism that is merely the formalism
of the state can incorporate the democratic element as a
*formal* element. But the democratic element should be the
actual element that acquires its *rational form* within the
state organism as a *whole.* If this element enters the state
organism or state formalism as a *"particular"* element, then
by "rational form" of its existence is meant a drill, an accommodation, a form in which the element does not exhibit the particularity of its essence. It would appear only
as a *formal* principle.

We have already indicated that Hegel develops merely a
*state formalism.* For him the only *material* principle is the
*Idea,* the abstract thought-*form* of the state as subject, the
absolute Idea lacking any passive, any *material* aspect. In
contrast to this abstract Idea, the definitions of the actual,
empirical state-formalism appear as *content.* Thus the *ac-*

*tual* content (here actual man, actual society, etc.) appears as formless, inorganic matter.

Hegel had seen the essence of the estates in the fact that the "empirical universality" becomes the subject of the completely existent universal. What else could that mean except that the state's concerns "are the concern of *all* and that they have a *right* to participate in them with their knowledge and will?" And shouldn't the estates constitute this actualized right? Is it surprising then that everyone claims the "actuality" of what is his by right?

"The idea that *all* as individuals should participate in deliberating and deciding on political matters of general concern . . ."

In a really rational state one could answer, "It is not the case that *all as individuals* should participate in deliberating and deciding on political matters of general concern," for the "individuals" participate in deliberating and deciding on political matters of *general concern* as "all," that is, within society and as parts of society. Not all as individuals, but the individuals as all.

Hegel presents himself with a dilemma. Either civil society (the mass, the multitude) participates through deputies in deliberating and deciding on political matters of general concern, or all do this as *individuals*. This is no contradiction in *essence*, such as Hegel attempts to present later, but rather a contradiction in *existence*, the most external existence, in *quantity*. The basis that Hegel himself has designated as *"external"—the multitude of members*—provides the best argument against the immediate participation of all. *The question* whether civil society is to participate in legislative power *either* through *deputies* or immediately through "all as individuals" is itself a question within the *abstraction of the political state* or within the *abstract political state;* it is an *abstract* political question.

In both cases, as Hegel himself has developed the matter, is found the political meaning of "empirical universality."

The contradiction essentially is: the *individuals participate as all,* or the *individuals* participate as *few, not all.* In either case the allness is only the *external* multiplicity or totality of individuals. The allness is no essential, no spiritual, no actual quality of the individual. The allness is not something that could deprive the individual of abstract individuality; rather it is only the *sum* total of *individuality*. *One* individuality, *many* individualities, *all* individualities. The one, the mass, the all—none of these qualifications alters the *essence* of the subject, individuality.

"All" should "as individuals . . . participate in deliberating and deciding on political matters of general concern." On this basis, then, *all* should not participate as all, but as "individuals."

The issue seems to contradict itself in two respects.

The political matters of general concern are the state's concern, the state as *actual concern*. Deliberations and decisions are the *effectuation* of the state as actual concern. It seems obvious that all members of the state have a *relationship* to the state as their *actual concern*. The term *member of the state* already implies being a *part* of the state and the state's including it as *its part*. However, if the member of the state is an *integral part* of the state, its social *presence* obviously is already *its actual participation* in the state. They *are* not only integral with the state, but the state is integral *with them*. To be consciously integral with something means to take part in it consciously, to be consciously integral with it. Without this consciousness the member of the state would be an *animal*.

With the phrase, "political matters of general concern," it appears as though the "matters of general concern" and the "state" are something *different*. But the *state* is the "matter of general concern," hence really, "matters of general concern."

To take part in the political matters of general concern and to take part in the state are identical. It is a *tautology* to say that a member of the state, a part of the state, takes part in the state, and this taking part can appear only in the form of deliberation or decision, or some such forms, and to say at the same time that every member of the state participates in *deliberating* and *deciding* on political matters of general concern (if these functions are conceived as functions of the *actual* participation of the state). If Hegel speaks of *actual* members of the state, he cannot speak of this participation as something that *should be*. Otherwise he would speak of subjects that *should* be or *want* to be *members of the state* but really *are* not.

Furthermore, if he is talking about *specific* concerns, about a single political act, it is obvious again that it is not accomplished by *all as individuals*. In that case the individual would be the *true* society, making society superfluous. The individual would have to do everything at once, while society has him act for others, just as it has others act for him.

The question whether *"all as individuals* participate in deliberating and deciding on political matters of general concern" arises from the separation of the political state from civil society.

We have seen how the state exists *only* as *political state*. The totality of the political state is the *legislative power*. To take part in this legislative power is therefore to take part in the political state, to prove and actualize one's *existence* as a *member of the political state* or as a *member of the state*. The fact that *all as individuals* wish to take part in legislative power is nothing but the will of *all* to be actual (active) *members of the state*, to give themselves a *political existence*, or to prove and effectuate their *political* existence. We have also seen that the element pertaining to the estates is *civil society* as legislative power, the *political existence* of civil society. The invasion of civil society *en masse*, where possible *totally*, into legislative power and its will to substitute itself as actual for a *fictitious* legislative power—this is nothing but the drive of civil society to give itself *political* existence or to make its *political existence* actual. The drive of *civil society* to become political or to make *political* society *actual* is evident as a drive toward participation in *legislative power* as *universal* as possible.

*Quantity* is not without significance. The increase of the *element pertaining to the estates* is already a physical and intellectual increase of one of the *hostile* forces, and we have seen that the different elements of the legislative power are divided into hostile forces. Hence the question as to whether all as individuals should be members of the legislative power or whether they should enter it through deputies throws into question the *representative* principle within the principle of representation and within the fundamental perspective of the political state existing in constitutional monarchy. 1. The view of the political state as an abstraction is the view that the *legislative power* is the *totality* of the political state. Since this *one* act is the only *political* act of civil society, *all* should and want to participate in it at once. 2. *All* as *individuals.* In the *element pertaining to estates* the legislative activity is not viewed as *social* or a function of *sociality,* but rather as the act in which individuals assume an actually and *consciously social* function, that is, a political function. The *legislative power* is here no outcome, no function of society, but only its *formation.* The formation into legislative power demands that *all* members of civil society regard themselves as *individuals* and act as such. "To be members of the state" is their "abstract definition," a definition which is not realized in living actuality.

There are two possibilities: (1) The political state and civil society are separated. In that case it is not possible that *all as individuals* participate in legislative power. The existence of the political state is *separated* from that of civil society. If all were to be legislators, civil society would have to abolish itself. On the other hand, the political state distinct from civil society can only tolerate it in a form that satisfies its *criterion.* Or the participation of civil society in the political state through *deputies* is precisely the *expression* of the separation and merely dualistic unity.

(2) The reverse may occur: Civil society is *actual* political society. Then it would be nonsense to make a claim which has emerged only from the notion of the political state as an existence separated from civil society and from the *theological* notion of the political state. In this situation the significance of *legislative* power as a *representative* power disappears altogether. The legislative power is here representation in the sense that *every* function is representative, as the cobbler, for example, is my representative when he meets a social need; as every specific social activity in a field represents only that field or a specification of my own nature; and as every man is the representative of oth-

ers. He is the representative not through something else that he appears to be, but through what he *is* and *does*.

"Legislative" power is something to be aimed at not because of its *content*, but because of its *formal* political significance. Concretely, the goal of popular desire has to be *governmental power* much more than the legislative, *metaphysical* political function. The legislative function is will, not in its practical but in its theoretical energy. Here *will* should not *displace law*, but the *discovery* and *formulation* of actual law is the important thing.

From this split nature of legislative power as actual *legislating* function and as *representative, abstract-political* function emerges a peculiarity especially important in France, the nation of political culture.

(There are always *two* things in *governmental power*: the actual deed and the reason of state for this deed, as another actual consciousness which in its entire structure is bureaucracy.)

If the prevailing special *interests* do not significantly conflict with the objectum quaestionis [object of investigation], the real content of legislative power is treated as something very much apart, as secondary. A problem attracts special attention only when it becomes *political,* that is, when ministerial responsibility is involved, in other words the force of legislative power over governmental power, or when it is a matter of rights in general connected with the political formalism. How does this happen? Because legislative power is also the representative of the political existence of civil society, because the political nature of an issue generally is found in its relationship to the different powers of the political state, and because legislative power represents political consciousness manifesting itself as *political* only in conflict with governmental power. The essential demand that every social need, law, etc., be *politically* evolved and *determined by the entire state* in the *social* sense, is modified in the state as political abstraction in that a *formal* stand against another force (content) is attributed to it besides its actual content. This is no French abstraction, but a necessary consequence because the actual state exists only as the *political state-formalism* as observed above. The *opposition* within the representative power is the κατ' ἐξοχὴν [principal] political existence of representative power. Within the representative constitution, however, the issue is somewhat different from the one that Hegel discusses. It is not a question whether civil society should exercise legislative power through deputies or through all as individuals. Rather it is a question of the *extent* and greatest possible *universalization* of *voting*, of *active* as well as *passive* suffrage. This is the real bone of contention of political *reform*, in France as well as in England.

If *voting* is immediately put into the context of *princely* or *governmental power*, it is not viewed philosophically, not in its own special nature. *Voting* is the *actual relationship* of *actual civil society* to the *civil society* of the *legislative power*, to the *representative element*. Or, *voting* is the *immediate, direct* relationship of civil society to the political state, not *only in appearance but in existence*. Hence it is obvious that *voting* is the paramount political interest of actual civil society. Only in *unlimited voting*, active as well as passive, does civil society *actually* rise to an abstraction of itself, to *political* existence as its true universal and essential existence. But the realization of this abstraction is also the transcendence of the abstraction. By making its *political existence* actual as its *true* existence, civil society also makes its civil existence *unessential* in contrast to its political existence. And with the one thing separated, the other, its opposite, falls. Within the *abstract political state* the reform of voting is the *dissolution* of the state, but likewise the *dissolution of civil society*.

# AN EXCHANGE OF LETTERS

[Having decided to resign from the *Rheinische Zeitung* and no longer "work in servitude" to censors, Marx wrote to Arnold Ruge in March 1843 about collaboration on a new journal to embody a "Gallo-German principle"—a union of the French heart in politics with the German head in philosophy—suggested by Feuerbach in the *Anekdota*. Ruge agreed to help finance the *Deutsch-Französische Jahrbücher* in Paris with Marx as salaried co-editor. A double issue of the *Jahrbücher*, the first and last, appeared in February 1844. In the prefatory "Plan of the *Jahrbücher*" Ruge spoke of stifling hypocrisy in Germany, the "cosmopolitan mission" of France in respect to liberty, and Hegelian philosophy as providing a "celestial map," which reason must move into earthly politics.

The first of the articles in the *Jahrbücher* was a series of letters among Marx, Ruge, Bakunin, and Feuerbach. Marx's letters, translated below, opened and closed the series. Their dates cover the period in which Marx married Jenny von Westphalen, completed his "Critique of Hegel's Philosophy of the State," and drafted his essay "On the Jewish Question." Marx probably revised his letters early in 1844, particularly the last letter criticizing "abstract" socialism and calling for action plus criticism to realize the "demands of reason" in the modern state "not yet conscious of socialistic demands." Marx's letters reveal his sensitivity to German events foreshadowing revolution. They also suggest that his nascent socialism, his dedication to "a community of men" inspired by freedom and aiming at democracy, was distinctly indebted to Feuerbach's humanism and to Hegel's conception of reason in history.]

On the barge to D. in March 1843

I am traveling in Holland now. As much as I can see from the local and French papers, Germany is deep in the mire and gets into it more and more. I assure you, even though one feels nothing of national pride, one does feel national shame, even in Holland. The least Hollander is still a citizen in comparison with the greatest German. And those judgments of foreigners on the Prussian government! A frightening agreement is prevailing concerning that; no longer is anyone deceived about this system and its simple nature. The new school was of some avail, after all. The splendid cloak of liberation has been dropped, and the most repulsive despotism stands in all its nakedness for the whole world to see.

This is also a revelation, though a perverted one. It is a truth that at least teaches us to recognize the hollowness of our patriotism, the unnatural character of our governmental system, and to turn our faces away in shame. Smiling, you look at me and ask, "What is gained thereby? No revolution results from shame." I answer, "Shame already is a revolution." Shame actually is the victory of the French Revolution over German patriotism by which the Revolution was conquered in 1813. Shame is a type of anger, introverted anger. And if a whole nation were really ashamed, it would be a lion crouched to spring. I admit, even shame is not yet present in Germany. On the contrary, the wretched Germans are still patriots. But what system could exercise patriotism except this ridiculous one of our new knight [Friedrich Wilhelm IV]? The comedy of despotism being performed with us is just as dangerous for him as the tragedy once was for the Stuarts and the Bourbons. And even if for a long time we would not see this comedy for what it is, it would still be a revolution. The state is too serious a thing to be made into a harlequinade. A shipload of fools might drift in the wind for quite a time, but it would meet its doom for the very reason that the fools do not believe this. This doom is the impending revolution.

[Ruge's answer to Marx was deeply pessimistic. Quoting bitter words on Germany from Hölderlin's *Hyperion*, Ruge insisted that there were no prospects whatsoever of a political revolution. He bewailed the Germans' "eternal submissiveness" and wondered whether one should not console himself with the thought that "man is not born to be free." In resignation he concluded: "You may reproach me as being no better than the others; you may challenge me to usher in a new era with a new principle and be a writer whom a free century follows; you may say as many bitter things as you please, but I am ready. Our nation has no future, so what is the use of our summons to it?" Responding to this "elegy" in the letter that follows, Marx finds hope in the present desperate situation because it contains promise of new life, a new humanity. "The system of industry and commerce, of property and the exploitation of men" foreshadows a rupture in society. Germany cannot indefinitely shackle "a suffering mankind which thinks and a thinking mankind which is suppressed."]

Cologne, in May 1843

Your letter, dear friend, is a good elegy, a choking funeral lay. But it is not political at all. No nation despairs. And if it should hope for a long time out of mere stupidity, it will at some time, perhaps after many years, realize its pleasant wishes out of sudden insight.

Yet, you have stimulated me. Your theme is still not finished. I should like to add the finale, and when all is done, you will give me your hand so that we may begin anew again. Let the dead bury their dead and mourn them. To be the first among the living to enter into new life, on the other hand, is enviable. This is to be our lot.

It is true: the old world belongs to the Philistine. But we must not treat him like a terror from which one flees in fear. Rather, we must face up to him bluntly. To study this master of the world is rewarding.

To be sure, he is master of the world only by filling it with his company, as worms fill a corpse. The society of these masters, therefore, needs nothing but a number of slaves whose property need not be free. If on account of their properties of land and people they are called masters in the eminent sense, they are for that reason no lesser Philistines than their people.

Human beings would have to be men of intellect; free men would have to be republicans. Old fogies want to be neither. What else is left to them but to exist and to be in want?

What they want, namely, to live and propagate themselves (and, as Goethe says, no one achieves more than this), the animal wants too. At most a German politician would still add that man *knows* that he wants to live and propagate himself and that the German is so sober-minded as to wish nothing further.

Freedom, the feeling of man's dignity, will have to be awakened again in these men. Only this feeling, which disappeared from the world with the Greeks and with Christianity vanished into the blue mist of heaven, can again transform society into a community of men to achieve their highest purposes, a democratic state.

The people, though, who do not feel themselves to be men, grow attached to their masters, like a herd of slaves or horses. The hereditary masters are the purpose of this whole society. This world belongs to them. They take it as it is and as it feels. They take themselves as they find themselves, and they stand where their feet have grown, on the necks of these political animals that know of no other destination than to be attached to the masters and subject to them, to be at their disposal.

The world of the Philistine is the *political animal kingdom,* and if we have to recognize its existence, we simply must acknowledge the status quo. Centuries of barbarism created and formed it, and now it exists as a consistent system, whose principle is the *world dehumanized.* The perfect world of the Philistine, our Germany, had to remain, of course, far behind the French Revolution, which again restored man to himself. A German Aristotle, who would derive his politics from our conditions, would start out by stating, "Man is a social, but completely apolitical animal." He could not explain the state more correctly than Herr Zöpfl has already done in his *Constitutional Law in Germany.* According to Zöpfl the state is an "association of families," which, so we continue to read, is the hereditary and proprietary possession of a most eminent family called the dynasty. The more prolific the families prove to be, the happier are the people; the bigger the state, the more powerful is the dynasty. For this very reason in normally despotic Prussia an award of fifty Reichstaler is paid for the seventh male offspring.

The Germans are such sober-minded realists that all their wishes and most high-flown thoughts do not go beyond the mere necessities of life. And those who govern this reality accept it and nothing else. These people, too, are realists. They are far removed from all thinking and human greatness; they are ordinary officers and landholders. But they are not mistaken; they are right. Just as they are they completely suffice to use and govern this animal kingdom, for ruling and using is *one* concept here as everywhere. And when they allow themselves to be venerated and gaze over the countless heads of those brainless creatures, what is then closer to them than Napoleon's thought at the Beresina? He is said to have pointed to a crowd of drowning soldiers and to have called out to his companion: *Voyez ces crapauds!* [Look at those toads!] This epithet is probably spurious, but it contains an element of truth nevertheless. Despotism's only idea is contempt for man, dehumanized man, and this idea further has the advantage over many others of being a fact. A despot always sees men as degraded. He sees them drown for him in the mud of common life from which they again and again emerge like toads. If this view forces itself even upon men capable of great achievements, like Napoleon before his dynastic fever, how could a very ordinary king be an idealist in such a reality?

The principle of monarchy in general is man despised, despicable, *dehumanized*. Montesquieu is quite wrong in honoring this principle. He avails himself of the differentiation of monarchy, despotism, and tyranny. But these are various terms for *one* concept. At most they constitute modal differences of the same principle. Where the monarchical principle is in the majority, men are in the minority; where it is not challenged, there are no men. Why should not someone like the King of Prussia, not having any evidence that he might be a problematic figure, simply give in to his caprice? And now that he does so, what happens? Contradictory purposes? Well, nothing comes of that. Feeble tendencies? They still are the only political reality. Disgraces and embarrassments? There is only *one* real disgrace and *one* real embarrassment, giving up the throne. As long as caprice stands its ground, caprice is in the right. However inconsistent, brainless, and contemptible it wants to be, it is still good enough to govern a people that has never known any other law than the arbitrariness of their kings. I do not say that a brainless system and the loss of respect, internally and externally, will remain without consequences. I do not claim the security of the ship of fools. I do assert, however, that the King of Prussia will be a man of his time as long as the perverted world is the actual one.

As you know, I am much concerned with this man. Already at the time when he had only the *Berliner politisches Wochenblatt* as his mouthpiece, I recognized his worth and destination. As early as the homage ceremony at Königsberg he justified my hunch that the matter might now become purely personal. He declared his heart and mind would be the future basic law of the domain of Prussia, *his* state. And in fact in Prussia the king is the political system. He is the only political person. His personality determines the system as this or that. Whatever he does or is allowed to do, whatever he thinks or is put into his mouth, is what in Prussia the state thinks or does. Hence it is actually a good thing that the present King has declared this so unequivocally.

One was only mistaken for a while in considering it important which wishes and thoughts the King would bring forth. This could not change anything in substance. The Philistine is the matériel of monarchy, the monarch always but the king of the Philistines. He can turn neither himself nor his people into free, real men if both parties remain what they are.

The King of Prussia has attempted to change the system with a theory his father [Friedrich Wilhelm III] did not have in mind at all. The outcome of this attempt is well known. It has failed completely, and quite naturally so. Once one has reached the threshold of the political animal kingdom, no further movement and no other withdrawal are possible than to leave its basis and enter the human world of democracy.

The old King did not want anything extravagant. He was a Philistine and made no claims as to his intellect. He knew that only a prosaic, quiet existence was required to possess the servants' state. The young King was more lively and agile. He had bigger ideas concerning the omnipotence of a monarch constrained only by his heart and reason. He loathed the old fossilized servants' and slaves' state. He wanted to bring life into the state and thoroughly penetrate it with his wishes, feelings, and thoughts; and as long as he would succeed, he could demand that much in *his* state. Hence his liberal speeches and outpourings. Not dead law, but the entire live heart of the King was to govern all subjects. He intended to set into motion all hearts and minds for his heart's wishes and plans many years old. A movement resulted, but the other hearts did not beat with his. The ruled could not open their mouths without speaking of the removal of the old rulership. The idealists spoke up with their brazenness of wanting to turn man into man. While the King indulged in old German fancies, they thought they were permitted to philosophize in new German terms. To be sure, this was unheard of in Prussia. For a moment the old order of things seemed to be reversed. Indeed, things began to assume human forms. There even were men with names of renown, although referring to persons by name is not permitted in parliamentary sessions. The servants of the old despotism, however, soon killed these un-German activities. It was not difficult to confront at close range the wishes of the King, who is in raptures about the great past of clergy, knights, and bondsmen, with the intentions of the idealists who merely want the results of the French Revolution, thus in the final analysis a republic and an order of free mankind instead of an order of dead things. When this conflict had become sharp and uncomfortable enough, and the rash King sufficiently excited, the servants who in former times had directed the course of events with so much ease approached him and declared: the King was misguided in enticing his subjects to inappropriate utterances. One would not be able to govern a generation of men who speak their mind. Even the ruler of all East Russians [Nicholas I] had become concerned about the commotion in the mind of the West Russians [i.e. Prussians] and demanded restoration of the old, quiet conditions. There resulted a new edition of the old disrespect of all men's wishes and thoughts about human rights and duties. That meant a regression to the old fossilized servants' state, in which the slave serves in silence and the owner of land and people rules as silently as possible, merely by the instrument of a well-trained, quietly obedient retinue. Neither party can say what it wants to say: neither the dehumanized, that they want to become human, nor the ruler, that he has no use for human beings in his country. Silence, therefore, is the only expedient. *Muta pecora, prona et ventri oboedientia* [The crowd is silent, submissive, and obeys its stomach].

This is an account of the miscarried attempt to lift the Philistine state up on its own foundation. It has led to an extreme point in that it has exemplified for despotism throughout the world the necessity of brutality and the impossibility of humaneness. A brutal relationship can be maintained only with brutality. And with this I have now finished our joint task of bluntly facing up to the Philistine and his state. You will not say that I value the present time too highly. And if I do not despair, it is only the desperate situation of the present that fills me with hope. I am not talking at all of the ineptness of the rulers and of the indolence of the servants and of the ruled who permit everything to run its course. Yet, together they would suffice to bring about a catastrophe. I only have to call your attention to the fact that the enemies of Philistinism, in other words all thinking and all suffering men, have arrived at an understanding for which formerly they lacked the means. Every day the passive system of perpetuation on the part of the old subjects raises recruits for the service of a new humanity. The system of industry and commerce, of property and the exploitation of men, however, leads much more rapidly to a rupture within the present society than the increase of the population. The old system cannot heal this rupture because it does not heal and create at all; it merely exists and enjoys itself. The existence of a suffering mankind that thinks and of a thinking mankind that is suppressed must necessarily become unpalatable and indigestible for the passive animal kingdom of Philistinism, which is thoughtlessly enjoying itself.

It is up to us to expose the old world to full daylight and to shape the new along positive lines. The more time the events allow for thinking men to reflect and for suffering men to rally, the better will be the product to be born which the present carries in its womb.

[The letters of Bakunin and Feuerbach in response to Ruge's "elegy" were encouraging and hopeful. "This is no time," wrote Bakunin, "for folding our arms, for cowardly despair." What is to be done? "We must root out metaphysical arrogance, which never makes the world warm; we must learn; we must work night and day so we can live like men with men, so we can be free and free others." Feuerbach granted that in Germany everything was rotten. "Everything needs to be rebuilt from the ground up, the work of united forces." This requires a purging of the head, of theory and philosophy. The head must be "yoked under practice [*Praxis*] and learn to live humanly in this world on the shoulders of active men." Practice unites many heads and has a mass effect in the world. A new journal for a new principle is itself indispensable practice. After Feuerbach's letter Ruge addressed himself to Marx. He has been converted to atheism and "the new philosophers," so Hegelian philosophy belongs to the past. "We must establish an organ here in Paris in which we can criticize ourselves and all Germany with complete freedom and honesty." Marx's reply in the following final letter, however, sees "criticism" as involving action and a Hegelian view of "reason in society."]

Kreuznach, in September 1843

I am glad that you are determined and turn your thoughts from retrospect on the past toward a new undertaking. Hence to Paris, the old high school of philosophy, *absit omen!* and the new capital of the new world. Whatever is necessary comes to pass. I do not doubt, therefore, that all obstacles, whose weight I do not underestimate, can be removed.

The undertaking may come about or not. At any rate I shall be in Paris at the end of this month, because the air here makes me a serf and I see no room at all for free activity in Germany.

In Germany everything is suppressed by force. A real anarchy of the mind, the regime of stupidity itself, has set in, and Zurich obeys the orders coming from Berlin. It is becoming clearer and clearer, therefore, that a new gathering point for the really thinking and independent minds must be sought. I am convinced that a real demand will be met by our plan, and it must be possible really to fulfill the real demand. I have no doubts about the undertaking, once we mean business.

Even greater than the external obstacles seem to be the inner ones. Even though there is no doubt about the "whence," there does prevail all the more confusion about the "whither." It is not only the fact that a general anarchy has broken out among the reformers; each one will have to admit to himself that he has no exact idea of what is to happen. But that is exactly the advantage of the new direction, namely, that we do not anticipate the world dogmatically, but rather wish to find the new world through criticism of the old. Until now the philosophers had the solution to all riddles in their desks, and the stupid outside world simply had to open its mouth so that the roasted pigeons of absolute science might fly into it. Philosophy has become secularized, and the most striking proof for this is the fact that the philosophical consciousness itself is drawn into the torment of struggle, not only outwardly but inwardly as well. Even though the construction of the future and its completion for all times is not our task, what we have to accomplish at this time is all the more clear: *relentless criticism of all existing conditions,* relentless in the sense that the criticism is not afraid of its findings and just as little afraid of the conflict with the powers that be.

I am not for setting up a dogmatic standard. On the contrary, we must attempt to help the dogmatists make their dogmas clear to themselves. Especially *communism* thus is a dogmatic abstraction; I have in mind the actually existing communism, as Cabet, Dézamy, Weitling, etc., teach it, not some other imagined or possible one. This communism is itself only a separate phenomenon of the humanistic principle, infected by its opposite, private advantage. Dissolution of private property, therefore, is in no way identical with communism, and communism saw the origin of other socialistic doctrines like those of Fourier, Proudhon, etc., not accidentally but necessarily in opposition to itself, because communism itself is only a special, one-sided realization of the socialistic principle.

And the entire socialistic principle, in turn, is only one side of the *reality* of true human nature. We have to be concerned just as much with the other side, the theoretical life of man. Hence, we have to make religion, science, etc., the object of our criticism. Moreover, we wish to influence our contemporaries, our German contemporaries. The question is how to go about it. Two facts cannot be denied; religion and politics are matters now forming focal points of Germany's interest. No matter how these may be, we must begin with them, not oppose them with any one fixed system, as for example the *Voyage to Icaria* [by Etienne Cabet].

Reason has always existed, but not always in rational form. The critic, therefore, can start with any form of theoretical and practical consciousness and develop the true actuality out of the forms *inherent* in existing actuality as its ought-to-be and goal. As far as actual life is concerned, the *political state* especially contains in all its *modern* forms the demands of reason, even where the political state is not yet conscious of socialistic demands. And the political state does not stop here. Everywhere it claims reason as realized. Equally, however, it everywhere gets into the contradiction between its ideal character and its real presuppositions.

Social truth, therefore, can be developed everywhere out of this conflict of the political state with itself. Just as *religion* is the table of contents of the theoretical struggles of mankind, the *political state* is that of the practical ones. The political state, therefore, expresses all social struggles, needs, and truths within its form *sub specie rei publicae*. By no means, then, is the most specific political problem—such as the difference between the estate system and the representative system—to be the object of our critique on account of the *hauteur des principes*. For this question merely expresses in a *political* way the difference between the control of man and the control of private property. The critic not only can but must enter into these political problems, which crass socialists regard as below their dignity. By developing the advantage of the representative system over the estate system the critic gets a large party *interested practically*. By elevating the representative system from its political context to a general context and by claiming the true significance that is due to it, he at the same time forces this party to go beyond itself, for its victory is simultaneously its loss.

Nothing prevents us, therefore, from starting our criticism with criticism of politics, with taking sides in politics, hence with *actual* struggles, and identifying ourselves with them. Then we do not face the world in doctrinaire fashion with a new principle, declaring, "Here is truth, kneel here!" We develop new principles for the world out of the principles of the world. We do not tell the world, "Cease your struggles, they are stupid; we want to give you the true watchword of the struggle." We merely show the world why it actually struggles; and the awareness of this is something the world *must* acquire even if it does not want to.

The reform of consciousness exists *merely* in the fact that one makes the world aware of its consciousness, that one awakens the world out of its own dream, that one *explains* to the world its own acts. Our entire purpose consists in nothing else (as is also the case in Feuerbach's criticism of religion) but bringing the religious and political problems into the self-conscious human form.

Our slogan, therefore, must be: Reform of consciousness, not through dogmas, but through analysis of the mystical consciousness that is unclear about itself, whether in religion or politics. It will be evident, then, that the world has long dreamed of something of which it only has to become conscious in order to possess it in actuality. It will be evident that there is not a big blank between the past and the future, but rather that it is a matter of *realizing* the thoughts of the past. It will be evident, finally, that mankind does not begin any *new* work but performs its old work consciously.

Therefore, we can express the aim of our periodical in *one* phrase: A self-understanding (critical philosophy) of the age concerning its struggles and wishes. This is a task for the world and for us. It must be the work of united forces. It is a *confession,* nothing else. To have its sins forgiven, mankind has only to declare them for what they are.

# ON THE JEWISH QUESTION

[Marx drafted the following review-essay in Kreuznach near the end of his work on the "Critique of Hegel's Philosophy of the State" and his reading on the French Revolution and American society. Criticizing Bauer's view of Jewish emancipation as incomplete, Marx here develops a major theme of his "Critique"—the split between "civil society" as the battle of individual interests and "the state" as an abstract, ideal universality. This split involves religion as Feuerbach viewed it, man's projection of his basic values into an ideal, heavenly realm to be recovered for man. But Feuerbach, Marx had already complained, was "too much concerned with nature and too little with politics." Marx regards political emancipation through a state with universal rights of conscience, property, and equality, as a step forward. But it demotes religion and property to "civil society," the private realm where man is egoistic, separated from his fellows, and alienated from himself in commodities and money as shown in politically emancipated America. Life in civil society is epitomized in Judaism, which is perfected in Christianity. This has been seen as Marx's anti-semitism, but his essential animus was against the dehumanizing alienation of civil society. With exclusively political emancipation, Marx argues, the state as a community uniting men remains alien and abstract. For full emancipation man must achieve community in everyday life and work, thus transcending the political state even with universal rights of man. Such emancipation, often identified as Marx's transition to socialism, was prefigured in his "Critique" of Hegel, in "democracy" as transforming civil society into "socialized man" through unrestricted voting.]

## Bruno Bauer, The Jewish Question, Braunschweig, 1843

The German Jews want emancipation. What kind of emancipation? *Civil, political* emancipation.

Bruno Bauer answers them: No one in Germany is politically emancipated. We are not free ourselves. How shall we liberate you? You Jews are *egoists* when you claim a special emancipation for yourselves as Jews. As Germans, you should work for the political emancipation of Germany, as men, for the emancipation of mankind; and you should feel the particular form of your oppression and shame not as an exception to the rule but rather as its confirmation.

Or do Jews desire to be put on an equal footing with *Christian subjects?* If so, they recognize the *Christian state* as legitimate, as the regime of general subjugation. Why should they be displeased at their particular yoke if the general yoke pleases them? Why should Germans be interested in the liberation of Jews if Jews are not interested in the liberation of Germans?

The *Christian* state takes cognizance only of *privileges.* In it the Jew has the privilege of being a Jew. As a Jew he has rights that Christians do not have. Why does he want rights he does not have and that Christians enjoy?

If the Jew wants to be emancipated from the Christian state, he is demanding that the Christian state abandon its *religious* prejudice. But does the Jew abandon *his* religious prejudice? Has he, then, the right to demand of another this abdication of religion?

By *its very nature* the Christian state cannot emancipate the Jew; but, Bauer adds, the Jew by his very nature cannot be emancipated. So long as the state remains Christian and the Jew remains Jewish, both are equally incapable of giving as well as receiving emancipation.

The Christian state can only behave toward the Jew in the manner of the Christian state—that is, permitting the separation of the Jew from other subjects as a privilege but making him feel the pressure of the other separate spheres of society, and feel them all the more heavily, since he stands in *religious* opposition to the predominant religion. But the Jew in turn can behave toward the state only in a Jewish manner, that is as a foreigner, since he opposes his chimerical nationality to actual nationality, his illusory law to actual law. He imagines that his separation from humanity is justified, abstains on principle from participation in the historical movement, looks to a future that has nothing in common with the future of mankind as a whole, and regards himself as a part of the Jewish people, the chosen people.

On what basis, then, do you Jews want emancipation? On the basis of your religion? It is the mortal enemy of the religion of the state. As citizens? There are no citizens in Germany. As men? You are not men, just as those to whom you appeal are not men.

After criticizing previous positions and solutions, Bauer formulates the question of Jewish emancipation in a new way. What is the *nature,* he asks, of the Jew who is to be emancipated and the Christian state that is to emancipate him? He answers with a critique of the Jewish religion, analyzes the *religious* antagonism between Judaism and Christianity, and explains the essence of the Christian state —all this with dash, acuteness, wit, and thoroughness in a style as precise as it is pregnant and energetic.

How then does Bauer settle the Jewish question? What is the result? The formulation of a question is its solution. Criticism of the Jewish question provides the answer to the Jewish question. The résumé thus follows:

We must emancipate ourselves before we can emancipate others.

The most persistent form of the antagonism between the Jew and the Christian is the *religious* antagonism. How is an antagonism to be resolved? By making it impossible. And how is a *religious* antagonism made impossible? By *abolishing religion.* Once Jew and Christian recognize their respective religions as nothing more than *different stages in the evolution of the human spirit,* as different snake skins shed by *history,* and recognize *man* as the snake that wore them, they will no longer find themselves in religious antagonism but only in a critical, *scientific,* and human relationship. *Science,* then, constitutes their unity. Contradictions in science, however, are resolved by science itself.

The *German* Jew is particularly affected by the general lack of political emancipation and the pronounced Christianity of the state. With Bauer, however, the Jewish question has a universal significance independent of specific German conditions. It is the question of the relation of religion to the state, of the *contradiction between religious prejudice and political emancipation*. Emancipation from religion is presented as a condition both for the Jew who seeks political emancipation and for the state which is to emancipate him and is to be emancipated itself as well.

"Very well, you say—and the Jew himself says it— the Jew should not be emancipated because he is Jew or because he has such excellent and universal ethical principles but rather because he takes second place to the *citizen* and becomes one in spite of being and wanting to remain a Jew. That is, he is and remains a Jew in spite of the fact that he is a *citizen* living in universally human relationships; his Jewish and restricted nature always triumphs in the end over his human and political obligations. The *prejudice* remains even though it has been overtaken by *universal* principles. But if it remains, it rather overtakes everything else." "The Jew could remain a Jew in political life only in a sophistical sense, only in appearance; thus if he wanted to remain a Jew, this mere appearance would become the essential thing and would triumph. In other words, his *life in the state* would be only a semblance or a momentary exception to the real nature of things, an exception to the rule." ("The Capacity of Present-day Jews and Christians to Become Free," *Twenty-one Sheets from Switzerland* [*Einundzwanzig Bogen aus der Schweiz*], p. 57.)

Let us see, on the other hand, how Bauer describes the role of the state:

"France," he says, "recently (Proceedings of the Chamber of Deputies, 26 December 1840) gave us, in connection with the Jewish question and all other *political* questions (since the July Revolution), a glimpse of a life which is free but which revokes its freedom by law, thus revealing it to be a sham, and on the other hand, denies its free law by its acts." (*The Jewish Question*, p. 64.)

"Universal freedom is not yet established as law in France, and the *Jewish question is not yet settled* because legal freedom—that all citizens are equal—is limited in actual life which is still dominated and fragmented by religious privileges, and because the lack of freedom in actual life reacts on the law, compelling it to sanction the division of inherently free citizens into the oppressed and the oppressors" (p. 65).

When, therefore, would the Jewish question be settled in France?

"The Jew, for instance, would really have ceased being a Jew if he did not let himself be hindered by his code from fulfilling his duties toward the state and his fellow citizens—if he went, for example, to the Chamber of Deputies and took part in public affairs on the Sabbath. Every *religious privilege,* including the monopoly of a privileged church, would have to be abolished, and if a few or many or *even the overwhelming majority still felt obliged to fulfill their religious duties,* such a practice should be left to *them* as a *purely private matter*" (p. 65). "There is no longer any religion if there is no privileged religion. Take from religion its power of excommunication and it ceases to exist" (p. 66). "Just as M. Martin du Nord saw the proposal to omit any mention of Sunday in the law as a declaration that Christianity had ceased to exist, with equal right (and one well-founded) a declaration that the Sabbath-law is no longer binding for the Jew would proclaim the end of Judaism" (p. 71).

Bauer thus demands, on the one hand, that the Jew give up Judaism and man give up religion in order to be emancipated *as a citizen.* On the other hand, he holds that from the *political* abolition of religion there logically follows the abolition of religion altogether. The state which presupposes religion is as yet no true, no actual state. "To be sure, the religious view reinforces the state. But what state? *What kind of state?*" (p. 97).

At this point Bauer's *one-sided* approach to the Jewish question becomes apparent.

It is by no means sufficient to ask: Who should emancipate and who should be emancipated? Criticism has to be concerned with a third question. It must ask: *What kind of emancipation* is involved and what are its underlying conditions? Criticism of *political emancipation* itself is primarily the final critique of the Jewish question and its true resolution into the *"universal question of the age."*

Since Bauer does not raise the question to this level, he falls into contradictions. He presents conditions that are not based on the essence of *political* emancipation. He raises questions that are irrelevant to his problem and solves problems that leave his question untouched. Bauer says of the opponents of Jewish emancipation, "Their mistake simply lay in assuming the Christian state to be the only true state without subjecting it to the same criticism they applied to Judaism" (p. 3). Here we find Bauer's mistake in subjecting *only* the "Christian state," not the "state as such," to criticism, in failing to examine the *relation between political emancipation and human emancipation,* and hence presenting conditions that are only explicable from his uncritical confusion of political emancipation with universal human emancipation. Bauer asks the Jews: Have you the right to demand *political emancipation* from your standpoint? We ask, on the contrary: Has the standpoint of *political* emancipation the right to demand from the Jews the abolition of Judaism and from man the abolition of religion?

The Jewish question has a different aspect according to the state in which the Jew finds himself. In Germany, where there is no political state and no state as such exists, the Jewish question is purely *theological.* The Jew finds himself in *religious* opposition to a state acknowledging Christianity as its foundation. This state is a theologian *ex professo.* Criticism is here criticism of theology, double-edged criticism of Christian and of Jewish theology. But however *critical* we might be, we are still moving in theology.

In France, a *constitutional* state, the Jewish question is a question of constitutionalism, a question of the *incompleteness of political emancipation.* As the *semblance* of a state religion is preserved there, if only by the meaningless and self-contradictory formula of a *religion of the majority,* the relation of the Jew to the state also retains the *semblance* of a religious or theological opposition.

Only in the free states of North America—or at least in some of them—does the Jewish question lose its *theological* significance and become a truly *secular* question. Only where the political state exists in its complete development can the relation of the Jew, and generally speaking the religious man, to the political state, that is, the relation of religion to state, appear in its characteristic and pure form. Criticism of this relation ceases to be theological once the state abandons a *theological* posture toward religion, once it relates itself to religion as a state, that is, *politically*. Criticism then becomes *criticism of the political state*. Where the question here ceases to be *theological*, Bauer's criticism ceases to be critical. *"In the United States there is neither a state religion, nor a religion declared to be that of the majority, nor a pre-eminence of one faith over another. The state is foreign to all faiths."* (Gustave de Beaumont, *Marie ou l'esclavage aux Etats-Unis . . .* [Brussels, 1835], p. 214.) There are even some states in North America where *"the constitution imposes no religious beliefs or sectarian practice as the condition of political rights"* (*loc. cit.*, p. 225). Yet *"no one in the United States believes that a man without religion can be an honest man"* (*loc. cit.*, p. 224). And North America is pre-eminently the land of religiosity as Beaumont, Tocqueville, and the Englishman Hamilton assure us unanimously. The North American states, however, serve only as an example. The question is: What is the relation of *complete* political emancipation to religion? If we find even in a country with full political emancipation that religion not only *exists* but is *fresh* and *vital*, we have proof that the existence of religion is not incompatible with the full development of the state. But since the existence of religion implies a defect, the source of this defect must be sought in the *nature* of the state itself. We no longer take religion to be the *basis* but only the *manifestation* of secular narrowness. Hence we explain religious restriction of free citizens on the basis of their secular restriction. We do not claim that they must transcend their religious restriction in order to transcend their secular limitations. We do claim that they will transcend their religious restriction once they have transcended their secular limitations. We do not convert secular questions into theological ones. We convert theological questions into secular questions. History has long enough been resolved into superstition, but now we can resolve superstition into history. The question of the *relation of political emancipation to religion* becomes for us a question of the *relation of political emancipation to human emancipation*. We criticize the religious weaknesses of the political state by criticizing the political state in its *secular* constitution *apart from* the religious defects. In human terms we resolve the contradiction between the state and a *particular religion* such as *Judaism* into the contradiction between the state and *particular secular* elements, the contradiction between the state and *religion generally* into the contradiction between the state and its *presuppositions*.

The *political* emancipation of the Jew, the Christian, or the *religious* man generally is the *emancipation of the state* from Judaism, from Christianity, from *religion* in general. In a form and manner corresponding to its nature, the *state* as such emancipates itself from religion by emancipating itself from the *state religion*, that is, by recognizing no religion and recognizing itself simply as the state. *Political* emancipation from religion is not complete and consistent emancipation from religion because political emancipation is not the complete and consistent form of *human* emancipation.

The limits of political emancipation are seen at once in the fact that the *state* can free itself from a limitation without man *actually* being free from it, in the fact that a state can be a *free state* without men becoming *free men*. Bauer himself tacitly admits this in setting the following condition of political emancipation: "Every religious privilege, including the monopoly of a privileged church, would have to be abolished. If a few or many or even the *overwhelming majority still felt obliged to fulfill their religious duties*, such a practice should be left to them as a *purely private matter*." The *state* can thus emancipate itself from religion even though the *overwhelming majority* is still religious.

And the overwhelming majority does not cease being religious by being religious *in private*.

But the attitude of the state, particularly the *free state*, toward religion is still only the attitude of the *men* who make up the state. Hence it follows that man frees himself from a limitation *politically, through the state*, by overcoming the limitation in an *abstract, limited*, and partial manner, in contradiction with himself. Further, when man frees himself *politically*, he does so *indirectly*, through an *intermediary*, even if the *intermediary* is *necessary*. Finally, even when man proclaims himself an atheist through the medium of the state—that is, when he declares the state to be atheistic—he is still captive to religion since he only recognizes his atheism indirectly through an intermediary. Religion is merely the indirect recognition of man through a *mediator*. The state is the mediator between man and the freedom of man. As Christ is the mediator on whom man unburdens all his own divinity and all his *religious ties*, so is the state the mediator to which man transfers all his unholiness and all his *human freedom*.

The *political* elevation of man above religion shares all the defects and all the advantages of any political elevation. If the state as state, for example, abolishes *private property*, man proclaims private property is *overcome politically* once he abolishes the *property qualification* for active and passive voting as has been done in many North American states. *Hamilton* interprets this fact quite correctly in political terms: *"The great majority of the people have gained a victory over property owners and financial wealth."*[*] Is not private property ideally abolished when the have-nots come to legislate for the haves? The *property qualification* is the last *political* form for recognizing private property.

Yet the political annulment of private property not only does not abolish it but even presupposes it. The state abolishes distinctions of *birth, rank, education*, and *occupation* in its fashion when it declares them to be *non-political*

---

[* Thomas Hamilton, *Men and Manners in America* (2 vols.; Edinburgh: William Blackwood, 1833). Marx quotes from the German translation, *Die Menschen und die Sitten in den Vereinigten Staaten von Nordamerika* (Mannheim: Hoff, 1834), Vol. I, p. 146.]

distinctions, when it proclaims that every member of the community *equally* participates in popular sovereignty without regard to these distinctions, and when it deals with all elements of the actual life of the nation from the standpoint of the state. Nevertheless the state permits private property, education, and occupation to *act* and manifest their *particular* nature as private property, education, and occupation in their *own* ways. Far from overcoming these *factual* distinctions, the state exists only by presupposing them; it is aware of itself as a *political state* and makes its *universality* effective only in opposition to these elements. *Hegel*, therefore, defines the relation of the *political state* to religion quite correctly in saying: "If the state is to have specific existence as the *self-knowing ethical actuality* of Spirit, it must be *distinct* from the form of authority and faith; this distinction emerges only as the ecclesiastical sphere is *divided* within itself; *only* thus has the state attained *universality* of thought, the principle of its form, *above particular* churches and only thus does it bring that universality into existence." (Hegel's *Philosophy of Law*, 1st ed., p. 346 [§ 270].) Exactly! Only thus *above* the *particular* elements is the state a universality.

By its nature the perfected political state is man's *species-life* in *opposition* to his material life. All the presuppositions of this egoistic life remain in *civil society outside* the state, but as qualities of civil society. Where the political state has achieved its full development, man leads a double life, a heavenly and an earthly life, not only in thought or consciousness but in *actuality*. In the *political community* he regards himself as a *communal being;* but in *civil society* he is active as a *private individual*, treats other men as means, reduces himself to a means, and becomes the plaything of alien powers. The political state is as spiritual in relation to civil society as heaven is in relation to earth. It stands in the same opposition to civil society and goes beyond it in the same way as religion goes beyond the limitation of the profane world, that is, by recognizing, reestablishing, and necessarily allowing itself to be dominated by it. In his *innermost* actuality, in civil society, man is a profane being. Here, where he counts as an actual individual to himself and others, he is an *illusory* phenomenon. In the state where he counts as a species-being, on the other hand, he is an imaginary member of an imagined sovereignty, divested of his actual individual life and endowed with an unactual universality.

The conflict in which man as believer in a *particular* religion finds himself—a conflict with his own citizenship and other men as members of the community—is reduced to the *secular* split between the *political* state and *civil society*. For man as *bourgeois* [or part of civil society], "life in the state is only a semblance or a momentary exception to the real nature of things, an exception to the rule." Certainly the *bourgeois*, like the Jew, participates in the life of the state only in a sophistical way just as the *citoyen* is only sophistically a Jew or *bourgeois;* but this sophistry is not personal. It is the *sophistry of the political state* itself. The difference between the religious man and the citizen is the difference between the shopkeeper and the citizen, between the day laborer and the citizen, between the landowner and the citizen, between the *living individual* and the *citizen*. The contradiction between the religious and political man is the same as that between *bourgeois* and *citoyen*, between the member of civil society and his *political lion skin*.

This secular conflict to which the Jewish question ultimately is reduced—the relation between the political state and its presuppositions, whether the presuppositions be material elements such as private property or spiritual elements such as education and religion, the conflict between *general* and *private interest*, the split between the *political state* and *civil society*—these secular contradictions Bauer leaves untouched while attacking their *religious* expression. "It is precisely its foundation, need, which assures the maintenance of *civil society* and *guarantees its necessity* but exposes its maintenance to constant danger, sustains an element of uncertainty in civil society, and produces that constantly alternating mixture of poverty and wealth, of adversity and prosperity, and change in general" (p. 8).

Consider his entire section, "Civil Society" (pp. 8–9), which closely follows the main features of Hegel's philosophy of law. Civil society in opposition to the political state is recognized as necessary since the political state is recognized as necessary.

*Political* emancipation is indeed a great step forward. It is not, to be sure, the final form of universal human emancipation, but it is the final form *within* the prevailing order of things. It is obvious that we are here talking about actual, practical emancipation.

Man emancipates himself *politically* from religion by banishing it from the sphere of public law into private right. It is no longer the spirit of the *state* where man—although in a limited way, under a particular form, and in a particular sphere—associates in community with other men as a species-being. It has become the spirit of *civil society*, of the sphere of egoism, of the *bellum omnium contra omnes*. It is no longer the essence of *community* but the essence of *division*. It has become what it was *originally*, an expression of the *separation* of man from his *community*, from himself and from other men. It is now only the abstract confession of particular peculiarity, of *private whim*, of caprice. The infinite splits of religion in North America, for example, already give it the *external* form of a purely individual matter. It has been tossed among numerous private interests and exiled from the community as a community. But one must not be deceived about the scope of political emancipation. The splitting of man into *public* and *private*, the *displacement* of religion from the state to civil society, is not just a step in political emancipation but its *completion*. It as little abolishes man's *actual* religiosity as it seeks to abolish it.

The *disintegration* of man into Jew and citizen, Protestant and citizen, religious man and citizen does not belie citizenship or circumvent political emancipation. It is *political emancipation itself*, the *political* mode of emancipation from religion. To be sure, in periods when the political state as such is forcibly born from civil society, when men strive to liberate themselves under the form of political self-liberation, the state can and must go as far as to *abolish* and *destroy religion*, but only in the way it abolishes private property by setting a maximum, confiscation, and progressive taxation or only in the way it abolishes life by the *guillotine*. In moments of special concern for itself political life seeks to repress its presupposition, civil society and its elements, and to constitute itself the actual, harmonious species-life of man. But it can do this only in *violent* contradiction with its own conditions of existence by declaring the revolution to be *permanent*, and thus the political drama is bound to end with the restoration of religion, private property, and all the elements of civil society just as war ends with peace.

Indeed, the perfected Christian state is not the so-called *Christian* state acknowledging Christianity as its foundation in the state religion and excluding all others. It is, rather, the *atheistic* state, the *democratic* state, the state that relegates religion to the level of other elements of civil society. The state that is still theological and still officially prescribes belief in Christianity has not yet dared to declare itself to be *a state* and has not yet succeeded in expressing in *secular* and *human* form, in its *actuality* as a state, those *human* foundations of which Christianity is the sublime expression. The so-called Christian state is simply a *non-state,* for it is only the *human foundation* of Christianity, not Christianity as a religion, which can realize itself in actual human creations.

The so-called Christian state is a Christian denial of the state, not in any way the political actualization of Christianity. The state that still professes Christianity in the form of religion does not profess it in political form because it still behaves religiously toward religion—that is, it is not the *actual expression* of the human basis of religion since it still deals with the *unreality* and *imaginary* form of this human core. The so-called Christian state is an *imperfect* one, which treats Christianity as the *supplement* and *sanctification* of its imperfection. Hence religion necessarily becomes a *means* to an end, and the state is a *hypocrite*. There is a great difference between a *perfected* state that counts religion as one of its *prerequisites* because of a lack in the general *nature* of the state and an *imperfect* state that proclaims religion as its *foundation* because of a lack in its *particular existence* as an imperfect state. In the latter, religion becomes *imperfect politics*. In the former, the inadequacy of even perfected *politics* is apparent in religion. The so-called Christian state needs the Christian religion to complete itself *as a state*. The democratic state, the real state, needs no religion for its political fulfillment. It can, rather, do without religion because it fulfills the human basis of religion in a secular way. The so-called Christian state, on the other hand, behaves toward religion in a political way and toward politics in a religious way. As it reduces political forms to mere appearance, it equally reduces religion to a mere appearance.

To express this contradiction clearly let us consider Bauer's construct of the Christian state, a construct derived from his perception of the Christian-Germanic state.

> "To prove the *impossibility* or *non-existence* of a Christian state," says Bauer, "we have recently and more frequently been referred to those passages in the Gospel which the [present] state *not only* does *not* follow but *also cannot unless it wants to dissolve itself completely*." "But the matter is not so easily settled. What do those Gospel passages demand? Supernatural self-renunciation and submission to the authority of revelation, turning away from the state, the abolition of secular relationships. But the Christian state demands and achieves all these things. It has made the *spirit of the Gospel* its own, and if it does not reproduce it in exactly the same words as the Gospel, that is because it expresses that spirit in political forms borrowed from the political system of this world but reduced to mere appearance by the religious rebirth they must undergo. This withdrawal from the state is realized through the forms of the state" (p. 55).

Bauer goes on to show how the people of a Christian state do not constitute a nation with a will of its own but have their true existence in the ruler to whom they are subject but who is alien to them by origin and nature since he was given to them by God without their consent. Further, the laws of this nation are not its own doing but are positive revelations. The supreme ruler requires privileged intermediaries in his relations with his own people, the masses, themselves split into a multitude of distinct spheres formed and determined by chance and differentiated from each other by their interests and particular passions and prejudices but permitted as a privilege to isolate themselves from each other, etc. (p. 56).

But Bauer himself says: "If politics is to be nothing more than religion, it cannot be politics any more than cleaning cooking pans can be regarded as an economic matter if it is to be treated religiously" (p. 108). But in the Christian-Germanic state, religion is an "economic matter" just as "economic matters" are religion. In the Christian-Germanic state, the dominance of religion is the religion of domination.

The separation of the "spirit of the Gospel" from the "letter of the Gospel" is an *irreligious* act. The state that permits the Gospel to speak in the letter of politics or in any other letter than that of the Holy Spirit commits a sacrilege if not in the eyes of men at least in the eyes of its own religion. The state that acknowledges Christianity as its highest rule and the *Bible* as its *charter* must be confronted with the *words* of Holy Writ, for the Writ is holy in every word. This state as well as the *human rubbish* on which it is based finds itself involved in a painful contradiction, a contradiction insoluble from the standpoint of religious consciousness based on the teaching of the Gospel, which it "not only does not follow but *also cannot unless it wants to dissolve itself completely as a state.*" And why does it not want to dissolve itself completely? It cannot answer this question either for itself or others. In its *own consciousness* the official Christian state is an *ought* whose realization is impossible. It knows it can affirm the *actuality* of its own existence only by lying to itself and hence remains dubious, unreliable, and problematic. Criticism is thus completely right in forcing the state that appeals to the Bible into a mental derangement in which it no longer knows whether it is an *illusion* or a *reality*, in which the infamy of its *secular* purposes cloaked by religion irreconcilably conflicts with the integrity of its *religious* consciousness viewing religion as the world's purpose. Such a state can only free itself of inner torment by becoming the *constable* of the

Catholic Church. In relation to that church, which claims secular power as its servant, the state, the *secular* power claiming to dominate the religious spirit, is impotent.

In the so-called Christian state what counts is indeed *alienation* but not *man*. The only man who does count, the *king,* is still religious, specifically distinguished from others and directly connected with heaven, with God. The relations prevailing here are still relations of *faith.* The religious spirit is still not actually secularized.

But the religious spirit cannot *actually* be secularized, for what is it, in fact, but the *unsecular* form of a stage in the development of the human spirit? The religious spirit can only be actualized if the stage of development of the human spirit it expresses religiously emerges into and assumes its *secular* form. This is what happens in the *democratic* state. The basis of the democratic state is not Christianity but the *human ground* of Christianity. Religion remains the ideal, unsecular consciousness of its members because it is the ideal form of the *stage of human development* attained in the democratic state.

The members of the political state are religious by virtue of the dualism between individual life and species-life, between the life of civil society and political life. They are religious inasmuch as man regards as his true life the political life remote from his actual individuality, inasmuch as religion is here the spirit of civil society expressing the separation and withdrawal of man from man. Political democracy is Christian in that it regards man—not merely one but every man—as *sovereign* and supreme. But this means man in his uncivilized and unsocial aspect, in his fortuitous existence and just as he is, corrupted by the entire organization of our society, lost and alienated from himself, oppressed by inhuman relations and elements—in a word, man who is not yet an *actual* species-being. The sovereignty of man—though as alien and distinct from actual men—which is the chimera, dream, and postulate of Christianity, is a tangible and present actuality, a secular maxim, in democracy.

In the perfected democracy the religious and theological

consciousness appears to itself all the more religious and theological for being apparently without political significance or mundane purposes—for being a spiritual affair eschewing the world, an expression of reason's limitation, a product of whim and fantasy, an actual life in the beyond. Christianity here achieves the *practical* expression of its universal religious meaning in that the most varied views are grouped together in the form of Christianity and, what is more, others are not asked to profess Christianity but only religion in general, any kind of religion (cf. Beaumont, *op. cit.*). The religious consciousness revels in the wealth of religious contradictions and multiplicity.

We have thus shown: Political emancipation from religion permits religion, though not privileged religion, to continue. The contradiction in which the adherent of a specific religion finds himself in relation to his citizenship is only *one aspect* of the universal *secular contradiction between the political state and civil society*. The fulfillment of the Christian state is a state that acknowledges itself as a state and ignores the religion of its members. The emancipation of the state from religion is not the emancipation of actual man from religion.

We thus do not say with Bauer to the Jews: You cannot be politically emancipated without radically emancipating yourselves from Judaism. Rather we tell them: Because you can be emancipated politically without completely and fully renouncing Judaism, *political emancipation* by itself is not *human* emancipation. If you Jews want to be politically emancipated without emancipating yourselves humanly, the incompleteness and contradiction lies not only in you but in the *essence* and *category* of political emancipation. If you are engrossed in this category, you share a general bias. Just as the state *evangelizes* when, in spite of being a state, it behaves toward the Jew in a Christian way, the Jew *acts politically* when, in spite of being a Jew, he demands civil rights.

But if man can be emancipated politically and acquire civil rights even though he is a Jew, can he claim and acquire the so-called *rights of man?* Bauer *denies* it.

"The question is whether the Jew as such—i.e. the Jew who avows that his true nature compels him to live in eternal separation from others—is able to acquire the *universal rights of man* and grant them to others."

"The idea of the rights of man was discovered in the Christian world only in the last century. It is not an innate idea but rather is acquired in struggle against historical traditions in which man has hitherto been educated. Thus the rights of man are neither a gift of nature nor a legacy from past history but the reward of struggle against the accident of birth and privileges transmitted by history from generation to generation up to the present. They are the result of culture, and only he can possess them who has earned and deserved them."

"But can the Jew actually take possession of them? As long as he remains a Jew the limited nature which makes him a Jew must triumph over the human nature which should link him as a man with others and must separate him from non-Jews. By this separation he proclaims that the special nature which makes him a Jew is his true and highest nature to which his human nature must yield."

"In the same way, the Christian as Christian cannot grant the rights of man." (Pp. 19, 20.)

According to Bauer man must sacrifice the *"privilege of faith"* to be able to acquire the universal rights of man. Let us consider for a moment these so-called rights and indeed in their most authentic form, the form they have among their *discoverers*, the North Americans and the French. In part these rights are *political* rights that can be exercised only in community with others. *Participation* in the *community*, indeed the *political* community or *state*, constitutes their substance. They belong in the category of *political freedom*, of *civil rights*, which by no means presupposes the consistent and positive transcendence of religion and thus of Judaism, as we have seen. There is left for consideration the other part, the *rights of man* as distinct from the *rights of the citizen*.

Among these is freedom of conscience, the right to practice one's chosen religion. The *privilege of faith* is expressly recognized either as a *right of man* or as a consequence of a right of man, freedom.

> *Declaration of the Rights of Man and of the Citizen,* 1791, Art. 10: "No one is to be disturbed on account of his beliefs, even religious beliefs." In Title I of the Constitution of 1791 there is guaranteed as a human right: "The liberty of every man to practice the *religious worship* to which he is attached."
>
> The *Declaration of the Rights of Man,* etc., 1793, includes among human rights, Art. 7: "Freedom of worship." Moreover, it even maintains in regard to the right to express views and opinions, to assemble, and to worship: "The need to proclaim these *rights* assumes either the presence or recent memory of despotism." Compare the Constitution of 1795, Title XIV, Art. 354.
>
> *Constitution of Pennsylvania,* Art. 9, § 3: "All men have a natural and indefeasible *right* to worship Almighty God according to the dictates of their own consciences; no man can of right be compelled to attend, erect, or support any place of worship, or to maintain any ministry against his consent; no human authority can, in any case whatever, interfere with the rights of conscience and control the prerogatives of the soul."
>
> *Constitution of New Hampshire,* Arts. 5 and 6: "Among the natural rights, some are in their very nature unalienable, because no equivalent can be conceived for them. Of this kind are the *rights* of conscience." (Beaumont, *loc. cit.,* pp. 213, 214.)

The incompatibility between religion and the rights of man is so little implied in the concept of the rights of man that the *right to be religious* according to one's liking and to practice a particular religion is explicitly included among the rights of man. The *privilege of faith* is a *universal human right.*

The *rights of man* as *such* are distinguished from the *rights of the citizen.* Who is this *man* distinguished from the *citizen?* None other than the *member of civil society.*

Why is the member of civil society called "man," man without qualification, and why are his rights called the *rights of man?* How can we explain this? By the relation of the political state to civil society and by the nature of political emancipation.

Let us note first of all that the so-called *rights of man* as distinguished from the *rights of the citizen* are only the rights of the *member of civil society,* that is, of egoistic man, man separated from other men and from the community. The most radical constitution, the Constitution of 1793, may be quoted:

*Declaration of the Rights of Man and of the Citizen.*
*Art. 2.* "These rights (the natural and imprescriptible rights) are: *equality, liberty, security, property.*"

What is this *liberty?*

*Art. 6.* "Liberty is the power belonging to each man to do anything which does not impair the rights of others," or according to the Declaration of the Rights of Man of 1791: "Liberty is the power to do anything which does not harm others."

Liberty is thus the right to do and perform anything that does not harm others. The limits within which each can act *without harming* others is determined by law just as the boundary between two fields is marked by a stake. This is the liberty of man viewed as an isolated monad, withdrawn into himself. Why, according to Bauer, is the Jew not capable of acquiring human rights? "As long as he remains a Jew the limited nature which makes him a Jew must triumph over the human nature which should link him as a man with others and must separate him from non-Jews." But liberty as a right of man is not based on the association of man with man but rather on the separation of man from man. It is the *right* of this separation, the right of the *limited* individual limited to himself.

The practical application of the right of liberty is the right of *private property.*

What is property as one of the rights of man?

*Art. 16* (Constitution of 1793): "The right of *property* is that belonging to every citizen to enjoy and dispose of his goods, his revenues, the fruits of his labor and of his industry *as he wills*."

The right of property is thus the right to enjoy and dispose of one's possessions as one wills, without regard for other men and independently of society. It is the right of self-interest. This individual freedom and its application as well constitutes the basis of civil society. It lets every man find in other men not the *realization* but rather the *limitation* of his own freedom. It proclaims above all the right of man "to enjoy and dispose of his goods, his revenues, the fruits of his labor and of his industry *as he wills*."

There still remain the other rights of man, equality and security.

"Equality"—here used in its non-political sense—is only the equal right to *liberty* as described above, viz., that every man is equally viewed as a self-sufficient monad. The Constitution of 1795 defines the concept of equality with this significance:

*Art. 3* (Constitution of 1795): "Equality consists in the fact that the law is the same for all, whether it protects or whether it punishes."

And security?

*Art. 8* (Constitution of 1793): "Security consists in the protection accorded by society to each of its members for the preservation of his person, his rights and his property."

*Security* is the supreme social concept of civil society, the concept of the *police*, the concept that the whole society exists only to guarantee to each of its members the preservation of his person, his rights, and his property. In this sense Hegel calls civil society "the state as necessity and rationality."

Civil society does not raise itself above its egoism through the concept of security. Rather, security is the *guarantee* of the egoism.

Thus none of the so-called rights of men goes beyond

the egoistic man, the man withdrawn into himself, his private interest and his private choice, and separated from the community as a member of civil society. Far from viewing man here in his species-being, his species-life itself—society —rather appears to be an external framework for the individual, limiting his original independence. The only bond between men is natural necessity, need and private interest, the maintenance of their property and egoistic persons.

It is somewhat curious that a nation just beginning to free itself, tearing down all the barriers between different sections of the people and founding a political community, should solemnly proclaim (Declaration of 1791) the justification of the egoistic man, man separated from his fellow men and from the community, and should even repeat this proclamation at a moment when only the most heroic sacrifice can save the nation and hence is urgently required, when the sacrifice of all the interests of civil society is highly imperative and egoism must be punished as crime (Declaration of the Rights of Man of 1793). This becomes even more curious when we observe that the political liberators reduce citizenship, the *political community,* to a mere *means* for preserving these so-called rights of man and that the citizen thus is proclaimed to be the servant of the egoistic man, the sphere in which man acts as a member of the community is degraded below that in which he acts as a fractional being, and finally man as bourgeois rather than man as citizen is considered to be the *proper* and *authentic* man.

"The *goal* of all *political association* is the *preservation* of the natural and imprescriptible rights of man." (Declaration of the Rights of Man, etc., of 1791, Art. 2.) "*Government* is instituted to guarantee man's enjoyment of his natural and imprescriptible rights." (Declaration, etc., of 1793, Art. 1.) Thus even at the time of its youthful enthusiasm fired by the urgency of circumstances political life is proclaimed to be a mere *means* whose end is life in civil society. To be sure, revolutionary practice flagrantly contradicts its theory. While security, for example, is proclaimed to be one of the rights of man, the violation of the privacy of correspondence is publicly established as the order of the day. While the *"unlimited* freedom of the press" (Constitution of 1793, Art. 122) as a consequence of the rights of man and individual freedom is guaranteed, freedom of the press is completely abolished because "freedom of the press should not be permitted to compromise public liberty." ("Robespierre jeune," *Parliamentary History of the French Revolution,* by Buchez and Roux, Vol. 28, p. 159.) This means that the human right of liberty ceases to be a right when it comes into conflict with *political* life while theoretically political life is only the guarantee of the rights of man, the rights of individual man, and should be abandoned once it contradicts its *end,* these rights of man. But the practice is only the exception, the theory is the rule. Even if we choose to regard revolutionary practice as the correct expression of this relationship, the problem still remains unsettled as to why the relationship is inverted in the consciousness of the political liberators so that the end appears as means and the means as the end. This optical illusion of their consciousness would always be the same problem, though a psychological, a theoretical problem.

The problem is easily settled.

Political emancipation is also the *dissolution* of the old society on which rests the sovereign power, the character of the state as alienated from the people. The political revolution is the revolution of civil society. What was the character of the old society? It can be described in one word. *Feudalism.* The old civil society had a *directly political* character, that is, the elements of civil life such as property, the family, the mode and manner of work, for example, were raised into elements of political life in the form of landlordism, estates, and corporations. In this form they determined the relation of the particular individual to the *state as a whole,* that is, his *political* relation, his separation and exclusion from other parts of society. For the feudal organization of national life did not elevate property or labor to the level of social elements but rather completed their *separation* from the state as a whole and established them as *separate* societies within society. Thus the vital functions and conditions of civil society always remained political, but political in the feudal sense. That is, they excluded the individual from the state as a whole and transformed the *special* relation between his corporation and the state into his own general relation to national life, just as they transformed his specific civil activity and situation into a general activity and situation. As a consequence of this organization, there necessarily appears the unity of the state as well as its consciousness, will, and activity—the general political power—likewise the *special* business of the ruler and his servants, separated from the people.

The political revolution, which overthrew this domination, turned the business of the state into the people's business, and made the political state the business of *all,* that is, an actual state—this revolution inevitably destroyed all estates, corporations, guilds, and privileges variously expressing the separation of the people from their community. The political revolution thereby *abolished* the *political character of civil society*. It shattered civil society into its constituent elements—on the one hand *individuals* and on the other the *material* and *spiritual elements* constituting the vital content and civil situation of these individuals. It released the political spirit, which had been broken, fragmented, and lost, as it were, in the various cul-de-sacs of feudal society. It gathered up this scattered spirit, liberated it from its entanglement with civil life, and turned it into the sphere of the community, the *general* concern of the people ideally independent of these *particular* elements of civil life. A *particular* activity and situation in life sank into a merely individual significance, no longer forming the general relation of the individual to the state as a whole. Public business as such rather became the general business of every individual and the political function became his general function.

But the fulfillment of the idealism of the state was at the same time the fulfillment of the materialism of civil society. The throwing off of the political yoke was at the same time the throwing off of the bond that had fettered the egoistic spirit of civil society. Political emancipation was at the same time the emancipation of civil society from politics, from the *appearance* of a general content.

Feudal society was dissolved into its foundation, into *man*. But into man as he actually was the foundation of that society, into *egoistical* man.

This *man,* the member of civil society, is now the basis and presupposition of the *political* state. He is recognized as such by the state in the rights of man.

But the freedom of egoistic man and the recognition of this freedom is rather the recognition of the *unbridled* movement of the spiritual and material elements forming the content of his life.

Thus man was not freed from religion; he received religious freedom. He was not freed from property. He received freedom of property. He was not freed from the egoism of trade but received freedom to trade.

The *constitution* of the *political state* and the dissolution of civil society into independent *individuals*—whose relation is *law* just as the relation of estates and guilds was *privilege* —is accomplished in *one and the same act.* As a member of civil society man is the *non-political* man but necessarily appears to be *natural* man. The *rights of man* appear to be *natural rights* because *self-conscious activity* is concentrated on the *political act.* The *egoistic* man is the *passive* and *given* result of the dissolved society, an object of *immediate certainty* and thus a *natural* object. The *political revolution* dissolves civil life into its constituent elements without *revolutionizing* these elements themselves and subjecting them to criticism. It regards civil society—the realm of needs, labor, private interests, and private right—as the *basis of its existence,* as a *presupposition* needing no ground, and thus as its *natural basis.* Finally, man as a member of civil society is regarded as *authentic* man, *man* as distinct from *citizen,* since he is man in his sensuous, individual, and *most intimate* existence while *political* man is only the abstract and artificial man, man as an *allegorical, moral* person. Actual man is recognized only in the form of an *egoistic* individual, *authentic* man, only in the form of *abstract citizen.*

The abstraction of the political man was correctly depicted by Rousseau:

"Whoever dares to undertake the founding of a nation must feel himself capable of **changing**,[*] so to speak, **human nature** and **transforming** each individual who is in himself a complete but isolated whole, into a **part** of something greater than himself from which he somehow derives his life and existence, substituting a **limited** and **moral existence** for physical and independent existence. **Man** must be deprived of **his own powers** and given alien powers which he cannot use without the aid of others." (*Social Contract*, Bk. II, London, 1782, p. 67.)

*All* emancipation is *restoration* of the human world and the relationships of *men themselves*.

Political emancipation is a reduction of man to a member of civil society, to an *egoistic independent* individual on the one hand and to a *citizen*, a moral person, on the other.

Only when the actual, individual man has taken back into himself the abstract citizen and in his everyday life, his individual work, and his individual relationships has become a *species-being*, only when he has recognized and organized his own powers as *social* powers so that social force is no longer separated from him as *political* power, only then is human emancipation complete.

*Bruno Bauer, "The Capacity of Present-day Jews and Christians to Become Free,"* Twenty-one Sheets [from Switzerland (*ed. Georg Herwegh*), *Zurich and Winterthur, 1843*], pp. 56–71.

Here Bauer deals with the relation between the *Jewish and Christian religion* and their relation to criticism. Their relation to criticism is their bearing "on the capacity to become free."

Accordingly: "The Christian has only one stage to surpass—namely, his religion—in order to abandon religion in general" and thus become free. "The Jew, on the other

[* Boldface type identifies Marx's emphasis in the quotation.]

hand, has to break not only with his Jewish nature but also with the development, the completion, of his religion, a development which has remained alien to him" (p. 71).

Thus Bauer here transforms the question of Jewish emancipation into a purely religious one. The theological difficulty as to whether the Jew or the Christian has the better prospect of salvation is here reproduced in the enlightened form: Which of the two is *more capable of emancipation?* It is thus no longer the question: Does Judaism or Christianity emancipate? but rather, on the contrary: Which emancipates more, the negation of Judaism or the negation of Christianity?

"If they want to be free, the Jews should not embrace Christianity but Christianity in dissolution, religion generally in dissolution—enlightenment, criticism and its results, free humanity" (p. 70).

For the Jew it is still a matter of *professing faith,* not Christianity but rather Christianity in dissolution.

Bauer requires the Jew to break with the essence of the Christian religion, a requirement which does not follow, as he says himself, from the development of the Jewish nature.

When Bauer, at the end of his *Jewish Question,* interpreted Judaism merely as a crude religious criticism of Christianity and hence gave it "only" a religious significance, it was to be expected that he would also transform the emancipation of the Jews into a philosophicotheological act.

Bauer views the *ideal* and abstract essence of the Jew, his *religion,* as his *whole* nature. Hence he correctly infers: "The Jew contributes nothing to mankind if he disregards his narrow law," if he cancels all his Judaism (p. 65).

The relation of Jews to Christians thus becomes the following: the sole interest of the Christian in the emancipation of the Jew is a general human interest, a *theoretical* interest. Judaism is an offensive fact to the religious eye of the Christian. As soon as the Christian's eye ceases to be religious, this fact ceases to offend it. In and for itself the emancipation of the Jew is not a task for the Christian.

The Jew, on the other hand, not only has to finish his

own task but also the task of the Christian—[Bruno Bauer's] *Critique of the [Gospel History of the] Synoptics* and [Strauss'] *Life of Jesus,* etc.—if he wants to emancipate himself.

"They can look after themselves: they will determine their own destiny; but history does not allow itself to be mocked" (p. 71).

We will try to break with the theological formulation of the issue. The question concerning the Jew's capacity for emancipation becomes for us the question: What specific *social* element is to be overcome in order to abolish Judaism? For the modern Jew's capacity for emancipation is the relation of Judaism to the emancipation of the modern world. This relation follows necessarily from the particular position of Judaism in the modern, subjugated world.

Let us consider the actual, secular Jew—not the *sabbath Jew,* as Bauer does, but the *everyday Jew.*

Let us look for the secret of the Jew not in his religion but rather for the secret of the religion in the actual Jew.

What is the secular basis of Judaism? *Practical need, self-interest.*

What is the worldly cult of the Jew? *Bargaining.* What is his worldly god? *Money.*

Very well! Emancipation from *bargaining* and *money,* and thus from practical and real Judaism would be the self-emancipation of our era.

An organization of society that would abolish the preconditions of bargaining and thus its possibility would render the Jew impossible. His religious consciousness would dissolve like a dull mist in the actual life-giving air of society. On the other hand, when the Jew recognizes this *practical* nature of his as futile and strives to eliminate it, he works away from his previous development toward general *human emancipation* and opposes the *supreme practical* expression of human self-alienation.

Thus we perceive in Judaism a general and *contemporary anti-social* element, which has been carried to its present high point by a historical development in which the

Jews have contributed to this element, a point at which it must necessarily dissolve itself.

The *emancipation of the Jews,* in the final analysis, is the emancipation of mankind from *Judaism.*

The Jew has already emancipated himself in a Jewish way. "The Jew who is only tolerated in Vienna, for example, determines the fate of the whole empire through his financial power. The Jew who may be without rights in the smallest German state decides the destiny of Europe. While corporations and guilds exclude the Jew or are unfavorable to him, audacity in industry mocks the obstinacy of these medieval institutions." (B. Bauer, *The Jewish Question,* p. 114.)

This is no isolated fact. The Jew has emancipated himself in a Jewish way not only by acquiring financial power but also because, with and without him, *money* has become a world power, and the practical Jewish spirit has become the practical spirit of Christian nations. The Jews have emancipated themselves insofar as the Christians have become Jews.

For example, the pious and politically free inhabitant of New England, Captain Hamilton reports, is a kind of *Laocoön* who does not make the slightest effort to free himself from the serpents strangling him. *Mammon* is his idol to whom he prays not only with his lips but with all the power of his body and soul. In his eyes the world is nothing but a stock exchange, and he is convinced that here below he has no other destiny than to become richer than his neighbor. Bargaining dominates his every thought, exchange in things constitutes his only recreation. When he travels, he carries his shop or office on his back, as it were, and talks of nothing but interest and profit. If he loses sight of his own business for a moment, it is only in order to poke his nose into that of others.

Indeed, the practical domination of Judaism over the Christian world in North America has achieved such clear and common expression that the very *preaching of the Gospel,* the Christian ministry, has become an article of commerce and the bankrupt merchant takes to the Gospel while the minister who has become rich goes into business.

*"That man whom you see at the head of a respectable con-
gregation began as a merchant; his business having failed, he
became a minister; the other started with the ministry, but
as soon as he had acquired a sum of money, he left the
pulpit for business. In the eyes of many, the religious ministry is a veritable commercial career."* (Beaumont, *loc.
cit.*, pp. 185, 186.)

According to Bauer it is a hypocritical situation when
the Jew is deprived of political rights in theory while he
wields enormous power in practice, when he exercises the
political influence *wholesale* denied to him in retail (*The
Jewish Question*, p. 114).

The contradiction existing between the practical political
power of the Jew and his political rights is the contradiction between politics and financial power in general. While
politics ideally is superior to financial power, in actual fact
it has become its serf.

Judaism has persisted *alongside* Christianity not only as
the religious critique of Christianity, not only as the concrete doubt concerning the religious descent of Christianity,
but equally because the practical Jewish spirit, Judaism,
has perpetuated itself in Christian society and there even
attained its highest development. The Jew, who exists as a
special member of civil society, is only the special manifestation of civil society's Judaism.

Judaism has survived not in spite of but by means of
history.

Out of its own entrails, civil society ceaselessly produces
the Jew.

What actually was the foundation of the Jewish religion?
Practical need, egoism.

Hence, the Jew's monotheism is actually the polytheism
of many needs, a polytheism that makes even the toilet an
object of divine law. *Practical need, egoism* is the principle
of *civil society* and appears purely as such as soon as
civil society has fully delivered itself of the political state.
The god of *practical need and self-interest* is *money*.

Money is the jealous god of Israel before whom no other
god may exist. Money degrades all the gods of mankind—
and converts them into commodities. Money is the gen-

eral, self-sufficient *value* of everything. Hence it has robbed the whole world, the human world as well as nature, of its proper worth. Money is the alienated essence of man's labor and life, and this alien essence dominates him as he worships it.

The god of the Jews has been secularized and has become the god of the world. The bill of exchange is the Jew's actual god. His god is only an illusory bill of exchange.

The view of nature achieved under the rule of private property and money is an actual contempt for and practical degradation of nature which does, to be sure, exist in the Jewish religion, but only in imagination.

In this sense Thomas Münzer declared it to be intolerable "that every creature should be turned into property, the fish in the water, the birds in the air, the plants of the earth—the creature must also become free."

That which is contained abstractly in the Jewish religion —contempt for theory, for art, for history, for man as an end in himself—is the *actual conscious* standpoint and virtue of the monied man. The species-relation itself, the relation between man and woman, etc., becomes an object of commerce! The woman is bought and sold.

The *chimerical* nationality of the Jew is the nationality of the merchant, particularly of the monied man.

The Jew's unfounded, superficial law is only the religious caricature of unfounded, superficial morality and law in general, the caricature of merely *formal* ceremonies encompassing the world of self-interest.

Here also the highest relation of man is the *legal* relation, the relation to laws which apply to him not because they are laws of his own will and nature but because they *dominate* him and because defection from them will be *avenged*.

Jewish Jesuitism, the same practical Jesuitism Bauer finds in the Talmud, is the relationship of the world of self-interest to the laws governing it, and the cunning circumvention of these laws is that world's main art.

Indeed, the movement of that world within its laws is necessarily a continuous abrogation of the law.

*Judaism* could not develop further as *religion*, could not develop further theoretically, because the perspective of practical need is limited by its very nature and soon exhausted.

By its very nature, the religion of practical need could not find fulfillment in theory but only in *practice* [*Praxis*], simply because practice is its truth.

Judaism could create no new world; it could only draw the new creations and conditions of the world into the compass of its own activity because practical need, whose rationale is self-interest, remains passive, never willfully extending itself but only *finding* itself extended with the continuous development of social conditions.

Judaism reaches its height with the perfection of civil society, but civil society achieves perfection only in the *Christian* world. Only under the reign of Christianity, which makes *all* national, natural, moral, and theoretical relationships *external* to man, was civil society able to separate itself completely from political life, sever all man's speciesties, substitute egoism and selfish need for those ties, and dissolve the human world into a world of atomistic, mutually hostile individuals.

Christianity arose out of Judaism. It has again dissolved itself into Judaism.

From the outset the Christian was the theorizing Jew. Hence, the Jew is the practical Christian, and the practical Christian has again become a Jew.

Christianity overcame real Judaism only in appearance. It was too *noble,* too spiritual, to eliminate the crudeness of practical need except by elevating it into the blue.

Christianity is the sublime thought of Judaism, and Judaism is the common practical application of Christianity. But this application could only become universal after Christianity as religion par excellence had *theoretically* completed the alienation of man from himself and from nature.

Only then could Judaism attain universal dominion and convert externalized man and nature into *alienable* and saleable objects subservient to egoistic need, dependent on bargaining.

Selling is the practice of externalization. As long as man is captivated in religion, knows his nature only as objectified, and thereby converts his nature into an *alien* illusory being, so under the dominion of egoistic need he can only act practically, only practically produce objects, by subordinating both his products and his activity to the domination of an alien being, bestowing upon them the significance of an alien entity—of money.

The Christian egoism of eternal bliss in its practical fulfillment necessarily becomes the material egoism of the Jew, heavenly need is converted into earthly need, and subjectivism becomes selfishness. We do not explain the Jew's tenacity from his religion but rather from the human basis of his religion, from practical need, from egoism.

Since the Jew's real nature has been generally actualized and secularized in civil society, civil society could not convince the Jew of the *unreality* of his *religious* nature which is precisely the ideal representation of practical need. Thus not only in the Pentateuch or Talmud but also in present society we find the nature of the contemporary Jew, not as an abstract nature but a supremely empirical nature, not only as the Jew's narrowness but as the Jewish narrowness of society.

When society succeeds in transcending the *empirical* essence of Judaism—bargaining and all its conditions—the Jew becomes *impossible* because his consciousness no longer has an object, the subjective basis of Judaism—practical need—is humanized, and the conflict between the individual sensuous existence of man and his species-existence is transcended.

The *social* emancipation of the Jew is the *emancipation of society from Judaism.*

# TOWARD THE CRITIQUE OF HEGEL'S PHILOSOPHY OF LAW: INTRODUCTION

[For the first time the following article, written in Paris at the end of 1843, identifies the proletariat as the means to actualize philosophy and achieve "full human emancipation." This important step in Marx's thought was the outcome of many factors—his reading on the working class in Lorenz von Stein and Flora Tristan, his own financial distress in exile, his association with socialist workers among whom "the brotherhood of man is no phrase but a truth," his humanitarian concern to bring Feuerbach's "man" into society and politics, and particularly his preoccupation with Hegel's political philosophy. Marx sees the following essay as introducing an examination of Hegel's philosophy of law developed from his previous "Critique of Hegel's Philosophy of the State." He had already concluded that Hegel's idea of a genuine state requires democracy where the universal class, in contrast to bureaucracy, can be actually universal in every citizen. Now Marx finds such a universal class in the proletariat, a class Hegel had seen as the opposite of "riches in a few hands," the outcome of industry and trade in civil society. Further, the movement of the proletariat follows Hegel's dialectic: a class in chains is to destroy all chains, the complete loss of humanity is to redeem humanity. Such "demands of reason" cannot be transcended without being actualized, and as they are actualized in practice—something neglected by Bauer and the Young Hegelians—philosophy itself is transcended, as suggested earlier in the Dissertation Notes. The dialectical synthesis of philosophy from Feuerbach and Hegel with actuality in historical practice is to be found, Marx concludes, in the emancipation of the proletariat.]

For Germany the *criticism of religion* has been essentially completed, and criticism of religion is the premise of all criticism.

The *profane* existence of error is compromised when its *heavenly oratio pro aris et focis* [defense of altar and hearth] has been refuted. Man, who has found only the *reflection* of himself in the fantastic reality of heaven where he sought a supernatural being, will no longer be inclined to find the *semblance* of himself, only the non-human being, where he seeks and must seek his true reality.

The basis of irreligious criticism is: *Man makes religion, religion does not make man.* And indeed religion is the self-consciousness and self-regard of man who has either not yet found or has already lost himself. But *man* is not an abstract being squatting outside the world. Man is *the world of men,* the state, society. This state and this society produce religion, which is an *inverted consciousness of the world* because they are an *inverted world.* Religion is the generalized theory of this world, its encyclopaedic compendium, its logic in popular form, its spiritualistic point d'honneur, its enthusiasm, its moral sanction, its solemn complement, its general ground of consolation and justification. It is the *fantastic realization* of the human essence inasmuch as the *human essence* possesses no true reality. The struggle against religion is therefore indirectly the struggle against *that world* whose spiritual *aroma* is religion.

*Religious* suffering is the *expression* of real suffering and at the same time the *protest* against real suffering. Religion is the sigh of the oppressed creature, the heart of a heartless world, as it is the spirit of spiritless conditions. It is the *opium* of the people.

The abolition of religion as people's *illusory* happiness is the demand for their *real* happiness. The demand to abandon illusions about their condition is a *demand to abandon a condition which requires illusions.* The criticism of religion is thus in *embryo* a *criticism of the vale of tears* whose *halo* is religion.

Criticism has plucked imaginary flowers from the chain, not so that man will wear the chain that is without fantasy or consolation but so that he will throw it off and pluck the living flower. The criticism of religion disillusions man so that he thinks, acts, and shapes his reality like a disillusioned man who has come to his senses, so that he revolves around himself and thus around his true sun. Religion is only the illusory sun that revolves around man so long as he does not revolve about himself.

Thus it is the *task of history,* once the *otherworldly truth* has disappeared, to establish the *truth of this world*. The immediate *task of philosophy* which is in the service of history is to unmask human self-alienation in its *unholy forms* now that it has been unmasked in its *holy form*. Thus the criticism of heaven turns into the criticism of the earth, the *criticism of religion* into the *criticism of law,* and the *criticism of theology* into the *criticism of politics*.

The following exposition—a contribution to this undertaking [developed from the unpublished "Critique of Hegel's Philosophy of the State" written in Kreuznach]—does not directly pertain to the original but to a copy, the German *philosophy* of the state and law, for the simple reason that it deals with *Germany*.

If one were to proceed from the *status quo* itself in Germany, even in the only appropriate way, *that is,* negatively, the result would still be an *anachronism*. Even the negation of our political present is already a dusty fact in the historical lumber room of modern nations. If I negate powdered wigs, I am still left with unpowdered wigs. If I negate German conditions of 1843, I am hardly, according to French chronology, in the year 1789 and still less in the focus of the present.

Indeed, German history plumes itself on a development no nation in the historical firmament previously exhibited or will ever copy. We have in point of fact shared in the restorations of the modern nations without sharing in their revolutions. We have been restored, first because other nations dared to make revolutions, and secondly because other nations suffered counter-revolutions—on the one hand because our masters were afraid, and on the other because they were not afraid. Led by our shepherds, we found ourselves in the company of freedom only once, on the *day of its burial*.

A school of thought that legitimizes today's infamy by yesterday's, a school of thought that explains every cry of the serf against the knout as rebellion once the knout is time-honored, ancestral, and historical, a school to which history shows only its *a posteriori*, as the God of Israel did to his servant Moses—the *Historical School of Law*—might have invented German history if it were not an invention of German history. A Shylock, but a servile Shylock, that school swears on its bond, on its historical bond, its Christian-Germanic bond, for every pound of flesh cut from the heart of the people.

Good-natured enthusiasts, German chauvinists by extraction and liberals by reflection, on the other hand, seek our history of freedom beyond our history in the primeval Teutonic forests. But how does the history of our freedom differ from the history of the wild boar's freedom if it is only to be found in the forests? As the proverb says, what is shouted into the forest, the forest echoes back. So peace to the primeval Teutonic forests!

*War* on German conditions! By all means! They are *below the level of history, beneath all criticism,* but they are still an object of criticism just as the criminal below the level of humanity is still an object of the *executioner.* In its struggle against these conditions criticism is not a passion of the head but the head of passion. It is not a lancet, it is a weapon. Its object is an *enemy* it wants not to refute but to *destroy.* For the spirit of these conditions has already been refuted. In and for themselves they are objects not *worthy of thought* but *existences* as despicable as they are despised. Criticism itself does not even need to be concerned with this matter, for it is already clear about it. Criticism is no longer an *end in itself* but simply a *means.* Its essential pathos is *indignation,* its essential task, *denunciation.*

It is a matter of describing the pervasive, suffocating pressure of all social spheres on one another, the general but passive dejection, the narrowness that recognizes but misunderstands itself—this framed in a system of government that lives on the conservation of all meanness and is nothing but *meanness in government.*

What a sight! Society is forever splitting into the most varied races opposing one another with petty antipathies, bad consciences, and brutal mediocrity, and precisely because of their mutually ambiguous and distrustful situation they are all treated by their *rulers* as merely *tolerated existences,* without exception, though with varying formalities. And they are forced to recognize and acknowledge their being *dominated, ruled,* and *possessed* as a *concession from heaven!* On the other side are the rulers themselves whose greatness is inversely proportional to their number!

The criticism dealing with this matter is criticism in *hand-to-hand* combat, and in such a combat the point is not whether the opponent is noble, equal, or *interesting,* the point is to *strike* him. The point is to permit the Germans not even a moment of self-deception and resignation. We must make the actual pressure more pressing by adding to it the consciousness of pressure and make the shame more shameful by publicizing it. Every sphere of German society must be shown as the *partie honteuse* of German society, and we have to make these petrified social relations dance by singing their own tune! The people must be taught to be *terrified* of themselves to give them *courage.* This will fulfill an imperative need of the German nation, and the needs of nations are themselves the ultimate grounds of their satisfaction.

And even for *modern* nations this struggle against the restricted content of the German *status quo* cannot be without interest, for the German *status quo* is the *open fulfillment of the Ancien Régime,* and the *Ancien Régime* is the *hidden deficiency of the modern state.* The struggle against the German political present is the struggle against the past of modern nations, and they are still burdened with reminders of that past. It is instructive for them to see the *Ancien Régime,* which lived through its *tragedy* with them, play its *comedy* as a German ghost. The history of the *Ancien Régime* was *tragic* so long as it was the established power in the world, while freedom on the other hand was a personal notion—in short, as long as it believed and had to believe in its own validity. As long as the *Ancien Régime* as an existing world order struggled against a world that was just coming into being, there was on its side a historical but not a personal error. Its downfall was therefore tragic.

On the other hand, the present German regime—an anachronism, a flagrant contradiction of generally accepted axioms, the nullity of the *Ancien Régime* exhibited to the whole world—only imagines that it believes in itself and demands that the world imagine the same thing. If it is believed in its own *nature*, would it try to hide that nature under the *semblance* of an alien nature and seek its salvation in hypocrisy and sophism? The modern *Ancien Régime* is merely the *comedian* in a world whose *real heroes* are dead. History is thorough and goes through many phases as it conducts an old form to the grave. The final phase of a world-historical form is *comedy*. The Greek gods, already tragically and mortally wounded in Aeschylus' *Prometheus Bound,* had to die again comically in Lucian's dialogues. Why this course of history? So that mankind may part from its past *happily.* This *happy* historical destiny we vindicate for the political authorities of Germany.

But once *modern* political and social reality itself is subjected to criticism, once criticism arrives at truly human problems, it either finds itself outside the German *status quo* or it would deal with its object at *a level below* its objects. For example! The relation of industry and the world of wealth in general to the political world is a major problem of modern times. In what form is this problem beginning to preoccupy the Germans? In the form of *protective tariffs,* the *system of prohibition,* and *political economy.* German chauvinism has gone from man to matter and thus one fine day our barons of cotton and heroes of iron saw themselves transformed into patriots. Thus in Germany we are beginning to recognize the sovereignty of monopoly at home by investing it with *sovereignty abroad.* We are about to begin in Germany where France and England are about to end. The old rotten condition against which these countries are revolting in theory and which they bear as chains is greeted in Germany as the dawn of a glorious future which as yet hardly dares to pass from *crafty* [*listigen:* Friedrich List] theory to the most ruthless practice. Whereas the problem in France and England reads: *political economy* or the *rule of society over wealth,* in Germany it reads: *political economy* or the *rule of private property over nationality*. Thus in France and England it is a question of abolishing monopoly that has developed to its final consequences; in Germany it is a question of proceeding to the final consequences of monopoly. There it is a question of solution; here, still a question of collision. This is an adequate example of the *German* form of modern problems, an example of how our history, like a raw recruit, still has had to do extra drill on matters threshed over in history.

If the *total* German development were not in advance of its *political* development, a German could at the most have a share in the problems of the present like that of a *Russian*. But if the single individual is not bound by the limitations of his nation, still less is the nation as a whole liberated by the liberation of one individual. The Scythians made no progress toward Greek culture even though Greece had a Scythian among her philosophers.

Fortunately we Germans are not Scythians.

As the ancient countries lived their pre-history in imagination, in *mythology,* so we Germans have lived our posthistory in thought, in *philosophy*. We are *philosophical* contemporaries of the present without being its *historical* contemporaries. German philosophy is the *ideal extension* of German history. If, therefore, we criticize the *œuvres posthumes* of our ideal history—*philosophy*—instead of the *œuvres incomplètes* of our real history, our criticism is in the center of questions of which the present says: *That is the question*. That which in progressive nations is a *practical* break with modern political conditions is in Germany, where these conditions do not yet exist, just a *critical* break with the philosophical reflection of those conditions.

The *German philosophy of law and of the state* is the only *German history* which stands *al pari* with the *official* modern present. The German nation must therefore join its dream-history to its present conditions and criticize not only these present conditions but also their abstract continuation. Its future can be *limited* neither to the direct negation of its real political and legal conditions nor to their direct fulfillment, for it has the direct negation of its real conditions in its ideal conditions and has almost *outlived* the direct fulfillment of its ideal conditions in the view of neighboring countries. Hence, the *practical* political party in Germany rightly demands the *negation of philosophy*. It is wrong not in its demand but in stopping at the demand it neither seriously fulfills nor can fulfill. It supposes that it accomplishes that negation by turning its back on philosophy, looking aside, and muttering a few petulant and trite phrases about it. Because its outlook is so limited it does not even count philosophy as part of *German* actuality or even imagines it is *beneath* German practice and its theories. You demand starting from *actual germs of life* but forget that the actual life-germ of the German nation has so far sprouted only inside its *cranium*. In short: *you cannot transcend [aufheben] philosophy without actualizing it*.

The same error, but with the factors *reversed,* was committed by the *theoretical* party which originated in philosophy.

In the present struggle the theoretical party saw *only* the *critical struggle of philosophy against the German world*. It did not consider that *previous philosophy* itself belongs to this world and is its *complement*, although an ideal one. Critical toward its counterpart, it was not critical of itself. Starting from the *presuppositions* of philosophy, it either stopped at philosophy's given results or passed off demands and results from somewhere else as direct demands and results from philosophy. But these latter—their legitimacy assumed—can only be obtained by the *negation of previous philosophy*, by the negation of philosophy as philosophy. We shall later give a closer account of this party. Its main defect may be summarized as follows: *It believed that it could actualize philosophy without transcending it*.

The criticism of the *German philosophy of the state and law*, which attained its most consistent, profound, and final formulation with *Hegel*, is at once a critical analysis of the modern state and the actuality connected with it and also the decisive negation of all previous *forms of German political and legal consciousness* whose most prominent and general expression at the level of *science* is precisely the *speculative philosophy of law.* If the speculative philosophy of law—that abstract and extravagant *thinking* about the modern state whose reality remains in the beyond, if only beyond the Rhine—was possible only in Germany, conversely the *German* conception of the modern state in abstraction from *actual man* was possible only because and insofar as the modern state abstracts itself from *actual man* or satisfies the *whole* man only in an illusory way. In politics the Germans have *thought* what other nations have *done.* Germany has been their *theoretical conscience.* The abstraction and presumption of its thought always kept pace with the one-sided and stunted character of their actuality. If the *status quo* of the *German political system* [*Staatswesen*] expresses *the completion of the Ancien Régime,* the thorn in the flesh of the modern state, the *status quo* of *German political science* [*Staatswissen*] expresses the *incompletion of the modern state,* the damage to the flesh itself.

As the resolute opponent of the previous mode of *German* political consciousness, the criticism of speculative philosophy of law does not proceed in its own sphere but proceeds to *tasks* that can be solved by only one means—*practice* [*Praxis*].

The question arises: Can Germany reach a practice *à la hauteur des principes, that is,* a *revolution,* which will raise it not only to the *official level* of modern nations but to the *human level* which will be their immediate future?

The weapon of criticism obviously cannot replace the criticism of weapons. Material force must be overthrown by material force. But theory also becomes a material force once it has gripped the masses. Theory is capable of gripping the masses when it demonstrates *ad hominem,* and it demonstrates *ad hominem* when it becomes radical. To be radical is to grasp things by the root. But for man the root is man himself. The clear proof of the radicalism of German theory and hence of its political energy is that it proceeds from the decisive *positive* transcendence of religion. The criticism of religion ends with the doctrine that *man is the highest being for man,* hence with the *categorical imperative to overthrow all conditions* in which man is a degraded, enslaved, neglected, contemptible being—conditions that cannot better be described than by the exclamation of a Frenchman on the occasion of a proposed dog tax: Poor dogs! They want to treat you like human beings!

Even historically, theoretical emancipation has a specific practical significance for Germany. For Germany's *revolutionary* past is theoretical—it is the *Reformation*. As the revolution then began in the brain of the *monk*, now it begins in the brain of the *philosopher*.

*Luther*, to be sure, overcame bondage based on *devotion* by replacing it with bondage based on *conviction*. He shattered faith in authority by restoring the authority of faith. He turned priests into laymen by turning laymen into priests. He freed man from outward religiosity by making religiosity the inwardness of man. He emancipated the body from its chains by putting chains on the heart.

But if Protestantism was not the true solution, it was the true formulation of the problem. The question was no longer the struggle of the layman against the *priest external to him* but of his struggle against *his own inner priest*, his *priestly nature*. And if the Protestant transformation of German laymen into priests emancipated the lay popes—the *princes* with their clerical set, the privileged, and the Philistines—the philosophical transformation of priestly Germans into men will emancipate the *people*. But little as emancipation stops with princes, just as little will *secularization* of property stop with the *confiscation of church property* set in motion chiefly by hypocritical Prussia. At that time the Peasants' War, the most radical fact of German history, came to grief because of theology. Today, when theology itself has come to grief, the most unfree fact of German history—our *status quo*—will be shattered by philosophy. On the eve of the Reformation official Germany was the most abject vassal of Rome. On the eve of its revolution Germany is the abject vassal of something less than Rome—of Prussia and Austria, of ignorant country squires and Philistines.

But a major difficulty seems to stand in the way of a *radical* German revolution.

Revolutions require a *passive* element, a *material* basis. Theory is actualized in a people only insofar as it actualizes their needs. But will the enormous discrepancy between the demands of German thought and the answers of German actuality correspond to a similar discrepancy between civil society and the state, and within civil society itself? Will theoretical needs be immediate practical needs? It is not enough that thought should seek its actualization; actuality must itself strive toward thought.

But Germany has not risen to the intermediate stages of political emancipation at the same time as the modern nations. It has not yet reached in practice even the stages it has surpassed in theory. How can it clear with a *salto mortale* not only its own limitations but also those of modern nations—limitations which in actuality it must experience and strive for as an emancipation from its actual limitations? A radical revolution can only be a revolution of radical needs whose preconditions and birthplaces appear to be lacking.

But if Germany has attended the development of modern nations only through the abstract activity of thought without taking an active part in the real struggles of this development, it has also shared the *sufferings* of this development without sharing its enjoyments or partial satisfaction. Abstract activity on one side corresponds to abstract suffering on the other. One fine day Germany will find itself at the level of European decadence before ever having reached the level of European emancipation. It will be comparable to a *fetishist* wasting away from the diseases of Christianity.

Considering *German governments,* we find that owing to the circumstances of the time, the situation of Germany, the outlook of German culture, and finally their own fortunate instinct they are driven to combine the *civilized deficiencies* of the *modern political order* (whose advantages we do not enjoy) with the *barbarous deficiencies* of the *Ancien Régime* (which we enjoy in full). Hence Germany must participate more and more if not in the sense [*Verstand*] at least in the nonsense [*Unverstand*] of those political forms transcending its *status quo.* Is there, for example, another country in the whole world which as naïvely as so-called constitutional Germany shares all the illusions of constitutional statehood without sharing its realities? And was it not, necessarily, a German government's bright idea to combine the tortures of censorship with the tortures of the French September laws [of 1835] presupposing freedom of the press? As the *gods* of all nations were found in the Roman Pantheon, the *sins* of all forms of the state will be found in the Holy German Empire. That this eclecticism will reach an unprecedented height is particularly guaranteed by the *politico-aesthetic gourmanderie* of a German king [Friedrich Wilhelm IV] who plans to play all the roles of monarchy—feudal or bureaucratic, absolute or constitutional, autocratic or democratic —if not in the person of the people at least in his *own,* and if not for the people at least for *himself. As the deficiency of the political present erected into a system, Germany* will not be able to shed the specifically German limitations without shedding the general limitations of the political present.

*Radical* revolution, *universal human* emancipation, is not a utopian dream for Germany. What is utopian is the partial, the *merely* political revolution, the revolution which would leave the pillars of the house standing. What is the basis of a partial and merely political revolution? It is *part of civil society* emancipating itself and attaining *universal* supremacy, a particular class by virtue of its *special situation* undertaking the general emancipation of society. This class emancipates the whole of society but only on the condition that the whole of society is in the same position as this class, *for example,* that it has or can easily acquire money and education.

No class in civil society can take this role without arousing an impulse of enthusiasm in itself and in the masses, an impulse in which it fraternizes and merges with society at large, identifies itself with it, and is experienced and recognized as its *general representative*—an impulse in which its claims and rights are truly the rights and claims of society itself and in which it is actually the social head and the social heart. Only in the name of the general rights of society can a particular class claim general supremacy. Revolutionary energy and intellectual self-confidence are not by themselves sufficient to seize this emancipatory position and hence the political control of all spheres of society in the interest of its own. If a *popular revolution* is to coincide with the *emancipation of a particular class* of civil society, if *one* class is to stand for the whole society, all the defects of society must conversely be concentrated in another class. A particular class must be the class of general offense and the incorporation of general limitation. A particular social sphere must stand for the *notorious crime* of society as a whole so that emancipation from this sphere appears as general self-emancipation. For *one* class to be the class of emancipation *par excellence,* conversely another must be the obvious class of oppression. The negative, general significance of the French nobility and clergy determined the positive, general significance of the *bourgeoisie* standing next to and opposing them.

But in Germany every class lacks not only the consistency, penetration, courage, and ruthlessness which could stamp it as the negative representative of society. There is equally lacking in every class that breadth of soul which identifies itself, if only momentarily, with the soul of the people—that genius for inspiring material force toward political power, that revolutionary boldness which flings at its adversary the defiant words, *I am nothing and I should be everything.* The main feature of German morality and honor in classes as well as individuals is rather a *modest egoism* displaying its narrowness and allowing it to be displayed against itself. The relationship of the different spheres of German society is therefore not dramatic but epic. Each of them begins to be aware of itself and place itself beside the others, not as soon as it is oppressed but as soon as circumstances, without its initiative, create a social layer on which it can exert pressure in turn. Even the *moral self-esteem of the German middle class* rests only on its awareness of being the general representative of the philistine mediocrity of all the other classes. Hence, not only do German kings ascend their thrones *mal à propos,* but every section of civil society goes through a

defeat before it celebrates victory, develops its own obstacles before it overcomes those facing it, asserts its
narrow-minded nature before it can assert its generosity so
that even the opportunity of playing a great role has always passed before it actually existed and each class is
involved in a struggle against the class beneath as soon as
it begins to struggle with the class above it. Hence princes
struggle against kings, the bureaucrat against the nobility,
and the bourgeoisie against them all, while the proletariat is
already beginning to struggle against the bourgeoisie. The
middle class hardly dares to conceive the idea of emancipation from its own perspective. The development of social
conditions and the progress of political theory show that
perspective to be already antiquated or at least problematic.

In France it is enough to be something for one to want
to be everything. In Germany no one can be anything unless he is prepared to renounce everything. In France partial emancipation is the basis of universal emancipation.
In Germany universal emancipation is the *conditio sine qua
non* of any partial emancipation. In France it is the actuality, in Germany the impossibility, of gradual emancipation which must give birth to complete freedom. In
France every class of the nation is *politically idealistic* and
experiences itself first of all not as a particular class but as
representing the general needs of society. The role of
*emancipator* thus passes successively and dramatically
to different classes of people until it finally reaches the class
which actualizes social freedom, no longer assuming certain conditions external to man and yet created by human
society but rather organizing all the conditions of human
existence on the basis of social freedom. In Germany, by
contrast, where practical life is as mindless as mental life is
impractical, no class in civil society has any need or capacity for general emancipation until it is forced to it by its
*immediate* condition, by *material* necessity, by its *very
chains*.

Where, then, is the *positive* possibility of German
emancipation?

*Answer:* In the formation of a class with *radical chains*, a class in civil society that is not of civil society, a class that is the dissolution of all classes, a sphere of society having a universal character because of its universal suffering and claiming no *particular* right because no *particular wrong* but *unqualified wrong* is perpetrated on it; a sphere that can invoke no *traditional* title but only a *human* title, which does not partially oppose the consequences but totally opposes the premises of the German political system; a sphere, finally, that cannot emancipate itself without emancipating itself from all the other spheres of society, thereby emancipating them; a sphere, in short, that is the *complete loss* of humanity and can only redeem itself through the *total redemption of humanity*. This dissolution of society as a particular class is the *proletariat*.

The proletariat is only beginning to appear in Germany as a result of the rising *industrial* movement. For it is not poverty from *natural circumstances* but *artificially produced* poverty, not the human masses mechanically oppressed by the weight of society but the masses resulting from the *acute disintegration* of society, and particularly of the middle class, which gives rise to the proletariat—though also, needless to say, poverty from natural circumstances and Christian-Germanic serfdom gradually join the proletariat.

Heralding the *dissolution of the existing order of things*, the proletariat merely announces the *secret of its own existence* because it *is* the *real* dissolution of this order. Demanding the *negation of private property*, the proletariat merely raises to the *principle of society* what society has raised to the principle *of the proletariat*, what the proletariat already embodies as the negative result of society without its action. The proletarian thus has the same right in the emerging order of things as the *German king* has in the existing order when he calls the people *his* people or a horse *his* horse. Declaring the people to be his private property, the king merely proclaims that the private owner is king.

As philosophy finds its *material* weapons in the proletariat, the proletariat finds its *intellectual* weapons in philosophy. And once the lightning of thought has deeply struck this unsophisticated soil of the people, the *Germans* will emancipate themselves to become *men*.

Let us summarize the result:

The only emancipation of Germany possible *in practice* is emancipation based on *the* theory proclaiming that man is the highest essence of man. In Germany emancipation from the *Middle Ages* is possible only as emancipation at the same time from *partial* victories over the Middle Ages. In Germany *no* brand of bondage can be broken without *every* brand of bondage being broken. Always seeking *fundamentals,* Germany can only make a *fundamental* revolution. The *emancipation of the German* is the *emancipation of mankind*. The *head* of this emancipation is *philosophy*, its *heart* is the *proletariat*. Philosophy cannot be actualized without the transcendence [*Aufhebung*] of the proletariat, the proletariat cannot be transcended without the actualization of philosophy.

When all the inner conditions are fulfilled, the *day of German resurrection* will be announced by the *crowing of the French rooster*.

# From EXCERPT-NOTES OF 1844

[From March into the summer of 1844—after his commitment to socialism as "full human emancipation" through the proletariat—Marx acted on the impetus to study economics that had come from his "Defense of the Moselle Correspondent." He studied and copied extensive excerpts from main writings of Engels, Say, Adam Smith, Ricardo, James Mill, and others. Engels' "Outlines of Political Economy" from the *Jahrbücher* drew letters from Marx that led to life-long collaboration. In the same months Marx became acquainted with Proudhon, associated with French workers and socialists, and became a father. Marx's excerpts from Mill's *Elements of Political Economy*, from the sections on money and consumption as involving production, stimulated him to write out his own views translated below. Going beyond his discussion of money in "The Jewish Question," Marx argues that the whole system of credit, banking, and wage-labor involves a demoralizing alienation which subordinates persons to things. Where production is only for possession and profit, men become slaves to things and labor is a torment. Without these premises, however, production would affirm individuality and provide that mutuality in which I would be "affirmed in your thought as well as your love." Marx thus brought Feuerbach's ethical humanism—"love" as well as the critical idea of "alienation"—into economic relationships which he analyzed more closely in the subsequent "Manuscripts."]

## Money and Alienated Man

In comparing money with precious metals, as well as in the discussion of the costs of production as the only factor in determining value, Mill makes the mistake—generally like Ricardo's school—of giving the *abstract law* without the variation and continuous suspension by which it comes into being. If it is an *independent* law, for example, that the costs of production ultimately—or rather with the periodic and accidental coincidence of supply and demand—determine price (value), it is equally an *independent* law that this relationship does not hold and that value and production costs have no necessary relationship. Indeed, supply and demand coincide only momentarily because of previous fluctuations of supply and demand, because of the discrepancy of costs and exchange value, just as this fluctuation and discrepancy in turn succeed the momentary coincidence of supply and demand. This *actual* process, in which this law is only an abstract, accidental, and one-sided factor, becomes something accidental, something unessential with the modern economists. Why? Since they reduce the economic order to precise and exact formulas, the basic formula, abstractly expressed, would have to be: In the economic order lawfulness is determined by its opposite, lawlessness. The real law of the economic order is *contingency* from which we scientists arbitrarily stabilize some aspects in the form of laws.

In designating *money* as the *medium* of exchange, Mill puts the matter very well and succinctly in a single concept. The essence of money is not primarily that it externalizes property, but that the *mediating activity* or process—the *human* and social act in which man's products reciprocally complement one another—becomes *alienated* and takes on the quality of a *material thing,* money, external to man. By externalizing this mediating activity, man is active only as he is lost and dehumanized. The very *relationship* of things and the human dealings with them become an operation beyond and above man. Through this *alien mediation* man regards his will, his activity, and his relationships to others as a power independent of himself and of them—instead of man himself being the mediator for man. His slavery thus reaches a climax. It is clear that this *mediator* becomes an *actual god,* for the mediator is the *actual power* over that which he mediates to me. His worship becomes an end in itself. Apart from this mediation, objects lose their value. They have value only insofar as they *represent* it while originally it appeared that the mediation would have value only insofar as *it* represents *objects*. This inversion of the original relationship is necessary. The *mediation,* therefore, is the lost, alienated *essence* of private property, exteriorated and *externalized* private property, just as it is the *externalized exchange* of human production with human production, the *externalized* species—activity of man. All qualities involved in this activity are transmitted to the mediator. Man as separated from this mediator thus becomes so much the poorer as the mediator becomes *richer.*

Christ originally *represents:* (1) man before God; (2) God for man; (3) man for man.

Likewise, *money* originally represents by its very concept: (1) private property for private property; (2) society for private property; (3) private property for society.

But Christ is God *externalized,* externalized *man.* God has value only insofar as he represents Christ; man has value only insofar as he represents Christ. It is the same with money.

Why must private property end up in *money?* Because man as a social being must resort to *exchange* and because exchange—under the presupposition of private property—must end up in value. The mediating process of man making exchanges is no social, no *human process,* no human relationship; rather, it is the *abstract relationship* of private property to private property, and this *abstract* relationship is the *value* whose actual existence as value is primarily *money.* Because men making exchanges do not relate to one another as men, *things* lose the significance of being human and personal property. The social relationship of private property to private property is a relationship in which private property has alienated itself. The reflexive existence of this relationship, money, is thus the externalization of private property, an abstraction from its *specific* and personal nature.

Despite all its cleverness, the modern economic order in opposition to the monetary system cannot achieve a decisive victory. The crude economic superstitions of people and their governments hold on to the *perceptible, palpable,* and *observable* moneybag and believe in the absolute value of precious metals and their possession as the only real form of wealth. The enlightened and knowledgeable economist comes along and proves to them that money is a commodity like any other and that its value, like that of any other commodity, depends on the relationship of the costs of production to demand (competition) and supply, and to the quantity or competition of other commodities. The correct reply to this economist is that the *actual* value of things, after all, is their *exchange value,* and the exchange value resides in money, just as money exists in precious metals. Money, therefore, is the *true* value of things and hence the most desirable thing. The economist's doctrines yield the same wisdom, except that he can abstractly recognize the existence of money in all forms of commodities and not believe in the exchange value of its official metallic existence. The metallic existence of money is only the official sensuous expression of the very soul of money existing in all branches of production and in all operations of civil society.

The modern economists, in opposition to the monetary system, have grasped *money* in its abstraction and generality and are enlightened about the *sensuous* superstition which believes that money exists only in precious metals. They substitute refined superstition for this crude one. But since both have a single root, the enlightened form of the superstition does not entirely replace the crude sensuous form because it does not deal with its essence but only with the particular form of its essence.—The *personal* existence of money as money—and not only as the inner, implicitly existing, and hidden relationship of commodities to one another in respect to their conversion and status—this existence more corresponds to the essence of money, the more abstract it is and the less *natural* relationship it has to other commodities. The more it appears as a product and yet again as something not produced by man, the less is its element of existence something *produced by nature*. The more it is produced by man or produced in economics, the greater is the *inverted* relationship of its *value as money* to the exchange value or to the monetary value of the material in which it exists. Hence *paper money* and *paper substitutes for money* such as bills of exchange, checks, promissory notes, etc., constitute the more *complete* existence of *money as money* and a necessary phase in the progressive development in the monetary system. In the *credit system,* fully expressed in *banking,* it appears as if the power of an alien, material force is broken, the relationships of self-alienation overcome, and man again is humanly related to man. The *followers of Saint-Simon,* misled by this *appearance,* consider the development of money, bills of exchange, paper money, paper substitutes for money, *credit,* and *banking* as a gradual transcendence of the separation of man from things, capital from labor, private property from money, and of money from man— a gradual transcendence of the separation of man from man. Hence the organized *bank system* is their ideal. But this transcendence of alienation, this *return* of man to himself and thus to other men is only *apparent.* Its self-alienation, its dehumanization is all the more *odious* and *extreme,* insofar as its element is no longer the commodity, metal, or paper, but the *moral* and *social* existence, the very *inwardness* of the human heart; insofar as it is the highest *distrust* of man for man and complete alienation, under the appearance of trust of man for man.

What is the nature of *credit?* We are here completely disregarding the *content* of credit which is again money. We thus disregard the *content* of this trust, wherein a man *recognizes* another by lending him values—let us assume that he does not take interest and is no profiteer—and by trusting that his fellow man is a "good" man and not a rascal. By a "good" man the trusting man here understands, like Shylock, the man who can pay.—Credit is possible under two relationships and under two distinct conditions. Take the case where a wealthy man gives credit to a poor man whom he considers diligent and reliable. This kind of credit belongs in the romantic and sentimental part of economics, belongs to its departures, excesses, *exceptions,* not to its *rule.* Even if this exception and this romantic possibility are assumed, the life, talent, and activity of the poor man *guarantee* for the rich man the repayment for the money loaned. All social virtues of the poor man, then, the substance of his living and his very existence, represent for the rich man the reimbursement of his capital with the usual interest. The death of the poor man is the worst possibility for the creditor. It is the death of his capital and the interest as well. Consider the ignominy in the *evaluation* of a man in terms of *money* as it takes place in the credit system. It is understood that in addition to *moral* guarantees the creditor also has the guarantee of *judicial* force and more or less *real* guarantees for his man. If the debtor is himself affluent, *credit* becomes merely a facilitating *medium* of exchange, and *money* itself acquires an *ideal* form. *Credit* is the *economic* judgment of man's morality. In credit, *man* himself instead of metal and paper has become the *medium* of exchange, but not as man, but rather as the *existence of capital* and interest. The medium of exchange is thus returned from its material form to man, but only because man has been externalized and has himself become a material form. Within the credit relationship, money is not transcended in man, but man is transformed into *money*, and money is *incorporated* in him. *Human individuality* and human *morality* have become an article of trade and the *material* in which money exists. Instead of money and paper, my very personal existence, my flesh and blood, my social virtue and reputation is the matter and the substance of the *monetary spirit*. Credit no longer reduces monetary value to money, but to human flesh and the human heart. All the progress and inconsequence of a false system thus constitute the extreme regression and consequence of ignominy.

The nature of the credit system as alienated from man is confirmed in the following manner under the appearance of the economic recognition of man: (1) The contrast between the capitalist and the laborer—between the big and the small capitalist—becomes even greater as credit is given only to the one who already has and is a new chance for accumulation for the wealthy, or as the poor person sees his *entire* existence confirmed or denied, and completely dependent upon the accidental caprice and judgment of the wealthy man. (2) Mutual dissimulation, hypocrisy, and sanctimoniousness are carried to the point that a moral judgment is added to the simple statement that a man without credit is poor, a judgment that he is untrustworthy and unworthy of recognition, a social pariah and bad man. On top of suffering from his destitution the poor man suffers from having to make a debasing *plea* to the rich for credit. (3) With this completely *ideal* existence of money, man must *counterfeit* his own person and must obtain credit by sneaking and lying. The credit relationship—for the creditor as well as for the debtor—becomes an object of trade, an object of mutual betrayal and misuse. Here *mistrust* is brilliantly apparent as the basis of economic trust; in the distrustful weighing as to whether credit should or should not be given; in the spying into the secrets of the private life of the one seeking credit; in the revealing of a rival's temporary misfortunes in order to wreck him by shaking his credit, etc.; the entire system of bankruptcy, pseudo-enterprises, etc. . . . In the *credit system on the state level* the state occupies completely the same position as shown above for man . . . The game with governmental bonds shows how far the state has become the plaything of men of commerce.

(4) The *credit system* is perfected in *banking*. The creation of the banker's position, state regulation of banking, concentration of fortunes in these hands—this economic *areopagus* of the nation—is the lauded perfection of the monetary system. As the *moral recognition of a man* and the *confidence in the state* has the form of *credit* in the credit system, the secret involved in the deception of that moral recognition, the *amoral* ignominy of that morality as well as the sanctimoniousness and egoism in the confidence in the state become apparent—and all this reveals itself for what it actually is.

The *exchange* of human activity within production itself as well as the exchange of *human products* with one another is equivalent to the *generic activity* and generic spirit whose actual, conscious, and authentic existence is *social* activity and *social* satisfaction. As *human* nature is the *true common life* [Gemeinwesen] of man, men through the activation of their *nature create* and produce a human *common life,* a social essence which is no abstractly universal power opposed to the single individual, but is the essence or nature of every single individual, his own activity, his own life, his own spirit, his own wealth. *Authentic common life* arises not through reflection; rather it comes about from the *need* and *egoism* of individuals, that is, immediately from the activation of their very existence. It is not up to man whether this common life exists or not. However, so long as man does not recognize himself as man and does not organize the world humanly, this *common life* appears in the form of *alienation*, because its *subject*, man, is a being alienated from itself. Men as actual, living, particular individuals, not in an abstraction, *constitute* this common life. It is, therefore, *what* men are. To say that *man* alienates himself is the same as saying that the *society* of this alienated man is the caricature of his *actual common life*, of his true generic life. His activity, therefore, appears as torment, his own creation as a force alien to him, his wealth as poverty, the *essential bond* connecting him with other men as something unessential so that the separation from other men appears as his true existence. His life appears as the sacrifice of his life, the realization of his nature as the diminution of his life, his production as the production of his destruction, his power over the object as the power of the object over him; the master of his creation appears as its slave.

Political economy understands the *common life of man*, the self-activating *human* essence and mutual redintegration toward generic and truly human life, in the form of *exchange* and *commerce*. *Society*, says Destutt de Tracy, is a *series of multilateral exchanges*. It is constituted by this movement of multilateral integration. *Society*, says Adam Smith, is a *commercial enterprise*. Each of its members is a *merchant*. It is evident that political economy *establishes* an *alienated* form of social intercourse as the *essential*, *original*, and definitive human form.

Economics—like the actual process itself—proceeds from the *relationship of man to man* and from the relationship of one *property owner to another*. Let us presuppose man as *property owner*, that is, as exclusive possessor who maintains his personality and distinguishes himself from other men and relates himself to them through this exclusive possession. Private property is his personal existence, his *distinguishing* and hence essential existence. The *loss* or *relinquishing* of private property, then, is an *externalization of man* as well as of *private property*. We are concerned here only with the latter. When I yield my private property to another person, it ceases being mine. It becomes something independent of me and *outside* my sphere, something *external* to me. I *externalize* my private property. So far as I am concerned, it is *externalized* private property. I see it only as something generally *externalized;* I only transcend my *personal* relationship to it; and I return it to the *elemental* forces of nature when I externalize it only in relation to myself. It only becomes externalized *private property* as it ceases being *my* private property without ceasing to be *private property* in general, that is, when it acquires the same relationship to *another* man *outside* of me, as it had to me—in a word, when it becomes the *private property* of *another* man. Apart from the situation of *force,* what causes me to externalize *my* private property to another person? Economics answers correctly: *need* and *want.* The other person is also a property owner, but of *another* object which I lack and which I neither can nor want to be without, an object which to me seems to be something *needed* for the redintegration of my existence and the realization of my nature.

The bond relating the two property owners to each other is the *specific nature of the object.* The fact that either property owner desires and wants objects makes him aware that he has another *essential* relationship to objects outside of property and that he is not the particular being he takes himself to be but rather a *total* being whose wants have a relationship of *inner* property to the products of the labor of the other person. For the need of an object is the most evident and irrefutable proof that the object belongs to *my* nature and that the existence of the object for me and its *property* are the property appropriate to my essence. Both owners are thus impelled to relinquish their property, but in such a way that at the same time they reaffirm that property; or they are impelled to relinquish that property within the relationship of private property. Each thus externalizes a part of his property in the other person.

The *social* relationship of both owners is thus the *mutuality of externalization*, the relationship of externalization on both sides—or *externalization* as the relationship of both owners—while in simple private property *externalization* takes place only one-sidedly, in relationship to itself.

*Exchange* or *barter*, therefore, is the social, generic act, the common essence, the social intercourse and integration of man within *private property*, and the external, the *externalized* generic act. For that very reason it appears as *barter*. And hence it is likewise the opposite of the *social* relationship.

Through the mutual externalization or alienation of private property, *private property* itself has been determined as *externalized* private property. First of all it has ceased being the product of labor and being the exclusive, distinctive personality of its owner because the owner has externalized it; it has been removed from the owner whose product it was and has acquired a personal significance for the person who did *not* produce it. It has lost its personal significance for the owner. In the second place it has been related to and equated with another private property. A private property of a *different* nature has taken its place, just as it itself takes the position of a private property of a *different* nature. On both sides, then, private property appears as a representative of private property of a different nature, as the *equivalence* of another natural product. Both sides are so related that each represents the existence of the *other* and they mutually serve as *substitutes* for themselves and the other. The existence of private property as such has thus become a *substitute*, an *equivalent*. Instead of its immediate self-unity it exists only in relationship to *something else*. As an *equivalent* its existence is no longer something peculiarly appropriate to it. It has become *value* and immediately *exchange value*. Its existence as *value* is a determination of *itself*, different from its immediate existence, outside of its specific nature, and *externalized*—only a *relative* existence.

It will be shown elsewhere how this *value* is more precisely determined and how it becomes *price*.

The relationship of exchange being presupposed, *labor immediately* becomes *wage-labor*. This relationship of alienated labor reaches its apex only by the fact (1) that on the one side *wage-labor*, the product of the laborer, stands in no *immediate* relationship to his need and to his *status* but is rather determined in both directions through social combinations alien to the laborer; (2) that the *buyer* of the product is not himself productive but exchanges what has been produced by others. In the crude form of *externalized* private property, *barter*, each of the two private owners produces what his need, his inclination, and the existing raw material induces him to produce. They exchange only the surplus of their production. To be sure, labor was for each one the immediate *source of his subsistence;* at the same time, however, it was also the confirmation of his *individual existence*. Through exchange, his *labor* has partly become his *source of income*. The purpose and existence of labor have changed. The product is created as *value, exchange value*, and an *equivalent* and no longer because of its immediate personal relationship to the producer. The more varied production becomes—in other words, the more varied the needs become on the one hand and the more one-sided the producer's output becomes on the other—the more does his labor fall into the category of *wage-labor*, until it is eventually nothing but wage-labor and until it becomes entirely *incidental* and *unessential* whether the producer immediately enjoys and needs his product and whether the *activity*, the action of labor itself, is his self-satisfaction and the realization of his natural dispositions and spiritual aims.

The following elements are contained in *wage-labor:* (1) the chance relationship and alienation of labor from the laboring subject; (2) the chance relationship and alienation of labor from its object; (3) the determination of the laborer through social needs which are an alien compulsion to him, a compulsion to which he submits out of egoistic need and distress—these social needs are merely a source of providing the necessities of life for him, just as he is merely a slave for them; (4) the maintenance of his individual existence appears to the worker as the *goal* of his activity and his real action is only a means; he lives to acquire the means of *living*.

The greater and the more articulated the social power is within the relationship of private property, the more *egoistic* and asocial man becomes, the more he becomes alienated from his own nature.

Just as the mutual exchange of products of *human activity* appears as *trading* and *bargaining*, so does the mutual redintegration and exchange of the activity itself appear as the *division of labor* making man as far as possible an abstract being, an automaton, and transforming him into a spiritual and physical monster.

Precisely the unity of human labor is regarded as being its *division* because its social nature comes into being only as its opposite, in the form of alienation. The *division of labor* increases with civilization.

Within the presupposition of the division of labor, the product and material of private property gradually acquire for the individual the significance of an *equivalent*. He no longer exchanges his *surplus*, and he can become *indifferent* to the object of his production. He no longer immediately exchanges his product for the product he *needs*. The equivalent becomes an equivalent in *money* which is the immediate result of wage-labor and the *medium* of exchange. (See above.)

The complete domination of the alienated object *over* man is evident in *money* and the complete disregard of the nature of the material, the specific nature of private property as well as the personality of the proprietor.

What formerly was the domination of one person over another has now become the general domination of the *thing* over the *person*, the domination of the product over the producer. Just as the determination of the *externalization* of private property lay in the *equivalent* and in value, so is *money* the sensuous, self-objectified existence of this *externalization*.

It is clear that economics can grasp this entire development only as a factum and as the offspring of chance need.

The separation of labor from itself = separation of laborer from capitalist = separation of labor from capital whose original form can be divided into *real property* and *chattel property* . . . The original determination of private property is monopoly; as soon as it acquires a political constitution, it is that of monopoly. Monopoly perfected is competition. —The economist distinguishes *production* and *consumption,* and as media of both he refers to *exchange* or *distribution.* The separation of production from consumption, and of activity from mind in various individuals and within the same individual is the *separation of labor* from its *object* and from itself as one mind. *Distribution* is the self-active power of private property. —The mutual separation of labor, capital, and real property as well as the separation of labor from labor, of capital from capital, of real property from real property, and finally the separation of labor from wages, of capital from profit, of profit from interest, and of real property from rent makes self-alienation appear in the form of self-alienation as well as in the form of mutual alienation.

## Free Human Production

It is the basic presupposition of private property that man *produces* only in order to *own.* The purpose of production is to *own.* It not only has such a *useful* purpose; it also has a *selfish* purpose. Man only produces in order to *own* something for himself. The object of his production is the objectification of his *immediate,* selfish *need.* Man—in his wild, barbaric condition—determines his production by the *extent* of his immediate need whose content is the *immediately* produced object itself.

In that condition man produces *no more* than he immediately needs. The *limit of his need* is the *limit of his production.* Demand and supply coincide. Production is *determined* by need. Either no exchange takes place or the exchange is reduced to the exchange of man's labor for the product of his labor, and this exchange is the latent form (the germ) of real exchange.

As soon as exchange occurs, there is an overproduction beyond the immediate boundary of ownership. But this overproduction does not exceed selfish need. Rather it is only an *indirect* way of satisfying a need which finds its objectification in the production of another person. Production has become a *source of income*, labor for profit. While formerly need determined the extent of production, now production, or rather the *owning of the product*, determines how far needs can be satisfied.

I have produced for myself and not for you, just as you have produced for yourself and not for me. The result of my production as such has as little direct connection with you as the result of your production has with me, that is, our production is not production of man for man as man, not *socialized* production. No one is gratified by the product of another. Our mutual production means nothing for us as human beings. Our exchange, therefore, cannot be the mediating movement in which it would be acknowledged that my product means anything for you because it is an *objectification* of your being, your need. *Human nature* is not the bond of our production for each other. Exchange can only set in *motion* and confirm the *relationship* which each of us has to his own product and to the production of the other person. Each of us sees in his product only his *own* objectified self-interest and in the product of another person, *another* self-interest which is independent, alien, and objectified.

As a human being, however, you do have a human relation to my product; you *want* my product. It is the object of your desire and your will. But your want, desire, and will for my product are impotent. In other words, your *human* nature, necessarily and intimately related to my human production, is not your *power*, not your sharing in this production, because the *power* of human nature is not acknowledged in my production. Rather it is the *bond* which makes you dependent upon me because it makes you dependent on my product. It is far from being the *means* of giving you *power* over my production; rather it is the *means* of giving me power over you.

When I produce *more* than I can consume, I subtly *reckon* with your need. I produce only the *semblance* of a surplus of the object. In truth I produce a *different* object, the object of your production which I plan to exchange for this surplus, an exchange already accomplished in thought. My *social* relationship with you and my labor for your want is just plain *deception* and our mutual redintegration is *deception* just as well. Mutual pillaging is its base. Its background is the intent to pillage, to defraud. Since our exchange is selfish on your side as well as mine and since every self-interest attempts to surpass that of another person, we necessarily attempt to defraud each other. The power I give my object over yours, however, requires your *acknowledgment* to become real. Our mutual acknowledgment of the mutual power of our objects is a battle and the one with more insight, energy, power, and cleverness is the winner. If my physical strength suffices, I pillage you directly. If there is no physical power, we mutually dissemble and the more adroit comes out on top. It makes no difference for the *entire* relationship who the winner is, for the *ideal* and *intended* victory takes place on both sides; in his own judgment each of the two has overcome the other.

On both sides exchange necessarily requires the *object* of mutual production and mutual ownership. The ideal relationship to the mutual objects of our production is our mutual need. But the *real* and *truly effective* relationship is only the mutually *exclusive ownership* of mutual production. It is your *object*, the *equivalent* of my object, that gives your want for my object *value*, *dignity*, and *efficacy* for me. Our mutual product, therefore, is the *means*, the *intermediary*, the *instrument*, the *acknowledged power* of our mutual needs. Your *demand* and the *equivalent of your property* are terms which for me are *synonymous* and equally valid, and your demand is effective only when it has an effect on me. Without this effect your demand is merely an unsatisfied effort on your part and without consequence for me. You have no relationship to my object as a human being because I *myself* have no human relation to it. But the *means* is the *real power* over an object, and we mutually regard our product as the *power* each one has over the other and over himself. In other words, our own product is turned against us. It appeared to be our property, but actually we are its property. We ourselves are excluded from *true* property because our *property* excludes the other human being.

Our objects in their relation to one another constitute the only intelligible language we use with one another. We would not understand a human language, and it would remain without effect. On the one hand, it would be felt and spoken as a plea, as begging, and as *humiliation* and hence uttered with shame and with a feeling of supplication; on the other hand, it would be heard and rejected as *effrontery* or *madness*. We are so much mutually alienated from human nature that the direct language of this nature is an *injury to human dignity* for us, while the alienated language of objective values appears as justified, self-confident, and self-accepted human dignity.

To be sure, from your point of view your product is an *instrument,* a *means* for the appropriation of my product and for the satisfaction of your need. But from my point of view it is the *goal* of our exchange. I regard you as a means and instrument for the production of this object, that is, my goal, and much more so than I regard you as related to my object. But (1) each of us actually *does* what the other thinks he is doing. You actually made yourself the means, the instrument, and the producer of *your* own object in order to appropriate mine; (2) for you, your own object is only the *sensuous shell* and *concealed form* of my object; its production *means* and *expressly* is the *acquisition* of my object. You indeed become the *means* and *instrument* of your object; your greed is the *slave* of this object, and you performed slavish services so that the object is never again a remission of your greed. This mutual servitude to the object is actually manifested to us at the beginning of its development as the relationship of *lordship* and *slavery,* and is only the *crude* and *frank* expression of our *essential* relationship.

Our *mutual* value is the *value* of our mutual objects for us. Man himself, therefore, is mutually *valueless* for us.

Suppose we had produced things as human beings: in his production each of us would have *twice affirmed* himself and the other. (1) In my *production* I would have objectified my *individuality* and its *particularity*, and in the course of the activity I would have enjoyed an individual *life;* in viewing the object I would have experienced the individual joy of knowing my personality as an *objective, sensuously perceptible,* and *indubitable* power. (2) In your satisfaction and your use of my product I would have had the *direct* and conscious satisfaction that my work satisfied a *human* need, that it objectified *human* nature, and that it created an object appropriate to the need of another *human* being. (3) I would have been the *mediator* between you and the species and you would have experienced me as a redintegration of your own nature and a necessary part of your self; I would have been affirmed in your thought as well as your love. (4) In my individual life I would have directly created your life; in my individual activity I would have immediately *confirmed* and *realized* my true *human* and *social* nature.

Our productions would be so many mirrors reflecting our nature.

What happens so far as I am concerned would also apply to you.

Let us summarize the various factors in the supposition above:

My labor would be a *free manifestation of life* and an *enjoyment* of *life*. Under the presupposition of private property it is an *externalization of life* because I work *in order to live* and provide for myself the *means* of living. Working *is not* living.

Furthermore, in my labor the *particularity* of my individuality would be affirmed because my *individual* life is affirmed. Labor then would be *true, active property*. Under the presupposition of private property my individuality is externalized to the point where I *hate* this *activity* and where it is a *torment* for me. Rather it is then only the *semblance* of an activity, only a *forced* activity, imposed upon me only by *external* and accidental necessity and *not* by an *internal* and *determined* necessity.

My labor can appear in my object only according to its nature; it cannot appear as something *different* from itself. My labor, therefore, is manifested as the objective, sensuous, perceptible, and indubitable expression of my *self-loss* and my *powerlessness*.

# ECONOMIC AND PHILOSOPHIC
## MANUSCRIPTS (1844)

[Developing and ordering basic themes of his Excerpt-Notes in critical relation to Feuerbach's humanism and Hegel's dialectic, Marx wrote the following analysis of labor, capital, property, and communism in Paris late in the summer of 1844. Since its first publication in 1932 this analysis has been frequently and copiously cited as revealing the fulcrum of Marx's thought and the essential premises of his *Capital*.

"Alienated Labor," the most substantial section of Marx's first manuscript, extends the kind of criticism Feuerbach had concentrated on religion. Property, wages, and the conflict between capital and labor are seen as effects of man's alienation from the tools, product, and social process of work, so the whole of human degradation and servitude is rooted in the relation of worker to production. In three shorter sections of the first manuscript, omitted below, Marx found Adam Smith and Ricardo delineating the struggle between capital and labor, the tendency of wages to seek the animal level for labor as a commodity, and the concentration of capital amidst expansion of the proletariat. The surviving fragment of Marx's second manuscript, omitted here, stressed previous conclusions on the struggle between capital and labor.

"Private Property and Communism," a major section of Marx's third manuscript, follows a brief discussion, omitted below, on Adam Smith as the Luther of economics. In contrast to the "crude," property-obsessed communism of Fourier and Proudhon, communism as "completed naturalism or humanism" fully overcomes human alienation, refuses to abstract "society" from individuals, develops all of man's capacities, and integrates man with industry and history, something Feuerbach had not done. Marx's third manuscript also had two shorter sections, omitted below, emphasizing fetishism in money, the real brotherhood of French workers, division of labor as depending on property, and money's perversion of love into hate.

Major points of Marx's fourth manuscript, a digest of the last chapter of Hegel's *Phenomenology*, are included in the extensive, final section of the third manuscript given below, a critique of Hegel's dialectic. Marx praises Hegel for seeing man as a result of his own work in a historical dialectic. His mistake, exposed by Feuerbach, lay in treating that dialectic as a relation of concepts, hence his "accommodation" and "false positivism." Marx's "completed naturalism" would unite the truth of Hegel's idealism, historical dialectic, with the truth of Feuerbach's "materialism," the primacy of sense perception.]

## Preface

In the *Deutsch-Französische Jahrbücher* I announced a critique of jurisprudence and political science in the form of a critique of the *Hegelian* philosophy of law. Preparing this for publication, I found that the combination of criticism directed solely against speculation with criticism of various subjects would be quite unsuitable; it would impede the development of the argument and render comprehension difficult. Moreover, the wealth and diversity of the subjects to be dealt with could have been accommodated in a *single* work only in a very aphoristic style, and such aphoristic presentation would have given the *impression* of arbitrary systematization. Therefore, I shall issue the critique of law, morals, politics, etc., in separate, independent brochures, and finally attempt to give in a separate work the unity of the whole, the relation of the separate parts, and eventually a critique of the speculative treatment of the material. Hence in the present work the relationships of political economy with the state, law, morals, civil life, etc., are touched upon only insofar as political economy itself, ex professo, deals with these subjects.

It is hardly necessary to assure the reader familiar with political economy that my conclusions have been obtained through an entirely empirical analysis, based on a thorough, critical study of political economy.

((The uninformed reviewer, however, who tries to hide his complete ignorance and poverty of thought by hurling *"utopian phrase"* at the positive critic's head or such phrases as "the entirely pure, entirely decisive, entirely critical criticism," the "not merely legal but social, entirely social society," the "compact, massy mass," the "outspoken spokesman of the massy mass"—this reviewer [Bruno

Bauer] has yet to furnish the first proof that outside his theological family affairs he has anything to contribute to *worldly* matters.))[*]

It is a matter of course that in addition to the French and English socialists I have also used German socialist works. The significant and *original* German contributions on this subject—apart from Weitling's writings—amount to no more than the essays by Hess in *Twenty-one Sheets [from Switzerland]* and Engels' "Outlines of a Critique of Political Economy" in the *Deutsch-Französische Jahrbücher* where I indicated the basic elements of the present work in a very general way.

((Besides the criticism concerned with political economy, positive criticism in general, and thus also German positive criticism of political economy, is really founded on the discoveries of *Feuerbach* against whose *Philosophy of the Future* and "Theses on the Reform of Philosophy" in the *Anekdota* the petty envy of some and the loud rage of others seem to have instigated an organized conspiracy of *silence*, despite the tacit use that is made of Feuerbach's works.))

*Positive* humanistic and naturalistic criticism begins with *Feuerbach*. The less vociferous *Feuerbach's* writings are, the more certain, profound, extensive, and lasting is their influence—the only writings since Hegel's *Phenomenology [of Spirit]* and *Logic* containing a real theoretical revolution.

In contrast to the *critical theologians* of our time [Bruno Bauer and followers] I have regarded the concluding chapter of the present work—the discussion of the *Hegelian dialectic* and philosophy in general—to be absolutely necessary because such a task has not yet been accomplished. This lack of *thoroughness* is inevitable because even the *critical* theologian remains a *theologian*. Either he must proceed from certain presuppositions of philosophy, accepting them as authoritative, or else, if in the course of criticism and as a result of other persons'

[* Material within double parentheses, from here on, vertically crossed out by Marx.]

discoveries doubts arise in his mind about the philosophical presuppositions, he abandons them in a cowardly, indefensible manner, *abstracts* from them, and manifests his servitude to these very presuppositions and his vexation over this servitude in a negative, unconscious, and sophistical way.

((manifests this only negatively and unconsciously, on the one hand, in constantly repeating the assurance of the *purity* of his own criticism, and on the other hand, in trying to present the appearance that criticism only has to do with a limited form of the criticism outside—say that of the eighteenth century—and with the obtuseness of the *mass,* in order to divert the observer's eyes as well as his own from the *necessary* clash between *criticism* and its birthplace—Hegelian *dialectic* and German philosophy in general—and from the necessary advancement of modern criticism beyond its own narrowness and natural origin. Finally, however, when discoveries such as *Feuerbach's* are made about the nature of his own philosophical presuppositions, the critical theologian may claim to have made the discovery *himself* and pretend this by hurling *catch phrases,* the results of the discovery which he was not able to develop, at writers who are still caught in philosophy. He may even manage to secure the sense of his superiority to that discovery, not by attempting, even if he could, to bring into their proper relations the elements of Hegelian *dialectic* which he still finds missing in the criticism of Hegelian dialectic not yet served up to him, but rather by employing those elements in veiled, mischievous, and sceptical ways, in a secretive manner, against the criticism of Hegelian dialectic—such as the category of mediating proof against the category of positive, self-originating truth, the [ . . . ?], etc.—in the form *peculiar* to Hegelian dialectic. The theological critic finds it quite natural that everything is to *be done* by philosophy so that he can *chatter* about purity, resoluteness, about the very critical criticism. He fancies himself the true *conqueror of philosophy* whenever he happens to *feel* that some moment in Hegel is lacking in relation to Feuerbach —for however much the theological critic practices the spiritualistic idolatry of *"Self-Consciousness"* and "Spirit," he can not go beyond feeling and achieve consciousness.))

Considered closely, *theological criticism*—while in the beginning of the movement an actual factor of progress—in the final analysis is nothing but the culmination and consequence of the old *philosophical* transcendence, particularly *Hegelian transcendence*, distorted into a *theological caricature*. On another occasion [subsequently in *The Holy Family*] I shall describe in detail this interesting historical justice, this historical nemesis, which is inducing theology, ever the sore point of philosophy, to exhibit in itself the negative dissolution of philosophy—that is, its decomposition process.

((To what extent *Feuerbach's* discoveries about the nature of philosophy still require—at least for their *proof*—a critical analysis of philosophical dialectic will be learned from my exposition itself.))

## Alienated Labor

We have proceeded from the presuppositions of political economy. We have accepted its language and its laws. We presupposed private property, the separation of labor, capital and land, hence of wages, profit of capital and rent, likewise the division of labor, competition, the concept of exchange value, etc. From political economy itself, in its own words, we have shown that the worker sinks to the level of a commodity, the most miserable commodity; that the misery of the worker is inversely proportional to the power and volume of his production; that the necessary result of competition is the accumulation of capital in a few hands and thus the revival of monopoly in a more frightful form; and finally that the distinction between capitalist and landowner, between agricultural laborer and industrial worker, disappears and the whole society must divide into the two classes of *proprietors* and propertyless *workers*.

Political economy proceeds from the fact of private property. It does not explain private property. It grasps the actual, *material* process of private property in abstract and general formulae which it then takes as *laws*. It does not *comprehend* these laws, that is, does not prove them as proceeding from the nature of private property. Political economy does not disclose the reason for the division between capital and labor, between capital and land. When, for example, the relation of wages to profits is determined, the ultimate basis is taken to be the interest of the capitalists; that is, political economy assumes what it should develop. Similarly, competition is referred to at every point and explained from external circumstances. Political economy teaches us nothing about the extent to which these external, apparently accidental circumstances are simply the expression of a necessary development. We have seen how political economy regards exchange itself as an accidental fact. The only wheels which political economy puts in motion are *greed* and the *war among the greedy, competition.*

Just because political economy does not grasp the interconnections within the movement, the doctrine of competition could stand opposed to the doctrine of monopoly, the doctrine of freedom of craft to that of the guild, the doctrine of the division of landed property to that of the great estate. Competition, freedom of craft, and division of landed property were developed and conceived only as accidental, deliberate, forced consequences of monopoly, the guild, and feudal property, rather than necessary, inevitable, natural consequences.

We now have to grasp the essential connection among private property, greed, division of labor, capital and land-ownership, and the connection of exchange with competition, of value with the devaluation of men, of monopoly with competition, etc., and of this whole alienation with the *money*-system.

Let us not put ourselves in a fictitious primordial state like a political economist trying to clarify things. Such a primordial state clarifies nothing. It merely pushes the issue into a gray, misty distance. It acknowledges as a fact or event what it should deduce, namely, the necessary relation between two things for example, between division of labor and exchange. In such a manner theology explains the origin of evil by the fall of man. That is, it asserts as a fact in the form of history what it should explain.

We proceed from a *present* fact of political economy.

The worker becomes poorer the more wealth he produces, the more his production increases in power and extent. The worker becomes a cheaper commodity the more commodities he produces. The *increase in value* of the world of things is directly proportional to the *decrease in value* of the human world. Labor not only produces commodities. It also produces itself and the worker as a *commodity,* and indeed in the same proportion as it produces commodities in general.

This fact simply indicates that the object which labor produces, its product, stands opposed to it as an *alien thing,* as a *power independent* of the producer. The product of labor is labor embodied and made objective in a thing. It is the *objectification* of labor. The realization of labor is its objectification. In the viewpoint of political economy this realization of labor appears as the *diminution* of the worker, the objectification as the *loss of and subservience to the object,* and the appropriation as *alienation* [*Entfremdung*], as externalization [*Entäusserung*].

So much does the realization of labor appear as diminution that the worker is diminished to the point of starvation. So much does objectification appear as loss of the object that the worker is robbed of the most essential objects not only of life but also of work. Indeed, work itself becomes a thing of which he can take possession only with the greatest effort and with the most unpredictable interruptions. So much does the appropriation of the object appear as alienation that the more objects the worker produces, the fewer he can own and the more he falls under the domination of his product, of capital.

All these consequences follow from the fact that the worker is related to the *product of his labor* as to an *alien* object. For it is clear according to this premise: The more the worker exerts himself, the more powerful becomes the alien objective world which he fashions against himself, the poorer he and his inner world become, the less there is that belongs to him. It is the same in religion. The more man attributes to God, the less he retains in himself. The worker puts his life into the object; then it no longer belongs to him but to the object. The greater this activity, the poorer is the worker. What the product of his work is, he is not. The greater this product is, the smaller he is himself. The *externalization* of the worker in his product means not only that his work becomes an object, an *external* existence, but also that it exists *outside him* independently, alien, an autonomous power, opposed to him. The life he has given to the object confronts him as hostile and alien.

Let us now consider more closely the *objectification*, the worker's production and with it the *alienation* and *loss* of the object, his product.

The worker can make nothing without *nature*, without the *sensuous external world*. It is the material wherein his labor realizes itself, wherein it is active, out of which and by means of which it produces.

But as nature furnishes to labor the *means of life* in the sense that labor cannot *live* without objects upon which labor is exercised, nature also furnishes the *means of life* in the narrower sense, namely, the means of physical subsistence of the *worker* himself.

The more the worker *appropriates* the external world and sensuous nature through his labor, the more he deprives himself of the *means of life* in two respects: first, that the sensuous external world gradually ceases to be an object belonging to his labor, a *means of life* of his work; secondly, that it gradually ceases to be a *means of life* in the immediate sense, a means of physical subsistence of the worker.

In these two respects, therefore, the worker becomes a slave to his objects; first, in that he receives an *object of labor*, that is, he receives *labor*, and secondly that he receives the *means of subsistence*. The first enables him to exist as a *worker* and the second as a *physical subject*. The terminus of this slavery is that he can only maintain himself as a *physical subject* so far as he is a *worker*, and only as a *physical subject* is he a worker.

(The alienation of the worker in his object is expressed according to the laws of political economy as follows: the more the worker produces, the less he has to consume; the more values he creates the more worthless and unworthy he becomes; the better shaped his product, the more mis-shapen is he; the more civilized his product, the more barbaric is the worker; the more powerful the work, the more powerless becomes the worker; the more intelligence the work has, the more witless is the worker and the more he becomes a slave of nature.)

*Political economy conceals the alienation in the nature of labor by ignoring the direct relationship between the worker* (labor) *and production.* To be sure, labor produces marvels for the wealthy but it produces deprivation for the worker. It produces palaces, but hovels for the worker. It produces beauty, but mutilation for the worker. It displaces labor through machines, but it throws some workers back into barbarous labor and turns others into machines. It produces intelligence, but for the worker it produces imbecility and cretinism.

*The direct relationship of labor to its products is the relationship of the worker to the objects of his production.* The relationship of the rich to the objects of production and to production itself is only a *consequence* of this first relationship and confirms it. Later we shall observe the latter aspect.

Thus, when we ask, What is the essential relationship of labor? we ask about the relationship of the *worker* to production.

Up to now we have considered the alienation, the externalization of the worker only from one side: his *relationship to the products of his labor.* But alienation is shown not only in the result but also in the *process of production,* in the *producing activity* itself. How could the worker stand in an alien relationship to the product of his activity if he did not alienate himself from himself in the very act of production? After all, the product is only the résumé of activity, of production. If the product of work is externalization, production itself must be active externalization, externalization of activity, activity of externalization. Only alienation—and externalization in the activity of labor itself —is summarized in the alienation of the object of labor.

What constitutes the externalization of labor?

First is the fact that labor is *external* to the laborer— that is, it is not part of his nature—and that the worker does not affirm himself in his work but denies himself, feels miserable and unhappy, develops no free physical and mental energy but mortifies his flesh and ruins his mind. The worker, therefore feels at ease only outside work, and during work he is outside himself. He is at home when he is not working and when he is working he is not at home. His work, therefore, is not voluntary, but coerced, *forced labor*. It is not the satisfaction of a need but only a *means* to satisfy other needs. Its alien character is obvious from the fact that as soon as no physical or other pressure exists, labor is avoided like the plague. External labor, labor in which man is externalized, is labor of self-sacrifice, of penance. Finally, the external nature of work for the worker appears in the fact that it is not his own but another person's, that in work he does not belong to himself but to someone else. In religion the spontaneity of human imagination, the spontaneity of the human brain and heart, acts independently of the individual as an alien, divine or devilish activity. Similarly, the activity of the worker is not his own spontaneous activity. It belongs to another. It is the loss of his own self.

The result, therefore, is that man (the worker) feels that he is acting freely only in his animal functions—eating, drinking, and procreating, or at most in his shelter and finery—while in his human functions he feels only like an animal. The animalistic becomes the human and the human the animalistic.

To be sure, eating, drinking, and procreation are genuine human functions. In abstraction, however, and separated from the remaining sphere of human activities and turned into final and sole ends, they are animal functions.

We have considered labor, the act of alienation of practical human activity, in two aspects: (1) the relationship of the worker to the *product of labor* as an alien object dominating him. This relationship is at the same time the relationship to the sensuous external world, to natural objects as an alien world hostile to him; (2) the relationship of labor to the *act of production* in *labor*. This relationship is that of the worker to his own activity as alien and not belonging to him, activity as passivity, power as weakness, procreation as emasculation, the worker's *own* physical and spiritual energy, his personal life—for what else is life but activity—as an activity turned against him, independent of him, and not belonging to him. *Self-alienation*, as against the alienation of the *object*, stated above.

We have now to derive a third aspect of *alienated labor* from the two previous ones.

Man is a species-being [*Gattungswesen*] not only in that he practically and theoretically makes his own species as well as that of other things his object, but also—and this is only another expression for the same thing—in that as present and living species he considers himself to be a *universal* and consequently free being.

The life of the species in man as in animals is physical in that man, (like the animal) lives by inorganic nature. And as man is more universal than the animal, the realm of inorganic nature by which he lives is more universal. As plants, animals, minerals, air, light, etc., in theory form a part of human consciousness, partly as objects of natural science, partly as objects of art—his spiritual inorganic nature or spiritual means of life which he first must prepare for enjoyment and assimilation—so they also form in practice a part of human life and human activity. Man lives physically only by these products of nature; they may appear in the form of food, heat, clothing, housing, etc. The universality of man appears in practice in the universality which makes the whole of nature his *inorganic* body: (1) as a direct means of life, and (2) as the matter, object, and instrument of his life activity. Nature is the *inorganic body* of man, that is, nature insofar as it is not the human body. Man *lives* by nature. This means that nature is his *body* with which he must remain in perpetual process in order not to die. That the physical and spiritual life of man is tied up with nature is another way of saying that nature is linked to itself, for man is a part of nature.

In alienating (1) nature from man, and (2) man from himself, his own active function, his life activity, alienated labor also alienates the *species* from him; it makes *species-life* the means of individual life. In the first place it alienates species-life and the individual life, and secondly it turns the latter in its abstraction into the purpose of the former, also in its abstract and alienated form.

For labor, *life activity,* and *productive life* appear to man at first only as a *means* to satisfy a need, the need to maintain physical existence. Productive life, however, is species-life. It is life begetting life. In the mode of life activity lies the entire character of a species, its species-character; and free conscious activity is the species-character of man. Life itself appears only as a *means of life*.

The animal is immediately one with its life activity, not distinct from it. The animal is *its life activity*. Man makes his life activity itself into an object of will and consciousness. He has conscious life activity. It is not a determination with which he immediately identifies. Conscious life activity distinguishes man immediately from the life activity of the animal. Only thereby is he a species-being. Or rather, he is only a conscious being—that is, his own life is an object for him—since he is a species-being. Only on that account is his activity free activity. Alienated labor reverses the relationship in that man, since he is a conscious being, makes his life activity, his *essence,* only a means for his *existence*.

The practical creation of an *objective world*, the *treatment* of inorganic nature, is proof that man is a conscious species-being, that is, a being which is related to its species as to its own essence or is related to itself as a species-being. To be sure animals also produce. They build themselves nests, dwelling places, like the bees, beavers, ants, etc. But the animal produces only what is immediately necessary for itself or its young. It produces in a one-sided way while man produces universally. The animal produces under the domination of immediate physical need while man produces free of physical need and only genuinely so in freedom from such need. The animal only produces itself while man reproduces the whole of nature. The animal's product belongs immediately to its physical body while man is free when he confronts his product. The animal builds only according to the standard and need of the species to which it belongs while man knows how to produce according to the standard of any species and at all times knows how to apply an intrinsic standard to the object. Thus man creates also according to the laws of beauty.

In the treatment of the objective world, therefore, man proves himself to be genuinely a *species-being*. This production is his active species-life. Through it nature appears as *his* work and his actuality. The object of labor is thus the *objectification of man's species-life:* he produces himself not only intellectually, as in consciousness, but also actively in a real sense and sees himself in a world he made. In taking from man the object of his production, alienated labor takes from his *species-life,* his actual and objective existence as a species. It changes his superiority to the animal to inferiority, since he is deprived of nature, his inorganic body.

By degrading free spontaneous activity to the level of a means, alienated labor makes the species-life of man a means of his physical existence.

The consciousness which man has from his species is altered through alienation, so that species-life becomes a means for him.

(3) Alienated labor hence turns the *species-existence of man,* and also nature as his mental species-capacity, into an existence *alien* to him, into the *means* of his *individual existence*. It alienates his spiritual nature, his *human essence,* from his own body and likewise from nature outside him.

(4) A direct consequence of man's alienation from the product of his work, from his life activity, and from his species-existence, is the *alienation of man* from *man*. When man confronts himself, he confronts *other* men. What holds true of man's relationship to his work, to the product of his work, and to himself, also holds true of man's relationship to other men, to their labor, and the object of their labor.

In general, the statement that man is alienated from his species-existence means that one man is alienated from another just as each man is alienated from human nature.

The alienation of man, the relation of man to himself, is realized and expressed in the relation between man and other men.

Thus in the relation of alienated labor every man sees the others according to the standard and the relation in which he finds himself as a worker.

We began with an economic fact, the alienation of the worker and his product. We have given expression to the concept of this fact: *alienated, externalized* labor. We have analyzed this concept and have thus analyzed merely a fact of political economy.

Let us now see further how the concept of alienated, externalized labor must express and represent itself in actuality.

If the product of labor is alien to me, confronts me as an alien power, to whom then does it belong?

If my own activity does not belong to me, if it is an alien and forced activity, to whom then does it belong?

To a being *other* than myself.

Who is this being?

*Gods?* To be sure, in early times the main production, for example, the building of temples in Egypt, India, and Mexico, appears to be in the service of the gods, just as the product belongs to the gods. But gods alone were never workmasters. The same is true of *nature*. And what a contradiction it would be if the more man subjugates nature through his work and the more the miracles of gods are rendered superfluous by the marvels of industry, man should renounce his joy in producing and the enjoyment of his product for love of these powers.

The *alien* being who owns labor and the product of labor, whom labor serves and whom the product of labor satisfies can only be *man* himself.

That the product of labor does not belong to the worker and an alien power confronts him is possible only because this product belongs to *a man other than the worker*. If his activity is torment for him, it must be the *pleasure* and the life-enjoyment for another. Not gods, not nature, but only man himself can be this alien power over man.

Let us consider the statement previously made, that the relationship of man to himself is *objective* and *actual* to him only through his relationship to other men. If man is related to the product of his labor, to his objectified labor, as to an *alien,* hostile, powerful object independent of him, he is so related that another alien, hostile, powerful man independent of him is the lord of this object. If he is unfree in relation to his own activity, he is related to it as bonded activity, activity under the domination, coercion, and yoke of another man.

Every self-alienation of man, from himself and from nature, appears in the relationship which he postulates between other men and himself and nature. Thus religious self-alienation appears necessarily in the relation of laity to priest, or also to a mediator, since we are here now concerned with the spiritual world. In the practical real world self-alienation can appear only in the practical real relationships to other men. The means whereby the alienation proceeds is a *practical* means. Through alienated labor man thus not only produces his relationship to the object and to the act of production as an alien man at enmity with him. He also creates the relation in which other men stand to his production and product, and the relation in which he stands to these other men. Just as he begets his own production as loss of his reality, as his punishment; just as he begets his own product as a loss, a product not belonging to him, so he begets the domination of the non-producer over production and over product. As he alienates his own activity from himself, he confers upon the stranger an activity which is not his own.

Up to this point, we have investigated the relationship only from the side of the worker and will later investigate it also from the side of the non-worker.

Thus through *alienated externalized labor* does the worker create the relation to this work of man alienated to labor and standing outside it. The relation of the worker to labor produces the relation of the capitalist to labor, or whatever one wishes to call the lord of labor. *Private prop-*

*erty* is thus product, result, and necessary consequence of *externalized labor,* of the external relation of the worker to nature and to himself.

*Private property* thus is derived, through analysis, from the concept of *externalized labor,* that is, *externalized man,* alienated labor, alienated life, and *alienated* man.

We have obtained the concept of *externalized labor* (*externalized life*) from political economy as a result of the *movement of private property*. But the analysis of this idea shows that though private property appears to be the ground and cause of externalized labor, it is rather a consequence of externalized labor, just as gods are *originally* not the cause but the effect of an aberration of the human mind. Later this relationship reverses.

Only at the final culmination of the development of private property does this, its secret, reappear—namely, that on the one hand it is the *product* of externalized labor and that secondly it is the *means* through which labor externalizes itself, the *realization of this externalization*.

This development throws light on several conflicts hitherto unresolved.

(1) Political economy proceeds from labor as the very soul of production and yet gives labor nothing, private property everything. From this contradiction Proudhon decided in favor of labor and against private property. We perceive, however, that this apparent contradiction is the contradiction of *alienated labor* with itself and that political economy has only formulated the laws of alienated labor.

Therefore we also perceive that *wages* and *private property* are identical: for when the product, the object of labor, pays for the labor itself, wages are only a necessary consequence of the alienation of labor. In wages labor appears not as an end in itself but as the servant of wages. We shall develop this later and now only draw some conclusions.

An enforced *raising of wages* (disregarding all other difficulties, including that this anomaly could only be maintained forcibly) would therefore be nothing but a *better slave-salary* and would not achieve either for the worker or for labor human significance and dignity.

Even the *equality of wages,* as advanced by Proudhon, would only convert the relation of the contemporary worker to his work into the relation of all men to labor. Society would then be conceived as an abstract capitalist.

Wages are a direct result of alienated labor, and alienated labor is the direct cause of private property. The downfall of one is necessarily the downfall of the other.

(2) From the relation of alienated labor to private property it follows further that the emancipation of society from private property, etc., from servitude, is expressed in its *political* form as the *emancipation of workers,* not as though it is only a question of their emancipation but because in their emancipation is contained universal human emancipation. It is contained in their emancipation because the whole of human servitude is involved in the relation of worker to production, and all relations of servitude are only modifications and consequences of the worker's relation to production.

As we have found the concept of *private property* through *analysis* from the concept of *alienated, externalized labor,* so we can develop all the *categories* of political economy with the aid of these two factors, and we shall again find in each category—for example, barter, competition, capital, money—only a *particular* and *developed expression* of these primary foundations.

Before considering this configuration, however, let us try to solve two problems.

(1) To determine the general *nature of private property* as a result of alienated labor in its relation to *truly human* and *social property.*

(2) We have taken the *alienation of labor* and its *externalization* as a fact and analyzed this fact. How, we ask now, does it happen that *man externalizes* his *labor,* alienates it? How is this alienation rooted in the nature of human development? We have already achieved much in resolving the problem by *transforming* the question concerning the *origin of private property* into the question concerning the relationship of *externalized labor* to evolution of humanity. In talking about *private property* one believes he is dealing with something external to man.

Talking of labor, one is immediately dealing with man himself. This new formulation of the problem already contains its solution.

On (1) *The general nature of private property and its relation to truly human property.*

We have resolved alienated labor into two parts which mutually determine each other or rather are only different expressions of one and the same relationship. *Appropriation* appears as *alienation, as externalization; externalization* as *appropriation; alienation* as the true *naturalization.*

We considered the one side, *externalized* labor, in relation to the *worker* himself, that is, the *relation of externalized labor to itself.* We have found the *property relation of the non-worker* to the *worker* and *labor* to be the product, the necessary result, of this relationship. *Private property* as the material, summarized expression of externalized labor embraces both relationships—the *relationship of worker to labor, the product of his work, and the non-worker;* and the relationship of the *non-worker to the worker* and *the product of his labor.*

As we have seen that in relation to the worker who *appropriates* nature through his labor the appropriation appears as alienation—self-activity as activity for another and of another, living as the sacrifice of life, production of the object as loss of it to an alien power, an *alien* man—we now consider the relationship of this *alien* man to the worker, to labor and its object.

It should be noted first that everything which appears with the worker as an *activity of externalization* and an *activity of alienation* appears with the non-worker as a *condition of externalization,* a *condition of alienation.*

Secondly, that the *actual, practical attitude* of the worker in production and to his product (as a condition of mind) appears as a *theoretical* attitude in the non-worker confronting him.

*Thirdly,* the non-worker does everything against the worker which the worker does against himself, but he does not do against his own self what he does against the worker.

Let us consider more closely these three relationships. [Here the manuscript breaks off, unfinished.]

## Private Property and Communism

The antithesis between *propertylessness* and *property*, however, still remains indifferent, not grasped in its *active connection* with its *internal* relationship as *contradiction*, so long as it is not understood as the antithesis of *labor* and *capital*. This antithesis can be expressed in the *first* form even without the advanced development of private property as in ancient Rome, in Turkey, etc. It does not yet *appear* as instituted by private property itself. But labor, the subjective essence of private property as exclusion of property, and capital, objective labor as the exclusion of labor, is *private property* as its developed relation of contradiction, hence a dynamic relation driving toward resolution.

The overcoming [*Aufhebung*] of self-alienation follows the same course as self-alienation. *Private property* is first considered only in its objective aspect—but still with labor as its essence. Its form of existence is therefore *capital* which is to be overcome "as such" (Proudhon). Or the *particular form* of labor—leveled down, parceled, and thus unfree labor—is taken as the source of the *perniciousness* of private property and its humanly alienated existence. *Fourier*, agreeing with the physiocrats, thus regards *agricultural labor* as being at least *exemplary*, while *Saint-Simon* on the other hand holds *industrial labor* as such to be the essence of labor and thus seeks the *exclusive* predominance of the industrialists and the improvement of the workers' condition. *Communism* is ultimately the *positive* expression of private property as overcome [*aufgehoben*]. Immediately it is *universal* private property. In taking this relation in its *universality* communism is: (1) In its first form only a *universalization* and *completion* of this relationship. As such it appears in a double pattern: On the one hand the domination of *material* property bulks so large that it wants to destroy *everything* which cannot be possessed by everyone as *private property*. It wants to abstract from talent, etc., by *force*. Immediate, physical *possession* is for it the sole aim of life and existence. The condition of the *laborer* is not overcome but extended to all men. The relationship of private property remains the relationship of the community to the world of things. Ultimately this movement which contrasts universal private property to private property is expressed in the animalistic form that *marriage* (surely a *form* of *exclusive private property*) is counterposed to the *community of women* where they become *communal* and *common* property. We might say that this idea of the *community of women* is the *open secret* of this still very crude, unthinking communism. As women go from marriage into universal prostitution, so the whole world of wealth—that is, the objective essence of man—passes from the relationship of exclusive marriage with the private owner into the relationship of universal prostitution with the community. This communism—in that it negates man's *personality* everywhere—is only the logical expression of the private property which is this negation. Universal *envy* establishing itself as a power is only the disguised form in which *greed* reestablishes and satisfies itself in *another* way. The thought of every piece of private property as such is *at the very least* turned against *richer* private property as envy and the desire to level so that envy and the desire to level in fact constitute the essence of competition. Crude communism is only the fulfillment of this envy and leveling on the basis of a *preconceived* minimum. It has a *definite delimited* measure. How little this overcoming of private property is an actual appropriation is shown precisely by the abstract negation of the entire world of culture and civilization, the reversion to the *unnatural* simplicity of the *poor* and wantless man who has not gone beyond private property, has not yet even achieved it.

The community is only a community of *labor* and an equality of *wages* which the communal capital, the *community* as universal capitalist, pays out. Both sides of the relationship are raised to a *supposed* universality—*labor* as the condition in which everyone is put, *capital* as the recognized universality and power of the community.

In the relationship with *woman,* as the spoil and hand-maid of communal lust, is expressed the infinite degradation in which man exists for himself since the secret of this relationship has its *unambiguous,* decisive, *plain,* and revealed expression in the relationship of *man* to *woman* and in the way in which the *immediate, natural* species-relationship is conceived. The immediate, natural, necessary relationship of human being to human being is the *relationship* of *man* to *woman.* In this *natural* species-relationship man's relationship to nature is immediately his relationship to man, as his relationship to man is immediately his relationship to nature, to his own *natural* condition. In this relationship the extent to which the human essence has become nature for man or nature has become the human essence of man is *sensuously manifested,* reduced to a perceptible *fact.* From this relationship one can thus judge the entire level of mankind's development. From the character of this relationship follows the extent to which *man* has become and comprehended himself as a *generic being,* as *man;* the relationship of man to woman is the *most natural* relationship of human being to human being. It thus indicates the extent to which man's *natural* behavior has become *human* or the extent to which his *human* essence has become a *natural* essence for him, the extent to which his *human nature* has become *nature* to him. In this relationship is also apparent the extent to which man's *need* has become *human,* thus the extent to which the *other* human being, as human being, has become a need for him, the extent to which he in his most individual existence is at the same time a social being.

The first positive overcoming of private property—*crude* communism—is thus only an *apparent form* of the vileness of private property trying to set itself up as the *positive community.*

(2) Communism (a) still of political nature, democratic or despotic; (b) with the overcoming of the state, but still incomplete and influenced by private property, that is, by the alienation of man. In both forms communism already knows itself as the reintegration or return of man to himself, as the overcoming of human self-alienation, but since

it has not yet understood the positive essence of private property and just as little the *human* nature of needs, it still remains captive to and infected by private property. It has, indeed, grasped its concept but still not its essence.

(3) *Communism* as *positive* overcoming of *private property* as *human self-alienation*, and thus as the actual *appropriation of the human* essence through and for man; therefore as the complete and conscious restoration of man to himself within the total wealth of previous development, the restoration of man as a *social*, that is, human being. This communism as completed naturalism is humanism, as completed humanism it is naturalism. It is the *genuine* resolution of the antagonism between man and nature and between man and man; it is the true resolution of the conflict between existence and essence, objectification and self-affirmation, freedom and necessity, individual and species. It is the riddle of history solved and knows itself as this solution.

The entire movement of history is therefore both its *actual* genesis—the birth of its empirical existence—and also for its thinking awareness the *conceived* and *conscious* movement of its *becoming* whereas the other yet undeveloped communism seeks in certain historical forms opposed to private property a *historical* proof, a proof in what explicitly exists. It thereby tears particular moments out of the movement (Cabet, Villegardelle, etc., particularly ride this horse) and marks them as proofs of its historical pedigree. Thus it makes clear that the far greater part of this movement contradicts its claims and that if it once existed, its *past* existence refutes the pretension of its *essence*.

It is easy to see the necessity that the whole revolutionary movement finds both its empirical as well as theoretical basis in the development of *private property*—in the economy, to be exact.

This *material*, immediately *perceptible* private property is the material, sensuous expression of *alienated human* life. Its movement—production and consumption—is the *sensuous* manifestation of the movement of all previous production, that is, the realization or actuality of man. Religion, family, state, law, morality, science, art, etc., are only *particular* forms of production and fall under its general law. The positive overcoming of *private property* as the appropriation of *human* life is thus the positive overcoming of all alienation and the return of man from religion, family, state, etc., to his *human*, that is, *social* existence. Religious alienation as such occurs only in the sphere of the inner human *consciousness*, but economic alienation belongs to *actual life*—its overcoming thus includes both aspects. It is obvious that the movement has its *first* beginning among different peoples depending on whether their true *acknowledged* life proceeds more in consciousness or in the external world, is more ideal or real. Communism thus begins (*Owen*) with atheism, but atheism is at the beginning still far from being *communism* since it is mostly an *abstraction*.*—The philanthropy of atheism is at first therefore only a *philosophical*, abstract philanthropy; that of communism is at once *real* and immediately bent toward *action*.

On the assumption that private property has been positively overcome we have seen how man produces man, himself, and other men; how the object, the immediate activity of his individuality, is at the same time his own existence for other men, their existence, and their existence for him. Similarly, however, both the material of labor and man as subject are equally the result and beginning of the movement (and the historical *necessity* of private property lies precisely in the fact that they must be this *beginning*). Thus is the *social* character the general character of the whole movement; *as* society itself produces *man* as *man*, so it is *produced* by him. Activity and satisfaction [*Genuss*], both in their content and *mode of existence*, are *social*, *social* activity and *social* satisfaction. The *human* essence of nature primarily exists only for *social* man, because only here is nature a *link* with *man*, as his existence for others

---

* Prostitution is only a *particular* expression of the *general* prostitution of the *laborer*, and since prostitution is a relationship which includes not only the prostituted but also the prostitutor—whose vileness is still greater—so also the capitalist, etc. falls in this category [Marx's footnote].

and their existence for him, as the life-element of human actuality—only here is nature the *foundation* of man's own *human* existence. Only here has the *natural* existence of man become his *human* existence and nature become human. Thus *society* is the completed, essential unity of man with nature, the true resurrection of nature, the fulfilled naturalism of man and humanism of nature.

Social activity and satisfaction by no means exist *merely* in the form of an *immediate* communal activity and immediate *communal* satisfaction. Nevertheless such activity and satisfaction, expressed and confirmed immediately in *actual association* with other men, will occur wherever that *immediate* expression of sociality is essentially grounded in its content and adequate to its nature.

Even as I am *scientifically* active, etc.—an activity I can seldom pursue in direct community with others—I am *socially* active because I am active as a *man*. Not only is the material of my activity—such as the language in which the thinker is active—given to me as a social product, but my *own* existence *is* social activity; what I make from myself I make for society, conscious of my nature as social.

My *general* consciousness is only the *theoretical* form of that whose *living* form is the *real* community, the social essence, although at present *general* consciousness is an abstraction from actual life and antagonistically opposed to it. Consequently the *activity* of my general consciousness is thus, as activity, my *theoretical* existence as a social being.

To be avoided above all is establishing "society" once again as an abstraction over against the individual. The individual *is* the *social being*. The expression of his life—even if it does not appear immediately in the form of a *communal* expression carried out together with others—is therefore an expression and assertion of *social life*. The individual and generic life of man are not *distinct*, however much—and necessarily so—the mode of existence of individual life is either a more *particular* or more *general* mode of generic life, or generic life a more *particular* or *universal* mode of individual life.

As *generic consciousness* man asserts his real *social life* and merely repeats his actual existence in thought just as, conversely, generic existence asserts itself in generic consciousness and in its universality exists explicitly as a thinking being. Though man is therefore a *particular* individual —and precisely his particularity makes him an individual, an actual *individual* communal being—he is equally the *totality*, the ideal totality, the subjective existence of society explicitly thought and experienced. Likewise he also exists in actuality both as perception and actual satisfaction of social existence and as a totality of human expression of life.

Thinking and being, to be sure, are thus *distinct* but at the same time in *unity* with one another.

*Death* seems to be a harsh victory of the species over the particular individual and to contradict the species' unity, but the particular individual is only a *particular generic being* and as such mortal.

(( (4) Just as *private property* is only the sensuous expression of the fact that man becomes *objective* for himself and at the same time becomes an alien and inhuman object for himself, that his expression of life is his externalization of life and his realization a loss of reality, an *alien* actuality, so the positive overcoming of private property—that is, the *sensuous* appropriation of the human essence and life, of objective man and of human *works* by and for man—is not to be grasped only as *immediate*, exclusive *satisfaction* or as *possession*, as *having*. Man appropriates to himself his manifold essence in an all-sided way, thus as a whole man. Every one of his *human* relations to the world—seeing, hearing, smelling, tasting, feeling, thinking, perceiving, sensing, wishing, acting, loving—in short, all the organs of his individuality, which are immediately communal in form, are an appropriation of the object in their *objective* relation [*Verhalten*] or their *relation to it*. This appropriation of *human* actuality and its relation to the object is the *confirmation of human actuality*. It is therefore as varied as are the *determinations* of the human *essence* and *activities*. It is human *efficacy* and human *suffering*, for suffering, humanly conceived, is a satisfaction of the self in man.

Private property has made us so stupid and one-sided

that an object is *ours* only if we have it, if it exists for us as a capital or is immediately possessed by us, eaten, drunk, worn, lived in, etc., in short, *used;* but private property grasps all these immediate forms of possession only as *means of living,* and the life they serve is the *life* of *private property,* labor, and capitalization.

Hence *all* the physical and spiritual senses have been replaced by the simple alienation of them *all,* the sense of *having.* Human nature had to be reduced to this absolute poverty so that it could give birth to its inner wealth. (On the category of *having,* see *Hess* in *Twenty-one Sheets.*)

The overcoming of private property means therefore the complete *emancipation* of all human senses and aptitudes [*Eigenschaften*], but it means this emancipation precisely because these senses and aptitudes have become *human* both subjectively and objectively. The eye has become a *human* eye, just as its *object* has become a social, *human* object derived from and for man. The *senses* have therefore become *theoreticians* immediately in their *praxis.* They try to relate themselves to their *subject matter* [*Sache*] for its own sake, but the subject matter itself is an *objective human* relation to itself and to man,* and vice versa. Need or satisfaction have thus lost their *egoistic* nature, and nature has lost its mere *utility* by use becoming *human* use.

Similarly the senses and satisfactions of other men have become my *own* appropriation. Besides these immediate organs, *social* organs are therefore developed in the *form* of society; for example, activity in direct association with others, etc., has become an organ of a *life-expression* and a way of appropriating *human* life.

It is obvious that the *human* eye appreciates differently from the crude, inhuman eye, the human *ear* differently from the crude ear, etc.

Only if man's object, we have seen, becomes for him a *human* object or objective man, is he not lost in it. This is possible only when the object becomes *social* and he himself becomes social just as society becomes essential for him in this object.

* I can practically relate myself to the subject matter in a human way only if it is itself humanly related to man [Marx's footnote].

On the one hand, therefore, it is only when objective actuality generally becomes for man in society the actuality of essential human capacities, human actuality, and thus the actuality of his *own* capacities that all *objects* become for him the *objectification* of himself, become objects which confirm and realize his individuality as *his* objects, that is, *he himself* becomes the object. *How* they become his depends on the *nature* of the *object* and the nature of the *essential capacity* corresponding to *it*, for it is precisely the *determinateness* of this relationship which shapes the particular, *actual* mode of affirmation. For the *eye* an object is different than for the *ear*, and the object of the eye *is* another object than that of the *ear*. The peculiarity of each essential capacity is precisely its *characteristic essence* and thus also the characteristic mode of its objectification, of its *objectively actual*, living *being*. Thus man is affirmed in the objective world not only in thought but with *all* his senses.

On the other hand and from the subjective point of view, as music alone awakens man's musical sense and the most beautiful music has *no* meaning for the unmusical ear—is no object for it, because my object can only be the confirmation of one of my essential capacities and can therefore only be so for me insofar as my essential capacity exists explicitly as a subjective capacity, because the meaning of an object for me reaches only as far as *my* senses go (only makes sense for a corresponding sense)—for this reason the *senses* of social man *differ* from those of the unsocial. Only through the objectively unfolded wealth of human nature is the wealth of the subjective *human* sensibility either cultivated or created—a musical ear, an eye for the beauty of form, in short, *senses* capable of human satisfaction, confirming themselves as essential *human* capacities. For not only the five senses but also the so-called spiritual and moral senses (will, love, etc.), in a word, *human* sense and the humanity of the senses come into being only through the existence of *their* object, through nature *humanized*. The *development* of the five senses is a labor of the whole previous history of the world. *Sense* subordinated to crude, practical need has only a *nar-*

*row* meaning.)) For the starving man food does not exist in its human form but only in its abstract character as food. It could be available in its crudest form and one could not say wherein the starving man's eating differs from that of *animals*. The care-laden, needy man has no mind for the most beautiful play. The dealer in minerals sees only their market value but not their beauty and special nature; he has no mineralogical sensitivity. Hence the objectification of the human essence, both theoretically and practically, is necessary to *humanize* man's *senses* and also create a *human sense* corresponding to the entire wealth of humanity and nature.

((Just as the coming society finds at hand all the material for this *cultural development* [*Bildung*] through the movement of *private property*, its wealth as well as its poverty both material and spiritual, *so* the fully *constituted* society produces man in this entire wealth of his being, produces the *rich*, deep, and *entirely sensitive* man as its enduring actuality.))

It is apparent how subjectivism and objectivism, spiritualism and materialism, activity and passivity lose their opposition and thus their existence as antitheses only in the social situation; ((it is apparent how the resolution of *theoretical* antitheses is possible *only* in a *practical* way, only through man's practical energy, and hence their resolution is in no way merely a problem of knowledge but a *real* problem of life which *philosophy* could not solve because it grasped the problem as *only* theoretical.))

((It is apparent how the history of *industry*, industry as *objectively* existing, is the *open* book of *man's essential powers*, the observably present human *psychology*, which has not been thus far grasped in its connection with man's *essential* nature but only in an external utilitarian way because in the perspective of alienation only the general existence of man—religion or history in its abstract-general character as politics, art, literature, etc.—was grasped as the actuality of man's essential powers and his *human generic action*. We have before us the *objectified essential powers* of man in the form of *sensuous, alien, useful objects*—in the form of alienation—in *ordinary material industry* (which can be conceived as a part of that general movement just as that movement can be grasped as a *particular* part of industry since all human activity up to the present has been labor, industry, activity alienated from itself). A *psychology* for which this book, that is, the most observably present and accessible part of history, remains closed cannot become an actual, substantial, and *real* science.)) What indeed should one think of a science which *arbitrarily* abstracts from this large area of human labor and is unaware of its own incompleteness while such an extended wealth of human activity means no more to it than can be expressed in one word—"*need*," "*common need*"?

The *natural sciences* have become enormously active and have accumulated an ever growing subject-matter. But philosophy has remained as alien to them as they have to it. Their momentary unity was only a *fantastic illusion*. The will was there, but the means were missing. Historiography itself only occasionally takes account of natural science as a moment of enlightenment, utility, some particular great discoveries. But natural science has penetrated and transformed human life all the more *practically* through industry, preparing for human emancipation however much it immediately had to accentuate dehumanization. *Industry* is the *actual* historical relationship of nature, and thus of natural science, to man. If it is grasped as the *exoteric* manifestation of man's *essential powers,* the *human* essence of nature or the *natural* essence of man can also be understood. Hence, natural science will lose its abstract material—or rather idealistic—tendency and become the basis of *human* science as it has already become, though in an alienated form, the basis of actual human life. One basis for life and *another* for *science* is in itself a lie. ((Nature developing in human history—the creation of human society—is the *actual* nature of man; hence nature as it develops through industry, though in an *alienated* form, is true *anthropological* nature.))

*Sense perception* (see Feuerbach) must be the basis of all science. Science is only *actual* when it proceeds from sense perception in the twofold form of both *sensuous* awareness and *sensuous* need, that is, from nature. The whole of history is a preparation for *"man"* to become the object of *sensuous* awareness and for the needs of "man as man" to become sensuous needs. History itself is an *actual* part of *natural history,* of nature's development into man. Natural science will in time include the science of man as the science of man will include natural science: There will be *one* science.

*Man* is the immediate object of natural science because immediately *perceptible nature* is for man, immediately, human sense perception (an identical statement) as the *other* man immediately perceptible for him. His own sense perception only exists as human sense perception for himself through the *other* man. But *nature* is the direct object of the *science of man.* The first object for man—man himself—is nature, sense perception; and the particular, perceptible, and essential powers of man can attain self-knowledge only in natural science because they are objectively developed only in *natural* objects. The element of thought itself, the element of the life-expression of thought, *language,* is perceptible nature. The *social* actuality of nature and *human* natural science or the *natural science of man* are identical expressions.

((It is apparent how the *rich man* and wide *human* need appear in place of economic *wealth* and *poverty.* The rich man is simultaneously one who *needs* a totality of human manifestations of life and in whom his own realization exists as inner necessity, as *need.* Not only the *wealth* but also the *poverty* of man equally acquire—under the premise of socialism—a *human* and thus social meaning. It is the passive bond which lets man experience the greatest wealth, the *other* human being, as need. The domination of the objective essence within me, the sensuous eruption of my essential activity, is *emotion* which thereby becomes the *activity* of my nature.))

(5) A *being* only regards himself as independent when he stands on his own feet, and he stands on his own feet only when he owes his *existence* to himself. A man who lives by the favor of another considers himself dependent. But I live entirely by the favor of another if I owe him not only the maintenance of my life but also its *creation,* its

*source*. My life necessarily has such an external ground if it is not my own creation. The notion of *creation* is thus very difficult to expel from popular consciousness. For such consciousness the self-subsistence of nature and man is *inconceivable* because it contradicts all the *palpable facts* of practical life.

The creation of the *earth* has been severely shaken by *geognosy* [rather: by *geogony*], the science which presents the formation and development of the earth as a self-generative process. Generatio aequivoca is the only practical refutation of the theory of creation.

It is easy indeed to tell a particular individual what Aristotle said: You were begotten by your father and mother, so in you the mating of two human beings, a generic act of mankind, produced another. You see therefore that man owes even his physical existence to another. Here you must not keep in view only *one* of the two aspects, the *infinite* progression, and ask further, Who begot my father? Who his grandfather? etc. You must also keep in mind the *circular movement* sensibly apparent in that process whereby man reproduces himself in procreation; thus *man* always remains the subject. But you will answer: I grant this circular movement but you must allow the progression which leads even further until I ask, Who created the first man and nature as a whole? I can only answer: Your question is itself a product of abstraction. Ask yourself how you arrive at that question, whether it does not arise from a standpoint to which I cannot reply because it is twisted. Ask yourself whether that progression exists as such for rational thought. If you ask about the creation of nature and man, you thus abstract from man and nature. You assert them as *non-existent* and yet want me to prove them to you as *existing*. I say to you: Give up your abstraction and you will also give up your question. Or if you want to maintain your abstraction, be consistent and if you think of man and nature as *non-existent,* think of yourself as non-existent as you too are nature and man. Do not think, do not question me, for as soon as you think and question, your *abstraction* from the existence of nature and man makes no sense. Or are you such an egoist that you assert everything as nothing and yet want yourself to exist?

You may reply to me: I do not want to assert the nothingness of nature, etc. I only ask about its *genesis* as I ask the anatomist about the formation of bones, etc.

Since for socialist man, however, the *entire so-called world history* is only the creation of man through human labor and the development of nature for man, he has evident and incontrovertible proof of his *self-creation*, his own *formation process*. Since the *essential dependence* of man in nature—man for man as the existence of nature and nature for man as the existence of man—has become practical, sensuous and perceptible, the question about an *alien* being beyond man and nature (a question which implies the unreality of nature and man) has become impossible in practice. *Atheism* as a denial of this unreality no longer makes sense because it is a *negation of God* and through this negation asserts the *existence of man*. But socialism as such no longer needs such mediation. It begins with the *sensuous perception, theoretically and practically*, of man and nature as *essential beings*. It is man's *positive self-consciousness*, no longer attained through the overcoming of religion, just as *actual life* is positive actuality no longer attained through the overcoming of private property, through *communism*. The position of communism is the negation of the negation and hence, for the next stage of historical development, the necessary *actual* phase of man's emancipation and rehabilitation. *Communism* is the necessary form and dynamic principle of the immediate future but not as such the goal of human development—the form of human society.

## Critique of Hegelian Dialectic and Philosophy in General

This is perhaps the place at which to make some comments explaining and justifying what has been said about Hegel's dialectic in general, particularly its exposition in the

*Phenomenology* [*of Spirit*] and *Logic,* and finally about its relation to the modern critical movement.

Modern German criticism has been so much preoccupied with the past, so much restricted by the development of its subject matter, that it has had a completely uncritical attitude toward methods of criticism and has been completely oblivious to the *seemingly formal* but actually *essential* question: How do we now stand in relation to the Hegelian *dialectic?* This lack of awareness concerning the relation of modern criticism to Hegel's philosophy in general and his dialectic in particular has been so great that critics like *Strauss* and *Bruno Bauer* have been completely entrapped in the Hegelian logic—the former completely and the latter at least implicitly in his [*Critique of the Gospel History of the*] *Synoptics* (where he substitutes the "self-consciousness" of abstract man for the substance of "abstract nature," in opposition to Strauss) and even in his *Revealed Christianity,* where you find, for example: "As though self-consciousness in producing the world did not produce its difference and thereby produce itself in what it produced since it again transcends the distinction between what is produced and itself, since it exists only in this production and movement—as though it should not have its purpose in this movement," etc. Or again: "They (the French materialists) could not yet see that the movement of the universe has only become actual for itself and unified with itself as the movement of self-consciousness." Such expressions not only verbally agree with the Hegelian perspective but reproduce it literally.

How little awareness there was in relation to the Hegelian dialectic during the act of criticism (Bauer, *Synoptics*) and how little this awareness appeared even after the act of substantial criticism is shown by Bauer in his *Good Cause of Freedom* [*and My Own Concern*] when he discusses Herr Gruppe's impertinent question—"What about logic now?"—and refers it to future critics.

But now that *Feuerbach* in his "Theses" appearing in the *Anekdota* and more fully in his [*Principles of the*] *Philosophy of the Future* has destroyed the inner principle of the old dialectic and philosophy, the school of criticism which was unable to do this by itself but has seen it done has proclaimed itself pure, decisive, absolute, and entirely clear with itself. In its spiritual pride it has reduced the entire process of history to the relation between the rest of the world—which falls under the category of "the Mass" —and itself and has reduced dogmatic antitheses into the one between its own cleverness and the stupidity of the world, between the critical Christ and "Humanity" as the "*rabble.*" Daily and hourly it has demonstrated its own excellence against the stupidity of the masses and has finally announced the critical *last judgment* to the effect that the day is at hand when the whole of fallen humanity will assemble before it and be divided into groups with each particular mob receiving its testimonium paupertatis. Now that this school of criticism has publicized its superiority to human feelings as well as to the whole world, above which it sits enthroned in sublime solitude, from time to time letting fall from its sarcastic lips the laughter of the Olympian gods—even now after all these entertaining antics of idealism (of Young Hegelianism) expiring in the form of criticism—even now it has not once expressed the suspicion that there must be a reckoning with its own source, the Hegelian dialectic. It has not even indicated a critical relation to Feuerbach's dialectic. This is a procedure with a completely uncritical attitude toward itself.

*Feuerbach* is the only one who has a *serious, critical* relation to Hegel's dialectic, who has made genuine discoveries in this field, and who above all is the true conqueror of the old philosophy. The magnitude of Feuerbach's achievement and the unpretentious simplicity with which he presents it to the world stand in a strikingly opposite inverse ratio.

Feuerbach's great achievement is: (1) proof that philosophy is nothing more than religion brought to and developed in reflection, and thus is equally to be condemned as another form and mode of the alienation of man's nature;

(2) the establishment of *true materialism* and *real science* by making the social relationship of "man to man" the fundamental principle of his theory;

(3) opposing to the negation of the negation, which claims to be the absolute positive, the self-subsistent positive positively grounded on itself.

Feuerbach explains Hegel's dialectic (and thereby justifies starting out from the positive, from sense certainty) in the following way:

Hegel proceeds from the alienation of substance (logically, from the infinite, abstract universal), from absolute and fixed abstraction—that is, in popular language, he proceeds from religion and theology.

Secondly, he transcends [*hebt auf*] the infinite and posits the actual, the perceptible, the real, the finite, the particular (philosophy, the transcendence of religion and theology).

*Thirdly*, he then transcends the positive and re-establishes abstraction, the infinite. Re-establishment of religion and theology.

Feuerbach thus views the negation of the negation as *merely* a contradiction of philosophy with itself, as philosophy which affirms theology (the transcendent, etc.) after having denied it, thus affirming it in opposition to itself.

The positing or self-affirmation and self-confirmation in the negation of the negation is taken to be a positing which is still not sure of itself and hence is burdened with its opposite, is still doubtful of itself and hence is in need of proof, and is thus not demonstrated by its own existence and not grasped as a self-justifying position and hence directly and immediately confronts the self-grounded position of sense certainty.

Because Hegel conceived the negation of the negation from the aspect of the positive relation inherent in it as the only true positive, and from the aspect of the negative relation inherent in it as the only true and self-confirming act of all being, he found only the *abstract, logical, speculative* expression of the movement of history, not the *actual* history of man as a given subject but only man's *genesis*, the *history of his origin*. We shall explain both the abstract form of this movement and the difference between this movement as conceived by Hegel and, in contrast, by modern criticism in Feuerbach's *Essence of Christianity*, or rather the *critical* form of this movement which is still uncritical with Hegel.

Let us take a look at Hegel's system. We must begin with his *Phenomenology*, the true birthplace and secret of his philosophy.

## Phenomenology

### A. *Self-consciousness*

I. *Consciousness.* ($\alpha$) Sense certainty or the "this" and *meaning.* ($\beta$) *Perception* or the thing with its properties and *illusion.* ($\gamma$) Force and understanding, phenomenon and supersensible world.

II. *Self-consciousness.* The truth of self-certainty. (a) Independence and dependence of self-consciousness, lordship and bondage. (b) Freedom of self-consciousness. Stoicism, scepticism, the unhappy consciousness.

III. *Reason.* Certainty and truth of reason. (a) Observational reason; observation of nature and self-consciousness. (b) The realization of rational self-consciousness through itself. Pleasure and necessity. The law of the heart and the frenzy of vanity. Virtue and the way of the world. (c) Individuality which is real in and for itself. The spiritual animal kingdom and deception or the real fact. Law-giving reason. Law-testing reason.

### B. *Spirit* [*Geist*]

I. *True* spirit, ethicality. II. Self-alienated spirit, culture. III. Spirit certain of itself, morality.

### C. *Religion*

*Natural* religion, *religion as art, revealed* religion.

### D. *Absolute Knowledge*

Since Hegel's *Encyclopedia* begins with logic, with *pure speculative thought*, and ends with *absolute knowledge*—with self-consciousness, self-comprehending or absolute, that is, superhuman, abstract mind [*Geist*]—it is altogether nothing but the *expanded essence* of the philosophical mind, its self-objectification. And the philosophical mind is only the alienated world-mind thinking within its self-alienation, that is, comprehending itself abstractly. *Logic*— the *currency* of mind, the speculative *thought-value* of man and nature, their essence indifferent to any actual determinate character and hence unreal—is *thought externalized* and hence *thought* abstracting from nature and actual men. It is *abstract* thinking. The *externality of this abstract thinking . . . nature* as it exists for this abstract thought. Nature is external to it, its self-loss, and is also conceived as something external, as abstract thought but as externalized abstract thought. Finally, [there is] *mind*, thinking which returns to its own birthplace and which as anthropological, phenomenological, psychological, ethical, and artistic-religious is not valid for itself until ultimately it finds itself and relates itself to itself as *absolute* knowledge in the absolute (i.e. abstract) mind containing its conscious and corresponding local existence. For its actual existence is *abstraction*.

Hegel makes a double mistake.

The first appears most clearly in the *Phenomenology*, the birthplace of the Hegelian philosophy. Where Hegel, to be specific, conceives wealth, state power, etc. as entities alienated from *man's* nature, this only happens in their thought form . . . They are thought-entities and hence merely an alienation of *pure*, that is, abstract, philosophical thinking. The whole movement, accordingly, ends with absolute knowledge. It is precisely abstract thought from which these objects are alienated and which they confront with their presumption of actuality. The *philosopher*—himself an abstract form of alienated man—sets himself up as the *measuring rod* of the alienated world. The entire *history of externalization* and the *withdrawal* from externalization is therefore nothing but the *history of the production* of abstract, that is, of absolute, logical, speculative thought. The *alienation* thus forming the real interest and transcendence of this externalization is the opposition of *in itself* and *for itself*, of *consciousness* and *self-consciousness*, of *object and subject*—that is, the opposition within thought itself between abstract thinking and sensuous actuality or actual sensibility. All other contradictions and their movements are only the *appearance,* the *cloak,* the *exoteric* form of these uniquely interesting opposites which constitute the *meaning* of the other profane contradictions. It is not that the human being *objectifies* himself *inhumanly* in opposition to himself, but that he *objectifies* himself by *distinction* from and in *opposition* to abstract thought—this is the essence of alienation as given and as to be transcended. The appropriation of man's essential capacities which have become things, even alien things, is thus primarily only an *appropriation* taking place in *consciousness,* in *pure thought,* that is, in *abstraction.* It is the appropriation of these objects as *thoughts* and *thought processes.* Hence there is already implicit in the *Phenomenology* as a germ, potentiality, and secret—despite its thoroughly negative and critical appearance and despite the actual criticism it contains which often anticipates later developments—the uncritical positivism and equally uncritical idealism of Hegel's later works, the philosophical dissolution and restoration of the existing empirical world.

*Secondly,* the vindication of the objective world for man —for example, the recognition that *sense* perception is no *abstract* sense perception but *human* sense perception, that religion, wealth, etc., are only the alienated actuality of *human* objectification, of *man's* essential capacities put to work, and therefore are only the *path* to genuine *human* actuality—this appropriation or insight into this process appears in Hegel as the affirmation that *sensuousness, religion,* state power, etc., are *mental* entities since *spirit* alone is the *genuine* essence of man and the true form of spirit is the thinking spirit, the logical, speculative mind. The *human quality* of nature, of nature produced through history, and of man's products appears in their being *products* of abstract spirit and hence phases of *mind, thought-entities.* The *Phenomenology* is thus concealed and mystifying criticism, unclear to itself, but inasmuch as it firmly grasps the *alienation* of man—even though man appears only as mind —*all* the elements of criticism are implicit in it, already *prepared* and *elaborated* in a manner far surpassing the

Hegelian standpoint. The sections on the "unhappy consciousness," the "honest consciousness," the struggle between the "noble and base consciousness," etc., etc., contain the *critical* elements—though still in an alienated form—of whole spheres such as religion, the state, civil life, etc. Just as the *entity* or *object* appears as a thought-entity, so is the *subject* always *consciousness* or *self-consciousness;* or rather the object appears only as *abstract* consciousness, man only as *self-consciousness,* and the diverse forms of alienation which make their appearance are therefore only different forms of consciousness and self-consciousness. Since abstract consciousness—the form in which the object is conceived—is *in itself* only a moment of distinction in self-consciousness, the result of the movement is the identity of self-consciousness with consciousness (absolute knowledge) or the movement of abstract thought no longer directed outward but proceeding only within itself. That is to say, the dialectic of pure thought is the result.

The great thing in Hegel's *Phenomenology* and its final result—the dialectic of negativity as the moving and productive principle—is simply that Hegel grasps the self-development of man as a process, objectification as loss of the object, as alienation and transcendence of this alienation; that he thus grasps the nature of *work* and comprehends objective man, authentic because actual, as the result of his *own work.* The *actual,* active relation of man to himself as a species-being or the confirmation of his species-being as an actual, that is, human, being is only possible so far as he actually brings forth all his *species-powers*—which in turn is only possible through the collective effort of mankind, only as the result of history—and treats them as objects, something which immediately is again only possible in the form of alienation.

We shall now indicate in detail Hegel's one-sidedness and limitations in the closing chapter of the *Phenomenology* on absolute knowledge—a chapter containing the pervasive spirit of the whole book, its relation to speculative dialectic, and Hegel's *consciousness* of both and their interrelationship.

Provisionally, let us say this much in advance: Hegel's standpoint is that of modern political economy. He views *labor* as the *essence,* the self-confirming essence of man; he sees only the positive side of labor, not its negative side. Labor is *man's coming-to-be for himself* within *externalization* or as *externalized* man. The only labor Hegel knows and recognizes is *abstract, mental* labor. So that which above all constitutes the *essence* of philosophy—the *externalization of man knowing himself* or *externalized* knowledge *thinking itself*—Hegel grasps as its essence. Therefore, he is able to collect the separate elements of preceding philosophy and present his own as *the* philosophy. What other philosophers did—grasp separate phases of nature and human life as phases of self-consciousness, indeed, abstract self-consciousness—Hegel *knows* from *doing* philosophy. Hence his science is absolute.

Let us now proceed to our subject.

*Absolute knowledge. The last chapter of the* Phenomenology.

The main point is that the *object* of *consciousness* is nothing else but *self-consciousness,* or that the object is only *objectified self-consciousness,* self-consciousness as object. (Assume man = self-consciousness.)

It is a question, therefore, of surmounting the *object of consciousness. Objectivity* as such is regarded as an *alienated* human relationship which does not correspond to the *essence of man,* to self-consciousness. *Reappropriation* of the objective essence of man, developed as something alien and determined by alienation, means not only the overcoming of *alienation* but also of *objectivity*—that is, man is regarded as a *non-objective, spiritual* being.

The process of *surmounting the object of consciousness* is described by Hegel as follows:

The *object* does not reveal itself as *returning* into the *self* (for Hegel that is a *one-sided* view of the movement, grasping only one aspect). Man is assumed as equivalent to self. But the self is only man conceived *abstractly,* derived through abstraction. Man is a *self.* His eye, his ear, etc., belong to a *self;* every one of his essential capacities has the quality of *selfhood.* But on that account it is quite false to say that *self-consciousness* has eyes, ears, essential capacities. Self-consciousness is rather a quality of human nature, of the human eye, etc.; human nature is not a quality of *self-consciousness*.

The self, abstracted and fixed for itself, is man as *abstract egoist*, purely abstract *egoism* raised to the level of thought. (We shall return to this later.)

For Hegel *human nature, man*, is equivalent to *self-consciousness*. All alienation of human nature is thus *nothing* but the *alienation of self-consciousness*. The alienation of self-consciousness is not taken to be an expression of the *actual* alienation of human nature reflected in knowledge and thought. *Actual* alienation, that which appears real, is rather in its *innermost* and concealed character (which philosophy only brings to light) only the *appearance* of the alienation of actual human nature, of *self-consciousness*. The science which grasps this is therefore called *phenomenology*. All reappropriation of that alienated objective nature thus appears as an incorporation into self-consciousness. The man who takes possession of his nature is *only* self-consciousness taking possession of its objective nature. Hence the return of the object into the self is its reappropriation.

Expressed *comprehensively*, the *surmounting* of the *object of consciousness* amounts to this: (1) that the object as such presents itself to consciousness as something vanishing; (2) that it is the externalization of self-consciousness which establishes thinghood; (3) that this externalization has not only a *negative* but a *positive* significance as well; (4) that it has this significance not only *for us* or in itself but *for self-consciousness itself*; (5) *for self-consciousness* the negative of the object or its self-transcendence thereby has *positive* significance—*self-consciousness* thus *knows* this negativity of the object—since self-consciousness externalizes itself and in this externalization establishes *itself* as object or establishes the object as itself on behalf of the indivisible unity of *being-for-self*; (6) on the other hand, there is also present this other moment in the process, that self-consciousness has transcended and reabsorbed into itself this externalization, this objectivity, and is thus at one with itself in *its* other-being *as such;* (7) this is the movement of consciousness, and consciousness is therefore the totality of its phases; (8) consciousness must similarly have related itself to the object in all its aspects and have grasped the object in terms of each of them. This totality of its aspects gives the object *implicitly* a *spiritual nature,* and it truly becomes this nature for consciousness through the apprehension of every one of these aspects as belonging to the *self* or through what was earlier called the *spiritual* relation to them.

ad (1) that the object as such presents itself to consciousness as something vanishing—this is the *return of the object into the self* mentioned above.

ad (2) the *externalization of self-consciousness* establishes *thinghood.* Since man equals self-consciousness, his externalized objective nature or *thinghood* is equivalent to externalized *self-consciousness* and *thinghood* is established through this externalization. (Thinghood is that which is *an object for man* and an object is truly only for him if it is essential to him and thus his *objective* essence. Since it is not *actual man* and therefore also not *nature*—man being *nature as human*—who as such becomes a subject but only the abstraction of man, self-consciousness, thinghood can only be externalized self-consciousness.) It is entirely to be expected that a living, natural being endowed with objective (i.e. material) capacities should have *real natural objects* corresponding to its nature and also that its self-externalization should establish an *actual* objective world but a world in the form of *externality,* one which does not belong to such a being's nature, an overpowering world. There is nothing incomprehensible or mysterious in this. The contrary, rather, would be mysterious. But it is equally clear that a *self-consciousness,* that is, its externalization, can only establish *thinghood,* that is, only an abstract thing, a thing of abstraction and no *actual* thing. It is further clear that thinghood thus completely lacks *independence, essentiality,* over and against self-consciousness but is a mere artifice *established* by self-consciousness. And what is established, instead of confirming itself, is only a confirmation of the act of establishing which for a moment, but only a moment, fixes its energy as product and *apparently* gives it the role of an independent, actual nature.

When actual, corporeal *man* with his feet firmly planted on the solid ground, inhaling and exhaling all of nature's energies *establishes* his actual, objective *essential capacities* as alien objects through his externalization, the *establishing* is not the subject but the subjectivity of *objective* capacities whose action must therefore also be *objective*. An objective being acts objectively and would not act objectively if objectivity did not lie in its essential nature. It creates and establishes *only objects because* it is established through objects, because it is fundamentally part of *nature*. In the act of establishing, this objective being does not therefore descend from its "pure activity" to the *creation* of the *object*, but its *objective* product merely confirms its *objective activity*, its activity as that of an objective, natural being.

We see here how a consistent naturalism or humanism is distinguished from both idealism and materialism as well, and at the same time is the unifying truth of both. We also see how only naturalism is able to comprehend the act of world history.

((Immediately, *man* is a *natural being*. As a living natural being he is, in one aspect, endowed with the *natural capacities* and *vital powers* of an *active* natural being. These capacities exist in him as tendencies and capabilities, as *drives*. In another aspect as a natural, living, sentient and objective being man is a *suffering*, conditioned, and limited creature like an animal or plant. The *objects* of his drives, that is to say, exist outside him as independent, yet they are *objects* of his *need*, essential and indispensable to the exercise and confirmation of his *essential capacities*. The fact that man is a *corporeal*, actual, sentient, objective being with natural capacities means that he has *actual, sensuous objects* for his nature as objects of his life-expression, or that he can only *express* his life in actual sensuous objects. *To be* objective, natural, sentient and at the same time have an object, nature, and sense outside oneself or be oneself object, nature, and sense for a third person is one and the same thing.)) *Hunger* is a natural *need;* it thus requires *nature* and an *object* outside itself to be satisfied and quieted. Hunger is the objective need of a body for an *object* existing outside itself, indispensable to its integration and the expression of its nature. The sun is the *object* of the plant, indispensable to it and confirming its life, just as the plant is object for the sun *expressing* its life-awakening, its *objective* and essential power.

A being which does not have its nature outside itself is not a *natural* one and has no part in the system of nature. A being which has no object outside itself is not objective. A being which is not itself an object for a third being has no being for its *object,* that is, is not related objectively, its being is not objective.

An unobjective being is a *nonentity.*

Suppose there is a being which is not an object itself and does not have one. First of all, such a being would be the *only* being; no other being would exist outside of it; it would be solitary and alone. For as soon as there are objects outside of me, as soon as I am not *alone,* I am *another, another actuality* from the object outside me. For this third object I am thus an *other actuality* than it, that is, *its* object. To assume a being which is not the object of another is thus to suppose that *no* objective being exists. As soon as I have an object, it has me for its object. But a *non-objective* being is an unactual, non-sensuous, merely conceived being. It is merely imagined, an abstraction. To be *sensuous* or actual is to be an object of sense or *sensuous* object and thus to have sensuous objects outside oneself, objects of sensibility. To be sentient is to *suffer.*

As an objective sentient being man is therefore a *suffering* being, and since he feels his suffering, he is a *passionate* being. Passion is man's essential capacity energetically bent on its object.

((But man is not only a natural being; he is a *human* natural being. That is, he is a being for himself and hence a *species-being;* as such he must confirm and express himself as much in his being as in his knowing. Accordingly, *human* objects are not natural objects as they immediately present themselves nor is *human* sense immediately and objectively *human* sensibility, human objectivity. Neither objective nor subjective nature is immediately presented in a form adequate to the *human* being.)) And as everything natural must *have its genesis, man* too has his genetic act, *history,* which is for him, however, known and hence consciously self-transcending. History is the true natural history of mankind. (We shall return to this later.)

Thirdly, since this establishment of thinghood is itself only an appearance, an act contradicting the essence of pure activity, it must again be transcended and thinghood must be denied.

ad 3, 4, 5, 6. (3) This externalization of consciousness has not only a *negative* significance but a *positive* significance as well, and (4) it has this positive significance not only *for us* or in itself but for consciousness itself. (5) *For consciousness* the negative of the object or its transcendence of its own self thereby has the *positive* significance or thereby *knows* the nullity of the object by the fact that it externalizes its *own self,* because in this externalization it *knows* itself as object or the object as its own self, serving the indivisible unity of *being-for-self.* (6) On the other hand there is equally present here the other moment or aspect, that consciousness has also transcended and reabsorbed this externalization and objectivity and is thus *at one with itself* in its *other-being as such.*

As we have already seen, the appropriation of alienated, objective being or the transcendence of objectivity in the mode of *alienation*—which must proceed from indifferent otherness to actual, antagonistic alienation—for Hegel means also or primarily the transcendence of *objectivity* since the *objective* character of the object for self-consciousness, not its *determinateness,* is the scandal of alienation. Hence the object is something negative, a self-transcendence, a *nullity.* This nullity of the object has not merely a negative but also a *positive* meaning for consciousness because it is precisely the self-*confirmation* of non-objectivity, of the *abstraction* of itself. For *consciousness itself* this nullity therefore has a positive significance in that it *knows* this nullity, objective being, as its *self-externalization* and knows that it exists only as a result of its self-externalization. . . .

The way in which consciousness is and the way in which

something is for it is *knowing*. Knowing is its only act. Hence something comes to exist for consciousness insofar as consciousness *knows* that *something*. Knowing is its sole objective relation. Consciousness knows, then, the nullity of the object (i.e. knows the non-existence of the distinction between object and itself, the non-existence of the object for it) because it knows the object is its *self-externalization;* that is, it knows itself—knowing as object—in that the object is only the *appearance* of an object, a deception, which essentially is nothing but knowing itself which has confronted itself with itself and hence with a *nullity,* with a something which has *no* objectivity outside the knowing. Or, knowing knows that in relating itself to an object it is merely *outside* itself externalized, that *it* only *appears* to *itself* as object or that what appears to it as object is only itself.

On the other hand, says Hegel, there is equally present here the other moment or aspect, that consciousness has also transcended and reabsorbed this externalization and objectivity and thus is *at one with itself* in its *other-being as such.*

All the illusions of speculation are assembled in this discussion.

*First,* consciousness—self-consciousness—is *at one with itself* in *its other-being as such.* Hence if we here abstract from Hegel's abstraction and replace consciousness with the self-consciousness of man, it is *at one with itself* in its *other-being as such.* This means, for one thing, that consciousness—knowing as knowing, thinking as thinking—claims to be immediately the *other* of itself, sensibility, actuality, life—thought surpassing itself in thought. (Feuerbach.) This aspect is present inasmuch as consciousness as mere consciousness is offended at *objectivity as such,* not alienated objectivity.

Secondly, this implies that self-conscious man, insofar as he has recognized and transcended the spiritual world—or the general spiritual existence of his world—as self-externalization, then reaffirms it in this externalized form and presents it as his authentic existence, re-establishes it, and pretends to be *at one in his other-being as such.* Thus after transcending religion, for example, and recognizing it as a product of self-externalization, he yet finds confirmation of himself in *religion as religion*. Here *is* the root of Hegel's *false* positivism or of his merely *apparent* criticism which Feuerbach noted as the positing, negation, and re-establishment of religion or theology—but which has to be conceived in more general terms. Thus reason is at one with itself in unreason as unreason. Having recognized that man leads an externalized life in law, politics, etc., man leads in this externalized life as such his truly human life. Self-affirmation and self-confirmation in *contradiction* with itself and with the knowledge and essence of the object is thus authentic *knowledge* and authentic *life*.

There can thus no longer be any question about Hegel's accommodation in regard to religion, the state, etc., since this lie is the lie of his principle.

If I *know* that religion is the *externalized* self-consciousness of man, what I know in it as religion is not my self-consciousness but my externalized self-consciousness confirmed in it. Then I know my own self and its essential self-consciousness not as confirmed in *religion* but rather in the *suppression* and *transcendence* of religion.

Thus with Hegel the negation of the negation is not the confirmation of my authentic nature even through the negation of its appearance. It is the confirmation of the apparent or self-alienated nature in its denial—the denial of the apparent nature as objective, as existing outside and independent of man—and its transformation into a subject. *Transcendence*, therefore, has a special role in which *denial* and preservation, denial and affirmation, are bound together.

Thus in Hegel's philosophy of law, for example, *private right* transcended is *morality*, morality transcended is the *family*, the family transcended is *civil society*, civil society transcended is the *state*, and the state transcended is *world history*. In *actuality* private right, morality, the family, civil society, the state, etc., remain in existence only as they have become *moments* or aspects, modes of the particular existence of man, which are meaningless in isolation but mutually dissolve and generate one another. They are *moments of process*.

In their actual existence their *process*-nature is hidden. It first appears and becomes manifest in thought, in philosophy. Hence my authentic religious existence is my existence in *philosophy of religion*, my authentic political existence is my existence in *philosophy of law*, my authentic natural existence is my existence in *philosophy of nature*, my authentic aesthetic existence is my existence in *philosophy of art*, and my authentic human existence is my existence in *philosophy*. Likewise the authentic existence of religion, the state, nature, and art is the *philosophy* of religion, of the state, of nature, and of art. But if the philosophy of religion, etc., is for me the only authentic existence of religion, I am only truly religious as a *philosopher of religion* and hence I deny *actual* religious feeling and the actually *religious* man. But at the same time I *assert* them, partly in my own particular existence or in the alien existence which I oppose to them—for this *is* only their *philosophical* expression—and partly in their particular original form, since for me they mean only the *apparent* other-being as allegories, forms of their own authentic existence concealed in sensuous coverings, that is, forms of my *philosophical* existence.

In the same way, *quality* transcended is *quantity*, quantity transcended is *magnitude*, magnitude transcended is *essence*, essence transcended is *phenomenon*, phenomenon transcended is *actuality*, actuality transcended is the *concept*, the concept transcended is *objectivity*, objectivity transcended is *absolute Idea*, the absolute Idea transcended is *nature*, nature transcended is *subjective* spirit, subjective spirit transcended is the *ethical* objective Spirit, the ethical objective Spirit transcended is *art*, art transcended is *religion*, and religion transcended is *absolute Knowledge*.

On the one hand this transcendence is transcendence of a thought-entity; thus private property as *thought* is transcended in the *thought* of morality. And because thought imagines itself to be immediately the other of itself or *sensuous actuality*—thus taking its own action for *actual, sensuous* action—this transcendence in thought which leaves its object intact in actuality believes it has actually overcome it. On the other hand, the object, having become a moment of thought for this transcendence, hence also becomes in its actuality a self-confirmation of the same transcendence, of self-consciousness, of abstraction.

From one aspect, the particular existence which Hegel *transcends* in philosophy is therefore not *actual* religion, not the *actual* state, and not *actual* nature but religion as already an object of knowledge, that is, *dogmatics*. (Similarly with *jurisprudence, political science,* and *natural science.*) In this respect he thus opposes both the *actual* nature of the object and the immediate unphilosophical *knowledge*—the unphilosophical concepts—of that nature. He therefore contradicts conventional *concepts*.

From the other aspect, the religious man, etc., can find his ultimate justification in Hegel.

Now the *positive* moments or aspects of the Hegelian dialectic—within the category of alienation—must be considered.

(a) *Transcendence* as an objective movement *reabsorbing* externalization into itself.—((This is the insight into the *appropriation* of objective being, expressed within alienation, through the transcendence of its alienation. It is the alienated insight into the *actual objectification* of man and into the actual appropriation of his objective nature by the destruction of the *alienated* character of the objective world, by the transcendence of the objective world in its alienated existence, just as atheism which transcends God is the emergence of theoretical humanism, and communism which transcends private property is the vindication of actual human life as man's property, the emergence of practical humanism. Or, atheism is humanism mediated through itself by the transcendence of religion, and communism is humanism mediated through itself by the transcendence of private property. Only through the transcendence of this mediation—which is, however, a necessary presupposition—emerges *positive* humanism, humanism emerging positively from itself.))

But atheism and communism are no flight from, no abstraction from, no loss of the objective world created by man as his essential capacities objectified. They are no impoverished return to unnatural, primitive simplicity. Rather they are primarily the actual emergence and the actual, developed realization of man's nature as something actual.

In grasping the *positive* significance of self-referring negation—even if again in an alienated way—Hegel thus grasps man's self-alienation, the externalization of his nature, his loss of objectivity and actualization as finding of self, expression of his nature, objectification, and realization. ((In short, he grasps labor, within the realm of abstraction, as man's *act of self-creation,* his relation to himself as something alien, and the manifestation of his developing *species-consciousness* and *species-life* as something alien.))

(b) But in Hegel—apart from or rather as a result of the inversion already described—this act of self-creation appears, first, as *merely formal* because it is abstract and because human nature itself is viewed only as *abstract,* as *thinking,* as self-consciousness.

Secondly, since the conception is *formal* and *abstract,* the transcendence of externalization affirms the externalization. Or, for Hegel the process of *self-creation* and *self-objectification* in the form of *self-externalization and self-alienation* is the *absolute* and hence final *expression of human life* which has itself as its goal, is at peace with itself, and is at one with its essence.

This movement in its abstract form as dialectic is therefore regarded as *authentic human life,* and since it is still an abstraction, an alienation of human life, it is regarded as a *divine process* and hence the divine process of mankind—a process carried out by man's abstract, pure, absolute nature as distinguished from himself.

*Thirdly:* This process must have a bearer, a subject. But the subject only emerges as a result—namely, the subject knowing itself as absolute self-consciousness which is therefore *God, Absolute Spirit, the self-knowing and self-manifesting Idea.* Actual man and actual nature become merely predicates or symbols of this concealed, unreal man and nature. Hence subject and predicate are absolutely inverted in relation to each other. There is a *mystical subject-*

*object* or a *subjectivity passing beyond the object*, the *absolute subject* as a *process* of self-*externalization* and returning from this externalization into itself but at the same time reabsorbing it into itself. And there is the subject as this process—a pure, restless revolving within itself.

*First*, the *formal and abstract* conception of man's act of self-creation or self-objectification.

With Hegel's identification of man and self-consciousness, the alienated object or alienated essence of man is nothing but *consciousness*, merely the thought of alienation, its *abstract* and hence empty and unreal expression, *negation*. The transcendence of externalization is thus also nothing but an abstract, empty transcendence of that empty abstraction, the *negation of the negation*. The rich, living, sensuous, concrete activity of self-objectification therefore becomes its mere abstraction, *absolute negativity*, an abstraction fixed as such and regarded as independent activity, as activity itself. Since this so-called negativity is only the *abstract, empty* form of that real living act, its content can only be *formal*, derived by abstraction from all content. Hence there are general, abstract *forms of abstraction*—thought forms and logical categories detached from *actual* spirit and *actual* nature—pertaining to any content and indifferent to all and valid for every content. (We shall develop the *logical* content of absolute negativity later.)

Hegel's positive achievement here (in his speculative logic) is his view that *determinate concepts*, universal *fixed thought-forms* independent of nature and spirit, are a necessary result of the universal alienation of human nature and human thought. Hegel has collated and presented them as moments of the abstraction process. For example, Being transcended is Essence, Essence transcended is Concept, Concept transcended . . . Absolute Idea. But what, then, is the Absolute Idea? It must again transcend its own self unless it wants to go through once more from the beginning the whole movement of abstraction and remain content with being a collection of abstractions or a self-comprehending abstraction. But a self-comprehending abstraction knows itself to be nothing; it must abandon itself as abstraction to arrive at something which is its exact opposite, *nature*. Hence the entire Logic is proof that abstract thought is nothing for itself, that the Absolute Idea is nothing for itself, and only *nature* is something.

The Absolute Idea, the *Abstract Idea* which "considered in its unity with itself is *intuiting*" [*Anschauen*] (Hegel's *Encyclopedia*, 3rd ed., p. 222 [¶ 244]) and which "in its own absolute truth *decides* to let the moment of its particularity or of initial determination and other-being, the *immediate idea* as its reflection, freely *proceed from itself* as *nature*" (*ibid*.)—this entire Idea which behaves in such a peculiar and extravagant way and has given the Hegelians such terrible headaches is from beginning to end nothing but *abstraction*, that is, the abstract thinker. It is abstraction which, wise from experience and enlightened concerning its truth, decides under various conditions, themselves false and still abstract, to *release* itself and establish its other-being, the particular, and the determinate, in place of its oneness with itself, non-being, universality, and indeterminateness. It decides to let *nature*, which it hid within itself as a mere abstraction or thought entity, *proceed freely from itself*—that is, it decides to forsake abstraction and for once pay attention to nature *free* of abstraction. The abstract idea which becomes unmediated *intuiting* is through and through nothing but abstract thought abandoning itself and deciding on *intuition*. This entire transition from Logic to Philosophy of Nature is nothing but the transition from *abstracting* to *intuiting*, very difficult for the abstract thinker and hence so quixotically described by him. The *mystical* feeling which drives a philosopher from abstract thinking to intuiting is *boredom*, the longing for a content.

(Man alienated from himself is also the thinker alienated from his *nature*, that is, from his natural and human essence. Hence his thoughts are fixed, ghostly spirits outside nature and man. Hegel has imprisoned all these spirits together in his Logic, conceiving each of them first as negation, as *externalization* of *human* thought, and then as the negation of the negation, the transcendence of this externalization as *actual* externalization of human thought. But since this negation of the negation is still itself imprisoned in alienation, it partly re-establishes these fixed spirits in their alienation and partly halts at the last step of alienation, self-reference, as their authentic existence.* Insofar as this abstraction apprehends itself and experiences an infinite boredom with itself, Hegel abandons abstract thinking moving solely within thinking—without eyes, teeth, ears, everything—as he decides to recognize *nature* as essential being and devote himself to intuition.)

But *nature* too, taken abstractly, for itself, and fixedly isolated from man, is *nothing* for man. It is obvious that the abstract thinker who has committed himself to intuiting, intuits nature abstractly. As nature lay enclosed in the thinker as absolute Idea, as a *thought-entity* in a form hidden and mysterious to the thinker himself, what he has in truth let proceed from himself was only this *abstract nature*, only nature as a thought-entity, but now with the significance of the other-being of thought, actual and perceived nature distinguished from abstract thought. Or, to speak in human terms, the abstract thinker perceives in his intuition of nature that the entities he thought he was creating out of nothing from pure abstraction, in a divine dialectic as pure products of the labor of thought weaving within itself and never perceiving outward actuality—these entities he thought he was creating are merely *abstractions* from *nature's characteristics*. The whole of nature thus only repeats logical abstractions to him in a sensuous, external form. —He again *analyzes* nature and these abstractions. His intuition of nature is thus only the act of confirming his abstraction by the intuition of nature, his conscious re-enactment of the process of producing his abstraction.

* That is, Hegel puts in place of these fixed abstractions the act of abstraction revolving within itself. He has thereby performed the service, in the first place, of having indicated the source of all these inappropriate concepts originally belonging to different philosophies, of having brought them together, and of having created the entire range of abstraction rather than some specific abstraction as the object of criticism. (Later we shall see why Hegel separates thinking from *subject*. But now it is already clear that if man is not human, his characteristic externalization cannot exist and hence thinking itself could not be viewed as the characteristic externalization of man as a human and natural subject with eyes, ears, etc., living in society, the world, and nature.) [Marx's parenthetical remark within the paragraph of the manuscript.]

Thus, for example, Time is its own self-related Negativity (*loc. cit.*, p. 238). To Becoming transcended as particular Being there corresponds, in natural form, Movement transcended as Matter. In *natural* form Light is *Reflection-in-itself*. Body as *Moon* and *Comet* is the *natural* form of the *opposition* which the Logic on one side calls the *positive grounded on itself* and on the other, the *negative* grounded on itself. The Earth is the *natural* form of the logical *ground* as the negative unity of the opposition, etc.

*Nature as nature*, that is, so far as it is sensuously distinguished from that secret meaning hidden within it, nature separated and distinguished from these abstractions, is *nothing*, a *nothing proving* itself to be *nothing*. It is *meaningless* or only means an externality which has been transcended.

"In the finite-*teleological* point of view is to be found the correct premise that nature does not contain in itself the absolute end or purpose" (p. 225 [¶ 245]). Its purpose is the confirmation of abstraction. "Nature has revealed itself as the Idea in the *form* of *other-being*. Since the *Idea* in this form is the negative of itself or *outside itself*, nature is not just relatively outside this Idea [ . . . ] but *externality* determines how it exists as nature" (p. 227 [¶ 247]).

*Externality* is not to be understood here as *self-externalizing sensuousness* open to the light and to the *sensibility* of sensuous man. It is here to be taken as externalization, error, a defect which ought not be. For what is true is still the Idea. Nature is only the *form* of the *other-being* of the Idea. And since abstract thought is the *essence* of things, something external to it is in essence merely *external*. The abstract thinker also recognizes that *sensuousness, externality* as distinguished from thought weaving *within itself*, is the essence of nature. But at the same time he expresses this distinction in such a way as to make this *externality of nature*, its *contrast* to thought, its *defect*. And inasmuch as nature is distinct from abstraction it is something defective. Something which is defective not only for me, in my eyes, but also in itself has something outside itself which it lacks. That is to say, its essence is something other than itself. For the abstract thinker nature must consequently transcend itself since it is already promulgated by him as a potentially *transcended* existence.

"*For us,* Spirit has *nature* as its *presupposition* since it is nature's *truth* and hence its *absolute prius*. In this truth nature has *disappeared* and Spirit has yielded to the Idea as Being-for-itself whose *object* as well as *subject* is the *Concept*. This identity is *absolute negativity* because in nature the Concept has its complete external objectivity but here its externalization has been transcended and in this transcendence the Concept has become self-identical. It is this identity only in being a return from nature" (p. 392 [¶ 381]).

"*Revelation,* as the *abstract* idea, is unmediated transition, the *becoming* of nature; as revelation of Spirit which is free it *establishes* nature as *its own* world. This establishing as reflection is likewise the *presupposition* of the world as independently existing nature. Revelation conceptually is the creation of nature as Spirit's own being in which Spirit gives itself the *affirmation* and *truth* of its freedom." "The *Absolute is Spirit;* this is the highest definition of the Absolute" [¶ 384].

# CRITICAL NOTES ON "THE KING OF PRUSSIA AND SOCIAL REFORM"* (1844)

[While Marx was at work on the "Economic and Philosophic Manuscripts," Arnold Ruge wrote an article for the Paris *Vorwärts* on the Silesian weavers' revolt and misleadingly signed it as written by "a Prussian." Marx and Ruge had quarreled over the finances of their *Jahrbücher*, and Ruge's hostility was aggravated by Marx's attachment to socialism as reflected in his discussions with Proudhon and his friendship with Heine. To clear up misunderstanding about the authorship of Ruge's article and Ruge's misconceptions about the relation of social reform to political action, Marx wrote the following "Critical Notes" for the *Vorwärts*. Using the view of the state he had developed in his critique of Hegel and essay "On the Jewish Question," Marx argues that the modern state is impotent against the debasement and slavery in the economic relations of civil society because it is premised on "the contradiction between public and private life." What is needed is not so much political revolt as social revolution involving "the standpoint of the *whole* because it is a protest of man against dehumanized life," the reaction of the individual against his separation from the "real community of man." Socialism, to be sure, requires political action against the existing ruling power. "But where its organizing activity begins, where its own aim and spirit emerges, there socialism throws the political hull away." In holding that socialism means a universal community involving labor and industry, Marx was insisting on a democracy that would go beyond the political state.]


Number 60 of the *Vorwärts* contains an article entitled "The King of Prussia and Social Reform" and signed *"A Prussian."*

The so-called Prussian chiefly restates the contents of the Royal Prussian Cabinet Order concerning the *Silesian*

---

* Special considerations lead me to explain that this article is the first I have contributed to the *Vorwärts*. K. M.

*weavers'* revolt and the view of the French journal *La Réforme* concerning that Order. *La Réforme* is reported to hold that the *"fears* and *religious* feeling" of the King are the source of the Cabinet Order. It even finds in this document the *anticipation* of great reforms which are in prospect for civil society. The "Prussian" instructs the *Réforme* as follows:

> "The King and German society has not yet reached the stage of 'anticipating its reform,'* and even the Silesian and Bohemian revolts have not created this state of mind. It is impossible to regard the *partial* misery of the factory districts as a general concern for an *unpolitical* country like Germany, let alone as a blot upon the entire civilized world. For Germans this event has the same character as any *local* drought or famine. Consequently the King regards it as an *administrative defect or lack of charity.* For this reason, and because a few soldiers dealt with the weak weavers, the destruction of factories and machines inspired no 'fears' in the King and the authorities. Even *religious feeling* did not dictate the Cabinet Order which is a very sober expression of Christian statecraft and a doctrine which lets no obstacle stand in the way of its own medicine, the 'good intentions of Christian hearts.' Poverty and crime are two great evils; who can remedy them? The state and the authorities? No, but the union of all Christian hearts."

The so-called Prussian denies the existence of the King's *"fears"* on the ground, among others, that a few soldiers dealt with the weak weavers.

In a country then where banquets with liberal toasts and liberal champagne—we recall the Düsseldorf celebration— provoke a Royal Cabinet Order, *without a single* soldier being required, to crush the aspiration of the *entire* liberal bourgeoisie for freedom of its press and a constitution; in a country where passive obedience is the order of the day; in such a country would the compulsory use of armed force against weak weavers not be an *event* and a *fearful* event?

* The stylistic and grammatical nonsense here is to be noted. "The King of Prussia and society *has* not yet reached the stage of anticipating *its* (to what does *its* refer?) reform."

And the weak weavers were victorious at the first encounter. They were suppressed by a later reinforcement of troops. Is the revolt of a crowd of workers less dangerous because it needs no army to stifle it? If the perceptive Prussian compares the Silesian weavers' revolt with the English labor revolts, the Silesian weavers will appear to be *strong* weavers.

On the basis of the *general* relation of *politics* to *social crime* we shall explain why the weavers' revolt could inspire no special *"fears"* in the King. Provisionally we only need say that the revolt was directed not immediately against the King of Prussia but against the bourgeoisie. As an aristocrat and absolute monarch, the King of Prussia can have no love for the bourgeoisie; he can have even less cause for alarm when their submission and impotence are enhanced by a strained and difficult relation to the proletariat. Further, an orthodox Catholic opposes an orthodox Protestant with greater enmity than he opposes an atheist, just as a legitimist opposes a liberal with greater enmity than he opposes a communist. Not because atheists and communists are more akin to the Catholic and legitimist but because they are more alien to him than the Protestant and liberal, because they are *outside* his circle. As a politician, the King of Prussia has his immediate opposition in politics itself, in liberalism. The opposition of the proletariat exists as little for the King as the King exists for the proletariat. The proletariat would have had to achieve decisive power to suppress antipathies, political oppositions, and turn against itself the entire enmity of politics. Finally, in view of the King's well-known character of hankering after what is *interesting* and *significant,* he must even be pleasantly surprised to find *"interesting"* and *"much discussed"* pauperism on his own soil and thus a new opportunity to make himself talked about. How pleased he must have been at the news that now he had his *"own"* Royal Prussian *pauperism.*

Our *"Prussian"* is even more unfortunate when he *denies "religious feeling"* to be the source of the Royal Cabinet Order.

Why is religious feeling not the source of this Cabinet

Order? Because it is a "very *sober* expression of Christian statecraft," a *"sober"* expression of the doctrine which "lets no obstacle stand in the way of its own medicine, the good intentions of Christian hearts."

Is not *religious feeling* the source of *Christian* statecraft? Is not a doctrine whose panacea lies in the good intentions of *Christian hearts* based on religious feelings? Does a *sober* expression of religious feeling cease to be an expression of religious feeling? Hardly! I maintain that it must be a religious feeling greatly infatuated with itself and highly *intoxicated,* which seeks in the *"union of Christian hearts"* the *"remedy for great evils"* it denies to the *"state and the authorities."* It is a highly *intoxicated* religious feeling that—according to the "Prussian's" admission —finds the entire evil in the lack of Christian sentiment and hence refers the authorities to the only means of strengthening this sentiment, *"exhortation."* The purpose of the Cabinet Order, according to the "Prussian," is *Christian conviction.* Obviously where religious feeling is intoxicated, when it is not sober, it regards itself as the sole good. Where it sees evil, it ascribes evil to its own *absence,* for if it is the only good, it alone can produce good. The Cabinet Order dictated by religious feeling thus consequently dictates the religious feeling. A politician of *sober* religious feeling would not, in his "perplexity," seek "help" in the "exhortation of pious preachers of Christian conviction."

How then does the so-called Prussian of *Réforme* prove that the Cabinet Order is not the result of religious feeling? By everywhere depicting it as the result of religious feeling. Is insight into social movements to be expected from so *illogical* a mind? Listen to his *chatter* about the relation of *German society* to the labor movement and to social reform in general.

Let us *distinguish,* which the "Prussian" neglects to do, among the various categories comprised in the expression *"German society":* government, bourgeoisie, the press, and finally the workers themselves. These are the *various* groups with which we are concerned here. The "Prussian" lumps them together and judges them en masse from his superior standpoint. *German society,* according to him, has "not yet even reached the stage of *anticipating* its 'reform.' "

Why is this instinct lacking?

"In an *unpolitical* country like Germany," answers the Prussian, "it is impossible to regard the *partial* misery of the factory districts as a *general concern,* let alone as a blot on the entire civilized world. For Germans this event has the same character as any *local* drought or famine. Consequently the King regards it as an *administrative defect* or *lack of charity.*"

The "Prussian" thus explains this *inverted* view of the misery of labor from the *peculiarity* of an *unpolitical* country.

It will be granted that England is a *political* country. It will be further granted that England is the *country of pauperism,* for even the word is of English origin. Investigation of England is thus the surest way of getting to know the *relationship* of a *political* country to *pauperism.* In England the misery of labor is not *partial* but *universal,* not confined to factory districts but extended to rural districts. The movements there are not at their beginning; they have recurred periodically for nearly a century.

Now how does the *English* bourgeoisie and the government and press associated with it view *pauperism?*

So far as the English bourgeoisie grants *politics any responsibility* for pauperism, the *Whig* regards the *Tory,* and the *Tory* the *Whig,* as the cause of pauperism. According to the Whig, the monopoly of large estates and the prohibition against the import of grain constitute the main source of pauperism. According to the Tory, the entire evil is due to liberalism, competition, and the factory system carried too far. Neither party finds the cause in politics generally, but each rather in the politics of its opponent; neither party lets itself dream of reforming society.

The most decisive expression of the English insight into pauperism—we are always referring to the insight of the English bourgeoisie and government—is *English political economy,* that is, the scientific reflection of English economic conditions.

MacCulloch, a follower of the cynical Ricardo, and one of the best and most famous of English economists, who knows existing conditions and should have a thorough grasp of the movement of civil society, ventured at a public lecture, amidst applause, to apply to economics what *Bacon* said of philosophy:

> "The man who suspends his judgment with true and untiring wisdom, who progresses gradually, and who successively surmounts obstacles which impede the course of study like mountains, will in time reach the summit of knowledge where rest and pure air may be enjoyed, where Nature may be viewed in all her beauty, and whence one may descend by an easy path to the final details of practice."

Good *pure air,* the pestilential atmosphere of English basement dwellings! *Great natural beauty,* the fantastic rags of the English poor, and the withered, wrinkled flesh of the women consumed by work and poverty; children lying in filth; monstrous creatures produced by overwork in the monotonous mechanism of the factories! And the most delightful *final details of practice:* prostitution, murder, and the gallows!

Even the sector of the English bourgeoisie most affected by the danger of pauperism views this danger and the means of remedying the situation not only in *particular* ways but, to speak bluntly, in *childish* and *silly* ways.

Thus Dr. *Kay* in his pamphlet on "Recent Measures for the Promotion of Education in England," for example, reduces everything to *neglected education.* Guess on what grounds! From lack of education the worker fails to comprehend the *"natural laws of commerce,"* laws which *necessarily* lead him to pauperism. Hence he resists. This can only *"disturb* the *prosperity* of English manufacturers and English commerce, shake the mutual confidence of businessmen, *diminish* the *stability* of political and social institutions."

So great is the thoughtlessness of the English bourgeoisie and its press concerning pauperism, England's national epidemic.

Granted, then, that the charges our "Prussian" directs at *German* society are well founded. Does the explanation lie in the *unpolitical* condition of Germany? But if the bourgeoisie of *unpolitical* Germany cannot grasp the general significance of a *partial* misery, the bourgeoisie of *political* England, on the other hand, has failed to appreciate the significance of a universal misery that has brought its universal significance to attention partly by periodic recurrence in time, partly by extension in space, and partly by the failure of all attempts to remedy it.

The "Prussian" further blames the *unpolitical* condition of Germany when the *King* of Prussia finds the cause of pauperism in an *administrative defect* and *lack of charity* and consequently seeks the remedy for pauperism in *administrative* and *charitable measures*.

Is this point of view peculiar to the King of Prussia? Take a quick look at England, the only country where one can refer to major *political* action on pauperism.

The present English Poor Law dates from the 43rd Act of the reign of Elizabeth.* What were the measures of this legislation? In the obligation laid on parishes to support their poor laborers, in the poor tax, in legal benevolence. This legislation—benevolence by way of government—has lasted two hundred years. After long and painful experience, what is the attitude of Parliament in its Amendment Bill of 1834?

First, the frightful increase of pauperism is explained from an *"administrative defect."*

The administration of the poor tax by officials of the respective parishes is hence reformed. *Unions* of about twenty parishes are formed, united in a single administration. A Board of Guardians, elected by the taxpayers, meets on a specified day in the residence of the Union and decides on the granting of relief. These Boards are guided and supervised by officials of the government, the Central Commission of Somerset House, the *Ministry of Pauperism* as it has been aptly designated by a Frenchman. The capital supervised by this administration about

* For our purpose it is not necessary to go back to the Statute of Labor under *Edward III*.

equals the amount which the French War Department costs. The number of local administrators it employs comes to 500, and each of these local administrators in turn keeps at least twelve officials busy.

The English Parliament did not stop with *external* reform of administration.

It found the main source of the *acute* condition of English pauperism in the *Poor Law* itself. The legal remedy for social crime, benevolence, encourages social crime. So far as pauperism *in general* is concerned, it is an *eternal law of nature* according to the theory of *Malthus:*

> "Since population continually tends to exceed the means of subsistence, benevolence is folly, an open encouragement to poverty. The state can therefore do nothing more than leave poverty to its fate and at most ease death for the poor."

With this philanthropic theory the English Parliament combines the view that pauperism is *poverty for which the laborer is himself responsible* and which therefore should not be regarded as a misfortune but rather be suppressed and punished as a crime.

Thus arose the system of workhouses, that is, poorhouses whose internal organization *deters* the poverty-stricken from seeking refuge from starving to death. In the workhouses benevolence is cleverly laced with the *revenge* of the bourgeoisie upon the poor who appeal to its charity.

Thus England first attempted to abolish pauperism by *benevolence* and *administrative measures*. Then it saw in the progressive increase of pauperism not the necessary consequence of modern *industry* but rather the consequence of the *poor tax*. It regarded universal misery as merely a *peculiarity* of English legislation. What was earlier attributed to *lack of charity* was now ascribed to an *overabundance of charity*. Finally, poverty was considered to be the fault of the poor and they were punished for being poor.

The general significance pauperism has achieved in *political* England is confined to the fact that in the course of development and in spite of administrative measures pauperism has become a *national institution* and hence has inevitably become the subject of a ramified and extensive administration, an administration, however, which *no longer* tries to suppress it but to *discipline* and perpetuate it. This administration has abandoned all effort to stop pauperism at its source by *positive* means; it is satisfied to dig a grave for it with a policeman's indifference whenever it gushes to the surface of the official territory. Instead of surpassing administrative and charitable measures, the English state is far from achieving them. Its administration still only touches *those* paupers who are so desperate as to allow themselves to be apprehended and imprisoned.

Thus far, the "Prussian" has not proved anything *peculiar* in the procedure of the King of Prussia. But *why*, exclaims the great man with *rare naïveté*, "Why doesn't the King of Prussia *immediately order the education of all destitute children?*" Why does he first turn to the authorities and wait upon their plans and proposals?

The overly shrewd "Prussian" may calm himself on learning that the King of Prussia in this respect is no more original than in his other actions, that he has even taken the only course a chief of state *can* take.

*Napoleon* wanted to eliminate begging at one stroke. He charged his officials to prepare plans for the *eradication of begging* throughout France. The project kept him waiting. Napoleon lost patience and wrote to his Minister of the Interior, Crétet, commanding him to eliminate begging within *one* month. He said:

> "One should not depart from this world without leaving marks behind which commend our memory to posterity. Do not keep me waiting another three or four months. You have young lawyers, wise prefects, well-trained engineers of roads and bridges; put them all to work and do not fall asleep doing the usual routine work."

In a few months everything was done. On July 5, 1808, a law was passed which suppressed begging. How? By means of *dépôts* which were so quickly transformed into penal establishments that soon the poor could only be admitted to them by way of the *police court*. And yet at that time M. Noailles du Gard, member of the legislature, exclaimed:

> "Eternal gratitude to the hero who provides the needy a place of refuge and means of life for the poor. Childhood will no longer be neglected, poor families will no longer be deprived of resources nor workers of encouragement and employment. We shall no longer be held up by the disgusting spectacle of need and shameful poverty."

The last cynical passage is the one truth in this eulogy.

If Napoleon seeks the judgment of his lawyers, prefects, and engineers, why shouldn't the King of Prussia go to his officials?

Why didn't Napoleon *immediately* order the abolition of begging? Of equal value is the "Prussian's" question: "Why doesn't the King of Prussia immediately order the education of destitute children?" Does the "Prussian" know what the King should order? Nothing less than the *abolition of the proletariat*. If children are to be educated, they must be *fed* and freed from *industrial labor*. The feeding and educating of destitute children, that is, the feeding and educating of the *entire growing* proletariat, would be the *abolition* of the proletariat and of pauperism.

For a moment the *Convention* had the courage to *order* the abolition of pauperism, not *"immediately,"* to be sure as the "Prussian" demands of his King, but only after entrusting the Committee of Public Safety with the preparation of the necessary plans and proposals and only after these had utilized the Constituent Assembly's extensive investigations of poverty in France and had proposed, through [Bertrand] Barère, the establishment of the "Livre de la bienfaisance nationale," etc. What was the upshot of the Convention's ordinance? Only that there was one more ordinance in the world and that *one* year later the Convention was besieged by starving women.

Yet the Convention represented the *maximum* of *political energy, political power,* and *political intelligence.*

*No* government in the world has issued *ordinances* on pauperism *immediately*, without consulting its officials. The

English parliament even sent commissioners to all the countries of Europe to get information about various administrative remedies for pauperism. Insofar as states have been concerned with pauperism, they have confined themselves to *administrative* and *charitable measures* or have done even less.

Can the *state* behave otherwise?

*The state* will *never* find the cause of *social ills* in the "*state* and the *organization of society*" as the "Prussian" requires of his King. Where there are political parties, each finds the cause of *every* evil in the fact that its opponent instead of itself, is at the *helm of state*. Even radical and revolutionary politicians seek the cause of the evil not in the *nature* of the state but in a specific *form of it* which they want to replace by *another* form.

The *state* and the *organization of society* are not, from the *political* standpoint, *two* different things. The state is the organization of society. So far as the state admits the existence of *social* evils, it attributes them either to *natural laws,* which no human power can change, or to *private life,* which is independent of the state, or to the *inadequacy of administration,* which is dependent on it. Thus England finds poverty rooted in the *natural law* according to which population continuously exceeds the means of subsistence. From another side, England explains *pauperism* as a consequence of the *ill will of the poor,* just as the King of Prussia explains it by the *unchristian spirit of the rich* and the Convention explains it by the *counter-revolutionary and equivocal attitude of property owners*. Hence England punishes the poor, the King of Prussia admonishes the rich, and the Convention decapitates property owners.

In the end, *every* state seeks the cause of its ills in *accidental* or *intentional defects* of *administration* and therefore seeks the remedy in *reprimand* of the administration. Why? Simply because the *administration* is the *organizing* activity of the state.

The state cannot transcend the *contradiction* between the aim and good intentions of the administration on the one hand and its means and resources on the other without transcending itself, for it *is based* on this contradiction.

It is based on the contradiction between *public* and *private life,* on the contradiction between *general interests* and *particular interests.* The *administration,* therefore, must confine itself to a *formal* and *negative* activity because its power ceases where civil life and its work begin. Indeed, as against the consequences which spring from the unsocial nature of this civil life, of private property, trade, industry, and the mutual plundering of different civil groups, as against these consequences *impotence* is the *natural law* of administration. This dismemberment, this debasement, this *slavery of civil society* is the natural foundation on which the *modern* state rests, just as the *civil society of slavery* was the foundation of the state in *antiquity.* The existence of the state and the existence of slavery are indivisible. The state and slavery of antiquity—open *classical* antitheses—were not more closely *joined* than are the modern state and the modern world of bargaining—sanctimonious *Christian* antitheses. If the modern state would want to transcend the *impotence* of its administration, it would have to transcend the present mode of *private life.* If it wanted to transcend this private life, it would have to transcend itself, for it exists *only* in contrast to that life. No *living person,* however, believes that the defect of his specific existence is rooted in the *principle* or essence of his life, but rather in circumstances *outside* his life. *Suicide* is unnatural. Thus the state cannot believe in the *innate* impotence of its administration, that is, of its own self. It can notice *only* formal, accidental defects of administration and seek to remedy them. If these modifications are fruitless, then the social ill is a natural imperfection independent of mankind, a *law of God,* or else the will of private individuals is too corrupted to advance the good aims of the administration. And what perverse private individuals! They grumble against the government whenever it restricts freedom, and they demand that the government prevent the necessary consequences of this freedom.

The more powerful the state and hence the more *political* a country is, the less is it inclined to seek the basis and grasp the *general* principle of *social* ills in the *principle of the state* itself, thus in the *existing organization of society* of which the state is the active, self-conscious, and official expression. *Political* thought is *political* precisely because it takes place *within* the bounds of politics. The more acute, the more vigorous it is, the more it is *incapable* of comprehending social ills. The *classical* period of political thought is the *French Revolution*. Far from perceiving the source of social defects in the principle of the state, the heroes of the French Revolution rather saw the source of political evils in social defects. Thus *Robespierre* saw in great poverty and great wealth only an obstacle to *pure democracy*. Hence he wanted to establish a general *Spartan* frugality. The principle of politics is *will*. The more one-sided and thus the more perfected *political* thought is, the more it believes in the *omnipotence* of will, the blinder it is to *natural* and spiritual *restrictions* on the will, and the more incapable it is of discovering the source of social ills. No further proof is needed against the foolish hope of the "Prussian," according to which *"political thought"* is called upon "to discover *the root of social misery* in Germany."

It was absurd to impute to the King of Prussia not only a power which the Convention and Napoleon together did not possess but also an insight exceeding the boundaries of *all* politics, an insight the wise "Prussian" no more nearly possesses than his King. This entire declaration was even more absurd, as the "Prussian" admits:

> "Good words and good intentions are *cheap*, insight and successful action are *dear*; in this case they are *more than dear*, they *are as yet unavailable*."

If they are as yet unavailable, one ought to give credit to anyone who tries to do what he can from his position. Besides, I leave it to the tact of the reader whether on this occasion the mercantile argot of "cheap," "dear," "more than dear," "as yet unavailable" belong in the category of *"good* words" and *"good* intentions."

Suppose that the "Prussian's" comments on the German government and the German bourgeoisie—the latter is certainly included in "German society"—are completely justified. Is this part of society more perplexed in Germany than in England and France? Is it possible to be more perplexed than, for example, in England where *perplexity* has been made into a system? If labor uprisings are now breaking out all over England, the bourgeoisie and government there are no better prepared than in the last third of the eighteenth century. Their only expedient is material force, and as material force diminishes at the same rate as pauperism spreads and the insight of the proletariat increases, English perplexity necessarily grows in geometrical proportion.

Finally, it is *untrue, factually untrue,* that the German bourgeoisie has entirely missed the general significance of the Silesian uprising. In several towns the masters are trying to unite with the journeymen. All the *liberal* German newspapers, the organs of the liberal bourgeoisie, are flowing over with the organization of labor, reform of society, criticism of monopoly and competition, etc. All this as a consequence of the labor movements. The newspapers of Trier, Aachen, Cologne, Wesel, Mannheim, Breslau, and even Berlin are frequently printing intelligently written articles on social affairs, from which the "Prussian" can always learn something. Indeed, letters from Germany constantly express astonishment at the meager opposition of the bourgeoisie against *social* tendencies and ideas.

If the "Prussian" were better acquainted with the history of the social movement, he would have put his question the other way around. Why does the German bourgeoisie itself interpret the partial misery as relatively universal? Whence the *animosity* and *cynicism* of the *political* bourgeoisie, whence the *lack of resistance* and *sympathies* of the *unpolitical* bourgeoisie in relation to the proletariat?

Now turn to the "Prussian's" oracular pronouncements concerning the *German workers.*

> *"The German poor,"* he puns, *"are no more intelligent than the poor Germans,* i.e., *nowhere* can they see beyond their hearth, their factory, their district: the whole question has thus far been neglected by the omnipresent *political* soul."

To be able to compare the situation of the German worker with that of the French and English, the "Prussian" must compare the *first form,* the beginning, of the English and French labor movement with the *German* movement that has *just begun.* He fails to do this. Hence his reasoning amounts to a triviality, such as that *industry* in Germany is not yet so developed as in England or that a movement in its beginning looks different from a movement well in progress. He wanted to talk about the *peculiarity* of the German labor movement. He says not one word on this subject.

But if the "Prussian" took the correct standpoint, he would find that *not a single* French and English labor revolt possessed such a *theoretical* and *conscious* character as the uprising of the Silesian weavers.

First of all, let us recall the *Weavers' Song* [by Heine], those bold *watchwords* of the struggle, in which hearth, factory, and district are not mentioned at all; rather the proletariat immediately screams out its opposition to the society of private property in a forceful, sharp, ruthless, and powerful way. The Silesian uprising *begins* precisely where the French and English labor revolts *end,* with the consciousness of the nature of the proletariat. The action itself bears this *superior* character. Not only the machines, the rivals of the worker, are destroyed but also *account books* and titles to property. While all other movements were directed first of all against the visible enemy, the *industrial lord,* this movement is at the same time directed against the hidden enemy, the banker. Finally, not a single English labor revolt has been conducted with equal courage, deliberation, and persistence.

As for the state of education or the capacity for education of the German workers generally, I recall *Weitling's* excellent writings which frequently surpass *Proudhon* in regard to theory, though they are inferior in execution. Where has the bourgeoisie—their philosophers and scholars included—produced a work similar to Weitling's *Guarantees of Harmony and Freedom* pertaining to the emancipation of the bourgeoisie—*political* emancipation? If one compares the insipid mediocrity of German political literature with this *tremendous* and brilliant literary debut of the German workers; if one compares these gigantic *child's shoes* of the proletariat with the dwarfed, worn-out political shoes of the German bourgeoisie, one must predict an *athletic figure* for the *German Cinderella*. It must be granted that the German proletariat is the *theorist* of the European proletariat, just as the English proletariat is its *economist* and the French proletariat its *politician*. It must be admitted that Germany, though incapable of *political* revolution, has a *classical* summons to *social* revolution. As the impotence of the German bourgeoisie is the *political* impotence of Germany, the talent of the German proletariat—even apart from German theory—is the *social* talent of Germany. The disparity between philosophical and political development in Germany is no *abnormality*. It is a necessary disparity. Only in socialism can a philosophical people find its suitable practice, thus only in the *proletariat* can it find the active element of its emancipation.

Yet at this moment I have neither the time nor the inclination to explain to the "Prussian" the relation of "German society" to social transformation, and from this relation to explain, on the one hand, the feeble reaction of the German bourgeoisie to socialism and, on the other hand, the unusual talent of the German proletariat for socialism. He will find the leading elements for the understanding of this phenomenon in my Introduction to The Critique of Hegel's Philosophy of Law (*Deutsch-Französische Jahrbücher*).

Thus the intelligence of the *German poor* is *inversely* proportional to the intelligence of the *poor Germans*. But people who must treat every subject as a public exercise in style get an inverted content through this *formal* activity while the inverted content, in its turn, impresses the seal of vulgarity on the form. Thus the "Prussian's" attempt to proceed in the form of antithesis on the occasion of the Silesian labor unrest led to the greatest antithesis against the truth. The only task of a thoughtful and truth-loving mind in regard to the first outbreak of the Silesian labor revolt was not to play the role of *schoolmaster* to the event but rather to study its *peculiar* character. For the latter some scientific insight and love of humanity is necessary, while for the other operation a glib phraseology, soaked in hollow egoism, is quite sufficient.

Why does the "Prussian" criticize the German workers so contemptuously? Because he finds that the "whole question"—namely the question of labor's misery—has *"up to now"* been left behind by the "omnipresent *political* soul." He explains in detail his Platonic love for the *political soul*:

> "All revolts breaking out in the disastrous *isolation of men from the community* and the separation of their *thought from social principles* will be suppressed in blood and irrationality; but if misery first creates understanding and the *political* understanding of the Germans discovers the root of social misery, then these events will also be felt in Germany as symptoms of a great transformation."

First of all, may the "Prussian" permit us to make a *stylistic* observation. His antithesis is incomplete. In the first half of the sentence he says: if *misery* creates *understanding;* and in the second half: if *political understanding* discovers the *root of social misery.* *Simple* understanding in the first half of the antithesis becomes *political* understanding in the second half, just as the simple *misery* of the first half becomes *social* misery in the second. Why has the artist of style so unequally endowed the two halves of the antithesis? I do not believe that he seriously thought about that. I shall interpret for him his real *intuition.* Had he written: "if *social* misery creates *political* understanding and if *political understanding* discovers the root of *social* misery," the *absurdity* of this antithesis could not have escaped any unprejudiced reader. In the first place such a reader would have wondered why the anonymous writer did not join social understanding with social misery and political understanding with political misery, as the simplest logic requires. Now to the point.

It is so false that *social misery* creates *political understanding* that the reverse is rather the case, *social well-being* creates *political* understanding. *Political* understanding is something spiritual and is given to him who already has, who is already in the clover. Our "Prussian" should listen to a French economist, M. *Michel Chevalier,* on this matter:

> "What the bourgeoisie lacked to be free, at their revolt in 1789, was a share in the government of the country. For them emancipation consisted in taking the direction of public affairs—the major civil, military, and religious functions—from the hands of the privileged who possessed the monopoly of these functions. *Wealthy* and *enlightened,* self-sufficient and self-governing, they wanted to get rid of the *régime du bon plaisir.*"

We have already shown the "Prussian" how incapable *political* understanding is of discovering the source of social misery. *One* word more about this opinion of his. The more developed and general the *political* intelligence of a people is, the more the *proletariat*—at least at the beginning of the movement—wastes its energies in irrational and useless uprisings which are suppressed in blood. Because it thinks politically, it sees the cause of all evils in *will* and all remedies in *force* and the *overthrow* of a *particular* form of the state. As evidence, consider the first outbreaks of the *French* proletariat. The workers of Lyons believed that they were pursuing only political aims, that they were only soldiers of the Republic, while actually they were soldiers of socialism. Thus their political understanding clouded the roots of their social misery, distorted their insight into their actual aims, and *deceived* their *social instinct.*

But if the "Prussian" expects the creation of understanding through misery, why does he put *"suppression in blood"* and *"suppression in irrationality"* together? If misery is generally a means, *bloody* misery is a *very acute* means to create understanding. The "Prussian" must thus say: Suppression in blood will suppress irrationality and provide the understanding a suitable air to breathe.

The "Prussian" prophesies the suppression of revolts that break out in the *"disastrous isolation of men from the community* and the *separation of their thought from social principles.*"

We have indicated that the Silesian uprising by no means came from the separation of thought from social principles. Further, we have only to deal with the *"disastrous isolation of men from the community."* By community is here to be understood the *political community,* the *state.* It is the old story of *unpolitical* Germany.

Do not *all* uprisings without exception, however, break out *in the disastrous isolation of men from the community?* Doesn't *every* uprising necessarily presuppose this isolation? Would the Revolution of 1789 have occurred without the disastrous isolation of the French citizens from the community? Its aim, after all, was to end this isolation.

But the *community* from which the worker is *isolated* is a community of a very different order and extent than the *political* community. This community, from which *his own labor* separates him, is *life* itself, physical and spiritual life, human morality, human activity, human enjoyment, *human* existence. *Human existence* is the *real community* of man. As the disastrous isolation from this existence is more final, intolerable, terrible, and contradictory than isolation from the political community, so is the ending of this isolation. And even a partial reaction, a *revolt* against it, means all the more, as *man* is more than *citizen* and *human life* more than *political life.* Hence, however *partial* the *industrial* revolt may be, it conceals within itself a *universal* soul: no matter how universal a *political* revolt may be, it conceals a *narrow-minded* spirit under the *most colossal* form.

The "Prussian" worthily closes his article with the following phrase: "A *social revolution without a political soul* (i.e. without organizing insight from the standpoint of the whole) is impossible."

We have seen that a *social* revolution involves the standpoint of the *whole* because it is a protest of man against dehumanized life even if it occurs in only *one* factory district, because it proceeds from the *standpoint* of the *single actual individual,* because the *community* against whose separation from himself the individual reacts is the *true* community of man, *human* existence. The *political soul* of a revolution, on the other hand, consists in the *tendency* of politically uninfluential classes to end their *isolation* from the *state* and from *power*. Its standpoint is that of the state, an *abstract* whole, which exists *only* through the separation from actual life and which is *unthinkable* without the *organized* antithesis between the universal idea and the individual existence of man. Hence a revolution of the *political soul* also organizes, in accordance with the *narrow* and *split* nature of this soul, a ruling group in society at the expense of society.

We would like to confide to the "Prussian" what a "*social revolution* with a *political* soul" is; at the same time we also suggest to him that he has not raised himself above the narrow political standpoint even in *phraseology*.

A "*social*" revolution with a *political* soul is either a compounded absurdity if the "Prussian" means by "social" revolution a "social" revolution in *contrast* to a political one and nevertheless attributes to this social revolution a political rather than a social soul. Or a "*social revolution with a political soul*" is nothing but a *paraphrase* of what used to be called a "*political revolution*" or a "*revolution pure and simple*." Any revolution breaks up the *old society;* to that extent it is *social*. Any revolution overthrows the *old ruling power;* to that extent it is *political*.

The "Prussian" may choose between the *paraphrase* and the *absurdity!* But though it is paraphrastic or senseless to speak of a *social revolution* with a *political soul,* it is sensible to talk about a *political revolution* with a *social* soul. *Revolution* in general—the *overthrow* of the existing ruling power and the *dissolution* of the old conditions—is a *political act*. Without *revolution,* however, *socialism* cannot come about. It requires this *political act* so far as it needs *overthrow* and *dissolution*. But where its *organizing activity* begins, where its *own aim* and *spirit* emerge, there socialism throws the *political* hull away.

Such long-windedness was necessary to break through the *web* of errors hidden in a single newspaper column. Not every reader can have the education and time to settle accounts with such *literary charlatanry*. For the time being, has not the anonymous "Prussian" the duty to the reading public to refrain from political and social writings, such as declamations about German conditions, and rather to begin with a conscientious self-analysis of his own condition?

# CRITICISM AND APPROPRIATION OF
# HEGEL AND FEUERBACH

# From THE HOLY FAMILY (1844), or
# CRITIQUE OF CRITICAL CRITICISM
# AGAINST BRUNO BAUER AND COMPANY

[After ten days of agreeable conversation in Paris early in September 1844, Marx and Engels began collaboration on the following critique of speculative idealism published in February 1845. Marx wrote most of the book, all but some sixteen pages contributed by Engels. The Foreword suggested their debt to Feuerbach. Their position was to be "real humanism," which pits "real individual man" against "disguised theology." In opposition to Bauer's "critical criticism" Marx praises Proudhon's discovery of basic contradictions in economics. Going further, Marx sees a dialectical antagonism between wealth and the proletariat reflected in man's self-alienation. The overcoming of this alienation depends on the objective development of property and the historically prescribed action of the proletariat. This view of historical development embodied Hegel's dialectic, but in seeking to ground it in perceptible events, Marx adhered to Feuerbach.

Attacking "speculative construction" in Bauer and company, Marx further appeals to sense perception, noting that Hegel himself often gave "a presentation of the *matter* itself." Marx finds Bauer treating history as "a person apart, a metaphysical subject," ignoring the effective role of interests. Engels notes how Feuerbach demolished such speculative history, the old "dialectic of concepts." Challenging Bauer's approach to materialism, Marx argues that the rootage of knowledge in sense perception, Feuerbach's position, logically leads to communism. In a chapter omitted below, however, Marx suggested the limitation of Feuerbach as well as Bauer: history must be linked with industry and "material production." In other omitted chapters Marx used themes he developed earlier—emancipation of the Jews and "rights of man" in the French Revolution—to criticize the "critical critics." Such chapters gave further scope to his exuberant style but also revealed his sensitivity to the miseries and ironies of industrialism along with his growing socialist convictions.]

## Critical Comment No. I on Proudhon

Just as the first criticism of any science is necessarily implicated in the premises of the science it is combating, so is Proudhon's work, *What Is Property?* a criticism of *political economy* from the standpoint of political economy. —We need not go further into the juridical part of the book criticizing law from the standpoint of law, since our major interest is the critique of political economy. —Thus Proudhon's work will be scientifically surpassed by criticism of *political economy,* even of political economy as conceived by Proudhon. This task only became possible through Proudhon himself, just as Proudhon's criticism presupposed the physiocrat's criticism of the mercantile system, Adam Smith's criticism of the physiocrats, Ricardo's criticism of Adam Smith as well as the works of Fourier and Saint-Simon.

All developments of political economy presuppose *private property*. This basic presupposition is regarded as an unassailable fact needing no further examination, indeed even a fact which is mentioned only "accidentally," as *Say* naïvely admits. Now Proudhon subjects the basis of political economy, *private property,* to a critical examination, in fact the first resolute, ruthless, and at the same time scientific examination. This is the great scientific advance he made, an advance revolutionizing political economy and making possible for the first time a real science of political economy. Proudhon's treatise, *What Is Property?* is as important for modern political economy as Sieyès' *What Is the Third Estate?* is for modern politics.

If Proudhon does not grasp the wider forms of private property—for example, wages, trade, value, price, money, etc.—as themselves forms of private property as is done, for example, in the *Deutsch-Französische Jahrbücher* (see F. Engels' "Outlines of a Critique of Political Economy") but uses these economic premises against political economists, this is entirely in keeping with his historically justified standpoint mentioned above.

Accepting the relationships of private property as human and rational, political economy moves in a continuous contradiction to its basic premise, private property, a contradiction analogous to that of a theologian who constantly gives a human interpretation to religious ideas and thereby constantly repudiates his fundamental assumption, the superhuman character of religion. Thus in political economy wages appear at the outset as the proportionate share of the produce due labor. Wages and profit on capital stand in the most friendly, mutually helpful, and apparently most human relationship to one another. Subsequently it turns out that they stand in the most hostile, *inverted* relationship. Value is determined at the beginning in an apparently rational way, by the costs of production of an article and its social utility. Subsequently it turns out that the determination of value is entirely fortuitous and need have no connection either with the costs of production or with social utility. The amount of wages is determined at the beginning by a *free* contract between the free laborer and free capitalist. Later it turns out that the laborer is forced to let the capitalist determine wages just as the capitalist is forced to set them as low as possible. *Freedom* of the contracting parties gives way to *coercion*. The same applies to trade and all other relationships of political economy. Political economists themselves occasionally sense these contradictions whose elaboration is the principal content of their mutual wrangling. But when economists become fully aware of these contradictions, *they themselves* tackle *private property* in some *partial* form as the falsifier of wages which are rational in themselves, namely in the conception they have formed of wages, or as the falsifier of value which is rational in itself, or as the falsifier of trade, rational in itself. Thus Adam Smith occasionally attacks the capitalists, Destutt de Tracy the bankers, Simonde de Sismondi the factory system, Ricardo landed property, and almost all modern economists attack the *non-industrial* capitalists who regard property as merely a *consumer*.

Thus sometimes, as an exception—when they are attacking some particular abuse—the political economists stress the humane appearance of economic conditions, but at other times and in most cases they conceive these conditions precisely in their pronounced *difference* from what is humane, in their strictly economic sense. They reel about within this contradiction, completely unaware of it.

Now *Proudhon* has once and for all put an end to this lack of awareness. He took seriously the *humane appearance* of economic conditions and sharply confronted it with their *inhumane reality*. He demanded that these conditions should be in actuality what they are in conception, or rather that their conception should be abandoned and their actual inhumanity be established. Hence, he was consistent when he presented as the falsifier of economic conditions not partly this or that kind of private property, as other economists do, but private property completely and universally. He accomplished everything a criticism of political economy can accomplish from the standpoint of political economy.

Wanting to *characterize* the *standpoint* of *What Is Property?* Herr Edgar [Bauer] naturally does not say a word about political economy or the distinctive character of this book—precisely that it has made the *essence of private property* the vital question of political economy and jurisprudence. Everything is self-evident for Critical Criticism. For it Proudhon has done nothing new with his negation of private property. He has only divulged one of Critical Criticism's concealed secrets.

"Proudhon," Herr Edgar immediately continues after his characterizing translation, "thus finds something absolute in history, an eternal foundation, a god, directing mankind—justice."

Proudhon's French writing of 1840 does not take the standpoint of German development of 1844. It is Proudhon's standpoint, a standpoint shared by countless French writers diametrically opposed to him, thus giving Critical Criticism the advantage of having characterized the most contradictory standpoints with one and the same stroke of the pen. Further, to deal with this Absolute in history one has only to apply consistently the law set forth by Proudhon himself—the realization of justice by its negation. If

Proudhon does not go that far, it is only because he had the misfortune of having been born a Frenchman and not a German.

For Herr Edgar, Proudhon has become *theological* with his Absolute in history and his faith in justice, and Critical Criticism which is ex professo criticism of theology can now seize upon him to express itself on "religious conceptions."

"It is characteristic of every religious conception that it establishes dogma in a situation where one antithesis comes out in the end as victorious and the only truth."

We shall see how religious Critical Criticism establishes dogma in a situation where in the end one antithesis, "*the* criticism," comes out victorious over the other, "the Mass," as the only truth. Proudhon, however, committed a still greater injustice in perceiving an Absolute, a God of history, in massy justice, since righteous Criticism had *expressly* reserved for itself the role of this Absolute, this God in history.

## Critical Comment No. II on Proudhon

"Proudhon arrives at his views one-sidedly through the fact of misery and poverty and sees in this fact a *contradiction* of equality and justice; it provides him with his weapons. Hence this fact becomes absolute and justified for him, and the fact of property becomes unjustified."

The "calm of understanding" [in Critical Criticism] tells us that Proudhon sees a contradiction of justice in the fact of misery and thus finds this fact unjustified; and in the same breath that "calm of understanding" assures us that this fact becomes absolute and justified for Proudhon.

Previous political economy proceeded from *wealth*, which the movement of private property supposedly created for *nations*, to arrive at an apology for private property. Proudhon proceeds from the opposite side, which is sophistically covered up in political economy, to arrive at the negation of private property. The first criticism of private property naturally proceeds from the fact which manifests its essence in the most perceptible and glaring form, the form most directly arousing human indignation—from the fact of misery and poverty.

"Criticism, on the other hand, merges both facts—poverty and property—into one, grasps the inner link between them, and makes them a single whole which it examines as such to find the conditions of its existence."

Criticism, which has previously comprehended nothing of the facts of property and poverty, "on the other hand" uses its imaginatively accomplished fact against Proudhon's actual fact. It merges *the two* facts into *one,* and having made *one* out of *two,* forthwith perceives the inner link between the *two.* Criticism cannot deny that Proudhon also perceives an inner link between the facts of poverty and property since he would abolish property because of this link in order to abolish poverty. Proudhon did even more. He demonstrated in detail *how* the movement of capital produces misery. Critical Criticism, on the other hand, does not concern itself with such trivialities. It recognizes that poverty and wealth are *antitheses:* a rather widespread acknowledgment. It *makes* poverty and wealth a *single whole* which it "examines *as such* to find the conditions of its existence"—an examination all the more superfluous since Critical Criticism has just *made* that "whole as such" and so its *making* is itself the condition of its existence.

In examining "the whole as such" to find the conditions of its existence, Critical Criticism is searching in truly theological fashion *outside* the whole for the conditions of its existence. Critical speculation moves outside the object with which it pretends to be dealing. While the *entire antithesis* is nothing but the *movement of both its sides* and the condition for the existence of the whole lies precisely in the nature of these two sides, Critical Criticism passes over the study of this actual movement constituting the whole in order to be able to declare that it is beyond both extremes of the antithesis as the "calm of understanding." And the activity of Critical Criticism which made "the whole as such" is now alone in position to transcend the abstraction it made.

Proletariat and wealth are antitheses. As such they constitute a whole. They are both manifestations of the world of private property. The question at issue is the specific position they occupy in the antithesis. It is not enough to describe them as two sides of a whole.

Private property as private property, as wealth, is compelled to *maintain* its *own existence* and at the same time that of its antithesis, the proletariat. It is the *positive* side of the contradiction—private property sufficient in itself.

The proletariat as proletariat, on the other hand, is compelled to abolish itself and at the same time its conditional antithesis, private property, which makes it the proletariat. It is the *negative* side of the contradiction, its internal restlessness—private property dissolved and dissolving.

The propertied class and the class of the proletariat represent the same human self-alienation. But the former feels comfortable and confirmed in this self-alienation, knowing that this alienation is *its own power* and possessing in it the *semblance* of a human existence. The latter feels itself ruined in this alienation and sees in it its impotence and the actuality of an inhuman existence. The proletariat, to use Hegel's words, is abased and *indignant* at its abasement —a feeling to which it is necessarily driven by the contradiction between its human *nature* and its situation in life, a situation that is openly, decisively, and comprehensively the negation of that nature.

Within this antithesis the property owner is therefore the *conservative* party, and the proletarian is the *destructive* party. From the *former* arises action to maintain the antithesis, from the *latter*, action to destroy it.

In its economic movement, private property is driven toward its own dissolution but only through a development which does not depend on it, of which it is unconscious, which takes place against its will, and which is brought about by the very nature of things—thereby creating the proletariat *as* proletariat, that spiritual and physical misery conscious of its misery, that dehumanization conscious of its dehumanization and thus transcending itself. The proletariat executes the sentence that private property inflicts on itself by creating the proletariat just as it carries out the verdict that wage-labor pronounces on itself by creating wealth for others and misery for itself. When the proletariat triumphs, it does not thereby become the absolute side of society because it triumphs only by transcending itself and its opposite. Then the proletariat and its determining antithesis, private property, disappear.

When socialist writers attribute this historic role to the proletariat, it is not, as Critical Criticism pretends to think, because they regard proletarians as *gods*. On the contrary. Because the abstraction of all humanity and even the *semblance* of humanity is practically complete in the fully developed proletariat, because the conditions of life of the proletariat bring all the conditions of present society into a most inhuman focus, because man is lost in the proletariat but at the same time has won a theoretical awareness of that loss and is driven to revolt against this inhumanity by urgent, patent, and absolutely compelling *need* (the practical expression of *necessity*)—therefore the proletariat can and must emancipate itself. But it cannot emancipate itself without transcending the conditions of its own life. It cannot transcend the conditions of its own life without transcending *all* the inhuman conditions of present society which are summed up in its own situation. It does not go through the hard but hardening school of *labor* in vain. It is not a question of what this or that proletarian or even the whole proletariat momentarily *imagines* to be the aim. It is a question of *what* the proletariat *is* and what it *consequently* is historically compelled to do. Its aim and historical action is prescribed, irrevocably and obviously, in its own situation in life as well as in the entire organization of contemporary civil society. There is no need to explain here in detail that a large part of the English and French proletariat is already *conscious* of its historic task and is continuously working to develop that consciousness into complete clarity.

"Critical Criticism" can even less admit this since it has proclaimed itself as the exclusive creative element of history. To it belong the historical contradictions and to it the activity of transcending them. Hence, it issues the following *public notice* through its incarnation, Edgar:

"Education and lack of education, property and lack of property as *antitheses* must *devolve wholly and completely* on Criticism if they are not to be *desecrated*."

Property and lack of property have received metaphysical consecration as critical, speculative antitheses. Hence only the hand of Critical Criticism can touch them without committing a sacrilege. Capitalists and workers must not meddle with their reciprocal relationships.

Far from expecting that his critical view of antitheses could be touched and that this holy thing could be desecrated, Herr Edgar lets his opponent make an objection which he only could make to himself.

"Is it then possible," asks the imaginary opponent of Critical Criticism, "to use other concepts than those already existing such as liberty, equality, etc.? I answer"—note Herr Edgar's answer—"that Greek and Latin became extinct as soon as the range of thought they sought to express was exhausted."

It is now clear why Critical Criticism does not present a single thought in *German*. The language of its thought has not yet appeared, however much Herr Reichardt with his Critical treatment of foreign words, Herr Faucher with his treatment of English, and Herr Edgar with his treatment of French have done to prepare the *new Critical* language.

## The Mystery of Speculative Construction

The mystery of the Critical presentation of the "Mysteries of Paris" is the mystery of *speculative,* of *Hegelian, construction*. Once Herr Szeliga has explained the "degeneracy within civilization" and lawlessness in the state as "mysteries", that is, has reduced them to the category of *"mystery,"* he lets "mystery" begin its *speculative career*. A few words will suffice to characterize speculative construction *in general*. Herr Szeliga's handling of the "Mysteries of Paris" will give the application *in detail*.

If I form the general idea *"Fruit"* from actual apples, pears, strawberries, and almonds, and if I go further to *imagine* that my abstract idea, *"the* Fruit," derived from actual fruits, is an external entity and indeed the *true* essence of the pear, the apple, etc., I am declaring—in the language of *speculation*—that "*the* Fruit" is the "*Substance*" of the pear, the apple, the almond, etc. Thus I am saying that it is unessential that the pear be a pear and the apple an apple. What is essential in these things is not their actual, sensuously perceptible particular existence, but the essence I have abstracted from and substituted for them, the essence of my idea, "*the* Fruit." I then declare apples, pears, almonds, etc. to be merely forms of existence, *modi,* of "*the* Fruit." Of course, my finite understanding, supported by my senses, *distinguishes* an apple from a pear and a pear from an almond, but my speculative reason declares these perceptual differences to be unessential and unimportant. My speculative reason sees in the apple *the same thing* as in the pear and in the pear the same thing as in the almond—namely, "*the* Fruit." Particular, actual fruits are taken to be only *apparent* fruits whose true essence is "*the* Substance," "*the* Fruit."

By this method one hardly achieves any particular *wealth* of *definition.* The mineralogist whose entire science is limited to asserting that all minerals are really *the* Mineral, would be a mineralogist—in *his imagination.* For every mineral the speculative mineralogist says "*the* Mineral," and his science is reduced to repeating this word as many times as there are actual minerals.

Having reduced different actual fruits to *one* abstract "Fruit," to *the* "Fruit," speculation must somehow try to get back again from *the* "Fruit," from *Substance,* to *different,* actual ordinary fruits such as the pear, the apple, the almond, etc., in order to give the appearance of having some actual content. It is as difficult to produce actual fruits from the abstract idea of "*the* Fruit" as it is easy to produce the abstract idea of "*the* Fruit" from actual fruits. In fact it is impossible to get from an abstraction to the *opposite* of an abstraction without *abandoning* the abstraction.

Hence the speculative philosopher abandons the abstraction, *the* "Fruit," but only in a *speculative, mystical* fashion, that is, with the appearance of *not* having abandoned it.

He actually rises above the abstraction only in appearance. He reasons somewhat as follows:

If the apple, pear, almond, and strawberry are really nothing but *"the* Substance," *"the* Fruit," then the question arises: How does it happen that *"the* Fruit" manifests itself to me now as apple, now as pear, and now as almond; whence this *appearance* of *diversity* so strikingly in contradiction with my speculative intuition of the *unity, "the* Substance" and *"the* Fruit"?

This, answers the speculative philosopher, is because *"the* Fruit" is no dead, undifferentiated static essence but living, self-differentiated, dynamic. The variety of ordinary fruits is significant not only for *my* sensuous understanding but also for *"the* Fruit" itself, for speculative reason. The different ordinary fruits are different life-forms of the *"one* Fruit;"* they are crystallizations formed by *"the* Fruit" itself. Thus, for example, in the apple *"the* Fruit" gives itself an appley existence, in the pear, a peary existence. One must no longer say as one did from the standpoint of Substance that a pear, an apple, and an almond is *"the* Fruit" but rather that *"the* Fruit" posits itself as pear, as apple, as almond. The differences which distinguish apple, pear, and almond from one another are really self-differentiations of *"the Fruit,"* converting the particular fruits into different members of the life-process of *"the* Fruit." So *"the* Fruit" is no longer an empty, undifferentiated unity; it is unity as *allness,* as *"totality"* of fruits constituting an *"organically ramified series."* In every member of that series *"the* Fruit" gives itself a more developed and explicit specific existence until it is finally the living *unity* as "summary" of all fruits, a unity containing those fruits as dissolved in and also produced from itself, just as all the organs of the body, for example, are continuously absorbed in and produced out of the blood.

Though the Christian religion knows of only *one* incarnation of God, speculative philosophy has as many incarnations as there are things, just as here it has an incarnation of Substance, of absolute Fruit, in every fruit. The speculative philosopher's main interest is thus to produce the *existence* of actual, ordinary fruit and to say in a mysterious way that there are such things as apples, pears, almonds, and raisins. But the apples, pears, almonds, and raisins we find again in the speculative world are nothing but *apparent* apples, *apparent* pears, *apparent* almonds, and *apparent* raisins because they are life-moments of *"the* Fruit," that abstract *creature of the understanding,* and are thus themselves abstract *creatures of the understanding.* What you enjoy in this speculation is to rediscover all the actual fruits but as fruits which have a higher mystical significance as incarnations of *"the* Fruit," the *absolute Subject,* grown from the ether of your brain and not from material ground and soil. Thus when you return to actual, *natural* fruits from the abstract *supernatural* creature of the understanding, *"the* Fruit," you thereby give the natural fruits a supernatural significance and transform them into pure abstractions. Your chief interest is then to establish the *unity* of *"the* Fruit" in all its life-forms—apple, pear, and almond —to prove the *mystical interconnection* among these fruits, and to show how in each *"the* Fruit" *gradually* and *necessarily* actualizes itself, for example, progresses from its specific existence as raisin to its specific existence as almond. The value of ordinary fruits *no longer* consists in their *natural* qualities *but* in the *speculative* quality by which they acquire a specific position in the life-process of *"the* absolute Fruit."

The ordinary man does not feel that he is saying anything extraordinary when he states that there are apples and pears. But when the philosopher expresses this existence in speculative fashion, he has said something *extraordinary.* He has accomplished a *miracle.* He has produced actual, *natural entities*—apples, pears, etc.—from an unreal *creature of the understanding, "the* Fruit." That is to say, he has *created* these fruits out of his *own abstract understanding* which he presents as an absolute Subject outside of himself, in this case as *"the* Fruit." And in every existence he articulates, he performs an act of creation.

It is obvious that the speculative philosopher accomplishes this constant creation only by introducing the properties of the apple, the pear, etc.—so well-known in actual experience—as determinations he has *invented;* by giving the *names* of actual things to abstract formulas of the understanding which only abstract understanding can create; and finally by declaring his *own* activity in passing from the notion of apple to that of pear to be the *self-activity* of the absolute Subject, *"the* Fruit."

In the language of speculation this operation is called conceiving *Substance* as *Subject,* as *inner Process,* as *Absolute Person* and this conceiving constitutes the essential character of the *Hegelian* method.

These preliminary remarks were necessary to make Herr Szeliga comprehensible. Having previously reduced such actual relationships as law and civilization to the category of mystery, thereby converting *"the* Mystery" into a substance, he now rises to a truly speculative, *Hegelian* height and transforms *"the* Mystery" into a self-existing Subject. This Subject *incarnates* itself in actual situations and persons and manifests its life in countesses, marquises, grisettes, porters, notaries, charlatans, love intrigues, dances, wooden doors, etc. Having created the category of *"the* Mystery" out of the actual world, he produces the actual world out of this category.

The mysteries of *speculative* construction in Herr Szeliga's account are disclosed all the *more apparently* in the *double* advantage he indisputably has over *Hegel.* First, Hegel knows how to present with sophistic mastery the process by which the philosopher passes from one object to another through sensuous perception and conception as a process of the imagined creature of the understanding itself, as a process of the absolute Subject. Besides, Hegel very often gives an *actual* presentation, a presentation of the *matter* itself, within his *speculative* presentation. This actual development *within* speculative development misleads the reader into taking the speculative development as actual and the actual as speculative.

With Herr Szeliga both these difficulties disappear. His dialectic has no hypocrisy or pretense whatsoever. He performs his tasks with the most laudable honesty and at the most worthy level. But *nowhere* does he develop any *actual content,* so his speculative construction is free from all disturbing complications, from all ambiguous disguises, and strikes the eye in its naked beauty. With Herr Szeliga it is also brilliantly clear how speculation apparently creates its object freely out of itself *a priori* and also how speculation, sophistically trying to avoid rational and natural dependence on the *object,* falls into the most unreasonable and unnatural *subservience* to the object whose most accidental and individual properties it must construe as absolutely necessary and universal.

## "Spirit" and "Mass"

Thus far Critical Criticism has seemed to deal more or less with the critical revision of various *massy* objects. Now we find it dealing with the absolutely critical object, *with itself.* Thus far it has drawn its relative fame from the critical degradation, rejection, and transformation of *definite* massy objects and persons. Now it draws its *absolute* fame from the critical degradation, rejection, and transformation of the mass in general. Relative criticism was confronted with relative limits. Absolute criticism is confronted with an absolute limit, the limit of the Mass, the Mass as limit. Relative criticism in its antithesis to definite limits was itself necessarily a *limited* individual. Absolute criticism in antithesis to the *general* limit, to limit without qualification, is necessarily an *absolute* individual. As the various massy objects and persons have coalesced in the *impure* mush of the *"Mass,"* so has seemingly objective and personal criticism changed into *"pure criticism."* Thus far criticism has appeared to be more or less a *quality* of critical individuals —Reichardt, Edgar, Faucher, et al. Now it is *Subject* and Herr Bruno [Bauer] is its incarnation.

Thus far *massiness* has seemed to be more or less the quality of the objects and persons criticized; now objects and persons have become *"Mass"* and *"Mass"* has become person and object. All previous critical relationships were resolved into the relationship between Absolute Critical wisdom and absolute mass stupidity. This *basic relationship* appears as the *meaning,* the *tendency,* the *watchword* of Criticism's deeds and struggles up to now.

In conformity with its absolute character, "pure" Criticism will give the decisive *"cue"* as soon as it comes on stage, but as Absolute Spirit it must nevertheless go through a dialectical process. Only at the end of its celestial movement will its original concept be truly actualized. (See Hegel's *Encyclopedia.*)

"Until a few months ago," proclaims Absolute Criticism, "the Mass believed itself to be gigantically strong and destined for mastery of the world within a time it could count on its fingers."

It was precisely Herr *Bruno Bauer* in the *Good Cause of Freedom* (obviously his *"own"* cause), the *Jewish Question,* and so on, who counted on his fingers the time till the mastery of the world, though he admitted that he could not give the exact date. To the record of the "Mass's" sins he adds the mass of his own.

"The Mass believed itself in possession of so many truths which seemed obvious to it." "But one *possesses* a *truth* completely only . . . if one follows it through *its* proofs."

For Herr Bauer as for Hegel truth is an *automaton* which proves itself. Man must *follow* it. As in Hegel, the result of actual development is nothing but *truth proven,* that is, *truth* brought to *consciousness.* Hence Absolute Criticism can ask with the most narrow-minded theologian:

*"Why* would there be any *history* if its task were not *to prove* precisely these simplest of all truths (such as the movement of the earth around the sun)?"

Just as plants, according to earlier teleologists, exist to be eaten by animals and animals by men, history exists to serve the consuming act of theoretical eating, *proving.* Man exists for the sake of history and history exists for the *proof of truths.* In this *critically* trivialized form is repeated the speculative wisdom that man and history exist so that *truth* may be brought to *self-consciousness.*

Hence *history* like *truth* becomes a person apart, a metaphysical subject of which actual human individuals are merely bearers. Hence Absolute Criticism uses such phrases as *"History* cannot be trifled with . . . *history* has exerted its greatest efforts to . . . *history* has been engaged in . . .

why would there be history . . . *history* explicitly proves for us; *history* introduces truths," etc.

If history, as Absolute Criticism asserts, has thus far been concerned with only a *few* such truths—the simplest of all —which in the end are self-evident, "this inadequacy to which previous human experiences are reduced directly proves only history's *own* inadequacy. From the uncritical standpoint the result of history is rather that the most complicated truth and epitome of all truth, *man,* in the end is self-evident."

"But truths," Absolute Criticism argues further, "which *seem* to the Mass to be so crystal-clear that they are self-evident *at the outset* . . . that their proof is superfluous, such truths are not worth history's explicitly supplying their proof; they form no part whatsoever of the problem which history is engaged in solving."

In holy zeal against the "Mass," Absolute Criticism flatters it in the nicest way. When a truth *is* crystal-clear because it *appears* crystal-clear to "the Mass," when history in the *judgment* of "the Mass" *relates* to truths, then the judgment of "the Mass" is absolute, infallible, and the *law* of history. History proves only what does *not* appear crystal-clear to "the Mass" and hence is in need of proof. "The Mass," therefore, prescribes history's "task" and its "occupation."

Absolute Criticism speaks of "truths which are self-evident *at the outset.*" In its Critical naïveté it invents an absolute *"at the outset"* and an abstract, immutable *"Mass."* In the eyes of Criticism there is as little difference between the "outset" of the sixteenth-century "Mass" and that of the nineteenth-century "Mass" as between those "Masses" themselves. It is precisely characteristic of a truth which has become *true, obvious,* and self-evident that it is "self-evident *at the outset.*" Absolute Criticism's polemic against truths self-evident at the outset is a polemic against truths which are "self-evident" in general.

A self-evident truth has lost its savor, its meaning, and its *value* for Absolute Criticism as well as for divine *dialectics.* It has become flat like stale water. Thus on the one hand Absolute Criticism proves everything which is self-evident and also many things which have the luck of being incomprehensible and never will be self-evident. On the other hand it considers everything self-evident which needs some proof. Why? Because it is *self*-evident that *actual problems* are *not* self-evident.

Since *the* truth, like history, is an ethereal subject separate from the material "Mass," it does not address itself to empirical man but to the *"depth of the soul."* To be *"truly apprehended"* it does not touch man's *gross body* which may dwell in the depths of an English cellar or in the height of a French attic, but "forces" itself "on and on" through his idealistic intestines. Absolute Criticism does maintain that "the Mass" thus far in its own way, that is, superficially, has been affected by truths which history so graciously "introduced"; but at the same time it prophesies "that the *relationship* of the *Mass* to *historical progress* will *completely change.*" It will not be long before the concealed meaning of this Critical prophecy becomes "crystal-clear" to us.

> "Up to the present all great actions of history," we are informed, "failed *at the outset* and had no marked success because they aroused the *interest* and *enthusiasm* of the Mass—in other words they had to come to a deplorable end because the idea at issue in them was such that it had to be content with a superficial perspective and thus rely on the approval of the Mass."

It appears that a perspective ceases to be superficial when it satisfies and corresponds to an idea. Herr Bruno only *apparently* brings out a *relationship* between the *idea* and its *perspective* just as he only *apparently* brings out a *relationship* between unsuccessful historical *action* and the *mass.* When Absolute Criticism thus condemns something as "superficial," it is simply previous history, whose actions and ideas were those of the "masses." It rejects *massy* history to replace it by *Critical* history (see Jules Faucher on English current issues). According to previous *un-Critical* history and thus history not conceived in the sense of Absolute Criticism, we must further distinguish precisely to what extent "the *Mass*" was *"interested"* in aims and to what extent it was *"enthusiastic"* about them. The *"idea"* always disgraced itself insofar as it was separate from *"interest."* But it is easy to understand that every massy, historically effective *"interest,"* when it first comes upon the scene in *"idea"* or *"conception,"* goes far beyond its actual limits and is mistaken for *human* interest in general. This *illusion* constitutes what *Fourier* calls the *tone* of each historical epoch. The *interest* of the bourgeoisie in the Revolution of 1789, far from having been a *"failure,"* *"won"* everything and had *"marked success,"* however much its *"pathos"* evaporated and the *"enthusiastic"* garlands with which it had decorated its cradle faded away. That *interest* was so powerful that it vanquished the pen of Marat, the guillotine of the Terrorists, the sword of Napoleon as well as the crucifix and the blueblood of the Bourbons. The Revolution was a "failure" only for *the mass* which did not find the idea of its actual *"interest"* in the *political* "idea" and whose real life-principle therefore did not coincide with the life-principle of the Revolution, whose real conditions of emancipation essentially differed from the conditions within which the bourgeoisie could emancipate itself and society. If the Revolution which can represent all great historical "actions" was a failure, it was a failure because the mass, within whose conditions of life it essentially remained, was an *exclusive* and *limited* mass, not an all-embracing one. If it failed, it was not because the mass was *"enthusiastic"* and *"interested"* but because the greatest part of the mass—the part distinct from the bourgeoisie—did not find its *actual* interest in the principle of the revolution and had no revolutionary principle of *its own* but *only* an *"idea,"* hence only an object of momentary *enthusiasm* and only an apparent *exaltation.*

Thus with the depth of historical action will increase the range of the mass whose action it is. In Critical history where historical actions are not a matter of the active mass, empirical action, or the empirical *interest* of that action but only *"an idea"* "in them," things must naturally take a different course.

*"In the Mass,"* we are informed, *"not elsewhere,* as its

former liberal spokesmen believed, *is to be found the true enemy of Spirit."*

The enemies of progress *outside* "the Mass" are precisely the *products* of the *self-degradation, self-rejection,* and *self-alienation* of the *mass,* endowed with an independent life of their *own.* In turning against the independently existing *products* of its *self-debasement,* the mass therefore turns against its *own* deficiency, just as man, turning against the existence of God, turns against his *own religiosity.* But since those *practical* self-alienations of the mass exist in the actual world in outward form, the mass must fight them in an *outward* way. It must by no means consider these products of its self-alienation as merely *ideal* phantasies, merely *alienations of self-consciousness.* It must not seek to abolish *material* alienation by a purely *inward spiritual* action. As early as 1789 Loustalot's gazette bore the motto:

> The great only appear great to us
> Because we are on our knees
> —Let us rise!—

But in order to rise it is not enough to do so in *thought* and leave hanging over one's *actual, sensuous* head the *actual, sensuous* yoke which is not refined away by ideas. Nevertheless *absolute criticism* has at least learned from Hegel's *Phenomenology* the art of transforming *real, objective* chains existing *outside me* into *merely ideal,* merely *subjective* chains existing *in me* and hence the art of transforming all *external,* sensuous struggles into mere struggles of thought.

This critical transformation is the basis of the *preestablished harmony* between *Critical Criticism* and *censorship.* From the Critical viewpoint the writer's struggle with the censor is not a struggle of "man against man." Rather the censor is nothing but *my own tact personified* for me by the provident police, my own tact struggling against my tactlessness and un-Criticalness. The struggle of the writer with the censor is only apparently, only for the wicked sensuous world, something else than the *inner* struggle of the writer *with himself. Insofar* as the censor is an *actual individual* distinct from me, a *policeman* who mishandles my intellectual product by applying an external standard irrelevant to the matter in question, he is only a *massy* conceit, an *un-Critical phantom.* When Feuerbach's "Theses on the Reform of Philosophy" were prohibited by the censor, the fault did not lie in the official barbarity of the censorship but in the lack of refinement of Feuerbach's "Theses." *"Pure"* Criticism, unsullied by all mass and matter, thus has in the censor a pure, "ethereal" form, free from all massy actuality.

Absolute Criticism has declared "the *Mass"* to be *the true enemy* of *Spirit.* It develops this in detail:

"Spirit now knows where it must *look* for *its* only *adversary*—in the self-deception and spinelessness of the Mass."

Absolute Criticism proceeds from the *dogma* of the absolute competency of the *"Spirit."* Further, it proceeds from *the dogma* of the *extramundane* existence of Spirit, that is, its existence outside the mass of humanity. Finally it transforms *"the* Spirit" and *"Progress"* on the one hand, and *"the* Mass" on the other into *fixed* essences, into concepts, and relates them one to the other as given fixed extremes. It does not occur to Absolute Criticism to investigate *the* "Spirit" itself to determine whether "the empty phrase," "self-deception," and "spinelessness" are not rooted in its own spiritualistic nature, its airy pretensions. Spirit, rather, is *absolute,* but unfortunately at the same time it continually turns into *spiritlessness:* it continually reckons without the host. Thus it must necessarily have *an adversary* intriguing against it. That *adversary* is "the Mass."

It is the same with *"Progress."* In spite of pretensions of *"Progress,"* there are continual *retrogressions* and *circular motions.* Not suspecting that the category of *"Progress"* is completely empty and abstract, Absolute Criticism is rather so profound as to recognize *"Progress"* as absolute and hence explain retrogression by supposing a *"personal adversary"* of Progress, *"the Mass."* Since *"the Mass"* is nothing but the *"antithesis of Spirit,"* the antithesis of "Criticism's" Progress, it can also only be defined by this imaginary antithesis, and outside this antithesis all that Criticism can say about the *meaning* and particular existence of "the Mass" is entirely *meaningless* because it is completely indeterminate: "the Mass in the sense in which the *'word'* also includes the *so-called* educated world." "Also" and "so-called" suffice for a Critical definition. *"The* Mass" is thus distinct from the *actual* masses and exists as *"the Mass"* only for *"the Criticism."*

All communist and socialist writers proceeded from the observation, on the one hand, that even the most favorable and brilliant deeds seemed to remain without brilliant results and end in trivialities, and on the other hand, that *all progress of the spirit* had thus far been *progress against the mass of mankind,* driving it into an ever *more dehumanized situation.* Hence, they declared *"Progress"* (see *Fourier*) to be an inadequate, abstract *phrase;* they assumed (see *Owen* among others) a fundamental flaw in the civilized world; hence, they subjected the *actual* foundations of contemporary society to an incisive *criticism.* The movement of the *great mass,* in contrast to which history had so far developed, responded immediately in practice to this communist criticism. One must be acquainted with the studiousness, the craving for knowledge, the moral energy, and the unceasing urge for development of the French and English workers to be able to form an idea of the *human* nobility of that movement.

How infinitely *profound,* then, is "Absolute Criticism" which, in face of these intellectual and practical facts, one-sidedly grasps only *one* aspect of the relationship—the continual foundering of Spirit—and in chagrin at this seeks in addition an *adversary* of "Spirit" which it finds in *"the* Mass"! In the end this great critical *discovery* amounts to a *tautology.* According to Criticism, Spirit has so far had a limit, an obstacle—that is, an *adversary—because* it has had an *adversary.* Who, then, is the adversary of the *Spirit? Spiritlessness.* "The Mass" is defined only as the "antithesis" of Spirit, as *spiritlessness* or, to use more precise definitions of spiritlessness, as "indolence," "superficiality," "self-complacency." What a fundamental advantage over communist writers not to have traced spiritlessness, indolence, superficiality, and self-complacency to their origin but to have rebuked them *morally* and *exposed* them as the antithesis of Spirit and Progress! If these qualities are declared to be qualities of *"the* Mass" as of a *subject* distinct from them, this distinction is nothing but a "Critical" *appearance* of distinction. Only in *appearance* has Absolute Criticism a *definite* concrete subject beyond the abstract qualities of spiritlessness, indolence, etc., because *"the Mass,"* in the Critical view, is *nothing* but those abstract qualities, another *word* for them, a *fantastic personification* of them.

Nevertheless, the relation between "Spirit and Mass" still has a *hidden* meaning which will be fully revealed in the course of development. We only indicate it here. The relation *discovered* by Herr Bruno is, in fact, nothing but the *Critically caricatured fulfillment of Hegel's view of history* which, in turn, is only the *speculative* expression of the *Christian-Germanic* dogma of the antithesis between *Spirit* and *Matter, God* and the *World.* This antithesis is expressed in history, in the very world of man, in such a way that only a few chosen *individuals* as *active* Spirit stand opposed to the rest of mankind as the *spiritless "Mass,"* as *matter.*

*Hegel's* view of history presupposes an *abstract* or *Absolute Spirit* which develops in such a way that mankind is only a *Mass,* a conscious or unconscious vehicle for Spirit. Hence Hegel provides for the development of a *speculative,* esoteric history within *empirical* exoteric history. The history of mankind becomes the history of the *abstract spirit* of mankind, thus a spirit *beyond* actual man.

Parallel with this Hegelian doctrine there developed in France the view of the *Doctrinarians* proclaiming the *sovereignty of reason* in opposition to the *sovereignty of the people* in order to exclude the masses and rule *by themselves.* This is quite consistent. If the activity of *actual* mankind is only the activity of a *mass* of human individuals, then *abstract universality,* Reason, Spirit must have an abstract expression exhausted in few individuals. Then it depends on the position and imaginative power of each individual whether he will pass for a representative of *"the* Spirit."

With *Hegel* the *Absolute Spirit* of history has its material in the *Mass* and its adequate expression only in *philosophy*. *The* philosopher, however, is only the organ whereby the creator of history, the Absolute Spirit, *retrospectively* becomes conscious after the movement of history has ended. The philosopher's participation in history is reduced to this retrospective consciousness, for the Absolute Spirit accomplishes the actual movement of history *unconsciously*. Thus the philosopher appears post festum.

Hegel is doubly inadequate, first because he declares that philosophy is the specific existence of the Absolute Spirit but then refuses to recognize the *actual philosophical individual* as the *Absolute* Spirit, and secondly because he allows the Absolute Spirit to make history only *in appearance* as Absolute Spirit. Since the Absolute Spirit becomes *conscious* as the creative World Spirit in the philosopher and only *post festum*, its making of history exists only in consciousness, in the opinion and conception of the philosopher, only in speculative imagination. Herr Bruno eliminates Hegel's inadequacy.

*First*, he proclaims Criticism to be the Absolute Spirit and *himself* to be *the* Criticism. Just as the element of Criticism is banished from "the Mass," so is the element of "Mass" banished from Criticism. Hence Criticism knows itself incarnate not in a *"Mass"* but exclusively in a *handful* of chosen men, in Herr *Bauer* and his disciples.

Herr Bruno further eliminates Hegel's other inadequacy in that he no longer makes history post festum and in the imagination like Hegel's Spirit but *consciously* takes the role of *World Spirit* in antithesis to the mass of the rest of mankind. He assumes a contemporary *dramatic* role, inventing and consummating history intentionally, after due deliberation.

On one side stands "the Mass" as the passive, spiritless, unhistorical, *material* element of history. On the other, stands *the* Spirit, *the* Criticism, Herr Bruno and Co. as the active element from which emerges all *historical* action. The act of social transformation is reduced to the *brain-activity* of Critical Criticism.

Indeed, the relationship of Criticism to "the Mass"—and

thus the relationship of Criticism incarnate, Herr Bruno Bauer and Co.—is in truth the *only* historical relationship of the present time. The whole of current history is reduced to the movement of these two sides one against the other. All antitheses have been resolved in this *Critical* antithesis.

Becoming *objective* only in its antithesis, "the Mass" and *stupidity,* Critical Criticism hence must continually *produce* this antithesis for itself, and Herr Faucher, Edgar and Szeliga have provided sufficient proof of virtuosity in the specialty of Critical Criticism, the *massive stupefaction* of persons and things.

## *"Criticism" and "Feuerbach"* [by Friedrich Engels]

As the consequence of its first campaign, *Absolute Criticism* can view *"philosophy"* as disposed of and flatly label it an ally of "the *Mass*."

> *"Philosophers* were predestined to realize the heart's desires of the '*Mass*.'" "The Mass *wants,*" in particular, "simple concepts so as to have nothing to do with the thing itself, shibboleths so as to be finished with everything at the outset, phrases so as to eliminate criticism *itself*. And 'philosophy' fulfills this desire of the Mass!"

Giddy from its victories, Absolute Criticism bursts out in a *Pythian* rage against philosophy. The hidden cauldron [*Feuerkessel*] whose fumes derange the victory-drunk brain of Absolute Criticism is *Feuerbach's Philosophy of the Future*. Absolute Criticism read Feuerbach's work in March. The fruit of that reading and the criterion of the seriousness with which it was undertaken is [Bruno Bauer's] Article No. II against Professor Hinrichs.

In this article Absolute Criticism, which has never freed itself from the cage of the Hegelian perspective, fumes at the iron bars and walls of its prison. The "simple concept," the terminology, philosophy's whole way of thinking, and even the whole of philosophy is rejected with loathing. In its place appear *"the actual wealth of human relation-*

ships," the *"immense content of history," "the meaning of man,"* etc. *"The mystery of the system"* is declared *"revealed."*

But then who revealed the mystery of the "system"? *Feuerbach.* Who destroyed the dialectic of concepts, the war of gods known to philosophers alone? *Feuerbach.* Who replaced the old trash and "infinite self-consciousness" not, to be sure, with *"the meaning of man"* —as though man had any other meaning than that of being man—but nevertheless with "Man"? *Feuerbach* and only *Feuerbach.* He did even more. He long ago destroyed the very categories with which "Criticism" now defends itself —the "actual wealth of human relationships, the immense content of history, the struggle of history, the struggle of Mass against Spirit," etc., etc.

Once man is understood as the essence, the basis of all human activity and situations, "Criticism" can only invent *new categories* and transform *man* himself into a category and into the principle of a whole series of categories, as it now does taking the only road to salvation still open for distressed and persecuted *theological* inhumanity. *History* does *nothing;* it "possesses *no* colossal riches," it "fights *no* battles"! Rather it is *man,* actual and living man, who does all this, who possesses and fights; "history" does not use man as a means for *its* purposes as though it were a person apart; it is *nothing* but the activity of man pursuing his ends. If *Absolute* Criticism, even after *Feuerbach's* gifted arguments, presumes to give us all the old trash in a new form and at the same moment abuse it as *"massy"* trash— which it has all the less right to do as it never moved a finger to destroy philosophy—that fact alone is enough to bring the *"Mystery"* of Criticism to light and assess the critical naïveté with which it can say to Professor Hinrichs whose *tiredness* once did it such great service:

> "The *damage* affects those who have not gone through any development and thus *could not change themselves even if they wanted to;* and if it gets as far as a *new* principle—still no! The new *cannot be turned into a phrase* and *particular turns of expression cannot be derived from it."*

In opposition to Professor Hinrichs, Absolute Criticism brags about its solution of *"the mystery of faculty sciences."* Has it then solved the "mystery" of philosophy, jurisprudence, politics, medicine, political economy, etc.? Not at all! It has shown—be it noted—in *The Good Cause of Freedom* that study to earn a living and free science, that academic freedom and faculty statutes contradict each other.

Were "Absolute Criticism" honest, it would have admitted where it got its supposed illumination on the "mystery of philosophy," although it is just as well that it did not put into *Feuerbach's* mouth, as it has put into others' such nonsense as the misunderstood and distorted statements it borrowed from him. While the German Philistines are now beginning to understand *Feuerbach* and adopt his conclusions, it is typical of "Absolute Criticism's" *theological* standpoint that it is not in position to grasp a single one of his sentences correctly or use it properly.

In comparison with the feats of its first campaign, Criticism makes real progress in "defining" the struggle between *"Mass"* and *"Spirit"* as *"the aim"* of all previous history, in declaring *"Mass"* to be "the *pure nothingness*" of "misery," and in contrasting *"Spirit"* as truth to "Mass" as *"Matter."* Is not Absolute Criticism thus *truly Christian-Germanic?* After the old antithesis between spiritualism and materialism has been fought out in all aspects and overcome once and for all by *Feuerbach,* "Criticism" again makes it a fundamental dogma in its most nauseating form and gives the victory to the *"Christian-Germanic spirit."*

We must finally consider, as a development of the mystery still concealed in Criticism's first campaign, that it now identifies the antithesis between *Spirit* and *Mass* with the antithesis between *"Criticism"* and "the Mass." It will later proceed to identify *itself* with *"the* Criticism" and hence represent itself as *"The Spirit"* as absolute and infinite and represent "the Mass," on the other hand, as finite, coarse, brutal, dead, and inorganic—for that is how *"the* Criticism" understands matter.

How colossal the riches of a history which is exhausted in the relationship of humanity to *Herr Bauer!*

## Critical Battle Against French Materialism

"*Spinozism* dominated the eighteenth century in its later French form which converted matter into substance, as well as in deism which endowed matter with a more spiritual name. . . . *Spinoza's French school* and the supporters of deism were simply two sects disputing over the true meaning of *his system*. . . . The simple fate of this Enlightenment was its decline in *Romanticism* after having had to surrender to the reaction which began with the French movement."

Thus far, the view of *Criticism*.

Against the Critical history of French materialism we shall present a brief outline of its profane, massy history. We shall respectfully acknowledge the gulf between history as it actually happened and history as it happened according to the decree of *the* "Absolute Criticism," the creator equally of the old as well as the new. Finally, obeying the prescriptions of *Criticism*, we shall make the "Why?" "Whence?" and "Whither?" of Critical history "an object of sustained study."

"To speak in an *exact* and *prosaic sense*," the French Enlightenment of the eighteenth century and particularly *French materialism* was not only a struggle against the existing political institutions as well as the existing religion and theology but was just as much an *open, outspoken* struggle against the *metaphysics of the seventeenth century* and against *all metaphysics*, particularly that of *Descartes, Malebranche, Spinoza* and *Leibniz. Philosophy* was opposed to *metaphysics* just as *Feuerbach* opposed *drunken speculation* with *sober philosophy* in his first decisive attack on *Hegel*. The *metaphysics* of the seventeenth century, swept from the field by the French Enlightenment and particularly by eighteenth-century *French materialism*, experienced a *triumphant and substantial restoration* in *German philosophy*, particularly in the *speculative German philosophy* of the nineteenth century. After *Hegel* had ingeniously combined previous metaphysics and German idealism and had established a universal realm of metaphysics, the attack on *speculative metaphysics* and on *all metaphysics* became once again, as in the eighteenth century, synonymous with an attack on theology. Metaphysics will succumb for good and all to *materialism,* now perfected by the effort of *speculation* itself and converging with *humanism.* French and English *socialism* and *communism* represented this convergence of *humanism* and *materialism* in the *practical* sphere, just as *Feuerbach* represented it in the *theoretical.*

"To speak in an *exact* and *prosaic sense,*" there are *two tendencies* in *French materialism, one* deriving its origin from *Descartes* and the other from *Locke.* The latter is *mainly* a *French* cultural element and leads directly into *socialism.* The former, *mechanical* materialism, merges into what is properly French *natural science.* The two tendencies intersect in the course of development. We need not deal more closely with the French materialism coming directly from *Descartes* any more than the French *Newtonian* school or the development of French natural science in general.

Therefore, only this much needs to be said: In his *physics Descartes* invested *matter* with self-creative power and viewed *mechanical* motion as its vital act. He completely separated his *physics* from his *metaphysics. Within* his physics *matter* is the sole *substance,* the only basis of being and knowing.

French *mechanical* materialism attached itself to *Descartes' physics* in contrast to his metaphysics. His followers were by profession *anti-metaphysicians,* viz., *physicists.*

This school begins with the *physician Le Roy* and reaches its peak with the physician *Cabanis.* The physician *La Mettrie* is its center. Descartes was still living when Le Roy transferred the Cartesian conception of *animals* to the human soul—as *La Mettrie* similarly did in the eighteenth century—declaring the soul to be a *mode of the body* and *ideas* to be *mechanical motions.* Le Roy even believed that Descartes had kept his real opinion secret. Descartes protested. At the end of the eighteenth century, *Cabanis* completed Cartesian materialism in his *Report on the Physique and Morality of Man.*

*Cartesian* materialism still exists in France today. It had great success in *mechanical natural science* which, to speak in an *exact* and *prosaic sense,* will least of all be reproached with being *romantic.*

The *metaphysics* of the seventeenth century, particularly as represented in France by *Descartes,* had *materialism* as its *antagonist* from its very birth. This antagonism to Descartes was personified in *Gassendi,* the restorer of *Epicurean* materialism. French and English materialism was always closely related to *Democritus* and *Epicurus.* Cartesian metaphysics had another opponent in *Hobbes,* the *English* materialist. Gassendi and Hobbes vanquished their opponent long after their death at the very moment when Cartesian metaphysics already predominated as the official power in all French schools.

*Voltaire* remarked that the indifference of Frenchmen to quarrels between Jesuits and Jansenists in the eighteenth century resulted less from philosophy than from [John] *Law's* financial speculations. Thus the overthrow of the metaphysics of the seventeenth century can be explained by the materialist theory of the eighteenth century only insofar as this theoretical movement itself is explained by the practical form of French life at the time. That life was directed to the immediate present, to worldly enjoyment and interests, to the *mundane* world. Its anti-theological, anti-metaphysical, materialistic practice required anti-theological, anti-metaphysical, materialistic theories. Metaphysics had *practically* lost all credit. Here we only have to indicate briefly its *theoretical* outcome.

In the seventeenth century, metaphysics was still tempered with *positive,* profane content (cf. Descartes, Leibniz, etc.). It made discoveries in mathematics, physics, and other exact sciences which appeared to belong to it. This appearance had already been destroyed by the beginning of the eighteenth century. The positive sciences had broken off from it and marked out their own territory. The whole metaphysical realm was reduced to thought-entities and heavenly things, precisely when real entities and earthly things began to be the center of all interest. Metaphysics had become stale. In the very year that Malebranche and Arnauld, the last of the great French seventeenth century metaphysicians, died, *Helvétius* and *Condillac* were born.

The man who ruined the *theoretical credit* of seventeenth-century metaphysics and all metaphysics was *Pierre Bayle*. His weapon was *scepticism,* forged out of the magical formulae of metaphysics itself. He even took Cartesian metaphysics as his immediate starting-point. As *Feuerbach* was driven to combat *speculative philosophy* by combating speculative theology precisely because he recognized speculation as the last prop of theology and because he had to force the theologians back from pseudo-science to *crude* and repulsive *faith,* so religious doubt forced Bayle into doubting the metaphysics that supported this faith. He therefore subjected metaphysics in its entire historical development to criticism. He became its historian in order to write the history of its death. Above all he refuted *Spinoza* and *Leibniz.*

*Pierre Bayle* not only prepared the way for acceptance of materialism and the philosophy of common sense in France by the sceptical disintegration of metaphysics. He heralded the *atheistic society* soon to come into existence by *proving* that a society of avowed atheists is *possible,* that an atheist *could* be an honest man, and that man degrades himself not by atheism but by superstition and idolatry.

In the words of one French writer, *Pierre Bayle* was *"the last metaphysician* in the seventeenth-century *sense* of the word and the *first philosopher in the eighteenth-century sense."*

In addition to the negative refutation of seventeenth-century theology and metaphysics, a *positive anti-metaphysical* system was needed. A book was needed which would systematize the practical activities of the time and give them a theoretical foundation. *Locke's* essay on the "Origin of Human Understanding" [*Essay Concerning Human Understanding*] came from across the Channel as if at call. It was welcomed enthusiastically like an eagerly awaited guest.

The question arises: Is *Locke* perhaps a disciple of *Spinoza?* "Profane" history can answer:

Materialism is the *natural-born* son of *Great Britain.* Even Britain's scholastic *Duns Scotus* [rather, William of Occam] wondered *"whether matter could not think."*

To effect this miracle, he took refuge in God's omnipotence, that is, he forced *theology* itself to preach *materialism.* Moreover, he was a *nominalist.* Nominalism is a main element with the *English* materialists, as it is generally the *first expression* of materialism.

The real ancestor of *English materialism* and all *modern experimental* science is Bacon. For him natural science is true science and *physics* based on sense perception is the outstanding part of natural science. *Anaxagoras* with his *homoeomeria* and *Democritus* with his atoms are frequently quoted as his authorities. According to his doctrine, the *senses* are infallible and the *source* of all knowledge. All science is *empirical* and consists in applying a *rational method* to sensuous data. Induction, analysis, comparison, observation, and experimentation are the principal requirements of rational method. Among the qualities inherent in *matter, motion* is the first and foremost, not only as *mechanical* and *mathematical* but even more as *impulse, vital spirit, tension,* or—to use Jakob Böhme's expression —*"Qual"* of matter. The primitive forms of matter are living, individualizing, *essential capacities* inherent in it, producing specific differences.

In *Bacon,* its first creator, materialism conceals within itself, still in a naïve way, the germs of an all-sided development. On the one hand, matter smiles upon the whole of man in poetic-sensuous splendor. On the other, this aphoristic doctrine itself is still full of theological inconsistencies.

In its further development materialism becomes *onesided.* *Hobbes* is the *systematizer* of *Baconian* materialism. Sensuous knowledge loses its bloom and becomes the abstract sensuousness of the *geometer.* *Physical* motion is sacrificed to *mechanical* or *mathematical* motion; *geometry* is proclaimed to be the chief science. Materialism becomes *misanthropic.* In order to overcome the *misanthropic, incorporeal* spirit on its own ground, materialism must mortify its own flesh and turn *ascetic*. It appears as a *creature of the understanding,* but it also develops the ruthless consistency of the understanding.

As Bacon's successor, Hobbes argues that if sensuousness is the source of all human knowledge, then perception, thought, representation, etc., are nothing but phantoms of the material world more or less divested of their sensuous form. Science can only name these phantoms. *One* name can be applied to several phantoms. There can even be names of names. But it would be a contradiction, on the one hand, to have all ideas originate in the world of the senses and, on the other, to maintain that a word is more than a word, and that there are also entities of a general nature in addition to those which are represented and always individual. An *incorporeal substance,* moreover, is the same absurdity as an *incorporeal body. Body, being, substance* are one and the same *real* idea. One cannot separate thought from matter *which* thinks. Matter is the subject of all changes. The word *infinite* is *meaningless* unless it refers to the capacity of our mind to go on adding without end. Since only what is material is perceptible and knowable, *nothing* is known of the existence of God. Only my own existence is certain. Every human passion is a mechanical movement which has a beginning and an ending. The objects of impulses are what we call good. Man is subject to the same laws as nature. Power and freedom are identical.

Hobbes systematized Bacon but without giving a firmer basis for his fundamental principle that our knowledge and ideas originate from the world of the senses.

In his essay on the origin of human understanding *Locke* provided the basis for Bacon and Hobbes' principle.

Just as Hobbes destroyed the *theistic* prejudices of Baconian materialism, so Collins, Dodwell, Coward, Hartley, Priestley, etc., removed the last theological barrier in Locke's sensationism. Anyway, for materialists, deism is no more than a convenient and easy way of getting rid of religion.

We have already mentioned how Locke's work came at an opportune time for the French. Locke had founded the philosophy of *bon sens,* of common sense; that is, he said indirectly that there are no philosophers in conflict with healthy human senses and the understanding based upon them.

*Condillac,* Locke's *immediate* follower and *French* interpreter, at once turned Locke's sensationism against the *metaphysics* of the seventeenth century. He proved that the French had rightly rejected metaphysics as a mere clumsy product of imagination and theological prejudice. He published a refutation of the systems of *Descartes, Spinoza, Leibniz,* and *Malebranche.*

In his "Essay on the Origin of Human Understanding" he developed Locke's ideas and proved that not only the soul but also the senses, not only the art of creating ideas but also the art of sensuous perception, are matters of *experience* and *habit.* The entire development of man, therefore, depends upon *education* and *environment.* Condillac was supplanted in the French schools only by the *Eclectic* Philosophy.

The difference between *French* and *English* materialism is the difference between the two nationalities. The French endowed English materialism with esprit, with flesh and blood, with eloquence. They gave it the temperament and grace which it lacked. They *civilized* it.

In *Helvétius,* who also took Locke as his starting point, materialism received its real French character. He comprehended it at once in its application to social life (Helvétius, *On Man* [*His Intellectual Capabilities and His Education*]). Sensuous qualities and self-love, pleasure and enlightened self-interest are the bases of all morality. The natural equality of human intelligence, the unity between the progress of reason and the progress of industry, the natural goodness of man, the omnipotence of education are the principal features of his system.

In the writings of *La Mettrie* we find a combination of Cartesian and English materialism. He makes use of Descartes' physics in detail. His *Man: A Machine* is an exposition modeled on the animal-machine of Descartes. In Holbach's *System of Nature* the section devoted to physics likewise consists of a combination of French and English materialism, just as the section on morals rests essentially on the morality of Helvétius. The French materialist *Robinet* (*On Nature*), who still remained closest to metaphysics and hence was praised for this by Hegel, explicitly refers to *Leibniz*.

We need not discuss Volney, Dupuis, Diderot, etc., any more than the physiocrats now that we have shown the dual derivation of French materialism from Descartes' physics and English materialism and the antithesis between French materialism and the seventeenth-century *metaphysics* of Descartes, Spinoza, Malebranche, and Leibniz. This antithesis could become apparent to the Germans only after they had themselves come into conflict with *speculative metaphysics*.

Just as *Cartesian* materialism passes into *natural science proper*, so the other tendency in French materialism flows directly into *socialism* and *communism*.

No great acumen is required to see the necessary connection of materialism with communism and socialism from the doctrines of materialism concerning the original goodness and equal intellectual endowment of man, the omnipotence of experience, habit and education, the influence of external circumstances on man, the extreme importance of industry, the justification of enjoyment, etc. If man forms all his knowledge, perception, etc., from the world of sense and experience in the world of sense, then it follows that the empirical world must be so arranged that he experiences and gets used to what is truly human in it, that he experiences himself as man. If enlightened interest is the principle of all morality, it follows that men's private interests should coincide with human interests. If man is unfree in the materialistic sense—that is, is free not through the negative capacity to avoid this or that but through the positive power to assert his true individuality—crime must not be punished in the individual but the antisocial sources of crime must be destroyed to give everyone social scope for the essential assertion of his vitality. If man is formed by circumstances, then his circumstances must be made human. If man is by nature social, then he develops his true nature only in society and the power of his nature must be measured not by the power of the single individual but by the power of society.

These and similar assertions are to be found almost word for word in the oldest French materialists. This is not the place to criticize them. The *apology for vice* by *Mandeville*, one of the early English followers of Locke, is significant for the socialist tendency of materialism. He proves that vice is *indispensable* and *useful* in *present-day* society. This is no justification for present-day society.

*Fourier* proceeds directly from the doctrines of French materialism. The followers of *Babeuf* were crude, uncivilized materialists, but even mature communism comes *directly* from *French materialism*. The latter returned to its mother-country, *England*, in the form *Helvétius* had given it. *Bentham* founded his system of *enlightened interest* on the morality of Helvétius, just as *Owen*, proceeding from *Bentham's* system, founded English communism. Exiled to England, the Frenchman *Cabet* came under the influence of communist ideas he found there and on his return to France became the most popular, if also the most shallow, representative of communism. Like Owen, the more scientific French communists—*Dézamy*, *Gay*, etc.—developed the doctrine of *materialism* as a doctrine of *real humanism*, the *logical* basis of *communism*.

Where, then, did Herr Bauer or *the* Criticism get the official documents for the Critical history of French materialism?

1. *Hegel's History of Philosophy* presents French materialism as the *realization* of Spinozistic Substance, which in any case is more comprehensible than the "French school of Spinoza."

2. Herr *Bauer* picked out French materialism as a *school* of Spinoza from Hegel's *History of Philosophy*. But when he found in another of Hegel's works that deism and materialism are *two parties with one and the same* fundamental principle, he concluded that Spinoza had *two* schools which disputed over the meaning of his system. Herr Bauer could have found the supposed explanation in the *Phenomenology* [*of Spirit*] where Hegel explicitly says:

"With regard to that Absolute Being, the *Enlightenment* comes into conflict with itself . . . and divides into *two parties*. . . . The one . . . calls a predicateless absolute . . . the *highest Absolute Being*. . . . The other calls it *matter*. . . . Both are *the same* concept—the distinction does not lie in the content but only in the different starting-points of the two developments." (Hegel, *Phenomenology*, pp. 420, 421, 422. [Ch. VI, Sec. B, ii, b. Ellipses and emphasis, except for *matter*, by Marx.])

3. Finally, again in Hegel, Herr Bauer could find that when substance does not develop into concept and self-consciousness, it merges into "Romanticism." The *Hallische Jahrbücher* [edited by Arnold Ruge, 1838–41] developed a similar view.

At all costs, however, *"Spirit"* had to decree a *"simple fate"* for its "adversary," *materialism*.

*Note.* The connection of French materialism with Descartes and Locke and the antithesis between the philosophy of the eighteenth century and the metaphysics of the seventeenth are set forth in detail in most of the recent *French* histories of philosophy. Here, as against Critical Criticism, we only have to repeat what is already known. But the connection of the materialism of the eighteenth century with English and French *communism* of the nineteenth still needs a detailed presentation. Here we limit ourselves to quoting a few short, pointed passages from Helvétius, Holbach, and Bentham.

(1) *Helvétius.* "Men are not wicked, but subject to their interests. One must not, therefore, complain of the wickedness of men but about the ignorance of lawmakers who have always put private interest in opposition to the general interest."—"Moralists have thus far had no success because one has to dig deep into legislation to pull out the roots which create vice. In New Orleans women have the right to repudiate their husbands as soon as they are tired of them. In such places there are no faithless wives because they have no interest in being so."—"Morality is only a frivolous science if it is not combined with politics and legislation."—"Hypocritical moralists can be rec-

ognized on the one hand by their indifference to the vices which disintegrate empires and on the other by the fury with which they condemn private vices."— "Men are born neither good nor wicked but ready to be one or the other according to the way they are united or divided by common interest."—"If citizens could not realize their private welfare without realizing the general welfare, there would be no wicked people except fools." (*On the Spirit*, Paris, 1822, Vol. I, pp. 117, 240, 241, 249, 251, 339 and 369 [with abridgments by Marx].) If according to Helvétius education forms man—education not only in the ordinary sense but the totality of an individual's conditions of life (cf. *loc. cit.*, p. 390)—and if a reform is necessary to abolish the contradiction between private and general interests, then a transformation of consciousness is necessary, on the other hand, to carry out such a reform: "Great reforms can be effected only by weakening people's stupid respect for old laws and customs" (*loc. cit.*, p. 260) or, as he says elsewhere, by removing ignorance.

(2) *Holbach.* "It is only himself that man can love in the objects he loves; it is only himself that he can cherish in the existence of his species." "Man can never for a single instant of his life separate himself from himself: he cannot lose sight of himself." "It is always our utility, our interest . . . that makes us hate or love things (*Social System*, Vol. I, Paris, 1822, pp. 80, 112), but: "In his own interest man must love others because they are necessary for his welfare. . . . Morality proves to him that of all beings *man is most necessary to man*" (p. 76). "True morality, like true politics, is that which seeks to bring men closer to one another to make them work for their mutual happiness with united efforts. Every morality which separates *our interests from those of our associates* is false, senseless, and contrary to nature" (p. 116). "To love others . . . is to *identify our interests with those of our associates* in order to work for *the common good.* . . . *Virtue* is only *the advantage of men united in society*" (p. 77). "A man without passion or desire would cease to be a man. . . . How could a man completely detached from himself be made to attach himself to others? A man who is indif-

ferent to everything, free of passion, and sufficient unto himself would cease to be a social being. . . . Virtue is only the *communication of goodness*" (*loc. cit.*, p. 118). "Religious morality never served to make mortals more sociable" (*loc. cit.*, p. 36).

(3) *Bentham*. We cite only one passage from Bentham in which he opposes the "general interest in the political sense." "The interest of individuals . . . should give way to the public interest. But . . . what does this mean? Is not each individual part of the public as much as any other? The public interest you personify is only an abstract term: it represents only the mass of individual interests. . . . If it were good to sacrifice the happiness of one individual to increase that of others, it would be still better to sacrifice that of a second, a third, and so on *ad infinitum*. . . . Individual interests are the only real interests." (Bentham, *Théorie des peines et des récompenses* . . . , 3rd ed.; Paris, 1826, Vol. II, p. [229,] 230.)

# From NOTEBOOKS OF 1844–45

## Points on the Modern State and Civil Society

[Marx probably wrote the following points in mid-January 1845 when he and other contributors to the *Vorwärts* were expelled from Paris to Brussels as a result of pressures from the Prussian government. The points may have been an outline for a book on the modern state he wanted to write but never did. They reflect his persistent interest in the course of the French Revolution and revive conclusions of his previous "Critique of Hegel's Philosophy of the State" concerning the relation of the state to civil society, sovereignty of the people, and suffrage.]

(1) *The genetic history of the modern state* or the *French Revolution.*

The presumption of the political sphere—its confusion with the state in antiquity. Relationship of the revolutionaries to civil society. Duplication of all elements in civil affairs and affairs of the state.

(2) The *proclamation* of the *rights of man* and the *constitution of the state.* Individual freedom and public power. *Freedom, equality* and unity. Sovereignty of the people.

(3) The *state* and *civil society.*

(4) The *representative state* and the *charter.*

The constitutional representative state, the democratic representative state.

(5) The *separation of powers.* Legislative and executive power.

(6) The *legislative power* and legislative bodies. Political clubs.

(7) The *executive power*. Centralization and hierarchy. Centralization and political civilization. The federal system and industrialism. *State administration* and *local government*.

(8′) *Judicial power* and *law*.

(8″) *Nationality* and the *people*.

(9′) *Political parties*.

(9″) *Suffrage*, the struggle to *overcome* [*Aufhebung*] the state and civil society.


## Theses on Feuerbach

[After moving to Brussels, Marx jotted down the following points around March 1845 for later elaboration. Engels saw in them "the brilliant germ of a new world-view" and published them with some revisions in 1888 as an appendix to his *Ludwig Feuerbach*. They became the best-known of Marx's early writings and the subject of extensive commentary as suggesting his special relationship to both Hegel and Feuerbach. Marx again refers to Feuerbach's position as "materialism" but finds it lacking in the active element for which he praised Hegel in the "Manuscripts." Hegel's "activity," however, is abstract, detached from *"practical,* human-sensuous activity." Feuerbach, too, in spite of his emphasis on "Praxis" in the *Jahrbücher*, is incomplete because "practice" must be seen as fundamentally social and historical action, pointing beyond isolated individuals of civil society toward "socialized humanity."]

### (1)

The chief defect of all previous materialism (including Feuerbach's) is that the object, actuality, sensuousness is conceived only in the form of the *object or perception* [*Anschauung*], but not as *sensuous human activity, practice* [*Praxis*], not subjectively. Hence in opposition to materialism the *active* side was developed by idealism—but only abstractly since idealism naturally does not know actual, sensuous activity as such. Feuerbach wants sensuous objects actually different from thought objects: but he does not comprehend human activity itself as *objective*. Hence in *The Essence of Christianity* he regards only the theoretical attitude as the truly human attitude, while practice is understood and fixed only in its dirtily Jewish form of appearance. Consequently he does not comprehend the significance of "revolutionary," of "practical-critical" activity.

### (2)

The question whether human thinking can reach objective truth—is not a question of theory but a *practical* question. In practice man must prove the truth, that is, actuality and power, this-sidedness of his thinking. The dispute about the actuality or non-actuality of thinking—thinking isolated from practice—is a purely *scholastic* question.

### (3)

The materialistic doctrine concerning the change of circumstances and education forgets that circumstances are changed by men and that the educator must himself be educated. Hence this doctrine must divide society into two parts—one of which towers above [as in Robert Owen, Engels added].

The coincidence of the change of circumstances and of human activity or self-change can be comprehended and rationally understood only as *revolutionary practice*.

### (4)

Feuerbach starts out from the fact of religious self-alienation, the duplication of the world into a religious and secular world. His work consists in resolving the religious world into its secular basis. But the fact that the secular basis becomes separate from itself and establishes an independent realm in the clouds can only be explained by the cleavage and self-contradictoriness of the secular basis. Thus the latter must itself be both understood in its contradiction and revolutionized in practice. For instance, after the earthly family is found to be the secret of the holy family, the former must then be theoretically and practically nullified.

### (5)

Feuerbach, not satisfied with *abstract thinking*, wants *perception*; but he does not comprehend sensuousness as *practical*, human-sensuous activity.

### (6)

Feuerbach resolves the religious essence into the *human* essence. But the essence of man is no abstraction inhering in each single individual. In its actuality it is the ensemble of social relationships.

Feuerbach, who does not go into the criticism of this actual essence, is hence compelled

1. to abstract from the historical process and to establish religious feeling as something self-contained, and to presuppose an abstract—*isolated*—human individual;

2. to view the essence of man merely as "species," as the inner, dumb generality which unites the many individuals *naturally*.

### (7)

Feuerbach does not see, consequently, that "religious feeling" is itself a social product and that the abstract individual he analyzes belongs to a particular form of society.

### (8)

All social life is essentially *practical*. All mysteries which lead theory to mysticism find their rational solution in human practice and the comprehension of this practice.

### (9)

The highest point attained by perceptual materialism, that is, materialism that does not comprehend sensuousness as practical activity, is the view of separate individuals and civil society.

### (10)

The standpoint of the old materialism is civil society; the standpoint of the new is human society or socialized humanity.

### (11)

The philosophers have only *interpreted* the world in various ways; the point is, to *change* it.

# THE GERMAN IDEOLOGY

## A Critique of the Most Recent German Philosophy as Represented by Feuerbach, B. Bauer, and Stirner

[Marx and Engels jointly wrote *The German Ideology* between November 1845 and October 1846 "to settle accounts" with their "philosophic conscience." They had recently returned to Brussels from a trip to England to study economics. While at work on the *Ideology,* they organized an international Communist Correspondence Committee through which they criticized Wilhelm Weitling and the "True Socialists." Marx, at the same time, was reading for a critique of political economy which did not appear until 1859. When the *Ideology* was declined by a Westphalian publisher, Marx and Engels left the manuscript, with little regret, "to the gnawing criticism of the mice," satisfied that they had achieved self-understanding.

The second and third parts of *The German Ideology,* omitted below, totalled about 450 book pages in which, as Franz Mehring put it, "oases in the desert" of super-polemics were rare. The part on "The Leipzig Council" dissected the views of Max Stirner, ironically canonized as Saint Max, at greater length than Stirner's own book, *The Ego and Its Own.* But among the "oases" there were sections on Kant's "good will" as reflecting the backwardness of German liberalism, the mystification in Hegelian speculation, utilitarianism as expressing the existing bourgeois world, and communism as full development of the individual based on the historical development of production. The "oases" in the third section on "True Socialism" directed against Karl Grün included criticism of Feuerbach's unhistorical and abstract "Man," sympathetic comments on Saint-Simon and Fourier, and references to Proudhon's failure, and Feuerbach's as well, to criticize "dialectics such as Hegel has already given us."

The part of *The German Ideology* on "Feuerbach" translated below, analyzes the "illusions" of Hegelian speculation and asserts the empirical premises of historical explanation. It criticizes Feuerbach's "Man" as an abstraction from the historical development of industry and society, bases men's ideas and consciousness on evolving modes of production, links history with economic development, and views communism as overcoming man's alienation in relation to the division of labor and the state. This part of the book, Engels noted later, was never finished and revealed the incompleteness of "our knowledge of economic history." By following the sequence, revisions, and newly found pages of the original manuscript, the translation below shows how the first and foundational part of *The German Ideology* was unfinished.]

## Preface

Until now men have constantly had false conceptions of themselves, about what they are or what they ought to be. They have related themselves to one another in conformity with their ideas of God, of normal man, etc. The phantoms of their imagination have gotten too big for them. They, the creators, have been bowing to their creations. Let us liberate them from their chimeras, from their ideas, dogmas, imaginary beings, under whose yoke they are languishing. Let us rebel against the rule of thoughts. Let us teach man, says one person, to exchange these imaginings for thoughts that correspond to man's essence; let us teach man to be critical toward them, says another; let us teach man to get rid of them altogether, says a third. Then—existing reality will collapse.

Such innocent and childlike fantasies make up the core of recent Young-Hegelian philosophy which not only is received with horror and awe by the German public, but is also propounded by the *philosophic heroes* themselves with a ceremonious consciousness of its cataclysmic dangerousness and criminal disregard. The first volume of the present publication attempts to unmask these sheep who consider themselves and are taken to be wolves, to show how their bleating only follows in philosophy the conceptions of the average German citizen, to indicate how the boasting of these philosophic exegetes simply mirrors the wretchedness of actual conditions in Germany. This publication aims to debunk and discredit that philosophic struggle with shadows of reality which so appeals to the dreamy, drowsy German people.

A clever fellow once got the idea that people drown because they are possessed by the *idea of gravity*. If they would get this notion out of their heads by seeing it as religious superstition, they would be completely safe from all danger of water. For his entire life he fought against the illusion of gravity while all statistics gave him new and abundant evidence of its harmful effects. That kind of fellow is typical of the new revolutionary philosophers in Germany.

## I. *Feuerbach: Opposition of Materialistic and Idealistic Outlook*[*]

German ideologists say that Germany experienced an unprecedented revolution during the past few years. The decomposition of the Hegelian philosophy that began with Strauss developed into a ferment of worldwide proportions affecting all "powers of the past." Gigantic empires grew in the general chaos, only to decline again. Heroes emerged momentarily, only to be hurled back again into obscurity by bolder and mightier rivals. The French Revolution was child's play in comparison with this revolution which dwarfs even that of the Diadochi [successors of Alexander the Great]. Principles ousted one another with unprecedented speed. Heroes of the mind speedily overthrew one another, and in three years, 1842–45, more of the past was swept away in Germany than in three centuries at other periods.

All this is said to have happened in the realm of pure thought.

We are certainly dealing with an interesting phenomenon: the rotting away of absolute Spirit. Its last spark having failed, the various components of this caput mortuum began to decompose, entered into new compounds, and formed new substances. The industrialists of philosophy, having lived off the exploitation of absolute Spirit, then

[* Title in the elder Engels' handwriting on the last manuscript page of Part I.]

seized on the new compounds. Each of them retailed his share with all possible zeal. Competition had to arise, and in the beginning it was rather bourgeois and traditional. Later when the German market was glutted and the commodity could not be sold on the world market despite all efforts, business was spoiled in typically German fashion by mass production or pseudo-production, by a lowering of quality, adulteration of raw materials, falsification of labels, fictitious purchases, bill-jobbing, and a credit system lacking any real basis. The competition turned into bitter fighting, which is now interpreted and extolled as a revolution of world-historical significance and as producing the most tremendous results and achievements. If we are to recognize fully this philosophical charlatanry which awakens even in the breast of the honest German citizen a warm feeling of national pride, and if we are to point out the pettiness, the parochial narrow-mindedness of the entire Young-Hegelian movement, and particularly the tragicomical contrast between the actual accomplishments of these heroes and the illusions they have about their achievements, we have to examine the whole spectacle from a standpoint outside of Germany.

## A. *Ideology in General, Particularly German Ideology*

Right up to its most recent efforts, German criticism never left the realm of philosophy. Far from examining its general philosophic premises, all of its inquiries were based on one philosophical system, that of Hegel. There was mystification not only in the answers but also even in the questions themselves. This dependence on Hegel is the reason why none of these modern critics even attempted a comprehensive criticism of the Hegelian system, though each of them claimed to have gone beyond Hegel. Their polemics against Hegel and against one another are rather limited. Each critic picks one aspect of the Hegelian system and applies it to the entire system as well as to the aspects chosen by other critics. In the beginning they took up pure and unfalsified Hegelian categories such as "Substance" or "Self-consciousness." Later they desecrated such categories by giving them more mundane names such as "Species," "the Unique," "Man," etc.

All German philosophical criticism from Strauss to Stirner is confined to criticism of *religious* conceptions. The critics proceeded from real religion and actual theology. As they went on, they determined in various ways what constitutes religious consciousness and religious conceptions. Their progress consisted of their subsuming the allegedly dominant metaphysical, political, juridical, moral, and other concepts under the class of religious or theological concepts. Similarly, they declared political, juridical, and moral consciousness to be religious or theological consciousness, and the political, juridical, and moral man, *"Man"* in the last resort, to be religious. They presupposed the governance of religion. Gradually every dominant relationship was held to be religious and made into a cult, such as the cult of law, the cult of state, etc. Eventually there was nothing but dogmas and belief in dogmas. The world was more and more sanctified until our honorable Saint Max [Stirner] was able to sanctify it en bloc and dismiss it once for all.

The Old Hegelians had *comprehended* everything once they reduced it to a Hegelian logical category. The Young Hegelians *criticized* everything by imputing religious conceptions to it or declaring everything to be theological. The Young Hegelians are in agreement with the Old Hegelians in believing in the governance of religion, concepts, a universal principle in the existing world. But one party attacks this governance as usurpation while the other party praises it as legitimate.

Since the Young Hegelians regard concepts, thoughts, ideas, and all products of consciousness, to which they give independent existence, as the real fetters of man—while the Old Hegelians pronounced them the true bonds of human society—it is obvious that the Young Hegelians have to fight only against the illusions of consciousness. In the Young Hegelians' fantasies the relationships of men, all their actions, their chains, and their limitations are products of their consciousness. Consequently they give men the moral postulate of exchanging their present consciousness for human, critical or egoistic consciousness to remove their limitations. This amounts to a demand to interpret what exists in a different way, that is, to recognize it by means of a different interpretation. The Young-Hegelian ideologists are the staunchest conservatives, despite their allegedly "world-shaking" statements. The most recent among them have found the correct expression for their doings in saying they are fighting only against "*phrases.*" They forget, however, that they fight them only with phrases of their own. In no way are they attacking the actual existing world; they merely attack the phrases of this world. The only results this philosophic criticism could achieve were some elucidations on Christianity, one-sided as they are, from the point of view of religious history. All their other assertions are only further embellishments of their basic claim that these unimportant elucidations are discoveries of world-historical significance.

Not one of these philosophers ever thought to look into the connection between German philosophy and German reality, between their criticism and their own material environment.

### 1. *Ideology in General, Especially German Philosophy.*[*]

((We know only one science, the science of history. History can be viewed from two sides: it can be divided into the history of nature and that of man. The two sides, however, are not to be seen as independent entities. As long as man has existed, nature and man have affected each other. The history of nature, so-called natural history, does not concern us here at all. But we will have to discuss the history of man, since almost all ideology amounts to either a distorted interpretation of this history or a complete abstraction from it. Ideology itself is only one of the sides of this history.))

The premises from which we start are not arbitrary; they are no dogmas but rather actual premises from which abstraction can be made only in imagination. They are the

[* This heading and subsequent material within double parentheses crossed out in the manuscript.]

real individuals, their actions, and their material conditions of life, those which they find existing as well as those which they produce through their actions. These premises can be substantiated in a purely empirical way.

The first premise of all human history, of course, is the existence of living human individuals. ((The first *historical* act of these individuals, the act by which they distinguish themselves from animals is not the fact that they think but the fact that they begin to *produce their means of subsistence*.)) The first fact to be established, then, is the physical organization of these individuals and their consequent relationship to the rest of nature. Of course, we cannot discuss here the physical nature of man or the natural conditions in which man finds himself—geological, orohydrographical, climatic, and others. ((These relationships affect not only the original and natural organization of men, especially as to race, but also his entire further development or non-development up to the present.)) All historiography must proceed from these natural bases and their modification in the course of history through the actions of men.

Man can be distinguished from the animal by consciousness, religion, or anything else you please. He begins to distinguish himself from the animal the moment he begins to *produce* his means of subsistence, a step required by his physical organization. By producing food, man indirectly produces his material life itself.

The way in which man produces his food depends first of all on the nature of the means of subsistence that he finds and has to reproduce. This mode of production must not be viewed simply as reproduction of the physical existence of individuals. Rather it is a definite form of their activity, a definite way of expressing their life, a definite *mode of life*. As individuals express their life, so they are. What they are, therefore, coincides with what they produce, with *what* they produce and *how* they produce. The nature of individuals thus depends on the material conditions which determine their production.

This production begins with *population growth* which in turn presupposes *interaction* [*Verkehr*] among individuals. The form of such interaction is again determined by production.[*]

The relations of various nations with one another depend upon the extent to which each of them has developed its productive forces, the division of labor, and domestic commerce. This proposition is generally accepted. But not only the relation of one nation to others, but also the entire internal structure of the nation itself depends on the stage of development achieved by its production and its domestic and international commerce. How far the productive forces of a nation are developed is shown most evidently by the degree to which the division of labor has been developed. Each new productive force, insofar as it is not only a quantitative extension of productive forces already known (e.g. cultivation of land) will bring about a further development of the division of labor.

The division of labor in a nation leads first of all to the separation of industrial-commercial labor from agricultural labor and consequently to the separation of *town* and *country* and to a clash of their interests. Its further development leads to the separation of commercial from industrial labor. At the same time, within these various branches, there develop through the division of labor further various divisions among the individuals co-operating in specific kinds of labor. The relative position of these individual groups is determined by the methods employed in agricultural, industrial, and commercial labor (patriarchalism, slavery, estates, classes). The same conditions can be observed in the relations of various nations if commerce has been further developed.

The different stages of development in the division of labor are just so many different forms of ownership; that is, the stage in the division of labor also determines the relations of individuals to one another so far as the material, instrument, and product of labor are concerned.

The first form of ownership is tribal ownership. It cor-

[* Break in manuscript text indicated by triple indentation of first line of the following paragraph. In all the text to follow some long paragraphs have been divided to facilitate reading, but in such cases the first lines of the new paragraphs have ordinary indentations.]

responds to the undeveloped stage of production where people live by hunting and fishing, by breeding animals or, in the highest stage, by agriculture. Great areas of uncultivated land are required in the latter case. The division of labor at this stage is still very undeveloped and confined to extending the natural division of labor in the family. The social structure thus is limited to an extension of the family: patriarchal family chieftains, below them the members of the tribe, finally the slaves. The slavery latent in the family develops only gradually with the increase in population, the increase of wants, and the extension of external relations in war as well as in barter.

The second form is the ancient communal and state ownership which proceeds especially from the union of several tribes into a *city* by agreement or by conquest; this form is still accompanied by slavery. Alongside communal ownership there already develops movable, and later even immovable, private property, but as an abnormal form subordinate to communal ownership. The citizens hold power over their laboring slaves only in community and are therefore bound to the form of communal ownership. The communal private property of the active citizens compels them to remain in this natural form of association over against their slaves. Hence the whole social structure based on communal ownership and with it the power of the people decline as immovable private property develops. The division of labor is developed to a larger extent. We already find antagonism between town and country and later antagonism between states representing urban interests and those representing rural interests. Within the cities themselves we find the antagonism between industry and maritime commerce. The class relation between citizens and slaves is then fully developed.

With the development of private property we encounter for the first time those conditions which we shall find again with modern private property, only on a larger scale. On the one hand, there is the concentration of private property which began very early in Rome (as proved by the Licinian agrarian law) and proceeded very rapidly from the time of the civil wars and particularly under the emperors. On the other hand, there is linked to this the transformation of the plebeian small peasantry into a proletariat that never achieved an independent development because of its intermediate position between propertied citizens and slaves.

The third form is feudal or estate ownership. Antiquity started out from the *town* and the small territory around it; the Middle Ages started out from the *country*. This different starting-point was caused by the sparse population at that time, scattered over a large area and receiving no large population increase from the conquerors. In contrast to Greece and Rome, the feudal development began in a much larger area, prepared by the Roman conquests and the spreading of agriculture initially connected with these conquests. The last centuries of the declining Roman Empire and its conquest by the barbarians destroyed many productive forces. Agriculture had declined, trade had come to a standstill or had been interrupted by force, and the rural and urban population had decreased. These conditions and the mode of organization of the conquest determined by them developed feudal property under the influence of the Germanic military constitution. Like tribal and communal ownership, it is based again on a community. While the slaves stood in opposition to the ancient community, here the serfs as the direct producing class stand in opposition. As soon as feudalism is fully developed, there also emerges antagonism to the towns. The hierarchical system of land ownership and the armed bodies of retainers gave the nobility power over the serfs. Like the ancient communal ownership this feudal organization was an association directed against a subjected producing class. But the form of association and the relation to the direct producers were different because of the different conditions of production.

This feudal organization of land ownership had its counterpart in the *towns* in the form of corporate property, the feudal organization of the trades. Property consisted mainly in the labor of each individual. The necessity for association against the organized robber nobility, the need for communal markets in an age when the industrialist was at the same time a merchant, the growing competition of escaped serfs pouring into the rising cities, and the feudal structure of the whole country gave rise to *guilds*. The gradually accumulated capital of individual craftsmen and their stable number in comparison to the growing population produced the relationship of journeyman and apprentice. In the towns, this led to a hierarchy similar to that in the country.

The main form of property during the feudal times consisted on the one hand of landed property with serf labor and on the other hand, individual labor with small capital controlling the labor of journeymen. The organization of both was determined by the limited conditions of production: small-scale, primitive cultivation of land and industry based on crafts. There was little division of labor when feudalism was at its peak. Every district carried in itself the antagonism of town and country. Though division into estates was strongly marked, there was no division of importance apart from the differentiation of princes, nobility, clergy, and peasants in the country, and masters, journeymen, apprentices, and soon the mob of day laborers in the cities. The strip-system hindered such a division in agriculture; cottage industry of the peasants themselves emerged; and in industry there was no division of labor at all within particular trades, and very little among them. The separation of industry and commerce occurred in older towns, and in newer towns it developed later when they entered into mutual relations.

The merger of larger territories into feudal kingdoms was a necessity for the landed nobility as well as for the cities. The organization of the ruling class, the nobility, had a monarch at its head in all instances.

The fact is, then, that definite individuals who are productively active in a specific way enter into these definite social and political relations. In each particular instance, empirical observation must show empirically, without any mystification or speculation, the connection of the social and political structure with production. The social structure and the state continually evolve out of the life-process of definite individuals, but individuals not as they may appear in their own or other people's imagination but rather as they *really* are, that is, as they work, produce materially, and act under definite material limitations, presuppositions, and conditions independent of their will.

((The ideas which these individuals form are ideas either about their relation to nature, their mutual relations, or their own nature. It is evident that in all these cases these ideas are the conscious expression—real or illusory—of their actual relationships and activities, of their production and commerce, and of their social and political behavior. The opposite assumption is possible only if, in addition to the spirit of the actual and materially evolved individuals, a separate spirit is presupposed. If the conscious expression of the actual relations of these individuals is illusory, if in their imagination they turn reality upside down, this in turn is a result of their limited mode of activity and their limited social relations arising from it.))

The production of ideas, of conceptions, of consciousness is directly interwoven with the material activity and the material relationships of men; it is the language of actual life. Conceiving, thinking, and the intellectual relationships of men appear here as the direct result of their material behavior. The same applies to intellectual production as manifested in a people's language of politics, law, morality, religion, metaphysics, etc. Men are the producers of their conceptions, ideas, etc., but these are real, active men, as they are conditioned by a definite development of their productive forces and of the relationships corresponding to these up to their highest forms. Consciousness can never be anything else except conscious existence, and the existence of men is their actual life-process. If men and their circumstances appear upside down in all ideology as in a camera obscura, this phenomenon is caused by their historical life-process, just as the inversion of objects on the retina is caused by their immediate physical life.

In direct contrast to German philosophy, which descends from heaven to earth, here one ascends from earth to heaven. In other words, to arrive at man in the flesh, one does not set out from what men say, imagine, or conceive, nor from man as he is described, thought about, imagined, or conceived. Rather one sets out from real, active men and their actual life-process and demonstrates the development of ideological reflexes and echoes of that process. The phantoms formed in the human brain, too, are necessary sublimations of man's material life-process which is empirically verifiable and connected with material premises. Morality, religion, metaphysics, and all the rest of ideology and their corresponding forms of consciousness no longer seem to be independent. They have no history or development. Rather, men who develop their material production and their material relationships alter their thinking and the products of their thinking along with their real existence. Consciousness does not determine life, but life determines consciousness. In the first view the starting point is consciousness taken as a living individual; in the second it is the real living individuals themselves as they exist in real life, and consciousness is considered only as *their* consciousness.

This view is not devoid of premises. It proceeds from real premises and does not abandon them for a moment. These premises are men, not in any fantastic isolation and fixation, but in their real, empirically perceptible process of development under certain conditions. When this active life-process is presented, history ceases to be a collection of dead facts as it is with the empiricists who are themselves still abstract, or an imagined activity of imagined subjects, as with the idealists.

Where speculation ends, namely in actual life, there real, positive science begins as the representation of the practical activity and practical process of the development of men. Phrases about consciousness cease and real knowledge takes their place. With the description of reality, independent philosophy loses its medium of existence. At best, a summary of the most general results, abstractions derived from observation of the historical development of men, can take its place. Apart from actual history, these abstractions have in themselves no value whatsoever. They can only serve to facilitate the arrangement of historical material and to indicate the sequence of its particular strata. By no means do they give us a recipe or schema, as philosophy does, for trimming the epochs of history. On the contrary, the difficulties begin only when we start the observation and arrangement of the material, the real description, whether of a past epoch or of the present. The removal of these difficulties is governed by premises we cannot state here. Only the study of the real life-process and the activity of the individuals of any given epoch will yield them. We shall select here some of these abstractions which we use in opposing ideology, and we shall illustrate them by historical examples.

### ⟪*Feuerbach*⟫[*]

[ . . . (at least two manuscript pages missing) ] in reality and for the *practical* materialist, that is, the *communist*, it is a question of revolutionizing the world as it is, of practically tackling and changing existing things. Though we sometimes find such views with Feuerbach, they never go beyond isolated surmises and have much too little influence on his general outlook to be considered here as anything but embryos capable of development. Feuerbach's "conception" of the sensuous world is confined to mere perception [*Anschauung*] of it on the one hand and to mere sensation [*Empfindung*] on the other. He speaks of "Man" instead of "real historical men." "Man" is actually "the German." In the first case, in the *perception* of the sensuous world, he necessarily encounters things which contradict his consciousness and feeling and disturb the harmony he presupposes of all parts of the sensuous world and especially of man with nature. ⟨Feuerbach's mistake is not that he subordinates the flatly obvious, the sensuous *appearance*, to the sensuous reality established by closer examination of the sensuous facts, but that he cannot, after all, cope with sensuousness except by looking

[* Double pointed brackets for adjacent addenda in Marx's handwriting in the right column of the manuscript page. Each manuscript page is halved lengthwise into two columns, the left filled with most of the text in Engels' script—he wrote more smoothly and quickly than Marx—from joint dictation.]

at it with the "eyes," that is, through the "eyeglasses" of the *philosopher*.)[*] To remove this disturbance, he must take refuge in a dual perception: a profane one which apprehends only the "flatly obvious" and a higher, philosophical one which gets at the "true essence" of things. He does not see that the world surrounding him is not something directly given and the same from all eternity but the product of industry and of the state of society in the sense that it is a historical product, the result of the activity of a whole succession of generations, each standing on the shoulders of the preceding one, developing further its industry and commerce, and modifying its social order according to changed needs. Even the objects of the simplest "sensuous certainty" are given to him only through social development, industry, and commercial relationships. The cherry tree, like almost all fruit trees, was transplanted into our zone by *commerce* only a few centuries ago, as we know, and only *by* this action of a particular society in a particular time has it become "sensuous certainty" for Feuerbach.

Incidentally, when we conceive things as they really are and happened, any profound philosophical problem is resolved quite simply into an empirical fact, as will be seen even more clearly below. For example, the important question of the relation of man to nature (Bruno [Bauer] even goes so far as to speak of the "antitheses in nature and history" as if these were two separate "things" and man did not always have before him a historical nature and a natural history) from which all the "unfathomably lofty works" on "Substance" and "Self-consciousness" were born, collapses when we understand that the celebrated "unity of man with nature" has always existed in industry in varying forms in every epoch according to the lesser or greater development of industry, just like the "struggle" of man with nature, right up to the development of his productive forces on a corresponding basis. Industry and commerce, production and the exchange of the necessities of life, determine distribution and the structure of the

[* Single pointed brackets for adjacent addenda in Engels' writing in the right column of the manuscript page.]

various social classes, and are in turn determined as to the mode in which they are carried on. And so it happens that in Manchester, for instance, Feuerbach sees only factories and machines, where a hundred years ago only spinning wheels and weaving looms could be seen, or in the Campagna di Roma he discovers only pasture and swamps, where in the time of Augustus he would have found nothing but the vineyards and villas of Roman capitalists.

Feuerbach speaks in particular of the viewpoint of natural science. He mentions secrets disclosed only to the eye of the physicist and chemist. But where would natural science be without industry and commerce? Even this "pure" natural science receives its aim, like its material, only through commerce and industry, through the sensuous activity of men. So much is this activity, this continuous sensuous working and creating, this production, the basis of the whole sensuous world as it now exists, that, were it interrupted for only a year, Feuerbach would find not only a tremendous change in the natural world but also would soon find missing the entire world of men and his own perceptual faculty, even his own existence. Of course, the priority of external nature remains, and all this has no application to the original men produced by generatio aequivoca [spontaneous generation]. But this differentiation has meaning only insofar as man is considered distinct from nature. And after all, the kind of nature that preceded human history is by no means the nature in which Feuerbach lives, the nature which no longer exists anywhere, except perhaps on a few Australian coral islands of recent origin, and which does not exist for Feuerbach either.

Feuerbach admittedly has a great advantage over the "pure" materialists because he realizes that man too is "sensuous object"; but he sees man only as "sensuous object," not as "sensuous activity," because he remains in the realm of theory and does not view men in their given social connection, not under their existing conditions of life which have made them what they are. He never arrives at the really existing active men, but stops at the abstraction "Man" and gets only to the point of recognizing the "true, individual, corporeal man" emotionally, that is, he knows no other "human relationships" "of man to man" than love and friendship, and these idealized. He gives no criticism of the present conditions of life. He never manages to view the sensuous world as the total living sensuous *activity* of the individuals composing it. When he sees, for example, a crowd of scrofulous, over-worked, and consumptive wretches instead of healthy men, he is compelled to take refuge in the "higher perception" and "ideal compensation in the species." Thus he relapses into idealism at the very point where the communistic materialist sees the necessity and at the same time the condition of transforming industry as well as the social structure.

As far as Feuerbach is a materialist he does not deal with history, and as far as he deals with history he is not a materialist. Materialism and history completely diverge with him, a fact which should already be obvious from what has been said.

### ⟪History⟫

In dealing with Germans devoid of premises, we must begin by stating the first premise of all human existence, and hence of all history, the premise, namely, that men must be able to live in order to be able "to make history." ⟪*Hegel.* Geological, hydrographical, etc., conditions. Human bodies. Needs, labor.⟫ But life involves above all eating and drinking, shelter, clothing, and many other things. The first historical act is thus the production of the means to satisfy these needs, the production of material life itself. This is a historical act, a fundamental condition of all history which must be fulfilled in order to sustain human life every day and every hour, today as well as thousands of years ago. Even when sensuousness is reduced to a minimum, to a stick as with Saint Bruno [Bauer], it presupposes the activity of producing the stick. The first principle therefore in any theory of history is to observe this fundamental fact in its entire significance and all its implications and to attribute to this fact its due importance. The Germans have never done this, as we all know, so they have never had an *earthly* basis for history and consequently have never had a historian. Though the French and the English grasped the connection of this fact with so-called history only in an extremely one-sided way, particularly so long as they were involved in political ideology, they nevertheless made the first attempts to give historiography a materialistic basis by writing histories of civil society, commerce, and industry.

The second point is that once a need is satisfied, which requires the action of satisfying and the acquisition of the instrument for this purpose, new needs arise. The production of new needs is the first historical act. Here we see immediately where the great historical wisdom of the Germans comes from. When they run out of positive material and are not dealing with theological, political, or literary nonsense, they do not think of history at all but of "prehistoric times," without explaining how we can get from the nonsense of "prehistory" to history proper. With their historical speculation, on the other hand, they seize upon "prehistory" because they believe that there they are safe from interference by "crude facts" and can give full rein to their speculative impulses to establish and tear down hypotheses by the thousand.

The third circumstance entering into historical development from the very beginning is the fact that men who daily remake their own lives begin to make other men, begin to propagate: the relation between husband and wife, parents and children, the *family*. The family, initially the only social relationship, becomes later a subordinate relationship (except in Germany) when increased needs produce new social relations and an increased population creates new needs. It must then be treated and developed in accordance with the existing empirical data and not according to the "concept of the family" as is customary in Germany. These three aspects of social activity are not to be taken as three different stages, but just for what they are, three aspects. To make it clear for the Germans we might call them three "moments" which have existed simultaneously ever since the dawn of history and the first men and still exist today.

The production of life, of one's own life in labor and of another in procreation, now appears as a double relationship: on the one hand as a natural relationship, on the other as a social one. The latter is social in the sense that individuals co-operate, no matter under what conditions, in what manner, and for what purpose. Consequently a certain mode of production or industrial stage is always combined with a certain mode of co-operation or social stage, and this mode of co-operation is itself a "productive force." We observe in addition that the multitude of productive forces accessible to men determines the nature of society and that the "history of mankind" must always be studied and treated in relation to the history of industry and exchange. It is also clear, however, why it is impossible in Germany to write such a history. The Germans lack not only the power of comprehension required and the material but also "sensuous certainty." On the other side of the Rhine people cannot have any experience of these matters because history has come to a standstill there. It is obvious at the outset that there is a materialistic connection among men determined by their needs and their modes of production and as old as men themselves. This connection is forever assuming new forms and thus presents a "history" even in absence of any political or religious nonsense which might hold men together in addition.

Having considered four moments, four aspects of the primary historical relationships, we now find that man also possesses "consciousness." ⟨⟨Men have history because they must *produce* their life, and [ . . . ?] in a *certain* way: this is determined by their physical organization; their consciousness is determined in the same way.⟩⟩ But this consciousness is not inherent, not "pure." From the start the "spirit" bears the curse of being "burdened" with matter which makes its appearance in the form of agitated layers of air, sounds, in short, in the form of language. Language is as old as consciousness. It *is* practical consciousness which exists also for other men and hence exists for me personally as well. Language, like consciousness, only arises from the need and necessity of relationships with other men. ⟨⟨My relationship to my surroundings is my consciousness.)) Where a relationship exists, it exists for me. The animal has no *"relations"* with anything, no relations at all. Its relation to others does not exist as a relation. Consciousness is thus from the very beginning a social product and will remain so as long as men exist. At first consciousness is concerned only with the *immediate* sensuous environment and a limited relationship with other persons and things outside the individual who is becoming conscious of himself. At the same time it is consciousness of nature which first appears to man as an entirely alien, omnipotent, and unassailable force. Men's relations with this consciousness are purely animal, and they are over-awed by it like beasts. Hence it is a purely animal consciousness of nature (natural religion)—for the very reason that nature is not yet modified historically. On the other hand it is consciousness of the necessity to come in contact with other individuals; it is the beginning of man's consciousness of the fact that he lives in a society. This beginning is as animalistic as social life itself at this stage. It is the mere consciousness of being a member of a flock, and the only difference between sheep and man is that man possesses consciousness instead of instinct, or in other words his instinct is more conscious.

((We here see immediately that this natural religion or particular relation to nature is determined by the form of society and vice versa. As it is the case everywhere, the identity of nature and man appears in such a way that the restricted behavior of men toward nature determines their restricted behavior to one another, and their restricted behavior to one another determines their restricted behavior to nature.)) This sheeplike or tribal consciousness receives further development and formation through increased productivity, the increase of needs, and what is fundamental to both, the increase of population. Along with these, division of labor develops which originally was nothing but the division of labor in the sexual act, then that type of division of labor which comes about spontaneously or "naturally" because of natural predisposition (e.g. physical strength), needs, accidents, etc., etc. The division of labor is a true division only from the moment a division of material and mental labor appears. ⟨⟨The first form of ideologists, *priests,* is concurrent.⟩⟩ From this moment on consciousness can really boast of being something other than consciousness of existing practice, of *really* representing something without representing something real. From this moment on consciousness can emancipate itself from the world and proceed to the formation of "pure" theory, theology, philosophy, ethics, etc. But even if this theory, theology, philosophy, ethics, etc., comes into conflict with existing relations, this can only occur because existing social relations have come into conflict with the existing force of production. Incidentally this can also occur in national relationships through a conflict not within the nation but between a particular national consciousness and the practice of other nations, that is, between the national and the general consciousness of a nation (as we observe now in Germany). ⟨⟨*Religion.* The Germans and *ideology* as such.⟩⟩ Since this contradiction appears only as a contradiction within national consciousness, and since the struggle seems to be limited to this na⟨⟨tional crap just because this nation is crap in and for itself.⟩⟩

Moreover it does not make any difference what consciousness starts to do on its own. The only result we obtain from all such muck is that these three moments—the force of production, the state of society, and consciousness—can and must come into conflict with one another because the *division of labor* implies the possibility, indeed the necessity, that intellectual and material activity ⟨⟨activity and thinking, that is, thoughtless activity and inactive thought [later deleted.]⟩⟩—enjoyment and labor, production and consumption—are given to different individuals, and the only possibility of their not coming into conflict lies in again transcending the division of labor. It is self-evident that words such as "specters," "bonds," "higher being," "concept," "scruple," are only the idealistic, spiritual expression, the apparent conception of the isolated individual, the image of very empirical fetters and restrictions within which the mode of production of life and the related form of interaction move. ⟨⟨This idealistic expression of existing economic restrictions is present not only in pure theory but also in practical consciousness; that is to say, having emancipated itself and having entered into conflict with the existing mode of production, consciousness shapes not only religions and philosophies but also states.))

With the division [*Teilung*] of labor, in which all these conflicts are implicit and which is based on the natural division of labor in the family and the partition of society into individual families opposing one another, there is at the same time distribution [*Verteilung*], indeed *unequal* distribution, both quantitative and qualitative, of labor and its products, hence property which has its first form, its nucleus, in the family where wife and children are the slaves of the man. The latent slavery in the family, though still very crude, is the first property. Even at this initial stage, however, it corresponds perfectly to the definition of modern economists who call it the power of controlling the labor of others. ⟨Division of labor and private property are identical expressions. What is said in the former in regard to activity is expressed in the latter in regard to the product of the activity.⟩

Furthermore, the division of labor implies the conflict between the interest of the individual or the individual family and the communal interest of all individuals having contact with one another. The communal interest does not exist only in the imagination, as something "general," but first of all in reality, as a mutual interdependence of those individuals among whom the labor is divided. And finally, the division of labor offers us the first example for the fact that man's own act becomes an alien power opposed to him and enslaving him instead of being controlled by him —as long as man remains in natural society, as long as a split exists between the particular and the common interest, and as long as the activity is not voluntarily but naturally divided. For as soon as labor is distributed, each person has a particular, exclusive area of activity which is imposed on him and from which he cannot escape. He is a hunter, a fisherman, a herdsman, or a critical critic, and he must remain so if he does not want to lose his means of livelihood. In communist society, however, where nobody has an exclusive area of activity and each can train himself in any branch he wishes, society regulates the general production, making it possible for me to do one thing today and another tomorrow, to hunt in the morning, fish in the afternoon, breed cattle in the evening, criticize after dinner, just as I like, without ever becoming a hunter, a fisherman, a herdsman, or a critic. This fixation of social activity, this consolidation of our own products into an objective power above us, growing out of our control, thwarting our expectations, and nullifying our calculations, is one of the chief factors in historical development so far, [ . . . (nine lines deleted and illegible) ]

⟨[beside previous paragraph] Out of this very contradiction between the interest of the individual and that of the community the latter takes an independent form as the *State*, separated from the real interests of individual and community, and at the same time as an illusory communal life, but always based on the real bonds present in every family and every tribal conglomeration, such as flesh and blood, language, division of labor on a larger scale, and other interests, and particularly based, as we intend to show later, on the classes already determined by the division of labor, classes which form in any such mass of people and of which one dominates all the others. It follows from this that all struggles within the State, the struggle between democracy, aristocracy and monarchy, the struggle for franchise, etc., etc., are nothing but the illusory forms in which the real struggles of different classes are carried out among one another (the German theoreticians do not have the faintest inkling of this fact, although they have had sufficient information in the *Deutsch-Französische Jahrbücher* and *The Holy Family*). Furthermore, it follows that every class striving to gain control—even when such control means the transcendence of the entire old form of society and of control itself, as is the case with the proletariat—must first win political power in order to represent its interest in turn as the universal interest, something which the class is forced to do immediately.⟩ ⟨⟨Just because individuals seek *only* their particular interest, which for them does not coincide with their communal interest, the latter will be imposed on them as something "alien" and "independent," as a "universal" interest of a particular and peculiar nature in its turn. Otherwise they themselves must remain within this discord, as in democracy. On the other hand, the *practical* struggle of these particular interests, which constantly *really* run counter to the communal and illusory communal interests, necessitates *practical* intervention and control through the illusory "universal" interest in the form of the State.

Communism is for us not a *state of affairs* still to be established, not an *ideal* to which reality [will] have to adjust. We call communism the *real* movement which abolishes the present state of affairs. The conditions of this movement result from premises now in existence.⟩⟩ The social power, that is, the multiplied productive force from the co-operation of different individuals determined by the division of labor, appears to these individuals not as their own united power but as a force alien and outside them because their co-operation is not voluntary but has come about naturally. They do not know the origin and the goal of this alien force, and they cannot control it. On the contrary, it passes through a peculiar series of phases and stages independent of the will and the action of men, even directing their will. X [Insertion mark for paragraph to follow] How else could property, for example, have a history at all and assume various forms? How else could landed property, according to different premises, have changed in France from parcellation to centralization in the hands of a few, and in England from centralization in the hands of a few to parcellation, as is actually the case today? Or how does it happen that trade, which after all is nothing more than the exchange of products of various individuals and countries, rules the entire world through supply and demand—a relation, as an English economist says, which hovers over the earth like the fate of antiquity, distributing fortune and misfortune with invisible hand, establishing and overthrowing empires, causing nations to rise and to disappear? How could this go on, while with the abolition of the basis of private property, with communistic regulation of production and hence with abolition of the alienation between men and their own products, the power of supply and demand is completely dissolved and men regain control of exchange, production, and the mode of their mutual relationships?

⟨⟨X This *"alienation,"* to use a term which the philosophers will understand, can be abolished only on the basis of two *practical* premises. To become an "intolerable" power, that is, a power against which men make a revolution, it must have made the great mass of humanity "propertyless" and this at the same time in contradiction to an existing world of wealth and culture, both of which presuppose a great increase in productive power and a high degree of its development. On the other hand, this development of productive forces (which already implies the actual empirical existence of men on a *world-historical* rather than local scale) is an absolutely necessary practical premise because, without it, *want* is merely made general, and with *destitution* the struggle for necessities and all the old muck would necessarily be reproduced; and furthermore, because only with this universal development of productive forces is a *universal* commerce among men established which produces in all nations simultaneously the phenomenon of a "propertyless" mass (universal competition), makes each nation dependent on the revolutions of the others, and finally replaces local individuals with *world-historical*, empirically universal individuals. Without this, (1) communism could only exist locally; (2) the *forces* of interaction themselves could not have developed as *universal* and thus intolerable powers, but would have remained homebred, superstitious "conditions"; (3) any extension of interaction would abolish local communism. Empirically, communism is only possible as the act of dominant peoples "all at once" and simultaneously, which presupposes the universal development of productive

## Communism

power and worldwide interaction linked with communism. Besides, the mass of *propertyless* workers—labor power on a mass scale cut off from capital or even limited satisfaction, and hence no longer just temporarily deprived of work as a secure source of life—presupposes a *world mar-*

*ket* through competition. The proletariat can thus only exist *world-historically,* just as communism, its activity, can only have a "world-historical" existence. World-historical existence of individuals means existence of individuals which is directly bound up with world history.⟩⟩

The form of interaction determined by and in turn determining the existing productive forces at all previous historical stages is *civil society.* It is clear from what has been said above, that civil society has as its premise and basis the simple family and the multiple family, the so-called tribe. More detailed definitions are contained in our remarks above. Already we see here how civil society is the true focus and scene of all history. We see how nonsensical is the old conception of history which neglects real relationships and restricts itself to high-sounding dramas of princes and states.

So far we have concerned ourselves mainly with one aspect of human activity, how man *affects nature.* ⟨⟨Interaction and productive power.⟩⟩ The other aspect, how *man affects man*—origin of the state and the relation of the state to civil society [ . . . ]

History is nothing but the succession of separate generations, each of which exploits the materials, capital, and productive forces handed down to it by all preceding generations. On the one hand, it thus continues the traditional activity in completely changed circumstances and, on the other, modifies the old circumstances with a completely changed activity. This can be speculatively distorted so that later history is made the goal of earlier history, for example, the goal ascribed to the discovery of America is to assure the outbreak of the French Revolution. History then obtains its own aims and becomes a "person ranking with other persons" (to wit: "Self-consciousness, Criticism, the Unique," etc.), while what is designated with the words "destiny," "goal," "germ," or "idea" of earlier history is nothing more than an abstraction formed from later history, an abstraction from the active influence which earlier history exercises on later history.

The further the separate spheres that interact on one another extend in the course of this development, the more the original isolation of separate nationalities is destroyed by the developed mode of production, commerce, and division of labor between various nations naturally brought forth by these and the more does history become world history. For instance, when a machine is invented in England to deprive countless workers of bread in India and China and revolutionize the entire life of these empires, it becomes a world-historical fact. Sugar and coffee proved their world-historical importance in the nineteenth century when the lack of these products, occasioned by the Napoleonic Continental System, caused the Germans to rise against Napoleon. Lack of sugar and coffee thus became the real basis of the glorious Wars of Liberation of 1813. Hence the transformation of history into world history is not a mere abstract act of the "Self-consciousness," the world spirit, or of any other metaphysical specter, but a completely material, empirically verifiable act, an act for which every individual furnishes proof as he comes and goes, eats, drinks, and clothes himself.

### ⟨⟨On the Production of Consciousness⟩⟩

In history up to the present it is certainly an empirical fact that separate individuals, with the broadening of their activity into world-historical activity, have become more and more enslaved to a power alien to them (a hardship they conceive as chicanery on the part of the so-called World Spirit, etc.), a power which has become increasingly great and finally turns out to be the *world market*. But it is just as empirically established that by the overthrow of the existing state of society by the communist revolution (more about this below) and the abolition of private property which is identical with it, this alien power so baffling to German theoreticians will be dissolved. Then the liberation of each single individual will be accomplished to the extent that history becomes world history. Hence it is clear that the real intellectual wealth of the individual depends entirely on the wealth of his real connections. Only in this way will separate individuals be liberated from the various national and local barriers, be brought into practical connection with the material and intellectual production of the whole world, and be able to enjoy this all-sided production of the whole earth (the creations of man). *All-around* dependence, that natural form of the *world-historical* co-operation of individuals, will be transformed by the communist revolution into the control and conscious governance of these powers, which, born of the interaction of men, have until now overawed and governed men as powers completely alien to them. Now this view can be expressed again speculatively and idealistically, that is, fantastically, as "self-generation of the species" ("society as the subject"), and thereby the consecutive series of inter-related individuals can be conceived as a single individual which accomplishes the mystery of generating itself. It is clear here that individuals certainly generate *one another,* physically and mentally, but do not generate themselves either in the nonsense of Saint Bruno [Bauer] ((or in the sense of the "Unique," of "made" Man)).

Finally, from the conception of history as developed above we obtain these further conclusions: (1) In the development of productive forces there comes a stage when productive forces and means of interaction are achieved which under the existing relationships cause nothing but mischief and are no longer productive forces but rather destructive ones (machinery and money). Connected with this is a class which has to bear all the burdens of society without enjoying its advantages. It is excluded from society and forced into extreme opposition to all other classes. It constitutes the majority of all members of society, and from it arises a consciousness of the necessity of fundamental revolution, communist consciousness, which may of course arise also in the other classes perceiving the situation of this class. (2) The conditions under which definite productive forces can be applied are the conditions of the rule of a definite class of society whose social power, deriving from its property, has its *practical*-idealistic expression in the form of the state as it happens to exist then. Therefore, every revolutionary struggle is directed against a class which until then has been in power. ((The people are interested in maintaining the present state of production.)) (3) In all revolutions up till now the mode of activity remained unchanged, and it was only a question of a different distribution of this activity, a new distribution of labor to other persons. But the communist revolution is directed against the preceding *mode* of activity, does away with *labor,* and abolishes the rule of all classes along with the classes themselves, because it is accomplished by the class which society no longer recognizes as a class and is itself the expression of the dissolution of all classes, nationalities, etc. (4) For the production of this communist consciousness on a mass scale and for the success of the cause itself, the alteration of men on a mass scale is required. This can only take place in a practical movement, in a *revolution.* A revolution is necessary, therefore, not only because the *ruling* class cannot be overthrown in any other way but also because the class *overthrowing* it can succeed only by revolution in getting rid of all the traditional muck and become capable of establishing society anew.

This conception of history depends on our ability to set forth the real process of production, starting out from the material production of life itself, and to comprehend the form of interaction connected with this and created by this mode of production, that is, by civil society in its various stages, as the basis of all history. We have to show civil society in action as State and also explain all the different theoretical products and forms of consciousness, religion, philosophy, ethics, etc., and trace their genesis from that basis. The whole thing can be depicted in its totality (and thus the reciprocal action of these various sides too). Unlike the idealistic view of history this conception does not look for a category in every historical period; rather it remains constantly on the real *ground* of history. It does not explain practice from the idea but explains the formation of ideas from material practice. Consequently it arrives at the conclusion that all forms and products of consciousness cannot be dissolved by mental criticism, by resolution into "Self-consciousness" or transformation into "apparitions," "specters," "fancies," etc., but only by the practical overthrow of the actual social relations which gave rise to this idealistic trickery. Not criticism but revolution is the driving force of history and also of religion, philosophy, and all other types of theory. It shows that history does not end by being resolved into "Self-consciousness" as "spirit of the Spirit," but that there is a material result at each historical stage, a sum of productive forces, a historically created relation of individuals to nature and to one another which is handed down to each generation from its predecessor—a mass of productive forces, capital funds, and conditions which on the one hand is modified by the new generation but on the other hand also prescribes its conditions of life, giving it a definite development and a special character. It shows, therefore, that circumstances make men just as much as men make circumstances.

The sum of productive forces, capital funds, and social forms of interaction which every individual and every generation finds existing is the real basis of what the philosophers have conceived as "Substance" and "essence of Man," what they have apotheosized and attacked, that is, a real basis which is not in the least disturbed in its effect and influence on the development of men by the fact that these philosophers revolt against it as "Self-consciousness" and the "Unique." These conditions of life which the various generations find in existence also decide whether periodical and recurring revolutionary tremors will be strong enough to overthrow the basis of the entire existing system. If these material elements of total revolution are not present (namely, the existing productive forces on the one hand and the formation of a revolutionary mass on the other, a mass which revolts not only against particular conditions of the prevailing society but against the prevailing "production of life" itself, the "total activity" on which it was based) then it is absolutely immaterial, so far as practical development is concerned, whether the *idea* of this revolution has already been expressed a hundred times, as the history of communism proves.

In the whole conception of history up to the present this actual basis of history has been either totally neglected or considered as a minor matter irrelevant to the course of history. Thus history must always be written according to an extraneous standard. The actual production of life appears as something unhistorical, while the historical appears as something separated from ordinary life, something extra-superterrestrial. Thus the relation of man to nature is excluded from history and the antithesis of nature and history is created. The exponents of this conception of history have only been able to see in history political action and religious or other theoretical struggles. In each historical epoch they have had to *share the illusion of that epoch.* For example, if an epoch imagines itself to be determined by purely "political" or "religious" motives, even though "religion" and "politics" are only forms of its actual motives, the historian accepts this opinion. The "notion" [*Einbildung*], the "conception" of the people about their real practice, is transformed into the sole determining and active force controlling and determining their practice. When the crude form in which the division of labor appears with the Indians and Egyptians brings about the caste system in their states and in their religions, the historian believes that the caste system is the power which produced this social form. While the French and the English at least adhere to a political illusion moderately close to reality, the Germans move in the realm of the "pure Spirit" and make religious illusion the driving force of history.

The Hegelian philosophy of history is the last consequence, the "purest expression," of all this German historiography which does not deal with real interests, not even political ones, but with pure thoughts which consequently must appear to Saint Bruno [Bauer] as a series of "thoughts" devouring one another and perishing in "Self-consciousness." The Blessed Max Stirner, who does not know a thing about real history, goes even farther. He sees history as a mere tale of "knights," robbers, and ghosts from whose visions he can escape only by "unholiness." ⟨⟨So-called *objective* historiography has just consisted in treating historical conditions as separate from activity. Reactionary character.⟩⟩ This conception is truly religious. It postulates religious man as the original man, the starting point of all history. In its imagination it puts the religious production of fancies in the place of the real production of the means of subsistence and of life itself. This whole conception of history together with its dissolution and the scruples and qualms resulting from it is a purely *national* affair of the Germans and has only *local* interest for Germany, as for example the important question which has been treated several times of late: How does one "pass from the realm of God to the realm of Man"? As if this realm of God had ever existed anywhere except in the imagination, and the learned gentlemen, without being aware of it, were not constantly living in the "realm of Man" which they are now seeking. As if the learned pastime, for it is nothing more, of explaining the mystery of this theoretical cloud-formation did not on the contrary lie in demonstrating its origin in actual earthly conditions. For these Germans it is always simply a matter of resolving some nonsense at hand into some other freak. In other words, they presuppose that all this nonsense has a special *sense* which can be discovered, while actually they should explain this theoretical talk from the actual existing conditions. The real, practical dissolution of these phrases, the removal of these notions from the consciousness of men will be effected by altered circumstances, not by theoretical deduction, as we have already said. Such theoretical notions do not exist and need not be explained to the mass of men, that is, the proletariat. If this mass ever had any theoretical notions, for example, religion, these have now long been dissolved by circumstances.

The purely national character of these questions and answers is shown also in the way these theorists believe in all seriousness that phantoms like "the God-Man," "Man," etc., have presided over individual epochs of history—Saint Bruno [Bauer] even goes so far as to assert that only "criticism and critics make history." When they construct historical systems, they skip over all earlier periods with greatest haste and jump immediately from "Mongoldom" to history "with meaningful content," to the history of the [young Hegelian] *Hallische* and *Deutsche Jahrbücher* [edited by Arnold Ruge] and the dissolution of the Hegelian school in a general squabble. They forget all other nations, all real events, and the theatrum mundi is confined to the

Leipzig Book Fair and the mutual quarrels of "criticism,"
"Man," and the "Unique." When these theorists attempt
to treat really historical subjects, as for example the eighteenth century, they merely give a history of the ideas of
the times, torn away from the facts and practical developments fundamental to them. They give such a history only
with the intention of representing that period as an imperfect preliminary stage, as the limited forerunner of the real
historical age, that is, the period of the German philosophical struggle from 1840 to 1844. When the history of an
earlier period is written with the aim of bringing out the
fame of an unhistoric person and his fantasies, the really
historical events, even the really historic invasions of politics into history, receive no mention. Instead we get a nar-
rative based not on studies but on conjectures and literary
gossip such as Saint Bruno presented in his now forgotten
history of the eighteenth century. These pompous and
haughty idea-peddlers who believe they are far above all
national prejudices are actually far more national than the
beer-philistines who dream of a united Germany. They do
not recognize the deeds of other nations as historical. They
turn the Rhine Song into a religious hymn and conquer
Alsace-Lorraine by robbing French philosophy instead of
the French state, by Germanizing French ideas instead of
French provinces. Venedey is a cosmopolitan compared
with the Saints Bruno [Bauer] and Max [Stirner] who in
the universal domination of theory proclaim the universal
domination of Germany.

It is also clear from this discussion how grossly Feuerbach deceives himself when he declares himself a communist (*Wigand's Vierteljahrsschrift,* II, 1845) by virtue of
the qualification "common man" converted into a predicate *"of"* Man, and thus he believes it possible to change
the word communist, which actually means the follower of
a definite revolutionary party, into a mere category. Feuerbach's whole deduction concerning the relation of men to
one another goes only so far as to prove that men need and
*always have needed* one another. He wants to establish
consciousness of this fact. Like other theorists he wants to
bring about a correct awareness of an *existing* fact,

whereas the real communist aims to overthrow the existing state of things. We appreciate fully that Feuerbach, trying to produce consciousness of just *this* fact, goes as far as a theorist possibly can without ceasing being a theorist and philosopher. It is characteristic, however, that Saint Bruno and Saint Max take Feuerbach's conception of the communist and substitute it for the real communist, partly so that they too can combat communism as "spirit of the Spirit," as a philosophical category, as an equal opponent —and in the case of Saint Bruno also for pragmatic reasons. As an example of Feuerbach's acceptance and at the same time misunderstanding of existing reality, something he still shares with our opponents, we recall the passage in his *Philosophy of the Future* where he develops the view that the existence of a thing or a man is at the same time its or his essence, that the conditions of existence, the mode of life, and the activity of an animal or human individual are those in which its or his "essence" feels satisfied. Here every exception is expressly conceived as an unfortunate accident and unalterable abnormality. If millions of proletarians in no way feel contented with their conditions of life, if their "existence"[*] does not in the least correspond to their "essence," this is an unavoidable misfortune which must be borne quietly. The millions of proletarians and communists, however, think differently and will prove this when they bring their "existence" into harmony with their "essence" in a practical way, by means of revolution. Feuerbach never speaks of the human world in such cases but always takes refuge in external nature, in nature *as such*, not yet subdued by men. But every new invention and every advance made by industry removes another portion of this domain so the ground which produces examples to illustrate Feuerbach's propositions is steadily shrinking. The "essence" of the fish is its "existence," water—to go no further than this one proposition. The "essence" of the freshwater fish is the water of a river. But this ceases to be the "essence" of the fish and is no longer a suitable medium

[* From here to paragraph below ending ". . . language of reality.))" are translated hitherto missing pages found in the International Institute of Social History, Amsterdam.]

of existence as soon as the river is made to serve industry, as soon as it is polluted by dyes and other waste products and navigated by steamboats, when its water is diverted into canals and the fish is deprived of its medium of existence by simple drainage. The explanation that all such contradictions are inevitable abnormalities does not essentially differ from the consolation which the Blessed Max Stirner offers [in *The Ego and Its Own*] to the discontented, saying that this contradiction is their own contradiction and this predicament their own predicament, that they should relax, or keep their disgust to themselves, or revolt against it in some fantastic way. It differs just as little from Saint Bruno's allegation [*op. cit.*] that these unfortunate circumstances arose because those concerned are stuck in the muck of "Substance," have not advanced to "absolute Self-consciousness," and do not realize that these adverse conditions are spirit of their spirit.

Of course, we shall not take the trouble to enlighten our wise philosophers by explaining to them that the "liberation" of "man" is not advanced a single step by their reducing Philosophy, Theology, Substance, and all that trash to "Self-consciousness" and by their liberating man from the domination of these phrases which have never held him in thrall. ⟨⟨Feuerbach. Philosophic and real liberation. *Man*. The *Unique*. The individual. Geological, hydrographical, etc., conditions. The human body. Need and labor.⟩⟩ Nor will we explain to them that real liberation can be achieved only in the real world and with real means, that slavery cannot be abolished without the steam engine and the spinning jenny, that serfdom cannot be abolished without improved agriculture, and that people on the whole cannot be liberated so long as they are unable to obtain food and drink, shelter and clothing in adequate quality and quantity. "Liberation" is a historical and not a mental act. It is effected by historical conditions, by the development of industry, commerce, agriculture, transportation [manuscript page damaged, unreadable]

In Germany, a country where only a shabby historical development is occurring, these mental developments, these glorified and ineffective trivialities, naturally serve as a substitute for the lack of historical development, and they take root and have to be combated. But this is a fight of local significance. ⟨⟨Phrases and real movement. The importance of phrases in Germany. Language is the language of reality.⟩⟩

In every epoch the ideas of the ruling class are the ruling ideas, that is, the class that is the ruling *material* power of society is at the same time its ruling *intellectual* power. The class having the means of material production has also control over the means of intellectual production, so that it also controls, generally speaking, the ideas of those who lack the means of intellectual production. The ruling ideas are nothing more than the ideal expression of the dominant material relationships grasped as ideas, hence of the relationships which make the one class the ruling one and therefore the ideas of its domination. The individuals who comprise the ruling class possess among other things consciousness and thought. Insofar as they rule as a class and determine the extent of a historical epoch, it is self-evident that they do it in its entire range. Among other things they rule also as thinkers and producers of ideas and regulate the production and distribution of the ideas of their age. Their ideas are the ruling ideas of the epoch. For example, in an age and in a country where royal power, aristocracy, and bourgeoisie are contending for domination and where control is shared, the doctrine of the separation of powers proves to be the dominant idea and is expressed as an "eternal law."

The division of labor, which we saw above (pp. [424–25]) as one of the chief forces of history up till now, is expressed also in the ruling class as the division of mental and material labor, so that within this class one part appears as the thinkers of the class (its active, conceptive ideologists who make perfecting the illusion of this class about itself their main source of livelihood), while the others' attitude toward these ideas and illusions is more passive and receptive because they are really the active members of this class and have less time to make up illusions and ideas about themselves. Within this class this split can even develop into opposition and hostility between the two parts, which disappears, however, in the case of a practical collision where the class itself is in danger. In this case the appearance that the ruling ideas were not ideas of the ruling class with a power distinct from the power of this class also vanishes. The existence of revolutionary ideas in a particular epoch presupposes the existence of a revolutionary class. About the premises for the latter we have made sufficient comment above (pp. [427–28]).

If in considering the course of history we detach the ideas of the ruling class from the ruling class itself and attribute to them an independent existence, if we confine ourselves to saying that these or those ideas prevailed in a certain epoch without bothering ourselves about their conditions of production or producers, if we ignore the individuals and world conditions which are the source of the ideas, we can say, for example, that during the time when aristocracy was dominant the concepts of honor, loyalty, etc., prevailed, during the dominion of the bourgeoisie, the concepts of freedom, equality, etc. The ruling class itself generally imagines this to be the case. This conception of history, common to all historians particularly since the eighteenth century, will necessarily come up against the phenomenon that increasingly the abstract ideas prevail, that is, ideas that increasingly take on the form of universality. Each new class which displaces the one previously dominant is forced, simply to be able to carry out its aim, to represent its interest as the common interest of all members of society, that is, ideally expressed. It has to give its ideas the form of universality and represent them as the only rational, universally valid ones. The class making revolution emerges at the outset simply because it is opposed to a *class* not as a class but as a representative of the whole of society. It appears as the whole mass of society confronting one ruling class. ⟨⟨Universality corresponds to (1) class versus estate, (2) competition, world trade, etc., (3) the great numerical strength of the ruling class, (4) the illusion of *common* interests (in the beginning this illusion is true), (5) the delusion of ideologists and the division of labor.⟩⟩ It can do this because in the beginning its interest really is more attached to the common interest of all other

non-ruling classes and because under the pressure of prevailing conditions its interest has not yet been able to develop as the particular interest of a particular class. Its
victory, therefore, benefits also many individuals of other
classes which do not win power but only insofar as it now
puts these individuals in a position to raise themselves into
the ruling class. When the French bourgeoisie overthrew
the power of the aristocracy, it permitted many proletarians
to raise themselves above the proletariat, but only insofar as they became bourgeois. Every new class, therefore,
achieves dominance only on a broader basis than that of
the previous class ruling, whereas the opposition of the
non-ruling class against the new ruling class later develops
all the more sharply and deeply. Both these factors mean
that the struggle to be waged against this new ruling class
aims at a more decided and more radical negation of the
previous conditions of society than could all previous
classes striving for dominance.

This entire appearance, that the rule of a certain class
is only the rule of certain ideas, comes to a natural end as
soon as class rule in general ceases to be the form in which
society is organized, as soon as it is no longer necessary
to represent a particular interest as general or "the general
interest" as dominant.

When ruling ideas are separated from ruling individuals
and above all from relationships resulting from a given
level of the mode of production and the conclusion has
been reached that ideas are always ruling history, it is very
easy to abstract from these various ideas "*the* ideas," the
Idea, etc., as the dominant force in history and thus understand all these separate ideas and concepts as "Self-
determinations" of *the* Concept developing in history. It
follows, of course, that all the relationships of men can
be derived from the concept of man, man as conceived,
the essence of man, *Man*. This has been done in speculative
philosophy. ⟨⟨Hegel himself admits at the end of the *Philosophy of History* that he "has considered the progress of
the *Concept* only" and has presented the "true *theodicy*"
in history (p. 446).⟩⟩ Now one can go back again to the
producers of "the Concept," to the theorists, ideologists,

and philosophers, and one comes to the conclusion that the philosophers, the thinkers as such, have always been dominant in history—a conclusion, as we see, already advanced by Hegel. Thus the whole trick of proving the hegemony (Stirner calls it hierarchy) of Spirit in history is confined to the following three efforts.

No. 1. One must separate the ideas of those ruling for empirical reasons, under empirical conditions, and as material individuals from the actual rulers; one must recognize the rule of ideas or illusions in history.

No. 2. One must put order into this rule of ideas, prove a mystical connection among the successive ruling ideas, which is managed by seeing them as "self-determinations of the Concept" (this is possible because these ideas are actually connected with one another by virtue of their empirical basis and because as *mere* ideas they become self-distinctions, distinctions made by thought).

No. 3. To remove the mystical appearance of this "self-determining Concept" one changes it into a person—"Self-Consciousness"—or, to make it appear thoroughly materialistic, into a series of persons who represent "the Concept" in history, into "the thinkers," "philosophers," ideologists who again are understood as the manufacturers of history, "the council of guardians," the rulers. ⟨⟨Man = the "rational human spirit."⟩⟩ Thus all materialistic elements have been removed from history and full rein can be given to one's speculative steed.

This historical method which prevailed in Germany and particularly the reason why it prevailed must be explained from its connection with the illusion of ideologists in general, for example, the illusions of jurists, politicians (even of the practical statesmen among them), and from the dogmatic dreamings and distortions of these fellows. It is very simply explained from their practical position in life, their employment, and the division of labor.

While in ordinary life every shopkeeper is very well able to distinguish between what somebody professes to be and what he really is, our historians have not yet achieved this trivial insight. They take every epoch at its word and believe everything it says and imagines about itself. [Pages 36 through 39 in Marx's pagination missing here.]

### [*Division of Labor*]

[ . . . ] are found. From the first, there follows the premise of a highly developed division of labor and extensive commerce; from the second, the locality. In the first case, individuals must be brought together; in the second, they find themselves alongside the given instrument of production as instruments of production themselves. Here arises the difference between natural instruments of production and those created by civilization. The *land* (water, etc.) can be regarded as a natural instrument of production. In the first case, with the natural instrument of production, individuals are subservient to nature; in the second, to a product of labor. In the first case, property (landed property) appears as direct natural domination; in the second, as domination of labor, particularly of accumulated labor, capital. The first case presupposes that the individuals are united by some bond: family, tribe, the land itself, etc. The second case presupposes that they are independent of one another and are only held together by exchange. In the first case, the exchange is mainly an exchange between men and nature in which the labor of men is exchanged for the products of nature; in the second, it is predominantly an exchange of men among themselves. In the first case, average human common sense suffices; physical activity is not as yet separated from mental activity. In the second, the division between physical and mental labor already must be practically completed. In the first case, the domination of the proprietor over non-proprietors may be based on a personal relationship or kind of community; in the second, it must have taken on physical shape in a third party: money. In the first case, small industry exists, but determined by the utilization of the natural instrument of production and hence without distribution of labor among various individuals; in the second, industry exists only in and through division of labor.

We started from instruments of production and showed that private property was a necessity for certain industrial stages. In *industrie extractive* private property still co-incides with labor. In small industry and agriculture up till now property is the necessary consequence of the existing instruments of production. Only with big industry does the contradiction between the instrument of production and private property appear; it is the product of big industry. In addition, big industry must be highly developed to produce it. Only with big industry is the abolition of private property possible.

The greatest division of material and intellectual labor is the separation of town and country. The opposition between the two begins with the transition from barbarism to civilization, from the tribe to the state, from locality to nation, and runs through the whole history of civilization to the present day (the Anti-Corn-Law League). With the existence of towns there is the necessity of administration, police, taxes, etc., in short of municipal life and thus politics in general. Here first became apparent the division of the population into two great classes directly based on the division of labor and the instruments of production. The town already shows in actual fact a concentration of population, of instruments of production, of capital, satisfactions, and needs, while the country demonstrates the opposite, isolation and separation. The antagonism between town and country can exist only with private property. It is the crassest expression of the subsumption of the individual under the division of labor, under a definite activity forced upon him, a subsumption making one man into a narrow town animal, the other into a narrow country animal, and every day creates anew the conflict between their interests. Labor is again the main thing here, power *over* individuals, and as long as this power exists, private property must exist. The overcoming of the antagonism between town and country is one of the first conditions of communal life, a condition depending on a mass of material premises. Mere will, as anyone can see at first glance, cannot fulfill this condition. (We will have to discuss these conditions.) Separation of town and country can also be understood as the separation of capital and landed property, as the beginning of capital's existence and development independent of landed property, the beginning of property based only on labor and exchange.

In towns that had not existed before but were newly built by freed serfs in the Middle Ages, each man's particular labor was his only property except for the small capital he brought with him consisting only of the most necessary tools of his craft. The competition of serfs constantly taking refuge in the towns, the constant war of the country against the town, and thus the necessity of an organized municipal military force, the bond of common ownership in a particular kind of labor, the necessity of sharing buildings for the sale of their wares when craftsmen were also traders, and consequently the exclusion of unauthorized persons from these buildings, the conflict of interests among various crafts, the necessity of protecting their laboriously acquired skill, and the feudal organization of the entire country—all these were causes of the union of workers of each craft into guilds. At this point we need not go further into the numerous modifications of the guild system with later historical developments. The flight of serfs into the towns continued without interruption through the entire Middle Ages. These serfs, persecuted by their lords in the country, came separately into the towns where they found an organized community against which they were powerless and in which they had to adjust to the station which their organized urban competitors assigned to them according to their need of labor and their interest. Arriving separately, these workers were never able to gain any power because if their labor was of the guild type and had to be learned, the guild masters put them in subjection and organized them according to their interest. If their labor was not of this type but rather day labor, they never managed to organize themselves and remained unorganized rabble. The need for day labor in the towns created the rabble.

These towns were true "associations" created by a direct need to provide for protection of property, multiply the means of production, and defend the individual members. The rabble of these towns was deprived of all power. It was composed of individuals who were strange to one another, had arrived separately, were unorganized, and faced an organized power armed for war and jealously supervising them. In each craft journeymen and apprentices were organized as best suited their master's interest. Their patriarchal relationship with their masters gave the masters a double power, first because of their direct influence on all aspects of life of the journeymen and secondly because there was a real bond uniting the journeymen who worked for the same master, a bond separating them from journeymen working for other masters. And finally the journeymen were bound to the existing order by their interest in becoming masters themselves. While the rabble at least carried out some revolts against the whole municipal order, revolts that remained completely ineffective because of their impotence, the journeymen had only insignificant squabbles within their guild and such as pertain to the nature of the system. The great revolts of the Middle Ages all started in the country. They, too, remained totally ineffective because of the dispersal and resulting cruelty of the peasants.

Capital in these towns consisted of a house, tools of the craft, and natural hereditary customers; it was natural capital. Since it was unrealizable because of the primitive form of commerce and lack of circulation, it had to descend from father to son. Unlike modern capital which can be appraised monetarily and invested in this thing or that, this natural capital was directly tied up with the particular work of the owner, was inseparable from it, and was thus *estate* capital.

In the towns the division of labor between the various guilds was quite natural; in the guilds themselves it was not at all carried out among the individual workers. Every worker had to be well versed in a whole round of tasks and had to be able to make all things that could be made with his tools. The limited commerce and the lack of good communications between individual towns, the lack of population, and limited needs did not permit a higher division of labor. Every man who set out to become a master craftsman had to be proficient in the whole of his craft. The medieval craftsmen still exhibited an interest in their special work and their skill in it which could develop to a certain limited artistic talent. For that very reason, however, every medieval craftsman was completely absorbed in his work, had a contented slavish relationship to it, and was subjected to it to a far greater extent than is the modern worker for whom his work is a matter of indifference.

The next extension of the division of labor was the separation of production and commerce and the formation of a special class of merchants, a separation which had been handed down (as for example with the Jews) in established towns and soon appeared in new ones. With this there was the possibility of commerce transcending the immediate neighborhood, and the realization of this possibility depended on existing means of communication, the state of public safety in the countryside determined by political conditions (throughout the Middle Ages the merchants traveled in armed caravans, as is well known), and on the cruder or more developed needs of the area accessible to commerce as determined by the stage of culture. With commerce as the proper business of a particular class and extension of trade through the merchants beyond the immediate surroundings of the town, an immediate reciprocal action between production and commerce appeared. The towns entered into relations *with one another*. New tools were brought from one town into the other. The division between production and commerce soon created a new division of production among individual towns, each exploiting a predominant branch of industry. Earlier local restrictions gradually broke down.

It depends entirely on the extension of commerce whether the productive forces, especially inventions, in a locality are lost for later development or not. As long as there is no commerce beyond the immediate neighborhood, every invention must be separately made in each locality. Pure accidents such as eruptions of barbaric peoples and even ordinary wars are enough to cause a country with advanced productive forces and needs to start all over again from the beginning. In primitive history every invention had to be made anew, independently, every day and in each locality. That well-developed productive forces are not safe from complete destruction even with relatively extensive commerce is proved by the Phoenicians ⟨⟨and glass painting in the Middle Ages⟩⟩ whose inventions were largely lost for a long time through the displacement of this nation from commerce, its conquest by Alexander, and its consequent decline. Glass painting in the Middle Ages had a similar fate. Only when commerce has become worldwide and is based on large-scale industry, when all nations are drawn into the competitive struggle, will the permanence of the acquired productive forces be assured.

## [*Manufacturing*]

A direct consequence of the division of labor between the various towns was the rise of manufactures, branches of production that had developed from the guild system. They first flourished in Italy and later in Flanders because of the historical condition of trade with foreign nations. In other countries, for example, England and France, manufacturing was at first confined to the domestic market. Besides the conditions already mentioned, manufacturing depends on an advanced concentration of population—particularly in the country—and of capital which began to accumulate in the hands of individuals, partly in the guilds despite their regulations, and partly among the merchants.

That kind of labor which from the beginning required a machine, even of the crudest kind, soon turned out to be most capable of development. Weaving, previously done by peasants in the country as a secondary job to provide clothing, was the first labor to receive an impetus and a further development through the extension of commerce. Weaving was the first and remained the main manufacturing. The rising demand for clothing materials from the growth of the population, the growing accumulation and mobilization of natural capital through accelerated circulation, the demand for luxuries caused by the accelerated circulation and generally facilitated by the gradual extension of commerce, gave weaving a quantitative and qualitative impetus which removed it from the prevailing form of production. Beside the peasants who continued, and still continue, to weave for their own use, a new class of weavers emerged in the towns whose fabrics were destined for the entire domestic market and usually also foreign markets. Weaving, a job usually requiring little skill, soon branched out into various kinds of jobs and resisted the restrictions of a guild. For this reason weaving was done mostly in villages and marketplaces, without guild organization. Villages grew into towns, and indeed the most flourishing ones in each country.

With guild-free manufacturing, property relations changed rapidly. The first advance beyond natural-estate capital was provided by the emergence of merchants whose capital was from the start movable, capital in the modern sense as far as we can speak of it in considering the circumstances of those times. The second advance came with manufacturing which again mobilized a great deal of natural capital and altogether increased the mass of movable capital as compared to that of natural capital. At the same time manufacturing became a refuge of the peasants from the guilds which excluded them or paid them poorly, just as earlier the guild towns had served as a refuge for the peasants from the landlords.

With the beginning of manufacturing there was immediately a period of vagrancy caused by the abolition of feudal retainers, the disbanding of armies which had served the kings against their vassals, the improvement of agriculture, and the transformation of large strips of arable land into pasture land. It is clear from this alone how this vagrancy coincides with the disintegration of the feudal system. Isolated epochs of this kind occurred as early as the thirteenth century. Only at the end of the fifteenth and beginning of the sixteenth centuries is it generally present and for quite some duration. These vagabonds were so numerous that, to give one example, Henry VIII of England had 72,000 of them hanged. They could be put to work only with the greatest difficulty and through most extreme destitution, and then after long resistance. The rapid rise of manufacturing, particularly in England, gradually absorbed them.

With the rise of manufacturing, the various nations entered into a competitive relationship, the fight for trade, which was fought out in wars, protective duties, and prohibitions, while the nations formerly had carried on an inoffensive exchange if they were in contact at all. From then on trade assumed political significance.

The relationship between worker and employer also changed. In the guilds the patriarchal relationship between journeyman and master continued to exist; in manufacturing the monetary relation between worker and capitalist took its place, a relationship which retained a patriarchal tinge in the country and the small towns but quite early lost almost all patriarchal coloration in the larger, the real manufacturing towns.

Manufacturing and the movement of production in general received an enormous stimulus through the extension of commerce with the discovery of America and a sea route to the East Indies. The new products imported from America and the Indies and particularly the large quantities of gold and silver which came into circulation completely changed the position of classes toward each other and dealt a hard blow to feudal landed property and laborers. The expeditions of adventurers, colonization, and above all the extension of markets into a world market, now possible and becoming more and more a fact with each day, called forth a new phase of historical development which we cannot further discuss here. Through the colonization of newly discovered lands, the commercial struggle of nations against one another received new fuel and thus became bigger and more bitter.

Expansion of trade and manufacturing accelerated the accumulation of movable capital while natural capital in the guilds remained stable or even decreased without any stimulus for increased production. Trade and manufacturing created the big bourgeoisie; the petty bourgeoisie was concentrated in the guilds, no longer a prevailing power in the cities but bowing to the power of big merchants and manufacturers. ⟨⟨[vertically] The petty bourgeois—Middle class—Big bourgeoisie⟩⟩ As soon as the guilds came into contact with manufacturing, they declined.

During the epoch under discussion the relationships of the nations to one another took on two different forms. In the beginning the small quantity of gold and silver in circulation brought about the ban on the export of these metals. Industry, mostly imported from abroad and needed to employ the increasing urban population, required those privileges which could be granted not only against competition at home but mainly against foreign competition. In the original prohibitions the local guild privilege was extended over the whole nation. Customs duties originated from levies which feudal lords exacted as protection money from merchants passing through their territories and from levies later imposed by towns as the most convenient method of raising money for their treasury. The appearance of American gold and silver on the European markets, the gradual development of industry, the rapid expansion of trade, and the consequent rise of the non-guild bourgeoisie and of money gave these measures a different significance. Being from day to day less able to do without money, the state now upheld the ban on the export of gold and silver for fiscal reasons. The bourgeois for whom these masses of money on the market became the chief object of speculation were thoroughly pleased. Privileges became a source of income for the government and were sold for money. In customs legislation export duties appeared which had a purely fiscal aim and were only a hindrance to industry.

The second period began in the middle of the seventeenth century and lasted almost to the end of the eighteenth. Commerce and navigation had expanded more rapidly than manufacturing which played a secondary role. Colonies were becoming important consumers. After long struggles the individual nations shared the opening world market. This period begins with the Navigation Laws and colonial monopolies. Competition of the nations among themselves was excluded so far as possible by tariffs, prohibitions, and treaties. In the last resort the competitive struggle was carried out and decided in wars (particularly in naval wars). The most powerful maritime nation, the English, held pre-eminence in trade and manufacturing. Here we already have concentration in one country.

Manufacturing was constantly protected at home by

tariffs, in the colonial market by monopolies, and abroad as much as possible by differential duties. The processing of domestic raw materials was encouraged (wool and linen in England, silk in France); the export of raw materials was forbidden (wool in England); and the processing of imported material was neglected or suppressed (cotton in England). The nation ruling in sea trade and colonial power naturally secured for itself also the greatest quantitative and qualitative expansion of manufacturing. Manufacturing could not do without protection. Through the slightest change taking place in other countries, it could lose its market and be ruined. It can be easily introduced into a country under reasonably favorable conditions and for this reason can be easily destroyed. Through the mode in which manufacturing was carried on particularly in rural areas of the eighteenth century, it was so much interwoven with the vital relationships of a great mass of individuals that no country dared jeopardize its existence by permitting free competition. When a country manages to export, this depends entirely on the extension or restriction of commerce and exercises a relatively small effect. [Corner of manuscript damaged.] Hence the secondary [importance] and influence of [the merchants] in the eighteenth century. More than anyone else the merchants and especially the shippers insisted on protection and monopolies. The manufacturers also demanded and received protection but were inferior in political importance at all times. The commercial towns, particularly the maritime towns, became to some degree civilized and big-bourgeois, but an extreme petty bourgeois outlook persisted in the factory towns. See Aikin [*Description of the Country from Thirty to Forty Miles round Manchester,* London, 1795], etc. The eighteenth century was a century of trade. Pinto says this expressly [*Traité de la circulation et du crédit,* Amsterdam, 1771]: "Commerce is the rage of the century," and: "for some time now people have been talking only about commerce, navigation, and the navy."

The movement of capital, although significantly accelerated, remained relatively slow. The splitting of the world market into separate parts, each of which was exploited by a particular nation, the exclusion of nations' competition among themselves, the clumsiness of production itself, and the fact that the financial system was only developing from its early stages—all this greatly impeded circulation. The consequence was a haggling, shabby, petty spirit which still clung to all merchants and the whole mode of carrying on trade. Compared with manufacturers and particularly craftsmen, they were certainly big bourgeois; compared with the merchants and industrialists of the next period they remain petty bourgeois. Cf. Adam Smith [*The Wealth of Nations*].

This period is also characterized by the cancellation of bans on the export of gold and silver, and the beginning of trade in money; by banks, national debts, paper money, speculation in stocks and shares, and jobbing in all articles; by the development of finance in general. Capital again lost a great part of the national character which it had still possessed.

The concentration of trade and manufacturing in one country, England, developed irresistibly in the seventeenth century and gradually created for that country a relative world market and thus a demand for its manufactured products which could no longer be met by the prevailing industrial forces of production. The demand outgrew the productive forces and was the motive power to bring about the third period of private ownership since the Middle Ages by producing big industry—the application of elemental forces to industrial purposes, machinery, and a very extensive division of labor. There already existed in England the remaining conditions for this new phase: freedom of competition within the nation and the development of theoretical mechanics (as perfected by Newton, the most popular science in France and England in the eighteenth century). (Free competition within the nation itself everywhere had to be obtained by revolution—1640 and 1688 in England, 1789 in France.) Competition soon forced every country that wanted to retain its historical role to protect its manufacturers by renewed customs regulations (the old duties were of little help against big industry) and soon introduce big industry under protective duties. Big industry universalized competition (practical free trade; the protective duty is only a palliative, a measure of defense *within* free trade) despite protective measures, established means of communication and the modern world market, subordinated trade to itself, transformed all capital into industrial capital, and thus produced the rapid circulation (development of finance) and centralization of capital funds. ⟨By universal competition it forced all individuals to strain their energy to the extreme. So far as possible, big industry destroyed ideology, religion, morality, etc., and where it could not, made them into a plain lie.⟩ It produced world history for the first time in that it made every civilized nation and every individual member of the nation dependent for the satisfaction of his wants on the whole world, thus destroying the former natural exclusiveness of separate nations. It subsumed natural science under capital and took from the division of labor the last semblance of its natural character. It destroyed natural growth in general, so far as this is possible in labor, and resolved all natural relationships into money relationships. In the place of naturally grown towns it created overnight modern, large industrial cities. Wherever big industry prevailed, it destroyed the crafts and all earlier stages of industry. It completed the victory [of the town] over the country. [Its premise] was the automatic system. [Its development] resulted in a mass of productive forces for which private property became just as much a fetter as the guild had been for manufacturer and the small rural shop for the developing craft. Under the system of private property these productive forces receive only a one-sided development and become destructive forces for the majority. A great multitude of such forces cannot find application at all under the system of private ownership. In general, big industry created everywhere the same relation between the classes of society and thus destroyed the particularity of each nationality. And finally, while the bourgeoisie of each nation still retained separate national interests, big industry created a class having the same interests in all nations and for which nationality is already destroyed; a class which is really rid of the entire old world and stands opposed to it. Big industry makes unbearable for the worker not only his relation to the capitalist but even labor itself.

It is clear that big industry does not develop equally in all districts of a country. However, this does not hinder the class movement of the proletariat, because the proletarians created by big industry assume leadership of this movement and carry the crowd with them, and because the workers excluded from big industry are put in a worse situation than the workers in big industry itself. Countries with big industries affect in a similar manner the more or less non-industrial countries, if the latter are swept by global commerce into universal competitive struggle. These different forms are only so many forms of the organization of labor and hence of property. In each period a unification of the existing productive forces takes place insofar as this has been made necessary by needs.

This contradiction between the productive forces and the form of commerce, which we observe occurring several times in past history without endangering the basis of history, had to burst out in a revolution each time, taking on at the same time various secondary forms, such as comprehensive collisions, collisions of various classes, contradictions of consciousness, battle of ideas, etc., political struggle, etc. From a narrow point of view one can isolate one of these secondary forms and consider it the basis of these revolutions. This is all the more easy as the individuals who started the revolutions had illusions about their own activity according to their degree of education and stage of historical development.

In our view all collisions in history have their origin in the contradiction between the productive forces and the form of interaction [*Verkehrsform*]. Incidentally, this contradiction does need to have reached its extreme in a particular country to lead to collisions in that country. Competition with industrially more developed countries brought about by expanded international commerce is sufficient to produce a similar contradiction in countries where industry is lagging behind (e.g. the latent proletariat in Germany brought out by the competition of English industry).

Competition isolates individuals, not only the bourgeois

but even more the proletarians, despite the fact that it brings them together. It takes a long time before these individuals can unite, apart from the fact that for this union —if it is not to be merely local—big industry must first produce the necessary means, the big industrial cities and inexpensive, quick communications. Therefore, every organized power standing in opposition to these isolated individuals, who live in relationships daily reproducing this isolation, can be conquered only after long struggles. To demand the opposite would be tantamount to demanding that competition should not exist in this definite historical period, or that the individuals should banish from their minds relationships over which they, the isolated, have no control.

### [Community]

The building of houses. With savages every family has its own cave or hut, just as with the nomads each family has a separate tent. This separate domestic economy is made even more necessary by the further development of private property. With agricultural people a communal domestic economy is just as impossible as is a communal cultivation of the soil. The building of towns was a great advance. In all previous periods, however, the abolition of individual economy, which cannot be separated from the abolition of private property, was impossible for the simple reason that the material conditions were not present. To establish a communal domestic economy presupposes the development of machinery, of the use of natural forces and of many other productive forces—for example, of water supplies, of gaslighting, steam heating, etc., the removal [of the antagonism] of town and country. Without these conditions a communal economy could not form a new productive force. Lacking any material basis and resting on a purely theoretical foundation, it would be only a freak and would not achieve more than a monastic economy achieves. —What was possible can be seen in the formation of cities which started when people moved close together and in the erection of communal buildings for various definite purposes (prisons, barracks, etc.). It is self-evident that the transcendence of individual economy cannot be separated from the transcendence of the family.

Saint Max's frequent statement that everyone is all that he is through the state is basically the same as the statement that the bourgeois is only a specimen of the bourgeois species, a statement presupposing that the *class* of the bourgeois existed before the individuals constituting it. ⟨⟨With the philosophers, *pre-existence* of a class.⟩⟩ In the Middle Ages the citizens of each town were compelled to unite against the landed nobility to save their skins. Extension of trade and establishment of communication acquainted separate towns with others which had asserted the same interests in the fight against the same opponent. Out of the many local corporations of burghers there gradually but very slowly arose the burgher *class*. The conditions of life of the individual burghers became conditions which were common to them all and independent of each individual because of their contradiction to the existing relationships and because of the mode of labor determined by these. The burghers had created these conditions insofar as they had freed themselves from feudal ties and had been created by them insofar as they were determined by their opposition to the existing feudal system. When the individual towns began to enter into associations, these common conditions developed into class conditions. These same conditions, the same antagonism, and the same interests had to call forth generally similar customs everywhere. With its conditions, the bourgeoisie itself develops only gradually, splits into various fractions according to the division of labor, ⟨⟨It absorbs, first of all, the branches of labor belonging directly to the state, then all more or less ideological estates.⟩⟩ and finally absorbs all existing propertied classes (while it develops most of the formerly propertyless class and part of the previously propertied class into a new class, the proletariat) to the extent that all existing property is transformed into industrial or commercial capital. Various individuals form a class only insofar as they have to carry on a joint battle against another class. Otherwise they are hostile, competing with each other. On the other hand, a class in turn achieves independent existence in relation to individuals so that they find their conditions of life predestined, have their position in life and their personal development assigned, and are subsumed under the class. This is the same phenomenon as the subsumption of particular individuals under the division of labor and can only be removed by the transcendence of private property and of labor itself. We have already indicated several times, how this subsuming of individuals under the class is accompanied by their subsumption under all kinds of ideas, etc.

If one considers this evolution of individuals *philosophically* in the common conditions of existence of estates and classes following one another and in the accompanying general conceptions forced on those individuals, it is certainly very easy to imagine that in these individuals the species or Man has evolved, or that they evolved Man. In this way one can give history some hard blows in the head. One can conceive these various estates and classes as specific terms of a general expression, as subordinate varieties of the species, as evolutionary phases of Man.

This subsuming of individuals under definite classes cannot be abolished until a class has taken shape which no longer has any particular class interest to assert against the ruling class.

The transformation of personal into material powers (relationships) through the division of labor cannot be transcended by dismissing the general idea of it from one's mind but only by individuals again controlling these material powers and transcending the division of labor. ⟨(Feuerbach: being and essence)⟩ This is not possible without the community. Only in community do the means exist for every individual to cultivate his talents in all directions. Only in the community is personal freedom possible. In previous substitutes for the community, in the state, etc., personal freedom has existed only for the individuals who developed within the ruling class and only insofar as they belonged to this class. The illusory community, in which individuals have come together up till now, always took on an independent existence in relation to them and was at the same time not only a completely illusory community but also a new fetter because it was the combination of one class against another. In a real community individuals obtained their freedom in and through their association.

Individuals have always started with themselves though within their given historical conditions and relationships, not with the "pure" individual in the sense of the ideologists. But in the course of historical development and precisely through the inevitable fact that in the division of labor social relationships assume an independent existence, there occurs a division in the life of each individual, insofar as it is personal and determined by some branch of labor and by the conditions pertaining to it. (This does not mean that, for example, the rentier, the capitalist, etc., cease to be persons; but their personality is conditioned and determined by very definite class relationships, and the differentiation appears only in their opposition to another class and, for themselves, only when they go bankrupt.) In the estate (and even more in the tribe) this is as yet concealed. A nobleman, for instance, will always remain a nobleman and a commoner always a commoner apart from his other relationships, a quality inseparable from his individuality. The differentiation between the personal and class individual and the accidental nature of the conditions of life for the individual appears only with the rise of the class which itself is a product of the bourgeoisie. Competition and the struggle of individuals among themselves engender and develop this accidental character. In imagination, individuals seem freer under the rule of the bourgeoisie than before because their conditions of life seem accidental to them. In reality they are less free, because they are more subjected to the domination of things. The difference from the estate is brought out particularly in the antagonism between the bourgeoisie and the proletariat.

When the estate of urban burghers, the corporations, etc., emerged in opposition to the landed nobility, their condition of existence, namely, movable property and craft labor already existing latently before their separation from feudal ties, appeared as something positive which was asserted against feudal landed property and hence at first took on a feudal form. Certainly the escaped serfs considered their previous servitude as something accidental to their personality. But they were only doing what every class freeing itself from a fetter does. And they did not free themselves as a class but as separate individuals. They did not rise above the system of estates, but merely formed a new estate and retained their previous mode of labor even in their new situation, developing it further by freeing it from its earlier fetters which no longer corresponded to the development already attained.

For the proletarians, on the other hand, the condition of their existence, labor, and thus all the conditions governing modern society have become something accidental, something over which they, as separate proletarians, have no control and over which no *social* organization can give them control. The contradiction between the personality of each separate proletarian and labor, the condition of life forced upon him, is very evident to him, for he is sacrificed from his youth on and within his class has no chance of arriving at conditions which would place him in another class.

N.B. It must not be forgotten that the serf's very need to exist and the impossibility of large-scale economy with distribution of allotments among the serfs soon reduced the duties of the serfs to an average of payments in kind and statute-labor for their lord. This enabled the serf to accumulate movable property, facilitated his escape from the possession of his lord, and gave him the prospect of making his way as a burgher. It also created gradations among the serfs; the runaway serfs were already half burghers. It is obvious that the serfs who were trained in a craft had the best chance of acquiring movable property.

While the runaway serfs only wished to become free in order to develop and assert those conditions of existence already present and hence in the end only arrived at free labor, the proletarians, if they are to assert themselves as individuals, must abolish the very condition of their existence which has been that of all society up to the present: labor. Thus they find themselves directly opposed to the form in which individuals composing society have given themselves collective expression, the state: and they must overthrow the state in order to realize their personality.

It is clear from what has been said that the communal relationship, into which the individuals of a class entered and which was determined by their common interests over against a third party, was always a community to which these individuals belonged only as average individuals, only insofar as they lived within the conditions of existence of their class—a relationship in which they participated not as individuals but as members of a class. On the other hand, it is just the reverse with the community of revolutionary proletarians who take their conditions of existence and those of all members of society under their control. The individuals participate in this community as individuals. It is this combination of individuals (assuming the present stage of productive forces, of course) which puts the conditions of the free development and movement of individuals under their control, conditions which were previously abandoned to chance and had acquired independent existence over against separate individuals because of their separation as individuals and because of the necessity of their combination which had been determined by the division of labor and through their separation had become a bond alien to them. Up till now the combination, by no means an arbitrary one as expounded in the *Contrat social* but a necessary one, was an agreement on these conditions within which the individuals were free to enjoy accidents of fortune (compare, for example, the formation of the North American state and the South American republics). This right to the undisturbed enjoyment of accidents of fortune, though within certain conditions, has been called personal freedom. —These conditions of existence are, of course, only the productive forces and forms of interaction of the particular time.

### [Communism: Production of the Form of Interaction Itself]

Communism differs from all previous movements because it overturns the basis of all previous relations of production and interaction, and for the first time consciously treats all natural premises as creations of men, strips them of their national character, and subjects them to the power of united individuals. Its organization, therefore, is essentially economic, the material production of the conditions of this unity. It turns existing conditions into conditions of unity. The reality that communism creates is the actual basis for making it impossible that anything should exist independently of individuals, insofar as this reality is only a product of the preceding interaction of individuals themselves. Communists in practice treat the conditions created until now by production and interaction as inorganic conditions, without imagining, however, that it was the plan or the destiny of previous generations to provide them material and without believing that these conditions were inorganic for the individuals creating them.

The difference between the individual as a person and what is accidental to him is not a conceptual difference but a historical fact. This distinction has a different significance in different periods, for example, the estate as something accidental to the individual in the eighteenth century and the family more or less accidental too. We do not have to make this distinction for each age; rather, each age itself makes it from the different elements which it finds in existence, not according to a concept but compelled by material collisions of life. Elements which appear accidental to a later age in comparison with an earlier one, including those handed down by the earlier age, constitute a form of interaction which corresponded to a particular stage of productive forces. The relation of the productive forces to the form of interaction is the relation of the form of interaction to the occupation or activity of the individuals. (Of course, the fundamental form of this activity is material; all other forms, intellectual, political, religious, etc., depend on it. The diverse shaping of material life is always dependent on needs already developed, and the production as well as satisfaction of these needs is itself a historical process not found with a sheep or a dog (the perverse principal argument of Stirner's *adversus* hominem) though sheep and dogs in their present form and in spite of themselves are products of a historical process.)

The conditions under which individuals interact so long as contradiction is still absent are nothing external to them but are conditions pertaining to their individuality, conditions under which these particular individuals living in particular circumstances can produce their material life and what is connected with it. They are the conditions of their self-activity and are produced by this self-activity. ⟨⟨Production of the form of interaction itself.⟩⟩ In the absence of contradiction the particular condition under which they produce thus corresponds to the actuality of their conditioned nature, their one-sided existence, the one-sidedness of which shows only when contradiction enters and thus only exists for later individuals. Then this condition appears as an accidental fetter, and the consciousness that it is a fetter is imputed to the earlier age.

These various conditions, which appear first as conditions of self-activity and later as fetters upon it, form in the whole evolution of history a coherent series of forms of interaction. The coherence consists of the fact that in the place of an earlier form of interaction, which has become a fetter, is put a new one corresponding to the more developed productive forces and thus to an advanced mode of the self-activity of individuals, a form which in turn becomes a fetter to be replaced by another. Since these conditions correspond at every stage to the simultaneous development of productive forces, their history is at the same time the history of the evolving productive forces taken over by each new generation and hence the history of the development of the forces of the individuals themselves.

Since this evolution proceeds naturally and is not subordinated to a general plan of freely united individuals, it starts out from various localities, tribes, nations, branches of labor, etc., each of which develops independently of the others and only gradually enters into relationship with the others. It proceeds only very slowly. The various stages and interests are never completely overcome but only subordinated to the winning interest and drag along with it for centuries. Thus we see that even within a nation the individuals, apart from their pecuniary circumstances, have quite different developments. We see that an earlier interest, whose peculiar form of interaction has already been supplanted by a form belonging to a later interest, remains for a long time afterwards in possession of a traditional power in the illusory community (state, law) which has become independent of individuals, a power that can only be broken by revolution. This explains why, with reference to particular points which permit a more general summary, consciousness can sometimes appear further advanced than contemporary empirical relationships so one can quote earlier theoreticians as authorities in the struggles of a later epoch.

In countries like North America which begin in an already advanced historical epoch, development proceeds very rapidly. Such countries have no other natural premises than the individuals who settled there and were induced to do so because the forms of interaction in the old countries did not correspond to their wants. Thus they begin with the most advanced individuals of the old countries and with the correspondingly most advanced form of interaction, even before this form of interaction has been established in the old countries. This is the case with all colonies which are not military or trading stations. Carthage, the Greek colonies, and Iceland in the eleventh and twelfth centuries are examples of this. A similar relationship is established by conquest when a form of interaction which has evolved elsewhere is introduced complete into the conquered country. While it was still encumbered with interests and relationships from earlier periods at home, it can and must be established completely and without hindrance in the conquered country to assure the conquerors' lasting power. (England and Naples after the Norman Conquest, when they received the most perfect form of feudal organization.)

This whole interpretation of history appears to be contradicted by the fact of conquest. Violence, war, pillage, murder, etc., have been seen as the motive force of history. We must limit ourselves here to the chief points and take up only the most striking example, the destruction of an old civilization by a barbarous people and the resulting formation of an entirely new organization of society (Rome and the barbarians; feudalism and Gaul; the Byzantine Empire and the Turks). As indicated above, with the conquering barbarian people, war is still a regular form of interaction which is the more eagerly exploited as the population increases and requires new means of production to take the place of the traditional and the only possible crude mode of production. In Italy, however, concentration of landed property (caused not only by purchases and indebtedness, but also by inheritance, since the old families died out from loose living and rare marriages and their possessions fell into the hands of a few) and its conversion into grazing land (caused not only by common economic forces still existing today but also by the importation of plundered and tribute grain and the resultant lack of demand for Italian grain) made the free population disappear almost completely. Slaves died out again and again and constantly had to be replaced by new ones. Slavery remained the basis of the entire productive system. The plebeians standing between freemen and slaves never succeeded in becoming more than proletarian rabble. Indeed, Rome never became more than a city. Its connection with the provinces was almost exclusively political and could easily be broken by political events.

Nothing is more common than the notion that in history up till now *taking* has been the thing that counts. The barbarians *take* the Roman Empire, and the transition from the old world to the feudal system is explained with this fact of taking. In this taking by barbarians it is important whether the conquered nation has industrial productive forces, as is the case with modern peoples, or whether its productive forces are based for the most part merely on association and community. Taking is further determined by the object taken. A banker's fortune consisting of paper cannot be taken without the taker's submitting to the conditions of production and interaction in the country taken. It is similar with the total industrial capital of a modern industrial country. Finally, taking very soon comes to an end, and when there is nothing more to take, one must begin to produce. From this necessity of producing, which comes about very soon, it follows that the form of community adopted by the settling conquerors must correspond to the stage of development of the productive forces they find in existence; or, if this is not the case from the start, it must change to accord with the productive forces. This explains what people say they have noticed everywhere in the period after the Great Migration, namely, that the servant was master and that the conquerors very soon adopted the language, culture, and manners of the conquered.

The feudal system was by no means brought complete from Germany. As far as the conquerors were concerned, it had its origin in the organization of the army during the conquest itself and developed after the conquest into the feudal system proper through the action of the productive forces found in the conquered countries. To what extent this form was determined by the productive forces is shown by the abortive attempts to institute other forms derived from reminiscences of ancient Rome (Charlemagne, etc.). To be continued.

In big industry and competition all the conditions of existence, the determining factors, and the biases of individuals are fused together into the two simplest forms: private property and labor. With money every form of interaction, and interaction itself, is considered accidental for individuals. Money implies that all previous interaction was only commerce of individuals under particular conditions, not of individuals as individuals. These conditions are reduced to two: accumulated labor or private property, and actual labor. Even if only one of these ceases, interaction comes to a standstill. The modern economists themselves, for example, Sismondi, Cherbuliez, etc., juxtapose "association of individuals" and "association of capital." On the other hand, the individuals themselves are completely subsumed under the division of labor and brought into complete dependence on one another. Private property, insofar as it is opposed to labor within labor itself, evolves out of the necessity of accumulation and has at first the form of community. But in its further development it approaches more and more the modern form of private property. From the outset, the division of labor implies division of the *conditions of labor,* of tools and materials, and the splitting up of accumulated capital into the hands of various owners, and thus the division between capital and labor and different forms of capital itself. The further division of labor proceeds and the more accumulation grows, the more pronounced does the fragmentation become. Labor itself can exist only under the premise of this fragmentation.

Personal energy of the individuals of various nations—Germans and Americans—energy generated already through crossbreeding—hence the cretinism of the Germans—in France, England, etc., foreign peoples transplanted to a land already developed, in America to virgin land—in Germany the native population quietly remained in its locale.

Thus two facts become clear. First, the productive forces appear as a world by themselves independent of, removed from, and alongside individuals because the individuals whose forces they are, exist as split up and opposed to one another. On the other hand these forces are only real forces in the interaction and association of the individuals. Thus we have, on the one hand, a totality of productive forces which, so to speak, have assumed material form and are for the individuals no longer the forces of individuals but of private property—of individuals only insofar as they are owners of private property. Never before have the productive forces taken on a form so indifferent to the interaction of individuals *as* individuals, because their interaction was still restricted. On the other hand, opposing the productive forces, there is the majority of the individuals from whom these forces have been wrested away and who have become abstract individuals deprived of all real life content. Only through this fact, however, are they enabled to enter into relation with one another *as individuals.* The only connection still linking them with the productive forces and with their own existence, labor, has lost all semblance of self-activity and sustains their life only by stunting it. While in earlier periods self-activity and the production of material life were separated by the fact that they devolved on different persons and because the production of material life was considered a subordinate mode of self-activity due to the narrowness of the individuals themselves, they now diverge to such an extent that material life appears as the end, and labor, the producer of this material life (now the only possible but negative form of self-activity, as we see), appears as means.

Things have come to the point where individuals must appropriate the existing totality of productive forces not merely to achieve self-activity but to secure their very existence. This appropriation is determined by the object to be appropriated—the productive forces developed to a totality and existing only within a universal interaction. From this aspect alone, this appropriation must have a universal character corresponding to the productive forces and interaction. The appropriation of these forces is itself nothing more than the development of individual capacities corresponding to the material instruments of production. For this very reason, the appropriation of a totality of instruments of production is the development of a totality of capabilities in the individuals themselves. It is further determined by the appropriating individuals. Only the proletarians of the present, completely deprived of any self-activity, can achieve a complete and unrestricted self-activity involving the appropriation of a totality of productive forces and consequently the development of a totality of capacities. All previous revolutionary appropriations were restricted. Individuals, whose self-activity was restricted by a crude instrument of production and limited interaction, appropriated this crude instrument of production and merely attained a new plateau of limitation. Their instrument of production became their property, but they themselves remained subject to the division of labor and their own instrument of production. In all appropriations up to now a mass of individuals remained subservient to a single instrument of production. In the appropriation by the proletarians, a mass of instruments of production must be subservient to each individual and the property of all. The only way for individuals to control modern universal inter-action is to make it subject to the control of all.

The appropriation is further determined by the manner in which it must be carried through. It can only be ac-complished by a union, universal because of the character of the proletariat itself, and through a revolution in which the power of the social organization and of earlier modes of production and interaction is overthrown and the prole-tariat's universal character and energy for the act of ap-propriation is developed. Furthermore, the proletariat must get rid of everything still clinging to it from its earlier position in society.

Not until this stage is reached will self-activity coincide with material life, will individuals become complete individ-uals. Only then will the shedding of all natural limitations be accomplished. The transformation of labor into self-activity corresponds to the transformation of the previous restricted interaction into the interaction of individuals as such. With the appropriation of the total productive forces through united individuals, private property ceases to exist. While in previous history a particular condition always ap-peared as accidental, now the isolation of individuals and the particular private gain of any individual have become accidental.

Individuals who are no longer subjected to the division of labor have been conceived by the philosophers as an ideal under the name of "Man." They have grasped the whole process described as the evolutionary process of "Man," so at every historical stage "Man" was substituted for individuals and presented as the motive force of his-tory. The whole process was seen as a process of the self-alienation of "Man," essentially because the average indi-vidual of the later stage was always foisted on the earlier stage and the consciousness of a later period on the individ-uals of an earlier. ⟨⟨Self-alienation⟩⟩ Through this inver-sion, which from the beginning has been an abstraction of the actual conditions, it was possible to transform all his-tory into an evolutionary process of consciousness.

Civil society comprises the entire material interac-tion among individuals at a particular evolutionary stage of the productive forces. It comprises the entire commercial and industrial life of a stage and hence transcends the state and the nation even though that life, on the other hand, is manifested in foreign affairs as nationality and organized within a state. The term "civil society" emerged in the eighteenth century when property relations had already evolved from the community of antiquity and medieval times. Civil society as such only develops with the bourgeoisie. The social organization, however, which evolves directly from production and commerce and in all ages forms the basis of the state and the rest of the idealistic superstructure, has always been designated by the same name.

## Relation of the State and Law to Property

The first form of property in antiquity as in the Middle Ages is tribal property, determined with the Romans chiefly by war and with the Germanic peoples by cattle breeding. Since several tribes lived together in one town in the ancient world, tribal property was state property and the right of the individual to it was mere Possessio, confined like tribal property as a whole to landed property only. With the ancients as with modern nations, real private property began with movable property—(slavery and community) (*dominium ex jure Quiritum* [ownership from the law of full Roman citizenship]). In nations evolving from the Middle Ages, tribal property developed through several stages—feudal landed property, corporative movable property, manufacturing capital—to modern capital determined by big industry and universal competition, pure private property free of all semblance of a communal institution and excluding the state from any influence on its development.

To such modern private property corresponds the modern state which has been gradually bought by property owners through taxes, has fallen entirely into their hands through the national debt, and has become completely dependent on the commercial credit they, the bourgeois, extend to it in the rise and fall of government bonds on the stock exchange. Being a *class* and no longer an *estate,* the bourgeoisie is forced to organize itself nationally rather than locally and give a general form to its averaged interest. Through the emancipation of private property from the community, the state has become a separate entity beside and outside civil society. But the state is nothing more than the form of organization which the bourgeois by necessity adopts for both internal and external purposes as a mutual guarantee of their property and interests. The independence of the state is found today only in countries where estates have not fully developed into classes, where estates, having disappeared in more advanced countries, still have a role to play, and where a mixture exists—countries where no one section of the population can attain control over the others. This is the case particularly in Germany. The perfect example of the modern state is North America. The modern French, English, and American writers all express the opinion that the state exists only for the sake of private property; this fact has entered into the consciousness of the ordinary man.

Since the state is the form in which the individuals of a ruling class assert their common interests and the entire civil society of an epoch is epitomized, the state acts as an intermediary in the formation of all communal institutions and gives them a political form. Hence there is the illusion that law is based on will, that is, on will divorced from its real basis, on *free* will. In a similar fashion, right in turn is reduced to statute law.

Civil law develops simultaneously with private property from the disintegration of the natural community. With the Romans the development of private property and civil law had no further industrial and commercial consequences because their whole mode of production remained unchanged. ⟨⟨Usury!⟩⟩ In modern nations where the feudal community was eliminated by industry and trade, there began with the rise of private property and civil law a new phase capable of further development. The very first town with extensive sea trade in the Middle Ages, Amalfi, also developed maritime law. As soon as industry and trade developed private property further, first in Italy and then in other countries, Roman civil law was adopted in a perfected form and made authoritative. When later the bourgeoisie had acquired so much power that princes took up the interests of the bourgeoisie in order to topple feudal nobility through the bourgeoisie, the real development of law began in all countries—in France in the sixteenth century. With the exception of England, it proceeded everywhere on the basis of the Roman Codex. Even in England, Roman legal principles had to be adopted to further the development of civil law, particularly in regard to movable property. (It must not be forgotten that law has just as little independent history as religion.)

In civil law the existing property relationships are declared to be the result of a general will. The *jus utendi et abutendi* [right of using and consuming] itself expresses, on the one hand, the fact that private property has become entirely independent of the community, and on the other the illusion that private property itself is based simply on private will, on the arbitrary disposition of the thing. In practice, the *abuti* has very definite economic limitations for the owner of private property if he does not wish to see his property and thus his *jus abutendi* pass into the hands of another person, because the thing, considered only with reference to his will, is not a thing at all but only becomes actual property through interaction and independently of the right to the thing (a *relationship* which the philosophers call an idea). ⟨⟨*Relationship for the philosophers* = *idea*. They only know the relationship *"of* Man" to himself, and thus all actual relationships become ideas for them.⟩⟩ This juridical illusion, which reduces law to mere will, in further development of property relationships necessarily leads to one's having legal title to a thing without actually having it. If for example the income from a piece of land is lost due to competition, the owner, to be sure, has his legal title to it along with the *jus utendi et abutendi*. But he cannot do anything with it. If he does not have enough capital to cultivate his land he owns nothing as a landed proprietor. This illusion of lawyers also explains why for them, as for every code, it is altogether accidental that individuals enter into relationships with one another, for example, make contractual agreements; why they hold the view that these relationships [can] be entered into or not at will and that their content [re]sts entirely on the individual free [will] of the contracting parties. Every time new forms of [com]merce evolved through the develop[ment] of industry and trade, for [example] insurance companies, etc., the law was compelled to admit them among the modes of acquiring property. [The continuous text in Engels' script ends here; directly below, in the left column, Marx added the following notes.]

Influence of division of labor on science.

*Repression* in state, law, morality, etc.

[In] law the bourgeois must present themselves as universal just because they rule as a class ⟨⟨⟨(Catholic) religious conceptions particularly correspond to the "community," to this bond, as it appears in the state of antiquity, in the feudal system, in absolute monarchy⟩⟩.

Natural science and history.

There is no history of politics, law, science, etc., of art, religion, etc.

*Why ideologists turn everything upside down.*

Religionists, lawyers, politicians.

Lawyers, politicians (government officials in general), moralists, religionists.

For this ideological subdivision within a class, 1. *Occupation becomes independent through the division of labor;* everybody thinks of his craft as the true one. Because it is determined by the nature of the craft itself, one necessarily has illusions about the connection of his craft with reality. In jurisprudence, politics, etc., relationships turn into concepts in consciousness. Since they do not transcend these relationships, the concepts become fixations. A judge, for example, applies the code. For him legislation is the true, active force. Respect for their goods because their occupation involves the universal.

Idea of law. Idea of state. In *ordinary* consciousness, the matter is turned upside down.

Religion from the outset is consciousness of *transcendence* [which] arises from a *real* necessity.

This in a more popular manner.

Tradition, in regard to law, religion, etc.

Individuals have always begun, always begin, with themselves. Their relationships are relationships of their actual life-process. How does it happen that their relationships become something independent over against them, that the forces of their own life overpower them?

Briefly: *the division of labor,* whose level depends on the productive power developed at the time.

Communal property.

Landed property, feudal, modern.

Estate property. Manufacturing property. Industrial capital.

# From THE POVERTY OF PHILOSOPHY: A REPLY TO M. PROUDHON'S *PHILOSOPHY OF POVERTY* (1847)

[Marx wrote the following critique of Proudhon's method in French from January to June 1847 in Brussels. He was then active in transforming the conspiratorial League of the Just into an open, democratic Communist League aimed at rule of the proletariat and a classless society. By the end of the year Marx had been elected president of the Brussels branch of the League and commissioned to write its international program, *The Communist Manifesto*.

Marx regarded *The Poverty of Philosophy* as the first scientific presentation of his theory. Its first chapter, omitted below, criticized Proudhon's notion of "constituted value" from Ricardo for neglecting class contradictions and failing to see that money reflects only a particular mode of production. The central section of the book, translated below, concentrates on Proudhon's adaptation of the Hegelian dialectic with which Marx had admittedly "infected" him. Marx finds Proudhon trapped in "speculative philosophy," transforming relations of production into a dialectic of abstractions. Here Marx utilizes objections to speculation he had adopted from Feuerbach. But he also adheres to Hegel's dialectic—of which Proudhon "has nothing . . . but the language"—and uses it to formulate "the real movement of things" in history, the dynamic antagonisms within feudal and bourgeois production. Such a movement foreshadows socialism which is not utopian but rather the outcome of observable developments. With this use of dialectic, Mehring well observed, Marx "went beyond Feuerbach by going back to Hegel."

In sections of *The Poverty of Philosophy* omitted below Marx criticized Proudhon's unhistorical views on division of labor, machinery, monopoly, and land. Proudhon opposed unions and strikes, but Marx foresaw their increase and looked forward to the achievement of a new society, an "association" without class antagonisms or a separate political power.]

## The Metaphysics of Political Economy:
### The Method

Now here we are, right in Germany! We have to talk metaphysics while talking political economy. And in this we still only follow the "contradictions" of M. Proudhon. He recently forced us to speak English, to become passably English ourselves. Now the scene changes. M. Proudhon takes us to our dear fatherland and forces us to become German again in spite of ourselves.

If the Englishman transforms men into hats, the German transforms hats into ideas. The Englishman is Ricardo, a rich banker and distinguished economist; the German is Hegel, a simple professor of philosophy at the University of Berlin.

Louis XV, the last absolute monarch and representative of the decadence of French royalty, had attached to his person a physician who was himself the leading economist of France. This physician and economist represented the imminent and certain triumph of the French bourgeoisie. Doctor Quesnay made a science of political economy; he summarized it in his famous "Economic Table." Besides the thousand and one commentaries which have appeared on this Table, we have one from the doctor himself. It is the "analysis of the economic table" followed by "seven *important observations.*"

M. Proudhon is another Doctor Quesnay. He is the Quesnay of the metaphysics of political economy.

Now according to Hegel, metaphysics, the whole of philosophy, is summed up in method. Hence we must try to elucidate M. Proudhon's method which is at least as obscure as the *Economic Table*. For this purpose we shall make seven more or less important observations. If Doctor Proudhon is not satisfied with our observations, well then, he will have to become an Abbé Baudeau and give "the explanation of the economico-metaphysical method" himself.

## First Observation

"We are not presenting *history according to the order in time* but *according to the succession of ideas*. Economic *phases* or *categories* are sometimes contemporary and sometimes inverted in their *manifestation*. . . . Nevertheless economic theories have their *logical succession* and *seriality in the understanding:* it is this order which we flatter ourselves to have discovered." (Proudhon, Vol. I, p. 146.)

Decidedly, M. Proudhon has wanted to frighten the French by throwing some quasi-Hegelian phrases in their faces. So we have to deal with two men, first with M. Proudhon and then with Hegel. How is M. Proudhon different from other economists? And what part does Hegel play in Proudhon's political economy?

The economists express the relations of bourgeois production, the division of labor, credit, money, etc., as fixed, immutable, eternal categories. M. Proudhon, who has before him these ready-made categories, wants to explain to us the act of formation and generation of these categories, principles, laws, ideas, thoughts.

The economists explain how production takes place in the relations given, but they do not explain how these relations themselves are produced, that is, the historical movement which gave birth to them. Having taken these relations for principles, categories, and abstract thoughts, M. Proudhon has only put *order* into thoughts which are already alphabetically arranged at the end of every treatise on political economy. The material of the economists is the active and busy life of men; the materials of M. Proudhon are the dogmas of the economists. But from the moment we do not pursue the historical movement of the relations of production which categories only express theoretically and from the moment we want to see in these categories only ideas and spontaneous thoughts independent of real relations, we are forced to attribute the origin of these thoughts to the movement of pure reason. How does pure reason, eternal and impersonal, give rise to these thoughts? How does it proceed in order to produce them?

If we had M. Proudhon's boldness in the case of Hegelianism, we should say: Reason is distinguished in itself from itself. What does this mean? Impersonal reason, having outside itself neither ground upon which to stand nor an object to which it can be opposed nor a subject with which it can be composed, finds itself forced to turn head over heels in posing, opposing, and composing itself—position, opposition, composition. To speak Greek, we have thesis, antithesis, and synthesis. For those who are not acquainted with the Hegelian language, we shall pronounce the sacramental formula: affirmation, negation, negation of the negation. That is real talking. It is certainly not Hebrew, apologies to M. Proudhon; but it is the language of that reason so pure as to be separated from the individual. Instead of the ordinary individual with his ordinary manner of speaking and thinking, we have nothing but this ordinary manner pure and simple, without the individual.

Is it surprising that everything in highest abstraction—for here there is abstraction and not analysis—presents itself in the form of a logical category? Is it surprising that in dropping little by little all that constitutes the individuality of a house, that in abstracting the materials of which it is composed and the form which distinguishes it, you end up with nothing but a body—that in abstracting the limits of this body you soon have nothing but a space—that finally in abstracting the dimensions of this space you end up with nothing but pure quantity, the logical category? By thus abstracting from every subject all the so-called accidents, animate or inanimate, men or things, we are right in saying that in the highest abstraction the only substance left is the logical categories. Thus the metaphysicians who imagine that in making these abstractions they are making an analysis and who imagine they approach the point of penetrating objects the more they are detached from them—these metaphysicians in turn are right in saying that the things of this earth are embroideries of which the logical categories form the canvas. This is what distinguishes the philosopher from the Christian. The Christian has but one incarnation of the *Logos,* in spite of logic; the philosopher has no end of incarnations. That everything which exists, all that lives on land and in water, can be reduced to a logical category by force of abstraction; that the whole real world can be drowned in the world of abstractions, in the world of logical categories—who will be surprised at that?

Everything which exists, all that lives on land and in water, lives only by some kind of movement. Thus the movement of history produces social relations, the industrial movement gives us the products of industry, etc.

Just as by force of abstraction we have transformed everything into a logical category, so one has only to make an abstraction of every characteristic distinguishing different movements to attain movement in the abstract, purely formal movement, the purely logical formula of movement. If one finds the substance of all things in logical categories, one imagines he has found in the logical formula of movement the *absolute method* that not only explains everything but also implies the movement of things.

Hegel speaks of this method as follows: "Method is the absolute, unique, supreme, infinite force which no object can resist; it is the tendency of reason to find itself again, to recognize itself in every object." (*Logic*, Vol. III.) With everything reduced to a logical category, with every movement and act of production reduced to method, it naturally follows that every aggregate of products and production, of objects and movement, is reduced to an applied metaphysics. What Hegel has done for religion, law, etc., M. Proudhon seeks to do for political economy.

What, then, is this absolute method? It is the abstraction of movement. What is the abstraction of movement? Movement in the abstract. What is movement in the abstract? The purely logical formula of movement or the movement of pure reason. In what does the movement of pure reason consist? In positing, opposing, and composing itself; in formulating itself as thesis, antithesis, and synthesis, or better still, in affirming itself, negating itself, and negating its negation.

How does reason manage to affirm itself, to posit itself

in a given category? That is the business of reason itself and its apologists.

But once reason has managed to posit itself in a thesis, this thesis, this thought, opposed to itself, splits itself into two contradictory thoughts—the positive and negative, yes and no. The struggle of these two antagonistic elements comprised in the antithesis constitutes the dialectical movement. The yes becoming no, the no becoming yes, the yes becoming at once yes and no, the no becoming at once no and yes, the contraries balance themselves, neutralize themselves, paralyze themselves. The fusion of these two contradictory thoughts constitutes a new thought, which is their synthesis. This new thought again splits itself into two contradictory thoughts, which in turn fuse into a new synthesis. From this labor is born a group of thoughts. This group follows the same dialectical movement as a simple category and has a contradictory group as its antithesis. From these two groups is born a new group of thoughts, their synthesis.

Just as from the dialectical movement of simple categories is born the group, so from the dialectical movement of the groups is born the series, and from the dialectical movement of the series is born the entire system.

Apply this method to the categories of political economy, and you get the logic and metaphysics of political economy, or, in other words, you get the economic categories known to everyone translated into a language hardly known to anyone, a language which makes those categories appear to have been freshly hatched in a head of pure reason, so much do they seem to engender one another, to enchain and entangle one another by the mere labor of the dialectical movement. The reader need not be alarmed at this metaphysics with all its scaffolding of categories, groups, series, and systems. In spite of all the trouble M. Proudhon has taken to scale the heights of the *system of contradictions,* he has never been able to raise himself above the first two steps of simple thesis and antithesis. Even these he has mounted only twice, and on one of these occasions he fell over backwards.

Up to this point we have set forth only Hegel's dialectic. We shall see later how M. Proudhon has succeeded in reducing it to the most paltry propositions. Thus for Hegel everything that has taken place and is still taking place is only just what is taking place in his own reasoning. Thus the philosophy of history is nothing but the history of philosophy, the history of his own philosophy. There is no longer a "history according to the order in time" but only "the succession of ideas in the understanding." He thinks he is constructing the world by the movement of thought, whereas he is merely systematically reconstructing and classifying by the absolute method the thoughts that are in everybody's head.

## Second Observation

Economic categories are only the theoretical expressions, the abstractions, of social relations of production. Holding things upside down like a true philosopher, M. Proudhon sees in real relations only the incarnation of these principles or categories which were slumbering—M. Proudhon the philosopher again tells us—in the bosom of "the impersonal reason of humanity."

M. Proudhon the economist has clearly understood that men make cloth, linen, and silk stuffs in definite relations of production. But what he has not understood is that these definite social relations are just as much produced by men as are the cloth, the linen, etc. Social relations are intimately bound up with productive forces. In acquiring new productive forces men change their mode of production, and in changing their mode of production, their manner of making a living, they change all their social relations. The windmill gives you society with the feudal lord; the steam mill, society with the industrial capitalist.

The same men who establish social relations in conformity with their material productivity also produce principles, ideas, and categories conforming to their social relations.

Hence these ideas, these categories are no more eternal than the relations which they express. They are *historical and transitory products*.

There is a continual movement of growth in productive forces, of destruction in social relations, and of formation in ideas; there is nothing immutable but the abstraction of the movement—*mors immortalis.*

### Third Observation

The productive relations of every society form a whole. M. Proudhon considers economic relations as so many social phases engendering one another, resulting from one another like antithesis from thesis, and realizing the impersonal reason of humanity in their logical succession.

The only drawback to this method is that when M. Proudhon comes to examine one of these phases he cannot explain it without having recourse to all the other relations of society, relations which, however, he has not yet generated by his dialectical movement. When afterwards M. Proudhon gives birth to these other phases by means of pure reason, he acts as if they were newborn babes and forgets that they are of the same age as the first.

Thus, in order to arrive at the constitution of value which for him is the basis of all economic evolutions, he could not do without division of labor, competition, etc. Yet in the *series,* in M. Proudhon's *understanding,* in the *logical succession,* these relations did not yet exist.

In constructing the edifice of an ideological system with the categories of political economy, one dislocates the members of the social system. The different members of society are converted into so many separate societies which follow one upon the other. How, indeed, could the single logical formula of movement, of succession, of time explain the composition of society in which all relations co-exist simultaneously and support one another?

### Fourth Observation

Now let us see the modifications to which M. Proudhon subjects Hegel's dialectic in applying it to political economy.

For M. Proudhon every economic category has two sides, one good, the other bad. He looks at these categories as the petty bourgeois looks at the great men of history:

*Napoleon* was a great man; he did a lot of good and he also did a lot of harm.

The *good side* and the *bad, the advantages* together with *the drawbacks,* form for M. Proudhon the *contradiction* in each economic category.

The problem to be solved: To conserve the good side while eliminating the bad.

*Slavery* is an economic category like any other. Thus it also has its two sides. Let us leave the bad side and talk about the beautiful side of slavery. Needless to say, it is only a question of direct slavery, the slavery of the blacks in Surinam, Brazil, and the southern states of North America.

Direct slavery is just as much the pivot of bourgeois industry as machinery, credit, etc. Without slavery you have no cotton; without cotton, you have no modern industry. It is slavery which gave colonies their value; it is colonies which created world trade; it is world trade which is the precondition of large industry. Thus slavery is an economic category of the highest importance.

Without slavery, North America, the most progressive country, would be transformed into a patriarchal land. Efface North America from the map of the world and you will have anarchy, the complete decay of modern commerce and civilization. Cause slavery to disappear and you will have wiped America off the map of nations.*

Thus slavery, because it is an economic category, has always existed among the institutions of nations. Modern nations have known how to disguise slavery in their own country, but they have imposed it on the New World without disguise.

* [Here Friedrich Engels put in the German edition of 1885 the following footnote:] This was entirely correct for the year 1847. Then the foreign trade of the United States was limited mainly to importing immigrants and industrial products and exporting cotton and tobacco, products of southern slave labor. The northern states produced mainly corn and meat for the slave states. Only when the North produced corn and meat for export and became an industrial land and only when the American cotton monopoly had to face strong competition in India, Egypt, Brazil, etc., was the abolition of slavery possible. And even then this led to the ruin of the South, which did not succeed in replacing open Negro slavery by the disguised slavery of Indian and Chinese coolies.

What will M. Proudhon do to save slavery? He will pose the *problem:* Conserve the good side of this economic category, eliminate the bad.

Hegel has no problems to pose. He only has the dialectic. M. Proudhon has nothing of Hegel's dialectic but the language. For him the dialectical movement is the dogmatic distinction between good and bad.

Let us for a moment take M. Proudhon himself as a category. Let us examine his good and his bad side, his advantages and his drawbacks.

If he has the advantage over Hegel of formulating problems which he reserves the right to solve for the greater good of humanity, he has the drawback of being stricken with sterility when it is a question of giving birth to a new category by dialectical labor. What constitutes dialectical movement is the co-existence of two contradictory sides, their conflict, and their fusion in a new category. Merely to formulate the problem of eliminating the bad side is to cut short the dialectical movement. It is not the category which poses and opposes itself by its contradictory nature, it is M. Proudhon who worries himself, disputes himself, and struggles between the two sides of the category.

Caught thus in an impasse from which it is difficult to escape by legal means, M. Proudhon performs a veritable somersault which carries him into a new category at one bound. The *seriality in the understanding* then unveils itself to his astonished eyes.

He takes the first category at hand and arbitrarily attributes to it the quality of providing a remedy for the drawbacks in the category to be purified. Thus taxes, if we are to believe M. Proudhon, remedy the drawbacks of monopoly; balance of trade, the drawbacks of taxes; landed property, the drawbacks of credit.

By thus taking the economic categories successively, one by one, and making one the *antidote* of the other, M. Proudhon succeeds in making with this mixture of contradictions and antidotes to contradictions two volumes of contradictions which he properly entitles: *The System of Economic Contradictions.*

### Fifth Observation

"In absolute reason all these ideas . . . are equally simple and general. . . . In fact, we attain scientific knowledge only by a *kind of scaffolding* of our ideas. But truth in itself is independent of these dialectical figures and free from the combinations of our minds." (Proudhon, Vol. II, p. 97.)

Here at one stroke, by a kind of turnabout of which we now know the secret, the metaphysics of political economy becomes an illusion! Never has M. Proudhon spoken more truly. Indeed, from the moment the process of dialectical movement is reduced to the simple process of opposing good to bad, of posing problems tending to eliminate the bad, and of giving one category as antidote to another, categories no longer have any spontaneity; the idea "no longer *functions*"; it no longer has any life in it. It no longer poses or decomposes itself in categories. The succession of categories has become a kind of *scaffolding*. The dialectic is no longer the movement of absolute reason. There is no longer any dialectic, at the most there is only pure ethics.

When M. Proudhon spoke of the *seriality in the understanding,* of *logical succession of categories,* he declared positively that he did not want to present *history according to the order in time,* that is to say, in M. Proudhon's view, the historical sequence in which the categories have *manifested* themselves. Thus for him everything took place in the *pure ether of reason.* Everything was to be derived from this reason by means of the dialectic. Now that he has put this dialectic into practice, reason fails him. The dialectic of M. Proudhon makes a false leap to the dialectic of Hegel, and M. Proudhon is led to say that the order in which he presents the economic categories is no longer the order in which they engender one another. Economic evolutions are no longer the evolutions of reason itself.

What, then, does M. Proudhon give us? Real history which is according to M. Proudhon's understanding, the sequence in which the categories are *manifested* in the order of time? No. History as it happens in the Idea itself? Still less. Thus neither the profane history of the categories nor their sacred history! What history does he give us then? The history of his own contradictions. Let us see how they march and how they drag M. Proudhon after them.

Before starting on this examination, which gives rise to the sixth important observation, we have still another but less important observation to make.

Let us admit with M. Proudhon that real history, history according to the order in time, is the sequence in which ideas, categories, and principles are manifested.

Each principle has had its century in which to manifest itself. The principle of authority, for example, had the eleventh century, just as the principle of individualism had the eighteenth. As a logical consequence it was the century which appertained to the principle and not the principle to the century. In other words, it was the principle which made history, it was not history which made the principle. When, further, to save principles as well as history we ask why a particular principle was manifested in the eleventh or eighteenth century rather than in another, we are of necessity compelled to examine minutely what men were like in the eleventh century, what they were like in the eighteenth, what their respective needs were, their productive forces, their mode of production, the raw materials of their production—in short, what the relations were between man and man resulting from all these conditions of existence. To get to the bottom of all these questions, what is this but to achieve the real, profane history of men in each century and present these men as both the authors and the actors of their own drama? But the moment you present men as the actors and authors of their own history, you arrive by a detour at the real point of departure since you have abandoned the eternal principles from which you first started.

M. Proudhon has not even gone far enough along the crossroad taken by the ideologist to reach the highway of history.

## Sixth Observation

Let us take the crossroad with M. Proudhon.

Let us grant that economic relationships viewed as *immutable laws, eternal principles,* and *ideal categories* existed before active and busy men; let us grant further that these laws, principles, and categories had slumbered "in the impersonal reason of humanity" since the beginning of time. We have already seen that with these immutable and immovable eternities, there is no longer any history: at the most there is only history in the Idea, that is, history reflected in the dialectical movement of pure reason. In saying that ideas are no longer *"differentiated"* in the dialectical movement, M. Proudhon has canceled both the *shadow of movement* and the *movement of shadows* by which one might at least have created a semblance of history. Instead of that he imputes to history his own impotence, he blames everything, even the French language. "It is not correct, then," says M. Proudhon the philosopher, "to say that something *happens,* something is *produced:* in civilization as in the universe everything exists and acts from eternity. *Thus it is with the entire social economy."* (Vol. II, p. 102.)

The productive force of the contradictions which *function* and make M. Proudhon function is such that in trying to explain history, he is forced to deny it; in trying to explain the successive movement of social relationships, he denies that *anything* can *happen;* in trying to explain production in all its phases, he questions whether *anything can be produced.*

Thus for M. Proudhon there is no longer any history, no longer succession of ideas, but there is still his book; and this book is precisely, to use his own expression, *"history according to the succession of ideas."* How can we find a formula—since M. Proudhon is a man of formulas —to help him clear all his contradictions *in a single leap?*

For this purpose he has invented a new kind of reason which is neither absolute reason, pure and chaste, nor the common reason of men living and acting in different centuries but a reason quite apart, the reason of society personified, of *humanity* as subject, which under M. Proudhon's pen appears also at times as *"social genius," "general reason,"* and finally *"human reason."* This reason, wrapped in so many names, is always to be recognized, however, as the individual reason of M. Proudhon, with its good and its bad side, its antidotes and its problems.

"Human reason does not create truth," hidden in the depths of absolute, eternal reason. It can only unveil it. But the truths it has unveiled up to now are incomplete, insufficient, and thus contradictory. Hence economic categories, being themselves truths discovered and revealed by human reason, by social genius, are equally incomplete and contain within themselves the germ of contradiction. Before M. Proudhon, social genius saw only the *antagonistic elements* and not the *synthetic formula*, both hidden in *absolute reason* simultaneously. Economic relationships which only realize on earth these insufficient truths, these incomplete categories, these contradictory ideas are hence contradictory in themselves and present two sides, one good, the other bad.

To find complete truth, the Idea in all its plenitude, the synthetic formula to annihilate contradiction—that is the problem of social genius. That again is why, in M. Proudhon's illusion, this same social genius has been driven from one category to another without having yet been able to extort from God a synthetic formula for absolute reason.

"At first, society (social genius) presents a primary fact, puts forward an *hypothesis* . . . a genuine antinomy whose antagonistic results develop in the social economy in the same way as its consequences could have been deduced in the mind; so that the industrial movement, everywhere following the deduction of ideas, splits into two currents, one of useful effects and the other of subversive results. . . . To make this two-sided principle harmonious and resolve this antinomy, society gives rise to a *second* which will soon be followed by a third, and such will be the *progress of social genius* until, having exhausted all its contradictions—I suppose, but it is not proved, that there is a limit to contradiction in humanity—it returns in one leap to all its former positions and solves all its problems *with a single formula.*" (Vol. I, p. 133.)

Just as the *antithesis* was earlier changed into an *antidote,* so now the *thesis* becomes a *hypothesis.* With M. Proudhon this change of terms can no longer surprise us. Human reason, being anything but pure and having only incomplete views, meets at every step new problems to be solved. Each new thesis which it discovers in absolute reason and which is the negation of the first thesis, becomes for it a synthesis which it naïvely accepts as the solution of the problem in question. Hence, this reason struggles in ever new contradictions until it perceives at the end of contradictions that all its theses and syntheses are only contradictory hypotheses. In its perplexity "human reason, the social genius, returns in one leap to all its former positions and solves all its problems with a single formula." This unique formula, we may say in passing, constitutes M. Proudhon's real discovery. It is *constituted value.*

Hypotheses are made only in view of some purpose. The goal which social genius, speaking through M. Proudhon, set itself in the first place was the elimination of the bad in each economic category in order to have only the good. For social genius, the good, the supreme good, the real practical purpose is *equality.* And why did social genius propose equality rather than inequality, fraternity, Catholicism, or any other principle? Because "humanity has successively realized so many separate hypotheses only in view of a superior hypothesis," which is precisely equality. In other words: because equality is M. Proudhon's ideal. He imagines that the division of labor, credit, the workshop, and all economic relationships were invented only to enhance equality, and yet they always ended up by turning against it. Since history and M. Proudhon's fiction contradict each other at every step, he concludes that there is a contradiction. If there is a contradiction, it is only between his fixed idea and the real movement of things.

Henceforth the good side of an economic relationship is that which affirms equality, the bad side, that which

denies it and affirms inequality. Every new category is a
hypothesis of social genius to eliminate the inequality engendered by the preceding hypothesis. In short, equality is
the *original intention,* the *mystical tendency,* the *providential purpose* which social genius constantly has before
its eyes in turning round and round in the circle of economic contradictions. Thus *Providence* is the locomotive
which moves the whole of M. Proudhon's economic bag-
gage better than his pure and airy reason. He has devoted
to Providence a whole chapter following the one on taxes.

Providence, providential purpose, this is the big word
used today to explain the movement of history. In actual
fact this word explains nothing. It is at most a rhetorical
form, one way among others of paraphrasing the facts.

It is a fact that landed property in Scotland acquired a
new value by the development of English industry. This
industry opened up new markets for wool. To produce
wool on a large scale, arable land had to be turned into
pasture. To effect this transformation, property had to be
concentrated. To concentrate property, small holdings had
to be abolished, thousands of tenants had to be driven
from their native soil, and a few shepherds tending millions
of sheep had to be put in their place. Thus by successive
transformations, landed property in Scotland has resulted
in men being driven out by sheep. Now say that the providential purpose of landlordism in Scotland was to have
men driven out by sheep and you will have made providential history.

Certainly the tendency toward equality belongs to our
century. To maintain now that all former centuries with
entirely different needs, means of production, etc., worked
providentially for the realization of equality is at once to
substitute the means and men of our century for the men
and means of earlier centuries and to misunderstand the
historical movement by which successive generations transformed the results acquired from the generations preceding
them. Economists know very well that the very thing which
was for one a finished product is for another only the raw
material of new production.

Suppose, as M. Proudhon does, that social genius produced, or rather improvised, the feudal lords with the providential purpose of transforming *peasants* into *responsible* and *equal workers* and you will have made a substitution of purposes and persons entirely worthy of that Providence which instituted landed property in Scotland to give itself the malicious pleasure of substituting sheep for men.

But since M. Proudhon takes such a tender interest in Providence, we refer him to the *History of Political Economy* of M. de Villeneuve-Bargemont who also runs after a providential purpose. This purpose, however, is not equality but Catholicism.

### Seventh and Last Observation

Economists have a peculiar method of procedure. There are only two kinds of institutions for them, artificial and natural. Feudal institutions are artificial institutions, those of the bourgeoisie are natural. In this they resemble theologians who also establish two kinds of religion. Every religion but theirs is an invention of men while their own is an emanation from God. In saying that existing conditions—the relationships of bourgeois production—are natural, the economists want it to be understood that these are the relationships in which wealth is created and productive forces are developed in conformity with laws of nature. Hence, these relationships are themselves natural laws, independent of the influence of time. They are eternal laws which must always govern society. Thus there has been history, but there is no history any longer. There has been history since there were feudal institutions, and in those feudal institutions we find quite different relationships of production from those of bourgeois society which the economists want to pass off as natural and therefore eternal.

Feudalism also had its proletariat—serfdom, which contained all the seeds of the bourgeoisie. Feudal production also had two antagonistic elements likewise designated as the *good side* and *bad side* of feudalism, regardless of the fact that the bad side always triumphs in the end over the good side. The bad side produces the movement which makes history by providing a struggle. If economists under feudalism, enthusiastic about knightly virtues, about the beautiful harmony between rights and duties, the patriarchal life of the towns, the prosperous condition of domestic industry in the countryside, the development of industry organized in corporations, guilds and companies, in short, everything that constitutes the good side of feudalism, had set themselves the problem of eliminating all that darkened this picture—serfdom, privilege, anarchy—what would have been the result? All the elements producing struggle would have been annihilated, and the development of the bourgeoisie would have been nipped in the bud. An absurd problem would have been set, the problem of eliminating history.

When the bourgeoisie triumphed, there was no longer any question of either the good or bad side of feudalism. The productive forces developed by the bourgeoisie under feudalism were acquired by the bourgeoisie itself. All the old economic forms, the corresponding civil relations, the political state which was the official expression of the old society were shattered.

Thus, to judge feudal production properly, it must be looked at as a mode of production based on antagonism. It must be shown how wealth was produced within this antagonism, how the productive forces were developed at the same time as class antagonisms, and how one of the classes—the bad side, the drawback of society—continued growing until the material conditions for its emancipation had achieved maturity. Is not this as much as saying that the mode of production, the relations in which productive forces are developed, are anything but eternal laws but that they correspond to a specific development of men and their productive forces, and that a change arising in men's productive forces necessarily leads to a change in their relations of production? As the main thing is not to be deprived of the fruits of civilization, of acquired productive forces, the traditional forms in which they were produced must be shattered. From this moment on, the revolutionary class becomes conservative.

The bourgeoisie begins with a proletariat which is itself a remnant of the working class of feudal times. In the course of its historical development, the bourgeoisie necessarily develops its antagonistic character which is more or less disguised in its first appearance and exists only in a latent condition. As the bourgeoisie develops there develops in its bosom a new proletariat, a modern proletariat: there develops a struggle between the proletarian class and the bourgeois class, a struggle which first only manifests itself in partial and momentary conflicts, in subversive acts, before it is felt, perceived, appreciated, comprehended, avowed, and proclaimed aloud by the two sides. On the other hand, if all the members of the modern bourgeoisie have an identity of interest inasmuch as they form one class opposed to another, they also have conflicting, antagonistic interests inasmuch as they are opposed to one another. This opposition of interests springs from the economic conditions of their bourgeois life. From day to day it thus becomes clearer that the relationships of production in which the bourgeoisie moves do not have a single, simple character but a double character; that in the same relationships in which wealth is produced, poverty is also produced; that in the same relationships in which there is a development of productive forces there is also a force producing repression; that these relationships produce *bourgeois wealth*, that is, the wealth of the bourgeois class, only by continually destroying the wealth of individual members of this class and by producing an ever growing proletariat.

The more this antagonistic character comes to light, the more the economists, the scientific representatives of bourgeois production, fall out with their own theory and different schools are formed.

We have the *fatalist* economists who are as indifferent in their theory to what they call the drawbacks of bourgeois production as the bourgeois themselves are in practice to the sufferings of the proletarians who help them acquire wealth. In this fatalist school there are classicists and romanticists. Classicists like Adam Smith and Ricardo represent a bourgeoisie which, still struggling with the remnants of feudal society, works only to purify economic relationships of feudal blemishes, to increase productive forces, and to give industry and commerce a new scope. The proletariat participating in this struggle and absorbed in this feverish labor undergoes only passing, accidental sufferings and itself regards them as passing and accidental. Economists like Adam Smith and Ricardo, who are the historians of this epoch, have no other mission than to show how wealth is acquired in the relationships of bourgeois production, to formulate these relationships in categories and laws, and to show how superior these laws and categories are to those of feudal society for the production of wealth. In their eyes poverty is merely the pang that accompanies every childbirth, in nature as well as in industry.

The romanticists belong to our epoch in which the bourgeoisie is directly opposed to the proletariat, in which poverty is engendered in as great abundance as wealth. The economists now pose as blasé fatalists who glance from their lofty position with arrogant disdain toward the human machines which manufacture wealth. They copy all the developments given by their predecessors, and the indifference which was naïveté in their predecessors becomes coquetry in them.

Next comes the *humanitarian school* which takes to heart the bad side of existing productive relationships. To ease its conscience, this school seeks, even if slightly, to excuse the real contrasts; it sincerely deplores the distress of the proletariat, the unbridled competition of the bourgeoisie among themselves; it counsels the workers to be sober, to work hard, and to have few children; it advises the bourgeoisie to put a deliberate zeal into production. The whole theory of this school rests on interminable distinctions between theory and practice, between principles and results, between idea and application, between form and content, between essence and reality, between right and fact, between the good side and the bad.

The *philanthropic* school is the humanitarian school perfected. It denies the necessity of antagonism; it would make all men bourgeois; it wants to realize theory insofar as it is distinguished from practice and contains no antagonism. It goes without saying that, in theory, it is easy to make an abstraction of the contradictions that are met with at every moment in reality. This theory would then become idealized reality. The philanthropists thus want to retain the categories expressing bourgeois relationships without the antagonism which constitutes those relationships and is inseparable from them. They imagine that they are seriously combating bourgeois practice, and they are more bourgeois than the others.

As the *economists* are the scientific representatives of the bourgeois class, so the *socialists* and *communists* are the theoreticians of the proletarian class. So long as the proletariat is not sufficiently developed to constitute itself as a class, consequently so long as the struggle itself between proletariat and bourgeoisie does not yet have a political character, so long as the productive forces are not yet sufficiently developed in the bosom of the bourgeoisie itself to permit a glimpse of the material conditions necessary for the emancipation of the proletariat and the formation of a new society—so long are these theoreticians merely utopians who improvise systems and pursue a regenerative science to meet the needs of the oppressed classes. But as history develops and with it the struggle of the proletariat becomes more clearly defined, they no longer need to seek science in their minds. They have only to give an account of what is happening before their eyes and give voice to it. So long as they seek science and merely make systems, so long as they are at the beginning of the struggle, they see in poverty nothing but poverty, without seeing in it the revolutionary, subversive side that will overthrow the old society. From this moment, science, produced by the historical movement and linking itself to that movement in full consciousness, has ceased to be doctrinaire and has become revolutionary.

Let us return to M. Proudhon.

Every economic relationship has a good side and a bad: this is the one point on which M. Proudhon does not contradict himself. The good side, he sees explained by the economists; the bad side, he sees denounced by the socialists. He borrows from the economists the necessity of eternal relationships; he borrows from the socialists the illusion of seeing in poverty nothing but poverty. He is in agreement with both in wanting to rely on the authority of science. Science, for him, is reduced to the insignificant proportions of a scientific formula; he is the man in search of formulas. Thus M. Proudhon flatters himself on having given a critique of both political economy and communism: he is beneath the one as well as the other. Beneath the economists, since as a philosopher with a magic formula in hand, he believed he could dispense with entering into purely economic details; beneath the socialists, since he has neither sufficient courage nor insight to rise, even if only speculatively, above the bourgeois horizon.

He wants to be the synthesis, he is a composite error. He wants to soar as man of science above the bourgeois and proletarians; he is merely the petty bourgeois, continually tossed between capital and labor, between political economy and communism.

# INDEX